S0-BXV-788

THE
WORLD'S
GREAT
RELIGIONS

Illinois Mathematics and Science Academy
1500 W. Sullivan Rd.
Aurora, IL 60506

Book belongs to H/SS Dept. S05-122

THE WORLD'S GREAT RELIGIONS

An Anthology of Sacred Texts

Compiled by
Selwyn Gurney Champion
and Dorothy Short

DOVER PUBLICATIONS, INC.
Mineola, New York

ACKNOWLEDGMENT

The quotations from *The Koran*, commencing on p. 260, are taken from the translation from the Arabic by the Rev. J. M. Rodwell, M.A., Everyman's Library, E. P. Dutton & Co. Inc., New York.

Bibliographical Note

This Dover edition, published in 2003, is an unabridged republication of the work originally published in 1952 by The Beacon Press, Boston under the title *Readings from World Religions.*

Library of Congress Cataloging-in-Publication Data

Readings from world religions.
The world's great religions : an anthology of sacred texts / compiled by Selwyn Gurney Champion and Dorothy Short.
    p. cm.
Originally published: Champion, Selwyn Gurney. Readings from world religions. Boston : Beacon Press, 1952.
Includes bibliographical references.
ISBN 0-486-42715-3 (pbk.)
1. Sacred books. 2. Religions. I. Champion, Selwyn Gurney. II. Short, Dorothy, 1884– III. Title.

BL70.R43 2003
291.8'2—dc21   2002041561

Manufactured in the United States of America
Dover Publications, Inc., 31 East 2nd Street, Mineola, N.Y. 11501

FOREWORD

THIS book is intended to be an introduction to the eleven living religions of the world. Three of these—Buddhism, Christianity, and Islam—aspire to universality, and the others are confined to special peoples or countries. The aim has been to present them all simply and with an equal lack of bias, as though for the information of someone newly come to the question of religion.

The inception of the book was due to Dr. S. Gurney Champion, whose authoritative work *The Eleven Religions and their Proverbial Lore* [1] is well known. This scheme was as follows. First there were to be introductions to each religion, giving its main doctrines and system and an account of the life of the founder, where there was one. These he asked me to write. Secondly, there was to be, in every case, a selection of short extracts, followed by longer passages, from the Scriptures. By including short as well as long excerpts, Dr. Champion hoped to draw attention to vital passages, which could easily be kept in the memory and form texts for discussion and comparison. His sudden death, in December, 1949, occurred just when this task of selection and arrangement had been completed. He has therefore been deprived of seeing the publication of the work which he had so much at heart, and by this sad loss, too, it falls to the lot of a collaborator to write this Foreword, which would have come so much better from his pen.

The book, as a whole, has been considerably shortened in order to meet present-day difficulties in publication, and, in particular, the short extracts have had to be reduced in number. It is hoped, however, that the present version will represent, as nearly as possible, what had been so ably planned and arranged by Dr. Champion and that here will be one more volume by which he will be remembered.

In order to maintain uniformity, and in the belief that this would have been Dr. Champion's wish, I have used capital

[1] Routledge (London), 1944.

letters for pronouns only when speaking of the Supreme Being in the primary aspect, and not where He is represented as incarnate in human form. It is hoped that this decision will be understood and that it will give offence to none.

Dr. Champion believed that a book such as this might be of special value today, when totalitarian ideology urges alternative solutions to man's need for spiritual satisfaction and security. In any case, the Readings from the Scriptures may provide refreshment for a distracted generation.

The Scriptures have been corrected and in many cases referenced by Mrs. Barbara C. Briault, one of Dr. Champion's executors.

Finally, I should like to express my gratitude to Dudley, my husband, whose help in preparing the work for publication has been invaluable.

DOROTHY SHORT.

Richmond, Surrey.
November 1950.

CONTENTS

CONTENTS

1

INTRODUCTION

WHAT is religion? This is a question hard to answer in a few words, and if a number of people were asked, each might give a different reply. Religion is hard to define, not because there is so little of it, but because there is so much : it has existed in some form or another since human history began, and geographically it covers the whole world, for there are no peoples entirely without it. It has wielded immense political power and swayed the rise and fall of Empires. If it has been associated with terrible wars and persecutions, it has also, and most profoundly, been a source of inspiration for the highest good of mankind : indeed, it is this very permeation of all history and social living that makes the word so difficult to define. It may be possible to arrive at a clearer picture if we go back to early origins and try to reconstruct the various stages of religious thought as they grew out of one another.

We all know that the concern of primitive man was mainly as to his own survival. Equipped with only the most elementary tools and weapons, he found that droughts, storms, or floods might at any time destroy the sources of his nourishment. Knowing nothing of the means of combating such catastrophes, or, on the other hand, of improving resources, it was inevitable that he should look upon Nature with extreme awe, as something that could either ruin or save him. Unlike the animal creation, he did not accept his precarious condition unquestioningly, because he had in him the germ of reasoning power. In his primitive way he may have said to himself : " Someone is doing this, a person rather like myself, only much more powerful; perhaps I can persuade him to give me the good things and withhold the bad." He would go on to imagine that there were Beings in the trees, the fire, the wind, and the river; spirits who might be approached and in some way bribed or placated. This first stage, which we now call *Animism*, was the worship of such spirits and it was the beginning of religion, for it assumed the presence of something outside humanity which could help or hinder at will. As knowledge increased and man learnt to control, to some extent, natural phenomena, these nature-spirits became less formidable. The next stage is sometimes described as *Animatism*. Here the nature-spirits were no longer confined to particular objects, but were thought of rather as *influences* over the sun, the moon, the storm, or the ocean, as the case might be. As their spheres widened still farther to cover more general conceptions, such as fertility, destruction, seasonal changes, and so on, they began to approach the dignity and status of gods.

The next stage is somewhat obscure. Some authorities claim that at this very early date certain tribes set up for their protection a single god, whom we may call a tribal deity. The theory is that when these tribes met together and united into larger groups they adopted the gods of one another, and so created Pantheons of many deities. If this were so, then a primitive form of *Monotheism*, the worship of One God only, came before the worship of many gods—the developed Polytheism so familiar in the history of the ancient world. The more usual view is, however, that Polytheism came next, being simply an extension of the original nature-spirits, who now acquired to the full the qualities, authority, and magnitude of gods. It is possible that both these things happened at different times and in different places. In any case, it is quite clear that very early in the history of the world a large number of deities are found together. This stage is *Polytheism*, which seems on the face of it to arise most naturally out of *Animatism*.

From Polytheism emerged what has been called *Monarchism*. This means that man, judging, no doubt, from experience in his own social life, came to erect one of the gods as king or head over all the others. This king-god increased in importance, while the lesser gods drifted into the background till they were little more than vassal-spirits resembling the angels and archangels of the Christian hierarchy. The character of the king-god began to change too. The nature-spirits had been the bestowers of favours and the creators of misfortune, and the first gods, too, were little more than this. They had none of what we should call " moral " qualities, but gradually a certain " rightness " was associated with them, and particularly with the king-god. This showed itself first, no doubt, in the idea of justice. The king-god was a "just" person; he would reward the righteous and punish the wicked. Man himself was beginning to find that, as a member of a community, he must make and keep certain rules and follow certain codes of behaviour, and he thus began to attribute to his god the rudiments of a moral and ethical code. This change of thought came about very slowly. Often the lower stages, when the gods were little more than capricious spirits, continued beside more advanced ones; indeed, this happens today when half-savage tribes, whose beliefs are still animistic, contact people with highly advanced religious ideas. To speak of stages is thus not merely to speak in terms of time.

While the king-god was advancing towards spiritual supremacy another question had apparently troubled men's minds. "Where do the gods live?" we can imagine them asking: "when trees and rivers were their homes, they were near at hand, but now where are they? We build for ourselves shelters; perhaps they also need dwellings of some kind." So shrines were erected —elementary buildings where the gods could be found and honoured by their worshippers—and these were the forerunners of the temples and sacred buildings of later times. But the question still arose: "Whence do the gods come to visit their shrines; do they not live somewhere all together just as we do?" So man imagined a god-world, very much like his own world, except that all good things could be obtained there at will. This god-world might be up in the sky, under the ground, or on some far-away mountain or island, but in any case it was remote, and the gods could only be called upon by prayer and sacrifice.

This belief in a god-world led to another development in religious thought. It hardly seemed enough to have built shrines and temples; the gods might or might not visit these, and meanwhile their presence was withdrawn from surrounding nature. Some way must be found by which they could come back and share to a greater degree the life of human beings. There are many stories, especially among the Greeks and Romans, of the gods coming down to earth, dealing with the problems of men, and even acting for a while as human kings. There they appeared much like men, but as religious ideas advanced the way was open for a more spiritual interpretation, by which the divine life could come nearer without the sacrifice of its majesty, mystery, and uniqueness. Thus arose the belief in Divine Incarnation, by which God becomes incarnate in a single person.

Another way in which the divine life could return to the human sphere was by Immanence, an indwelling in all visible, as well as invisible, things. The original nature-spirits had inhabited natural objects, but they were separate entities and had no unity of being. The belief in Divine Immanence meant that One Universal Spirit permeated all nature and everything beyond it.

When the king-god no longer shared his authority with other deities, when he stood alone as the supreme ruler of the universe, the monotheistic principle was established. Religious thought had passed through phases of Animism, Animatism, and Polytheism to the worship of the One God. During the process of development three ways of regarding the divine life had emerged. Firstly, God was eternal, apart from and above His creation; secondly, He could become incarnate in a human being; and, thirdly, He was the indwelling Spirit, present in all things. These three aspects of the One Being became the foundation of the doctrine of the Trinity, which was fully expressed later in the Christian creed.

Meanwhile belief as to the nature of man himself had also changed. In primitive times he had approached the nature-spirits with prayer and sacrifice and without questioning his ability to do this. Now he came to realize that the animals around him made no such efforts; they were satisfied with their condition and felt no further need. He, then, must possess something more than his animal nature, another order of being, a spiritual entity which could desire the divine life and respond to it. That second nature was what we now call the Soul; it was the soul which could distinguish between right and wrong, desire God, and even survive death.

The single God of Monotheism had now not only power attributed to Him but also Holiness, Wisdom, and Foreknowledge. He became the source of all good things, the Creator of the universe, and the ultimate goal of mankind. But it was not without a struggle that He rose in men's minds to the height of unfettered spirituality. Too often the conception of Him sank to the plane of anthropomorphism; He was presented in the likeness of a man with the limitations of men. Belief in the indwelling Spirit was a spiritualizing influence, and, reacting against anthropomorphism, it sometimes became isolated and appeared as Pantheism—the doctrine that God is All and All is God. In some later phases of religion this idea is highly developed, accompanied by emphasis on mystical experience and religious exaltation.

The brief outline which has been given is offered as an attempt at simplification, and it must be understood that there can be no definite chronological order. Religious phases, as has been said, exist simultaneously, and there are constant reactions and interactions. It is hoped, however, that it may help to clear the ground and prepare the way for a statement as to what the word " religion " should be held to imply.

Religion involves, in the first place, a belief in the Divine Life—omnipotent, eternal, and dwelling apart; a divine nature which can draw near to man through incarnation and immanent presence. Secondly, as a corollary to this, it asserts that man himself has a spiritual nature which is derived from this divine life and can, and indeed must, respond to it. Upon this dual foundation the separate religions build their systems and present different aspects with varying degrees of emphasis. Each has its prophets, its scriptures, its temples, its rule of life, its special way. Each is coloured by language, geographical position, race, national temperament, and even, perhaps, by climate. Within every fold there are widely differing degrees of understanding, and this is true even among people of the same nation and education. Elementary ideas exist beside highly advanced ones, and popular and esoteric versions are often linked by parable, symbolism, and ritual observance.

The following chapters give some account of eleven existing religions with extracts from their sacred writings. Greatly as the ways differ, the likenesses are more remarkable, and it is probably true to say that there is more similarity between two men sincerely professing different creeds than between a religious man and one who professes no religion at all. It may be added that the attempt to dispense with religion altogether is too modern a movement to show its full possibilities: the religious way of thought is deeply embedded in human consciousness and is an integral part of the history of the human race.

2

HINDUISM

THE Introduction was intended to give an outline of the major conceptions of the religions of the world, and to suggest how these may have developed out of one another. The pattern can only be chronological in the most general sense, for various stages may exist at the same time, and what to one man is a symbol of living truth, to another may be little more than an idol.

The religion which best illustrates not only the general line, but also the immense diversity and complexity within that pattern, is Hinduism. Hinduism is prehistoric, and India has been called the " cradle of religion " : indeed, four of the eleven religions to be described in this book originated there. The word, of course, means the religion of the Hindus. Some religions derive their names from their founders, some from an aspect of doctrine, and some, as in this case, from a race. Hinduism thus belongs to a particular people and does not make converts of outsiders. It is *non-proselytizing*.

The Hindus have been described as the most religious people in the world. Innumerable acts of daily life, as well as the social system as a whole, have a religious sanction. There are, however, very many different schools of thought within Hinduism. Different gods are recognized as the Supreme Being ; temples and observances vary widely ; indeed, were it not for certain fundamental co-ordinating ideas, one would have to say that in India there are a large number of distinct religions. The two main ideas that unite Hindu religious thought are *Reincarnation* and the principle of *Caste*.

The doctrine of Reincarnation assumes that man's destiny is not confined to a single earth-life, but is worked out in many.[1] Thus he goes on from one shape to another, according to his deserts, in a succession of existences stretching from the far past into the distant future. As he sows, so shall he reap. If he acts

[1] The number given in the Scriptures is 8,400,000.

well and develops spiritually, he will be reborn into a better position in life, but if he deteriorates, then he will worsen his lot and he may become an animal or even a plant. Thus he makes his own world. The law which governs this inexorable working out of cause and effect is called *Karma*, which means literally *Works*. Reincarnation and Karma are bound up together, and their existence is assumed in all forms of Hinduism. There have been, it is true, some attempts at modification; indeed, many movements have been founded on an attempt to short-cut the long succession of lives and so to " break the wheel of transmigration." For to the Hindu there is no advantage in this lengthy series; the goal is rather to be released altogether from the power of Karma, *whether good or bad*, for then the self of man will be absorbed into, or united with, the divine life from whence it sprang. Modifications have, however (except in certain cases to be noticed later), largely been embodied in Hinduism, and have failed seriously to undermine the prevailing conceptions of Karma and Reincarnation.

Closely connected with the concept of Reincarnation is the idea of Caste, which is held to reveal on the social plane the working out of Karma. A man is born into a certain position in life—or class, as we should call it—according to his acts in a former life, and he can no more change his caste than a bird can become a beast. Caste is closely connected with occupation—a potter remains a potter; a sweeper, a sweeper; a Brahman, a Brahman. Only after death—that is, *in the next incarnation*—can a man rise in the social scale. Accustomed as the Westerner is to the idea of social " climbing " and " social betterment," this seems to us a harsh law, yet it is only part of the doctrine that as a man sows so shall he reap. The caste system must be thought of in connection with the laws of Reincarnation and Karma. When a man is reborn into higher and higher castes he draws nearer to the divine life, for the highest caste of all is the priesthood, the Brahmans, who are in a special relation to the Godhead and therefore guardians of religious truth. Thus the Hindu conception of social life is founded on a religious concept.

The history of Hinduism is extremely complicated, yet it is possible to simplify it by dividing it into three main periods— Vedism, Brahmanism, and modern Hinduism. Vedism means the period of the Vedas, the Vedas being a collection of very early

hymns, the earliest of which dates from about 1000 B.C.   There
are four Vedas—the Rig-Veda, Atharva-Veda, Sama-Veda, and
Yajur-Veda.   These hymns were compiled for the worship of
the Aryan tribes who invaded India from the north-west, and
those of the Rig-Veda are the oldest : they are mostly addressed
to nature-spirits, such as the God of the Rain, of the Dawn, of
the Sun, the Wind, the Sky, and so on.   But even in the Rig-
Veda (the earliest scripture, not only of India, but of the Aryan
race as a whole) there are signs that suggest a long previous period.
For instance, there is already a tendency for the gods to extend
their sphere of influence and to be associated with wider cosmic
forces, or for one to become supreme over all the others, or, again,
there is the foreshadowing of the doctrine of One Immanent
Spirit which pervades everything.   In the sphere of conduct the
concepts of good and evil are already established, with suitable
rewards in some after-life.   Man is thus already thought of as
more than his physical body—as possessing something which
we should now call the soul.   Thus the first Scriptures of the
Hindus, early as they are, are much in advance of the most
elementary stages of religion which were described in the first
chapter.

As Vedism passes into Brahmanism we find the veneration for
these ancient Scriptures increasing; indeed, they have never been
disowned or superseded, and they still form part of the sacred
books of the Hindus.   A more profound meaning began, however, to be seen in them, and a class of poets and priests arose who
professed to be their special interpreters.   These poets and
priests developed the idea suggested in the Rig-Veda of an indwelling Spirit which moved through the whole universe, including man himself, and they gave to this impersonal spirit the name
of *Brahm*, which means literally " breath."   Thus the priests
themselves became known as Brahmans.   It was realized that
people in the lower stages of development—many of them half-
savage—could hardly be expected to grasp the abstract idea of a
World-Self, or Spirit.   So, in order to meet the needs of elementary minds, the Brahmans developed a system of detailed observances and sacrifices, and about 800 B.C. they compiled huge
volumes elaborating these, which were called *Brahmanas*.   The
priests professed to derive their authority from the Vedas, and each
Veda had a Brahmana of its own.   Somewhat later the Brahmanas

were followed by the *Upanishads* (lit. Sessions), which set forth in full the esoteric philosophy of the Brahmans. The World-Self, Brahm, was held to be identical with the individual self, or soul of man, and the realization of this truth was essential to final happiness and emancipation. All things were in fact One; there was only Brahm, and there was no secondary principle. Thus the Brahmans taught a form of Pantheism, the doctrine that God is All and All is God. But they went farther than this. They insisted that man should *know the Truth*—that is, *grasp it in its full significance*; only when he was able to do this would he reunite with that All of Being, that impersonal entity from which he came. Meanwhile what had happened to the gods of Rig-Veda ? Gradually they had faded into the background, retaining only a relative immortality, only a relative power as compared with the indwelling Brahm. Yet all the while the hearts of ordinary people yearned for the warm experience of love and devotion to a personal God; the idea of the World-Spirit was too abstract for them, and the elaborate ritual of the Brahmans appeared to need some sanction which they could understand. So they seized upon two deities from the dying Pantheon of the Vedas : Vishnu, who had been a god of grace, and Siva, who had inherited the characteristics of Rudra, the god of the wild mountains. Each of these seemed to offer what was now the urgent spiritual need, a personal Deity and Creator, and their cults have divided India ever since into two rival Churches.

Perhaps no god has been worshipped with greater fervour than the adored Vishnu, or received more love and devotion on the part of so large a number of people. All the factors which go to make up personality were now attributed to him. Many Brahmans came to acknowledge him as the Supreme Self, the individual self and the All of Being, and therefore identical with the indwelling Brahm. A new element arose in connection with this worship, the element of *Bhakti*, which means a kind of passionate devotion. Vishnu was also the god who incarnated from time to time in order to show the way to men. Ten incarnations have been attributed to him, the most important of which was his incarnation as Krishna, while one of them is yet to come. As Krishna, he was supposed to have uttered what is one of the great Scriptures of India—the Bhagavad-Gita (Lord's Song)—when acting as charioteer to a Prince engaged in a battle. The Prince hesitated in the fight, which is described in the great epic known as the Mahabharata, and Krishna, in this remarkable work, comforts him and sets forth the principles of religious truth. The Bhagavad-Gita shows a compromise between the doctrine of a personal God and the abstraction of the indwelling Brahm.[1] The worship of Siva is harder to understand; the character of the god seems to be so full of contradictions. His name means " gracious one," yet he is fierce and terrible. He is known as the Destroyer, yet he is also the bringer of life. He is probably connected with the whole cycle of change, just as Vishnu is the preserver of whatever is. His worship tended to drift southward, while the Vishnuite Churches held the more northerly parts of India.

Meanwhile the Brahmans had evolved a personal God of their own. They had given to Brahm (the impersonal World-Spirit) a masculine counterpart, Brahma, an active deity, the Creator of the universe. In the later Upanishads, Brahma, Vishnu, and Siva appear as a kind of triad—Creator, Preserver, and Destroyer, emanations of the indwelling Brahm. There was even an effort to develop the idea of a Trinity, three in one and one in three. But the Trinitarian concept never sank deeply into the Hindu consciousness, and Brahm, the Creator, as an independent deity, was no rival to the other two. In practice men worshipped either Vishnu or Siva as supreme, Brahma being in each case an emanation of the chosen deity. Many other gods and god-like beings, survivals from the Vedic period, retained a subordinate position, somewhat corresponding to that of the angels and archangels of Christendom. At its highest level the worship of either Vishnu or Siva reached the stage of Monotheism—belief in one Supreme God as Creator and ruler of the universe.

During the early stages of the Brahmanical period the priests had established the social system by clearly marking out the divisions of the four great castes—the Brahmans, the Warriors, the Traders, and the Manual Workers. Sub-castes grew up in time, and also an increasing number of those who, by reason of mixed marriage or other causes, belonged to no caste at all. These came to be regarded as the lowest of all humanity—the " Untouchables "—even the shadow of whom must not cross the Brahman's path.

---

[1] It is a superlative work and one of the " five jewels " of the Indian scriptures.

The power of the priests was not lessened by the cults of Vishnu and Siva, for they merely accommodated themselves to popular ideas. When it is firmly believed that all things are One, it is easy to substitute one name for another and thus to declare dogmas to be interchangeable. Hinduism became one of the most all-embracing systems in the world. Almost any religious element was absorbed into it, and this is one of the chief difficulties of Christian missionaries, who have made comparatively little progress in India. A new god can always be regarded as merely another aspect of the indwelling Brahm, and a new creed as a restatement of truths already held. Thus the Brahmans, by attaching themselves to the Churches of Vishnu or of Siva, remained the guardians of religion and of their position as the highest caste. Rebellions against their power and efforts at reform of their metaphysics were, after some resulting modifications, usually quietly absorbed into Hinduism. There were, however, certain movements which were strong enough to break away and to form separate religions altogether. These were Buddhism and Jainism, which date from the sixth century B.C., both originating from the warrior caste, and, much later, Sikhism, which arose from the same source, in the fifteenth century A.D. These three religions are dealt with in other chapters. Suffice it to say here that Buddhism was by far the most important of the three; indeed, it made such progress during some centuries that it seemed as if it would finally conquer India, but the Brahmans prevailed, and in the end Buddhism was expelled to other parts of Asia. Jainism, which had at first much in common with Buddhism, never gained a very large number of adherents, and finally settled down quietly in a small part of the country. Sikhism was too late a development to overthrow the strongly established Brahman position. As the result of the impact of Muhammadanism—which came to India from the north-west—upon Hindu ideas, it made considerable progress for a time and was important historically, but it was confined to certain localities and failed to permeate India as a whole.

Muhammadanism should perhaps be mentioned in passing. This great religion, which is dealt with in Chapter 11, was of a foreign origin, and came to India with the invasion of the Moghul emperors. Though many Hindus became converted to the new faith, and though its fanatical Monotheism strengthened the idea

of the singleness of a personal God within Hinduism, the two
faiths remained distinct and incompatible. Muhammadanism
failed to destroy Brahmanism, and rivalry between the followers
of the two religions has existed up to the present day.

Brahmanism, then, continued along the main lines of its own
tradition, and in the ninth century A.D. there arose a Brahman,
named Sankara, who developed further, and finally fixed, the
Upanishad philosophy. To him we owe the theory of Maya, or
Illusion. The earlier philosophers had thought of the universe
as a single reality, appearing in a plurality of manifestations.
To Sankara the manifestations were *in themselves unreal*; they
were only a mirage—the visible universe was, in fact, a phantom.
It was Maya, Illusion, which caused men to think of themselves
as separate from one another, and to believe that the vision
around them had actual existence. This was an effort to
explain why, if there were only the one Brahm, sin, suffering,
and divisions should exist in the world at all. But actually
the theory of Maya only put the question one stage farther
back, for it has still to be asked *why and how* such illusion
came to arise. The difficulty of reconciling the presence of
disunity, sin, and suffering with the existence of a single just
principle has been the major problem, not only of Brahmanism,
but of almost all religions. The theory of Maya, which was
variously interpreted, was only a partial solution; nevertheless
it was welcomed by the Brahmans, who, in their uncompromising
Monism, were determined to admit of no secondary principle.
On Sankara's version of the Upanishad philosophy modern
Hinduism rests.

The second main period which followed the age of the Vedas
and which we have called in a very general sense Brahmanism
now merges, in our historical survey, into modern Hinduism, the
Hinduism of later centuries. Later Hinduism presents such an
immensely complicated picture that one would despair of attempting to simplify it were it not for the prevailing ideas of Caste,
Reincarnation, and Karma which were described earlier and for
the historical pattern which has been briefly outlined. An
enormous number of elements have been absorbed and retained,
some even dating to cults existing among the aboriginals in pre-
Aryan times. Every possible religious concept from the highest
to the lowest may be found among the Hindus, and there is hardly

any object which the uneducated are not prepared to worship. Nowhere are there greater inequalities of outlook. Crude, complicated, and even, to us, repulsive observances exist simultaneously with profound mysticism and a philosophy which, regarded from some angles, is the most spiritual in the world. One always has to remember the divergences caused by the caste system and how illiterate and half-savage people need to express themselves at the same time as initiates who give their whole lives to meditation and religious contemplation. The latter tolerate hideous idols and repulsive or childish ceremonies because social inequality is felt to be inevitable, even divine in its origin, and because it is understood that the practice of religion corresponds to the mind of the worshipper. Advanced religious Hindus (and there are no more keenly intellectual, tolerant, and spiritual men in the world) see in all these contradictions the working out of the law of Karma and the multiple and mysterious manifestations of Brahm—the all-pervading Spirit. Hinduism is intensely conservative. The Vedas, the Brahmanas, and the Upanishads remain the inspired Scriptures, and to the later Upanishads is given the term Vedanta, or Veda's End. The central philosophy of Brahmanism, the doctrine of the World-Self, remains the background of the advanced man's faith, added to which there is often the belief in a more personal God and Creator as an emanation of that All-Spirit—the name of Whom will vary according to the particular Church to which the worshipper belongs. The cultured Hindu may thus be said to be a Monotheist with a background of mystical Pantheism.

A few words should perhaps be added concerning the influence of modern European culture and " Westernization." This began to show itself early in the nineteenth century by the founding of the Brahma-samaj and the Arya-samaj Churches. These and certain other theistic sects were influenced by Christianity, and they made various efforts to simplify Hinduism by abolishing " idolatry," modifying the caste system, introducing high ethical principles, and insisting on the holiness and singleness of the One God. In still more recent times scientific materialism with its idea of " progress " has affected India to some extent. Hindus who receive a European education, in theory lose caste by their contacts with European countries. A ceremony may re-initiate them, but, with frequent travel and inter-communication, barriers

must lose their strength. It is easier, however, for a Hindu to
resist the encroachments of materialistic scepticism than for many
other people, because his system is so elastic and absorbent. Since
there is always an " unknown " in the last resort, the Hindu can
fall back on the doctrine of the all-pervading Brahm. He is so
naturally religious that contradictions tend to resolve themselves
in his mind with less difficulty than they would in the mind of a
Westerner, who sees in sharp opposition the doctrine of a personal
God and all that that implies on the one hand, and the conclusions
derived from scientific discovery on the other. It is possible,
therefore, that scepticism, atheism, materialism, and agnosticism
will present less of a problem here than elsewhere and that the
accommodating Brahmans will survive the test, however greatly
India may become Westernized and " educated " in our modern
sense. Meanwhile religion, both at its lowest and at its highest,
is more variously exemplified in Hinduism than anywhere else in
the world.

Verses from the Scriptures

ABBREVIATIONS TO REFERENCES

B.G.	= Bhagavadgita	*Panchat.*	= Panchatantra
Bh. Nit.	= Bhartrihari's Niti-Sataka	*Rāmāy.*	= Rāmāyana
Bri. Up.	= Brihadaranyaka-Upani-	*R.V.*	= Rig-Veda
	shad	*Sri. Bhag.*	= Srimad-Bhagavatam
Hitop.	= Hitopadesa	*Svet. Up.*	= Svetasvatara-Upanishad
Mahabh.	= Mahabharata	*Tait. Up.*	= Taittiriyaka-Upanishad
N.S.	= Narada Smriti	*V.P.*	= Vemana's Padyamulu

Let him (**ascetic**) patiently bear hard words, let him not
insult anybody, and let him not become anybody's enemy for
the sake of this perishable body. Against an angry man let him
not in return show anger, let him bless when he is cursed, and
let him not utter speech devoid of truth. *Manu* 6, 47–8.

Blessings give for curses. *Manu* 6, 48.

Be eyes to the **blind**, friend to the friendless, father and mother
to all who do well. *Panchat.* 1, 12.

Compassion is the root of religion, pride the root of sin.
Tulsi Das.

Kine are of divers colours, but all milk is alike; the kinds of
flowers vary, yet all worship is one; systems of faith are different,

but the **deity** is one. (Flowers are commonly used as offerings in worship of the gods.) *V.P.*

Desire is never extinguished by the enjoyment of desired objects; it only grows stronger like a fire fed with clarified butter. If one man would obtain all those sensual enjoyments and another should renounce them all, the renunciation of all pleasure is far better than the attainment of them. *Manu* 2, 94–5.

Deliver, mighty lord, thy worshippers, purge us from taint of sin, and when we **die**, deal mercifully with us on the pyre, burning our bodies with their load of guilt, but bearing our eternal part on high to luminous abodes and realms of bliss, for ever there to dwell with righteous men. *Manu.*

This is the sum of **duty** : do naught to others which if done to thee, would cause thee pain. *Mahabh.* 5, 1517.

Non-injury, truthfulness, freedom from theft, lust, anger, and greed, and an effort to do what is agreeable and beneficial to all creatures—this is the common **duty** of all castes. *Sri. Bhag.* 11, 17, 21.

One's **duty**, though defective, is better than another's duty well performed. Performing the duty prescribed by nature, one does not incur sin. O son of Kunti! one should not abandon a natural duty though tainted with evil; for all actions are enveloped by evil, as fire by smoke. *B.G.* 18, 47–8.

A **friend** who is the elixir of love to the eyes, the joy of the heart, a vessel of sympathy whether in pleasure or pain, is hardly to be found. Others—filled with the hope of gain—friends in prosperity—these abound everywhere. Truly misfortune is the touchstone of friendship. *Hitop.* 1, 224.

Just heaven is not so pleased with costly **gifts**, offered in hope of future recompense, as with the merest trifle set apart from honest gains, and sanctified by faith. *Mahabh.* 14, 2788.

Conquer a man who never gives by **gifts**; subdue untruthful men by truthfulness; vanquish an angry man by gentleness; and overcome the evil man by goodness. *Mahabh.* 3, 13253.

I **God** am of even mind towards all beings; none is hateful to me nor dear; but they who worship me with devotion are in me and I also in them. *B.G.* 9, 29.

He is the one **God** hidden in all beings, all-pervading, the self within all beings, watching over all worlds, dwelling in all beings, the witness, the perceiver.   *Svet. Up.* 6, 11.

He who is the same to foe and friend, honour and dishonour, who is the same in cold and heat, pleasure and pain, and is without attachment, who holds blame and praise equal, silent, content with anything, without a home, of firm thought and full of devotion, to me (**God**) that man is dear.   *B.G.* 12, 18–19.

The study of the Vedas, austerity, the pursuit of knowledge, purity, control over the organs, the performance of meritorious acts and meditation on the soul, are the marks of the quality of **goodness.** *Manu* 12, 31.

For not by years, nor by **grey hair**, not by wealth or kindred is superiority; the seers made the rule—who knows the Veda completely, he is great among us. . . . One is not, therefore, aged because his head is grey; whoever, although a youth, has perused the Vedas, him the gods consider an elder.   *Manu* 2, 154, 156.

Even to foes who visit us as **guests** due hospitality should be displayed; the tree screens with its leaves, the man who fells it. *Mahabh.* 12, 5528.

True **happiness** consists in making happy.   *Bharavi's Kiratarjuniya* 7, 28.

The instructor, the learner, the hearer and the enemy are always within the **heart.** *Anugita* 11, 17.

From the unreal, lead me to the real, from darkness lead me to light, from death lead me to **immortality.** *Bri. Up.* 1, 3, 28.

Knowledge only on the surface : love bought for money : food at the expense of another : these are three miseries of men. *Hitop.* 1, 147.

He (God) is the **light** of all lights and luminous beyond all the darkness of our ignorance. He is knowledge and the object of knowledge. He is seated in the hearts of all. *B.G.* 13, 17.

To him, who sees **Me** in everything and everything in Me, I am never lost, and he is not lost to Me. *B.G.* 6, 30.

Let **mutual fidelity** continue until death, this may be considered as the summary of the highest law for husband and wife.

Let man and woman, united in marriage, constantly exert themselves, that they may not be disunited and may not violate their mutual fidelity. *Manu* 9, 101–2.

Let him carefully avoid all undertakings the success of which depends on **others**; but let him eagerly pursue that the accomplishment of which depends on himself. Everything that depends on others gives pain, everything that depends on oneself gives pleasure; know that this is the short definition of pleasure and pain. *Manu* 4, 159–60.

Wound not **others**, do no one injury by thought or deed, utter no word to pain thy fellow-creatures. *Manu* 2, 161.

The good of **others** leads to religious merit, causing pain to others is sin. *Rishi Veda Vyas.*

Enjoy thou the **prosperity** of others, although thyself unprosperous; noble men take pleasure in their neighbour's happiness. *Mahabh.* 12, 3880.

Purity of body comes by water, purity of mind by truthfulness. The lamp of truth is a lamp of the wise. *Vedas.*

Honour thy father and mother. Forget not the favours thou hast received. Seek the society of the good. Live in harmony with others. Remain in thy own place. Speak ill of none. The sweetest bread is that earned by labour. Knowledge is riches, what one learns in youth is engraven on stone. The wise is he who knows himself. There is no tranquil sleep without a good conscience, nor any virtue without **religion**. *Avaiyar.*

Our lives are for the purpose of **religion**, labour, love and salvation. If these are destroyed, what is not lost? If these are preserved, what is not preserved? *Hitop.* 1, 2.

Sacrifice, study of the sacred scriptures, almsgiving and penance; truth, fortitude, patience, and freedom from covetousness. This is the eightfold road leading to **righteousness**. *Hitop* 1, 7.

Charity done in secret, eager courtesy to the visitor of his house, silence after doing kindness and public mention after receiving it; modesty in fortune, conversation without spice of insolence, who taught good men this **rule of life**, hard as a sword's edge to tread? *Bh. Nit.* 28.

A man should elevate his **self** by his self; he should not debase his self, for even a man's own self is his friend. A man's own self is also his enemy. *B.G.* 6, 5.

Thus he who by means of **self** sees self in all created things, after attaining equality with the all, enters into Brahma, the highest place. *Manu* 12, 125.

Depend not on another, rather lean upon thyself; trust to thine own exertions . . . true happiness consists in **self-reliance.** *Manu* 4, 160.

Bear **shame** and glory with an equal peace and an ever tranquil heart. *B.G.* 12, 1.

The embodied **soul** casts away old and takes up new bodies as a man changes worn-out raiment for new. Weapons cannot cleave it, nor the fire burn, nor do the waters drench it, nor the wind dry. It is uncleavable, it is incombustible, it can neither be drenched nor dried. Eternally stable, immobile, all-pervading, it is for ever and ever . . . therefore knowing it as such thou should'st not grieve. *B.G.* 2, 22-5.

If you ask whether among all these virtuous actions, performed here below, there be one which has been declared more efficacious than the rest for securing supreme happiness to man, the answer is that the knowledge of the **soul** is stated to be the most excellent among all of them; for that is the first of all sciences because immortality is gained through that. *Manu* 12, 84-5.

Thou canst not gather what thou dost not **sow**; as thou dost plant the tree so will it grow. *Manu* 9, 40.

Truth, self-control, asceticism, generosity, non-injury, constancy in virtue,—these are the means of **success**, not caste nor family. *Mahabh.* 3, 181, 42.

He by whom the **swans** were formed white—by whom the parrots were made green—by whom the varied hues were given to the peacocks, he will give thee thy subsistence. *Hitop.* 1, 189.

Thou art **thyself** a stream whose sacred ford is self-restraint, whose water is veracity, whose bank is virtue, and whose waves are love; here practise thy ablutions; by mere water the inner man can ne'er be purified. *Hitop.* 4, 90.

Truth is said to be the one unequalled means of purification of the soul. Truth is the ladder by which man ascends to heaven, as a ferry plies from one bank of a river to the other. *N.S.* 1, 210.

From the **unreal** lead me to the real. From darkness lead me to light. From death lead me to immortality. *Bri. Up.* 1, 3, 38.

Virtue is spotlessness of mind; all else is mere noise. *Tiruvalluvar.*

Brahmin **vows** :

1. Not to injure living beings.
2. Not to lie.
3. Not to steal.
4. To be continent.
5. To be liberal.

How can true happiness proceed from **wealth,** which in its acquisition causes pain; in loss, affliction; in abundance, folly. *Hitop.* 1, 192.

Where **women** are honoured, there the gods rejoice; but where they are not honoured, there all rites are fruitless. Where women grieve, that family quickly perishes; but where they do not grieve, that family ever prospers. *Manu* 3, 56–7.

To carry out an enterprise in **words** is easy; to accomplish it by acts is the sole test of man's capacity. *Rāmāy.* 4, 67, 10.

Looking upon all beings as myself, in thought, word and deed is the best of all methods of **worship.** *Sri. Bhag.* 11, 29, 19.

Readings from the Scriptures

In the beginning there was neither naught nor aught;
Then there was neither sky nor atmosphere above.
What then enshrouded all this teeming Universe ?
In the receptacle of what was it contained ?
Was it enveloped in the gulf profound of water ?
Then was there neither death nor immortality,
Then was there neither day, nor night, nor light, nor darkness,
Only the existent One breathed calmly, self-contained.
Naught else than him there was—naught else above, beyond.
Then first came darkness hid in darkness, gloom in gloom.

Next all was water, all a chaos indiscrete,
In which the One lay void, shrouded in nothingness.
Then turning inwards, He by self-developed force
Of inner fervour and intense abstraction, grew.
And now in Him Desire, the primal germ of mind
Arose, which learned men, profoundly searching, say
Is the first subtle bond, connecting Entity
With Nullity.　This ray that kindled dormant life,
Where was it then ? before ? or was it found above ?
Were there parturient powers and latent qualities,
And fecund principle beneath, and active forces
That energized aloft ?　Who knows ?　Who can declare ?
How and from what has sprung this Universe ? the gods
Themselves are subsequent to its development.
Who then can penetrate the secret of its rise ?
Whether t'was framed or not, made or not made, He only
Who in the highest heaven sits, the omniscient Lord,
Assuredly knows all, or haply knows He not.　*R.V.*

What god shall we adore with sacrifice ?
Him let us praise, the golden child that rose
In the beginning, who was born the lord—
The one sole lord of all that is—who made
The earth, and formed the sky, who giveth life,
Who giveth strength, whose bidding gods revere,
Whose hiding place is immortality.
Whose shadow, death; who by his might is king
Of all the breathing, sleeping, waking, world—
Who governs men and beasts, whose majesty
These snowy hills, this ocean with its rivers,
Declare; of whom these spreading regions form
The arms; by whom the firmament is strong,
Earth firmly planted, and the highest heavens
Supported, and the clouds that fill the air
Distributed and measured out; to whom
Both earth and heaven, established by his will,
Look up with trembling mind; in whom revealed
The rising sun shines forth upon the world.
Where'er let loose in space, the mighty waters
Have gone, depositing a fruitful seed,

And generating fire, there He arose,
Who is the breath and life of all the gods,
Whose mighty glance looks round the vast expanse
Of watery vapour—source of energy,
Cause of the sacrifice—the only God
Above the gods. May he not injure us!
He the Creator of the earth—the righteous
Creator of the sky, Creator too
Of oceans bright, and far-extending waters.

R.V.

Agni, thou art a sage, a priest, a king,
Protector, father of the sacrifice.
Commissioned by us men, thou dost ascend
A messenger, conveying to the sky
Our hymns and offerings. Though thy origin
Be threefold, now from air, and now from water,
Now from the mystic double Arani,
Thou art thyself a mighty god, a lord,
Giver of life and immortality;
One in thy essence, but to mortals three;
Displaying thine eternal triple form,
As fire on earth, as lightning in the air,
As sun in heaven. Thou art the cherished guest
In every household—father, brother, son,
Friend, benefactor, guardian, all in one.
Deliver, mighty lord, thy worshippers,
Purge us from taint of sin, and when we die,
Deal mercifully with us on the pyre,
Burning our bodies with their load of guilt,
But bearing our eternal part on high
To luminous abodes and realms of bliss,
For ever there to dwell with righteous men.

R.V.

To Yama, mighty king, be gifts and homage paid.
He was the first of men that died, the first to brave
Death's rapid rushing stream, the first to point the road
To heaven, and welcome others to that bright abode.
No power can rob us of the home thus won by thee.
O king, we come; the born must die, must tread the path

That thou hast trod—the path by which each race of men,
In long succession, and our fathers, too, have passed.
Soul of the dead! depart; fear not to take the road—
The ancient road—by which thy ancestors have gone;
Ascend to meet the god—to meet thy happy fathers,
Who dwell in bliss with him. Fear not to pass the guards—
The four-eyed brindled dogs—that watch for the departed.
Return unto thy home, O soul! Thy sin and shame
Leave thou behind on earth; assume a shining form—
Thy ancient shape—refined and from all taint set free.

R.V.

The mighty Varuna, who rules above, looks down
Upon these worlds, his kingdom, as if close at hand.
When men imagine they do aught by stealth, he knows it.
No one can stand, or walk, or softly glide along,
Or hide in dark recess, or lurk in secret cell,
But Varuna detects him, and his movements spies.
Two persons may devise some plot, together sitting,
And think themselves alone; but he, the king, is there—
A third—and sees it all. His messengers descend
Countless from his abode, for ever traversing
This world, and scanning with a thousand eyes its inmates.
What'er exists within this earth, and all within the sky,
Yea, all that is beyond, king Varuna perceives.
The winkings of men's eyes are numbered all by him :
He wields the universe as gamesters handle dice.

Atharva-Veda 4, 16.

Say what is true! Do thy duty. Do not swerve from the
truth. Do not swerve from duty. Do not neglect what is useful.
Do not neglect greatness. Let thy mother be to thee like unto
a god! Let thy father be to thee like unto a god! Let thy
teacher be to thee like unto a god. Let thy guest be to thee like
unto a god. Whatever actions are blameless, those should be
regarded, not others. Whatever is given should be given with
faith, not without faith—with joy, with modesty, with kindness.
Thus conduct thyself. This is the true rule. This is the teaching. This is the true purport of the Veda. This is the command.
Thus should you observe. Thus should this be observed. *Tait.
Up.* Valli I, Anuvaka 10.

A person is made not of acts, but of desires only. As is his
desire, such is his resolve; as is his resolve, such the action
he performs; what action he performs, that he procures for
himself.

> Where one's mind is attached—the inner self
> Goes thereto with action, being attached to it alone.
> Obtaining the end of his action,
> Whatever he does in this world,
> He comes again from that world
> To this world of action.

So the man who desires.

Now the man who does not desire.—He who is without desire,
who is freed from desire, whose desire is satisfied, whose desire
is the Soul—his breaths do not depart. Being very Brahma, he
goes to Brahma.

> When are liberated all
> The desires that lodge in one's heart,
> Then a mortal becomes immortal!
> Therein he reaches Brahma!

Bri. Up. 4, 4, 5–7.

> May Sun and Anger, may the lords of anger
> Preserve me from my sins of pride and passion.
> What'er the nightly sins of thought, word, deed,
> Wrought by my mind, my speech, my hands, my feet,
> Wrought through my appetite and sensual organs,
> May the departing Night remove them all!
> In thy immortal light, O radiant Sun,
> I offer up myself and this my guilt.

Taittiriya Aranyaka 10, 25.

At the end of that day and night he who was asleep, awakes
and, after awaking, creates mind, which is both real and unreal.
Mind, impelled by Brahman's desire to create, performs the
work of creation by modifying itself, thence ether is produced;
they declare that sound is the quality of the latter. But from
ether, modifying itself, springs the pure, powerful wind, the
vehicle of all perfumes; that is held to possess the quality of
touch. Next from wind, modifying itself, proceeds the brilliant
light, which illuminates and dispels darkness; that is declared to
possess the quality of colour; and from light, modifying itself,

is produced water, possessing the quality of taste, from water earth which has the quality of smell; such is the creation in the beginning. *Manu* 1, 74-8.

Learn that sacred law which is followed by men learned in the Veda and assented to in their hearts by the virtuous, who are ever exempt from hatred and inordinate affection. To act solely from a desire for rewards is not laudable, yet an exemption from that desire is not to be found in this world : for on that desire is grounded the study of the Veda and the performance of the actions, prescribed by the Veda. The desire for rewards, indeed, has its root in the conception that an act can yield them, and in consequence of that conception sacrifices are performed; vows and the laws prescribing restraints are all stated to be kept through the idea that they will bear fruit. Not a single act here below appears ever to be done by a man free from desire; for whatever man does, it is the result of the impulse of desire. He who persists in discharging these prescribed duties in the right manner, reaches the deathless state and even in this life obtains the fulfilment of all the desires that he may have conceived. *Manu* 2, 1-5.

The gift of the Veda surpasses all other gifts, water, food, cows, land, clothes, sesamum, gold, and clarified butter. For whatever purpose a man bestows any gift, for that same purpose he receives in the next birth with due honour its reward. Both he who respectfully receives a gift, and he who respectfully bestows it, go to heaven; in the contrary case they both fall into hell. . . . Giving no pain to any creature, let him slowly accumulate spiritual merit, for the sake of acquiring a companion to the next world, just as the white ant gradually raises its hill. For in the next world neither father, nor mother, nor wife, nor sons, nor relations stay to be his companions; spiritual merit alone remains with him. Single is each being born; single it dies; single it enjoys the reward of its virtue; single it suffers the punishment of its sin. Leaving the dead body on the ground like a log of wood, or a clod of earth, the relatives depart with averted faces; but spiritual merit follows the soul. Let him therefore always slowly accumulate spiritual merit, in order that it may be his companion after death; for with merit as his companion he will traverse a gloom difficult to traverse. That companion speedily conducts the man who is devoted to duty and effaces his sins by austerities, to the next world, radiant and clothed with an ethereal body. *Manu* 4, 233–43.

He who injures innoxious beings from a wish to give himself pleasure, never finds happiness, neither living nor dead. He who does not seek to cause the sufferings of bonds and death to living creatures, but desires the good of all beings, obtains endless bliss. He who does not injure any creature, attains without an effort what he thinks of, what he undertakes, and what he fixes his mind on. Meat can never be obtained without injury to living creatures, and injury to sentient beings is detrimental to the attainment of heavenly bliss; let him therefore shun the use of meat. *Manu* 5, 45–8.

Punishment alone governs all created beings, punishment alone protects them, punishment watches over them while they sleep; the wise declare punishment to be identical with the law. If punishment is properly inflicted after due consideration, it makes all people happy; but inflicted without consideration, it destroys everything. . . . The whole world is kept in order by punishment, for a guiltless man is hard to find; through fear of punishment the whole world yields the enjoyments which it owes. *Manu* 7, 18–19, 22.

By confession, by repentance, by austerity, and by reciting the Veda a sinner is freed from guilt, and in case no other course is possible, by liberality. In proportion as a man who has done wrong, himself confesses it, even so far he is freed from guilt, as a snake from its slough. In proportion as his heart loathes his evil deed, even so far is his body freed from that guilt. He who has committed a sin and has repented, is freed from that sin, but he is purified only by the resolution of ceasing to sin and thinking " I will do so no more." Having thus considered in his mind what results will arise from his deeds after death, let him always be good in thoughts, speech, and actions. . . . If his mind be uneasy with respect to any act, let him repeat the austerities prescribed as a penance for it until they fully satisfy his conscience. . . . Whatever is hard to be traversed, whatever is hard to be attained, whatever is hard to be reached, whatever is hard to be performed, all this may be accomplished by austerities; for austerity possesses a power which is difficult to surpass. (Both those who have committed mortal sin (Mahapataka) and all other offenders are severally freed from their guilt by means of well-performed austerities.) Whatever sin men commit by thoughts, words, or deeds, that they speedily burn away by penance, if they keep penance as their only riches. . . . The daily study of the Veda, the performance of the great sacrifices according to one's ability, and patience in suffering quickly destroys all guilt, even that caused by mortal sins. *Manu* 11, 228–32, 234, 239–42, 246.

Even though wronged, treat not with disrespect thy father, mother, teacher, elder brother. (2, 226.)

From poison thou mayest take the food of life, the purest gold from lumps of impure earth, examples of good conduct from a foe, sweet speech and gentleness from e'en a child, something from all; from men of low degree lessons of wisdom, if thou humble be. (2, 238–9.)

Wound not another, though by him provoked, do no one injury by thought or deed, utter no word to pain thy fellow-creatures. (2, 161.)

Treat no one with disdain, with patience bear reviling language; with an angry man be never angry; blessings give for curses. (6, 47–8.)

When asked, give something, though a very trifle, ungrudgingly and with a cheerful heart, according to thy substance; only see that he to whom thou givest worthy be. (4, 227–8).

Pride not thyself on thy religious works, give to the poor, but talk not of thy gifts, by pride religious merit melts away, the merit of thy alms by ostentation. (4, 236–7.)

The soul is its own witness; yea, the soul itself is its own refuge; grieve thou not, O man, thy soul, the great internal Witness. (8, 84.)

When thou hast sinned, think not to hide thy guilt under a cloak of penance and austerity. (4, 198.)

Contentment is the root of happiness, and discontent the root of misery. Wouldst thou be happy, be thou moderate. (4, 12.)

Honour thy food, receive it thankfully, eat it contentedly and joyfully ne'er hold it in contempt; avoid excess, for gluttony is

hateful, injures health, may lead to death, and surely bars the
road to holy merit and celestial bliss. (2, 54, 57.)

The man who keeps his senses in control, his speech, heart,
actions pure and ever guarded, gains all the fruit of holy study;
he needs neither penance nor austerity. (2, 160.)

Contentment, patience under injury, self-subjugation, honesty,
restraint of all the sensual organs, purity, devotion, knowledge of
the Deity, veracity, and abstinence from anger, these form the
tenfold summary of duty. (6, 92.)

Precepts of Manu.

As a man, casting off old clothes, puts on others and new ones,
so the embodied self casting off old bodies, goes to others and new
ones. Weapons do not divide it into pieces; fire does not burn
it; waters do not moisten it; the wind does not dry it up. It is
not divisible; it is not combustible; it is not to be moistened; it
is not to be dried up. It is everlasting, all-pervading, stable,
firm, and eternal. It is said to be unperceived, to be unthinkable,
to be unchangeable. . . . For to one that is born, death is certain;
and to one that dies, birth is certain. . . . This embodied self,
O descendant of Bharata! within every one's body is ever in-
destructible. . . . Looking alike on pleasure and pain, on gain
and loss, on victory and defeat, then prepare for battle, and thus
you will not incur sin. . . . He who has obtained devotion in
this world casts off both merit and sin. Therefore apply yourself
to devotion; devotion in all actions is wisdom. The wise who
have obtained devotion cast off the fruit of action; and released
from the shackles of repeated births, repair to that seat where
there is no unhappiness. . . . He whose heart is not agitated in
the midst of calamities, who has no longing for pleasures, and from
whom the feelings of affection, fear, and wrath have departed, is
called a sage of steady mind. *B.G.* 2, 22–5, 27, 30, 38, 49–51, 56.

Perform all necessary acts, for action
Is better than inaction, none can live
By sitting still and doing nought; it is
By action only that a man attains
Immunity from action. Yet in working
Ne'er work for recompense; let the act's motive
Be in the act itself. Know that work
Proceeds from the Supreme. I am the pattern

For man to follow; know that I have done
All acts already, nought remains for me
To gain by action, yet I work for ever
Unweariedly, and this whole universe
Would perish if I did not work my work.

                                        B.G. 3, 19.

He who even in this world, before his release from the body,
is able to bear the agitations produced from desire and wrath, is
a devoted man, he is a happy man. The devotee whose happiness
is within himself, whose recreation is within himself, and whose
light of knowledge also is within himself, becoming one with the
Brahman, obtains the Brahmic bliss. The sages whose sins have
perished, whose misgivings are destroyed, who are self-restrained,
and who are intent on the welfare of all beings, obtain the Brahmic
bliss. To the ascetics, who are free from desire and wrath, and
whose minds are restrained, and who have knowledge of the self,
the Brahmic bliss is on both sides of death. *B.G.* 5, 23–6.

There is nothing higher than I (God), O winner of wealth.
All this universe is strung upon me as rows of jewels upon a
string. I am the taste in water, the light in sun and moon, the
A U M in the Vedas, manhood in man. The might of the mighty
and the heat of the fire, the wisdom of the wise, the splendour of
the magnificent. From me come the moods of goodness, fire
and melancholy. I am not in them but they are in me. And
bewildered by these three moods the whole universe fails in
understanding that I sit above them and am changeless. For
divine magic of moods is hard to see through, but they who cling
to me transcend this magic. *B.G.* 7, 6–14.

I am the Kratu,[1] I am the Yagna,[2] I am the Svadhâ,[3] I the
product of the herbs.[4] I am the sacred verse. I too am the
sacrificial butter, and I the fire, I the offering. I am the father
of this universe, the mother, the creator, the grandsire, the thing
to be known, the means of sanctification, the syllable Om, the
Rik, Sâman, and Yagus also; the goal, the sustainer, the lord,
the supervisor, the residence, the asylum, the friend, the source,

---

[1] Kratu is a Vedic sacrifice.
[2] Yagna, a sacrifice laid down in Smritis.
[3] Svadhâ is an offering to the manes (Good People).
[4] Product of the herbs is food prepared from vegetables, or medicine.

and that in which it merges, the support, the receptacle, and the inexhaustible seed. I cause heat and I send forth and stop showers. I am immortality and also death; and I, O Arguna! am that which is and that which is not. *B.G.* 9, 16–19.

That devotee of mine, who hates no being, who is friendly, and compassionate, who is free from egoism, and from the idea that this or that is mine, to whom happiness and misery are alike, who is forgiving, contented, constantly devoted, self-restrained, and firm in his determinations, and whose mind and understanding are devoted to me, he is dear to me. He through whom the world is not agitated, and who is not agitated by the world, who is free from joy and anger, and fear and agitation, he too is dear to me. He who is full of devotion to me, who feels no joy and no aversion, who does not grieve and does not desire, who abandons both what is agreeable and what is disagreeable, he is dear to me. He who is alike to friend and foe, as also in honour and dishonour, who is alike in cold and heat, pleasure and pain, who is free from attachments, to whom praise and blame are alike, who is taciturn, and contented with anything whatever that comes, who is homeless, and of a steady mind, and full of devotion, that man is dear to me. *B.G.* 12, 13–19.

Absence of vanity, absence of ostentatiousness, absence of hurtfulness, forgiveness, straightforwardness, devotion to a preceptor, purity, steadiness, self-restraint, indifference towards objects of sense, and also absence of egoism; perception of the misery and evil of birth, death, old age, and disease; absence of attachment, absence of self-identifying regard for son, wife, home, and so forth; and constant equability on the approach of both what is agreeable and what is disagreeable; unswerving devotion to me, without meditation on any one else; resorting to clean places, distaste for assemblages of men, constancy in knowledge of the relation of the individual self to the supreme, perception of the object of knowledge of the truth, this is called knowledge; that is ignorance which is opposed to this. *B.G.* 13, 7–11.

Who is self-contained; to whom pain and pleasure are alike; to whom a sod and a stone and gold are alike; to whom what is agreeable and what is disagreeable are alike; who has discernment; to whom censure and praise of himself are alike; who is alike in honour and dishonour; who is alike towards the sides of friends and foes; and who abandons all action. And he who worships me with an unswerving devotion, transcends these qualities, and becomes fit for entrance into the essence of the Brahman. *B.G.* 14, 23–7.

Freedom from fear, purity of heart, perseverance in pursuit of knowledge and abstraction of mind, gifts, self-restraint, and sacrifice, study of the Vedas, penance, straightforwardness, harmlessness, truth, freedom from anger, renunciation, tranquillity, freedom from the habit of backbiting, compassion of all beings, freedom from avarice, gentleness, modesty, absence of vain activity, noblemindedness, forgiveness, courage, purity, freedom from a desire to injure others, absence of vanity, these, O descendant of Bharata! are his who is born to godlike endowments. *B.G.* 16, 1–3.

> Entangled in a hundred worldly snares,
> Self-seeking men, by ignorance deluded,
> Strive by unrighteous means to pile up riches.
> Then, in their self-complacency, they say,
> "This acquisition I have made to-day,
> That I will gain to-morrow; so much pelf
> Is hoarded up already, so much more
> Remains that I have yet to treasure up.
> This enemy I have destroyed, him also,
> And others in their turn I will despatch.
> I am a lord; I will enjoy myself;
> I'm wealthy, noble, strong, successful, happy;
> I'm absolutely perfect; no one else
> In all the world can be compared to me.
> Now I will offer up a sacrifice,
> Give gifts with lavish hand and be triumphant."
> Such men, befooled by endless vain conceits,
> Caught in the meshes of the world's illusion,
> Immersed in sensuality, descend
> Down to the foulest hell of unclean spirits.
>
> *B.G.* 16, 12–16.

The unperceived is the source of the worlds; and the same is also the end of everything. Days end with the sun's setting;

the night ends with the sun's rising; the end of pleasure is ever grief; the end of grief ever pleasure. All accumulations end in exhaustion; all ascents end in falls; all associations end in dissociations; and life ends in death. All action ends in destruction; death is certain for whatever is born; everything movable or immovable in this world is ever transient. Sacrifice, gift, penance, study, observances and regulations, all this ends in destruction. There is no end for knowledge. Therefore one whose self is tranquil, whose senses are subjugated, who is devoid of the idea that this or that is mine, who is devoid of egoism, is released from all sins by pure knowledge. *Anugita* 29.

The wheel of life moves on; a wheel of which the spoke is the understanding, of which the pole is the mind, of which the bonds are the group of the senses, of which the outer rim is the five great elements, of which the environment is home; which abounds in old age and grief, which moves in the midst of disease and misfortune, which rotates in space and time; the noise of which is trouble and toil, the rotations of which constituted day and night; which is encircled with cold and heat; of which pleasure and pain are the joints, and hunger and thirst the nails fixed into it, of which sunshine and shade are the ruts; which staggers in the opening or closing of an eyelid, which is enveloped in the fearful waters of delusion, which is ever revolving and void of consciousness, which is measured by months and half months, is ever-changing, which moves through all the worlds; the mud for which is penance and regulations, the mover of which is the force of the quality of passion; which is lit up by the great egoism, which is sustained by the qualities; the fastenings in which are vexations; which revolves in the midst of grief and destruction, which is full of actions and instruments of action, which is large, and which is extended by means of attachments, which is rendered unsteady by avarice and desire, which is produced by ignorance of various matters, which is attended upon by fear and delusion, and which is the cause of the delusion of all beings, which moves towards joy and pleasure, which has desire and wrath as its appurtenances, which is made up of the entities beginning with the Mahat and ending with the gross elements, which is unchecked, the imperishable source of all, the speed of which is like that of the mind, and which is never fatigued. This wheel of life, which is associated with the pairs of opposites, and which is devoid of consciousness, all the world, together with the immortals, should cast away, abridge, and check. That man, among all creatures, who always accurately understands the movement and stoppage of the wheel of life is never deluded. *Anugita* 30.

A dispute once arose among the sages which of the three gods was greatest. They applied to the greatest of all sages—Bhrigu—to determine the point. He undertook to put all three gods to a severe test. He went first to Brahma, and omitted all obeisance. The god's anger blazed forth, but he was at length pacified. Next he went to the abode of Siva, and omitted to return the god's salutation. The irascible god was enraged, his eyes flashed fire, and he raised his Trident weapon to destroy the sage. But the god's wife, Pārvatī, interceded for him. Lastly, Bhrigu went to the heaven of Vishnu, whom he found asleep. To try his forbearance, he gave the god a good kick on his breast, which awoke him. Instead of showing anger, Vishnu asked Bhrigu's pardon for not having greeted him on the first arrival. Then he declared he was highly honoured by the sage's blow. It had imprinted an indelible mark of good fortune on his breast. He trusted the sage's foot was not hurt, and began to rub it gently. ' This ', said Bhrigu, ' is the mightiest god; he overpowers his enemies by the most potent of all weapons—gentleness and generosity.' *Bhagavata-purana* 10, 89.

No disciple of mine must ever intentionally kill any living thing whatever, not even a flea or the most minute insect. (11.)

The killing of any animal for the purpose of sacrifice to the gods is forbidden by me. Abstaining from injury is the highest of all duties. (12.)

No flesh meat must ever be eaten, no spirituous or vinous liquor must ever be drunk, not even as medicine. (15.)

All theft is prohibited, even under pretence of contributing to religious objects. (17.)

No male or female followers of mine must ever commit adultery. (18.)

No false accusation must be laid against any one from motives of self-interest. (20.)

A truth which causes serious injury to one's self or others

ought not to be told. Wicked men, ungrateful people, and persons in love are to be avoided. A bribe must never be accepted. (26.)

A trust must never be betrayed. Confidence must never be violated. Praise of one's self with one's own lips is prohibited. (37.)

Holy men should patiently bear abusive language, or even beating, from evil-minded persons, and wish good to them. (201.)

Wives should honour their husbands as if they were gods, and never offend them with improper language, though they be diseased, indigent, or imbecile. (159.)

They should only eat one meal a day, and should sleep on the ground. (168.)

An act promising good reward, but involving departure from proper duties, must never be committed. (73.)

If by the great men of former days anything unbecoming has been done, their faults must not be imitated, but only their good deeds. (74.)

If knowingly or unintentionally any sin, great or small, be committed, the proper penance must be performed according to ability. (92.)

Every man ought to worship Krishna by means of that soul at all times. (116.)

Towards him alone ought all worship to be directed by every human being on the earth in every possible manner. Nothing else except devotion (bhakti) to him can procure salvation. (113.)

Almsgiving and kind acts towards the poor should always be performed by all. (83.)

A tithe of one's income should be assigned to Krishna; the poor should give a twentieth part. (147.)

Those males and females of my followers who will act according to these directions shall certainly obtain the four great objects of all human desires—religious merit, wealth, pleasure, and beatitude. (206.)

Siksha-patri.

Where'er we walk, Death marches at our side;
Where'er we sit, Death seats himself beside us;
However far we journey, Death continues

Our fellow-pilgrim and goes with us home.
Men take delight in each returning dawn,
And with admiring gaze, behold the glow
Of sunset.   Every season, as it comes,
Fills them with gladness, yet they never reck
That each recurring season, every day
Fragment by fragment bears their life away.
As drifting logs of wood may haply meet
On Ocean's waters, surging to and fro,
And having met, drift once again apart;
So fleeting is a man's association
With wife and children, relatives and wealth,
So surely must a time of parting come.

Rāmāy. 2, 24–7.

Triple restraint of thought and word and deed,
Strict vow of silence, coil of matted hair,
Close shaven head, garments of skin or bark,
Keeping of fasts, ablutions, maintenance
Of sacrificial fires, a hermit's life,
Emaciation—these are all in vain,
Unless the inward soul be free from stain.

Mahabh. 3, 13445.

To injure none by thought or word or deed,
To give to others, and be kind to all—
This is the constant duty of the good.
High-minded men delight in doing good,
Without a thought of their own interest;
When they confer a benefit on others,
They reckon not on favours in return.

Mahabh. 3. 16782, 16797.

Who in this world is able to distinguish
The virtuous from the wicked, both alike
The fruitful earth supports, on both alike
The sun pours down his beams, on both alike
Refreshing breezes blow, and both alike
The waters purify ?   Not so hereafter—
Then shall the good be severed from the bad;
Then in a region bright with golden lustre—

Centre of light and immortality—
The righteous after death shall dwell in bliss.
Then a terrific hell awaits the wicked—
Profound abyss of utter misery—
Into the depths of which bad men shall fall
Headlong and mourn their doom for countless years.
Mahabh. 12, 2798.

This is the sum of all true righteousness—
Treat others, as thou would'st thyself be treated.
Do nothing to thy neighbour, which hereafter
Thou would'st not have thy neighbour do to thee.
In causing pleasure, or in giving pain,
In doing good, or injury to others,
In granting, or refusing a request,
A man obtains a proper rule of action
By looking on his neighbour as himself.
Mahabh. 13, 5571.

Before infirmities creep o'er thy flesh;
Before decay impairs thy strength and mars
The beauty of thy limbs; before the Ender,
Whose charioteer is sickness, hastes towards thee,
Breaks up thy fragile frame and ends thy life,
Lay up the only treasure; do good deeds;
Practise sobriety and self-control;
Amass that wealth which thieves cannot abstract,
Nor tyrants seize, which follows thee at death,
Which never wastes away, nor is corrupted.
Mahabh. 13, 12084.

Heaven's gate is very narrow and minute,
It cannot be perceived by foolish men,
Blinded by vain illusions of the world.
E'en the clear-sighted who discern the way,
And seek to enter, find the portal barred
And hard to be unlocked. Its massive bolts
Are pride and passion, avarice and lust.
Mahabh. 14, 2784.

Blinded by self-conceit and knowing nothing,
Like elephant infatuate with passion,

I thought within myself, I all things knew;
But when by slow degrees I somewhat learnt,
By aid of wise preceptors, my conceit,
Like some disease, passed off; and now I live
In the plain sense of what a fool I am. . . .
The attribute most noble of the hand
Is readiness in giving; of the head,
Bending before a teacher; of the mouth,
Veracious speaking; of a victor's arms,
Undaunted valour; of the inner heart,
Pureness the most unsullied; of the ears,
Delight in hearing and receiving truth—
These are adornments of high-minded men
Better than all the majesty of Empire. . . .
Now for a little while a child, and now
An amorous youth; then for a season turned
Into the wealthy householder; then stripped
Of all his riches, with decrepit limbs
And wrinkled frame, man creeps towards the end
Of life's erratic course; and, like an actor,
Passes behind Death's curtain out of view.

Precepts from Bh. Nit. 2, 8, 55, and 3, 51.

The noble-minded dedicate themselves
To the promotion of the happiness
Of others—e'en of those who injure them.
True happiness consists in making happy. . . .
Let not a little fault in him who does
An act of kindness, minish aught its value. . . .
Riches and pleasure are the root of evil;
Hold them not dear, encourage not their growth;
They are aggressors hard to be subdued,
Destroyers of all knowledge and of truth.

Kiratarjuniya of Bharavi 13, 28, and 7, 15, and 11, 20.

That energy which veils itself in mildness
Is most effective of its object; so
The lamp that burns most brightly owes its force
To oil drawn upwards by a hidden wick. . . .
Wise men rest not on destiny alone,
Nor yet on manly effort, but on both. . . .

Weak persons gain their object when allied
With strong associates; the rivulet
Reaches the ocean by the river's aid.
Sisupāla-badha of Māgha, 2, 85, 86, 100.

Praise not the goodness of the grateful man
Who acts with kindness to his benefactors.
He who does good to those who do him wrong
Alone deserves the epithet of good. . . .
Hear thou a summary of righteousness,
And ponder well the maxim : Never do
To other persons what would pain thyself. . . .
The little-minded ask : Belongs this man
To our own family ?   The noble-hearted
Regard the human race as all akin.
Panchat. 1, 277, and 3, 104, and 5, 38.

A man of truest wisdom will resign
His wealth, and e'en his life, for good of others;
Better abandon life in a good cause,
When death in any case is sure to happen. . . .
He has all wealth who has a mind contented.
To one whose foot is covered with a shoe
The earth appears all carpeted with leather.
Hitop. 1, 45, 152.

3

SHINTOISM

WE saw in the last chapter that Hinduism is the national religion of the Hindus : it belongs to them only and to their country. It has no definite founder, and its origins are prehistoric. In the same way Shintoism is the religion of Japan : it belongs to the Japanese only; it is prehistoric, and has no definite founder. Neither of these religions is concerned with making converts : each is the natural expression of a particular people, part of a social culture which does not admit foreigners.

The word Shinto is an adaptation of two Chinese words—*Shin* and *To*, the Way of the Spirits—and the native form is *Kami-no-michi*. Shintoism, like Hinduism, has shown in the course of its long history, though on a smaller scale, many of the phases described in the Introduction. It started with a primitive nature-worship, similar to that found in the ancient Scriptures of the Hindus, and the Divine Thing was the sky, the sun, the wind, the serpent, the silkworm, or even the insect. From this it passed to a Polytheism, which has never been clearly resolved into a unity, although certain sects and exceptional religious thinkers have attempted at times to assert the existence of a single principle lying behind the plurality of the many gods. Thus the Shinto writer, Izawa-Nagahide, says that the Divine Being " is at one and the same time the 800 myriads of deities. It is the One Great Root of Heaven and Earth and all things in the Universe are in this One God." [1] Again, Shirai-Soin, writing in 1670, says : " The Deity is the Absolute. It transcends human words. It is incomprehensible, and yet it permeates all things." In the Shinto-Gobusho, dating from the thirteenth century, we read that the Divine is " the Spiritual Existence, the Incorporeal Unity, revealing itself in thousands of forms."

[1] This and the following quotations are from Mr. Genchi Kato's *A Study of Shinto, the Religion of the Japanese Nation*. Meiji Japan Society, 1926.

These utterances are, however, exceptional : the main stream of Shintoism remains polytheistic and embodies up to its latest phases the culture of many deities. In defence of Polytheism, Mr. Genchi Kato, in his book *A Study of Shinto, the Religion of the Japanese Nation*, first published in 1926, quotes the words of the New Zealand chief who is reported to have said to a Christian missionary : " Is there one maker of all things amongst you Europeans ? Is not one a carpenter, another a blacksmith, another a shipbuilder, and another a house-builder ? And so it was in the beginning : one made this, another that." [1]

A remarkable feature of Shinto Polytheism is the number of deities involved. In the Kojiki (A.D. 712) and the Nihongi (completed A.D. 720), which are books containing both mythical and historical material, and which are regarded as Scriptures comparable in some ways to the Old Testament, the number is variously given as eighty myriads of deities and eight hundred myriads of deities. In a history of Japan, compiled in the thirteenth century, the number of deities prayed to on the occasion of earthquakes (in A.D. 1215) is cited as thirty-six thousand, historical books quoting 1,370, and again " more than 1,400." It must be remembered, however, that these gods include spirits of all kinds. The word used is *Kami*, which means " above," " superior," and the *Kami* are not only powers derived from early nature-deities, but also the souls of many of the dead, especially those who made sacrifices for their country. A *Kami* may even be a living person. Thus the Emperor and Empress were, at any rate until recently, regarded as *Kami* in their own life-time. The worship of the heroic man, sometimes an ancestor, is thus an addition to the Pantheon of deities, and many of the shrines have their origins in graves.

There have been in the history of Shintoism two broad divisions —the Sectarian or Denominational Shinto (formerly sub-divided into thirteen sects), and the national faith of the Japanese as a nation, the State religion, taught in the schools as national ethics. The latter has been associated with the idea of loyalty to the Jinno (Mikado) or Divine Ruler, and centred in patriotic reverence and a belief in the Japanese as the Chosen People. This is also Shrine Shinto, for it involved respect paid to all the shrines and the countless *Kami* associated with them. In State Shinto, while the

[1] The story is told in Stratton's *Psychology of the Religious Life.*

gods remained manifold, the idea of divinity became unified in the ruler and the nation. Despite its emphasis on national ethics, State Shinto has always been rooted in religious conceptions: it never became purely secular, although the ceremonies were performed by Government officials. The thirteen sects, while accepting the national faith, built upon it systems involving some deity, for whom they sometimes claim supremacy and universality. Thus the Kanko sect worship a " Heaven-and-Earth-including-Deity " the " Boundless One, Absolute Divinity." Most of the sects had individual founders, and believers followed their teachers closely. Thus Sectarian Shinto was a qualification of the main stream of Shinto and super-imposed upon it.

In 1930 State Shinto became part of the totalitarian apparatus and all Japanese were compelled to adopt it. After the defeat of Japan in 1945 it was " abolished " in this form by General MacArthur's decree, but in the post-war revival of religion the number of sects increased rapidly—to 85 in 1948. Shintoism remains a form of religious expression which grew up and developed with the Japanese sense of nationality.

The position of man in relation to divinity has already been referred to as being high in Shintoism. In many religions God and man are thought of as widely separated—God is above, man is below; God is supreme, man, by himself, nothing. Shintoism tends to exalt man to the sphere of divinity, and this is the only sense in which there is Divine Incarnation. A man, it has been said, may *become* divine and be worshipped not only after his death, but also during his life-time. The Emperor was, till lately, a God " visible in the flesh," and many men, especially those who have served their country well, have been similarly regarded. Thus we read : " A righteous man, pure in mind and just in conduct, is himself a Deity ". Moreover, men help to make the gods great by their worship, for we read : " Devotional reverence on the part of man makes a deity more and more supreme."

Traditionally, the head of each family was both father and priest, and became a guardian deity after his death. It should be noticed, however, that the ancestor was worshipped because he had become a *Kami*—rather than as an ancestor as such. Ancestor-worship is not, as often supposed, a fundamental doctrine of the Japanese. It is of Chinese origin, and has been developed mainly under the influence of Chinese ideas. In Shinto it is the *Kami* who rule, and the ancestor may, or may not, be one of these.

Just as the spirits of men may attain divinity and mingle with the gods, so the gods themselves are remarkably human in their attributes, and the books sometimes describe them as having been rewarded with decorations and official grades of honour. The divine and earthly worlds are thus closely interrelated, but it is in the State and nation that the idea of divinity finds fullest and most visible expression; for, as one writer says: " The worship of the Gods is the source of Government, nay, it is Government itself."

The high value set on man and his life in the world and nation largely accounts for the lack of interest in life after death. Personal salvation has never been a distinct aim in Shintoism. The Japanese adore their Land of the Rising Sun, and the place of the dead was originally described as eternal darkness. Divine men may rise to the plane of high Heaven, where the deities dwell, but the emphasis is always on the present life. The Shintoist, like the Chinese, does not regard this world as a vale of tears, but as something highly precious and not willingly to be exchanged for anything else. Nevertheless, the good life on earth is essentially part of religion, and prayers should be made to the gods for divine grace. For such prayer sincerity is the first essential. " The Deity," says the Emperor Nimmyo (A.D. 810–850), " though unseen, is ever ready to respond to prayer from a truthful heart." And again Prince Kane-akira (A.D. 914–987) writes: " Gods or Spirits are impartial and just in mind, pleased only with a man's religious piety. Approach and pray to them with a sincere heart and be sure that you will gain their favour."

Sincerity is, indeed, the leading Shinto virtue and, in the words of Yamaga-Soko, the " surest passport for entrance into communion with the Divine." It is continually stressed by Shinto writers, and a Shinto priest, writing in 1845, says :

> Simplicity the simple virtue is
> That binds Divinity and Man in one.

Purity and impurity are other fundamental conceptions of Shintoism. Purity is the " right and moral way " and pollution " moral evil or vice." " The gods dislike evil deeds because they are impure." The sense of sin was shown in early times by the existence of a ceremony of purification, which was revived by imperial decree in 1872, at the time of the Shinto revival. This was ordered to take place on June 30th and December 31st at all Shinto shrines.

Despite the vast number of deities, the worship in Shintoism is very simple. The shrines are simple too; some of them are so small as to be portable. Priests are attached to them and public prayers offered at them, but they contain no images and involve little in the way of ritual except the State ceremonies on special occasions. A sacred mirror which signifies sincerity hangs in the shrine—otherwise there is little of symbolical significance. The sacred Imperial Regalia, consisting of the Mirror, the Sword, and the Jewel, are the great national symbols—the heirlooms of the imperial line, and are held to symbolize wisdom (or sincerity), courage, and benevolence. There is no table of commandments in Shintoism, no formulated creed, and, except in the cases of particular sects, no Supreme Deity. None the less, it is quite clear that the Way of the Spirits is a religious way, which is epitomized in the national consciousness.

Something must now be said about foreign influence, especially that of Buddhism, which, coming from India, is sometimes claimed to be the real religion of the Japanese. When Buddhism was first introduced, during the sixth century of our era, there was considerable opposition, and even after it had made some progress, Buddhist temples were forbidden near the Ise (principal) shrine, and also the use of Buddhist terminology in the precincts. Both religions were, however, extremely tolerant, and a way was soon found to form a synthesis. Many Buddhist priests accepted the *Kami* as revelations of the Buddhas[1] and took charge of Shinto shrines. Some of them were authorities on Shintoism. On the other hand, Shintoists came to accept the Buddhas as manifestations of their own deities. A Japanese might therefore describe himself as both a Shintoist and a Buddhist.[2] Actually, however, Shinto remains distinct as a culture and a faith, particularly in its aspect as the life of the nation.

Confucianism was another foreign influence, coming this time

[1] Japanese Buddhism recognizes many Buddhas.
[2] These religions were well blended in Bushido, the Knightly code of old Japan.

from China about the sixth century of our era. The sayings of Confucius, which we shall be considering in another chapter, filled a gap in the old Japanese teaching by supplying a large number of ethical maxims. There was no suggestion of a rival deity here, and these were absorbed quite naturally and became part of the general religious approach.

We cannot do better than conclude with some of the words of Hirata (1776–1843), the Japanese Shinto teacher of the nineteenth century, which are quoted by Dr. Estlin Carpenter in his *Comparative Religion*. " Everything," he says, " depends on the *Kami* of Heaven and Earth and therefore the worship of the *Kami* is a matter of primary importance." Hirata's morning prayer before the Kami-dana, a wooden shelf fixed against a wall in a Shinto home and bearing a small model of a temple, ran thus :—

> " Reverently adoring the great God of the two palaces of Ise in the first place, the 800 myriads of celestial *Kami*, the 800 myriads of ancestral *Kami*, all the 1500 myriads to whom are consecrated the great and small temples in all provinces, all islands and all places in the great land of eight islands, the 1500 myriads of *Kami* whom they cause to serve them . . . I pray with awe that they will deign to correct the faults which, heard and seen by them, I have committed, and, blessing and favouring me according to the powers which they severally wield, cause me to perform good works in the way." [1]

This is a true Shinto prayer—the prayer of a polytheist.

Verses from the Scriptures

What is **ablution** ? It is not merely the cleansing of one's body solely with lustral water, it means one's following the Right and Moral Way. Pollution means moral evil or vice. Though a man wash off his bodily filth, he will yet fail to please the Deity if he restrain not his evil desires. *Shinto-Shoden-Kuju.*

Every little yielding to **anxiety** is a step away from the natural heart of man. *God of Fujiyama.*

I have no corporeal existence, but Universal **benevolence** is my divine body. I have no physical power, but Uprightness is

[1] *Comparative Religion*, J. Estlin Carpenter, Williams and Norgate.

my strength. I have no religious clairvoyance beyond what is bestowed by Wisdom, I have no power of miracle other than the attainment of quiet happiness, I have no tact except the exercise of gentleness. *Tōshōgū-Goikun, Oracle of the Deity of Sumi-yoshi.*

Our eyes may see some uncleanness, but let not our mind see things that are not **clean.** Our ears may hear some uncleanness, but let not our mind hear things that are not clean. *Most common Shinto Prayer.*

Deem not that only in this earthly shrine the **Deity** doth reign; the earth entire, and all the Heavens Divine, his presence do proclaim. *Shima-Shigeoyu.*

E'en in a single leaf of a tree, or a tender blade of grass, the awe-inspiring **Deity** manifests Itself. *Urabe-no-Kanekuni.*

What is **faith** ? It literally means true heart, implying sincerity in heart, which itself again is the essence of divine heart. *Inoue-Masakane-Zaitoki.*

If we keep unperverted the human heart—which is like unto heaven and received from earth—that is **God.** *A Revelation to Mikado Seiwa.*

Think not **God** is something distant, but seek for him in your heart, for the heart is the abode of God. That which in Heaven begets all things is, in man, that which makes him love his neighbour, so doubt not that Heaven loves goodness of heart and hates its opposite. Reverence for Heaven and one's ancestors is the foundation of the Way of the sages. *Muro-Kiuso.*

When the sky is clear, and the wind hums in the fir trees, 'tis the heart of **God** who thus reveals himself. *Oracle at a Tajima Shrine.*

All ye under the heaven! Regard **heaven** as your father, earth as your mother, and all things as your brothers and sisters. *Oracle of the Deity Atsuta.*

Attend strictly to the commands of your parents and the instructions of your teachers. Serve your chief with diligence; be upright of heart; eschew falsehood; and be diligent in study; that you may conform to the wishes of the **Heavenly Spirit.** *Oracle of the Deity Temmangu.*

We (the gods) will surely visit the dwellings without invitation, if **lovingkindness** is there always. We make lovingkindness our representative. *Oracle of the Gods of Kasuga.*

Those who do not abandon **mercy** will not be abandoned by me. *Oracle of Itsukushima.*

If that which is within is not perfect, it is useless to **pray** for that which is without. *Oracle of Tatsuta.*

Prayer is of the foremost importance in appealing for the Divine Grace; and uprightness is a fundamental quality in one who would obtain the unseen protection. Although the Sun and Moon continually circle round the four quarters, and illuminate every corner of the globe, yet do they unfailingly shine upon the heads of the upright. *Yamatohime-no-Mikoto-Seiki in the Shinto-Gobusho.*

Prayers to the Deity accompanied by monetary gifts secured by injustice are sure not to be granted. Pray in all righteousness and the Deity will be pleased to listen to your supplication. Foolish is he who, in impatient eagerness and without following the path of righteousness, hopes to obtain divine protection. *Shinto-Uden-Futsujosho.*

If you desire to obtain help, put away **pride**. Even a hair of pride shuts you off, as it were by a great cloud. *Oracle of the Gods of Kasuga.*

All ye who come before me, hoping to attain the accomplishment of your desires, pray with hearts **pure** from falsehood, clean within and without, reflecting the truth like a mirror. *Oracle of the Deity Temmantenjin.*

To do good is to be **pure**; to commit evil is to be impure. The deities abhor evil deeds because they are impure. *The Shinto-Gubusho.*

The surest passport for entrance into communion with the Divine is **sincerity**. If you pray to the Deity with Sincerity, you will assuredly realize the divine presence. *Chūchō-Jijitsu.*

I am none but Benevolence Itself. **Sincerity** is my own divine body. *Oracle of God Hachiman. Jingishoju.*

Sincerity is the single virtue that binds divinity and man in one. *Senge-Takatomi.*

The noblest attribute possessed in life most surely is **sincerity** of mind—that shines serenely through the whole world's strife and man to man in brotherhood doth bind. *Kurozumi Munetada.*

So long as a man's mind is in accord with the way of **truthfulness** the gods will guard him though he may not pray. *Sugawarano-Michizane.*

What pleases the deity is **virtue** and sincerity, and not any number of material offerings. *The Shinto-Gobusho.*

Leave the things of this **world**, and come to me daily and monthly with pure bodies and pure hearts. *Oracle of the Deity Atago.*

> In each of the three wondrous **worlds of life**—
> The past, the present, and that yet to come—
> The first before our birth, the second now,
> The next to open when we breathe our last—
> Through all are we maintained by Grace Divine!
> *Tachibana-no-Sanki.*

If the poorest of mankind come here once for **worship**, I will surely grant their heart's desire. *Oracle of Itsukushima in Aki.*

Readings from the Scriptures

Precepts of Jyegasu (Nikko, Japan)

(There are twenty miles of cryptomeria trees leading up to the red lacquer bridge, with its temple above.)

Life is like unto a long journey with a heavy load. Let your footsteps be slow and steady that you stumble not. Persuade yourself that imperfection and not inconvenience, are the natural lot of mortals, then there will be no room for discontent neither for despair. When ambitious desires arise in thy heart, recall the days of extremity thou hast passed through. Forbearance is the root of quietness and lasting happiness. Look upon wrath as thy enemy. If thou knowest only what it is to conquer and knowest not what it is to be defeated, woe unto thee, it will fare ill with thee. Find fault with thyself rather than with others.

If the Sovran Gods will bestow in ears many a hand's breadth long and ears abundant the latter harvest which they will bestow, the latter harvest produced by the labour of men from whose arms the foam drips down, on whose opposing thighs the mud is gathered, I will fulfil their praises by humbly offering first fruits, of ears a thousand, of ears many a hundred, raising up the tops of the sake-jars and setting in rows the bellies of the sake-jars, in juice and in ear will I present them, of things growing in the great moor-plain, sweet herbs and bitter herbs, of things that dwell in the blue sea-plain, the broad of fin and the narrow of fin, edible seaweed, too, from the offing and seaweed from the shore, of clothing, bright stuffs and shining stuffs, soft stuffs and coarse stuffs—with these I will fulfil your praises.

The Toshigohi—prayer for harvest.

Ten Negative Precepts of Shinto

1. Do not transgress the will of the gods.
2. Do not forget your obligations to ancestors.
3. Do not transgress the decrees of the state.
4. Do not forget the profound goodness of the gods, whereby misfortune is averted and sickness is healed.
5. Do not forget that the world is one great family.
6. Do not forget the limitations of your own person.
7. Even though others become angry do not become angry yourself.
8. Do not be slothful in your business.
9. Do not be a person who brings blame to the teaching.
10. Do not be carried away by foreign teachings.

4

JUDAISM

IN the second chapter of this book we tried to obtain in broad outline a view of Hinduism. We saw that it is a religion belonging to a particular people and that it does not go outside its own borders to obtain converts. In the third chapter we found that the same was true of the Shintoists of Japan. The religion of the Jews is also associated with a particular people, as its name, Judaism (or Hebraism), implies, and it is thus, like the first two, a non-proselytizing religion. But whereas both the Hindus and the Japanese have been settled in lands of their own from very early times, the Jews have suffered continual disruption, having been captive both in Egypt and Babylon, and finally losing their country altogether when the Roman Emperor Titus took Jerusalem in A.D. 70. Their country of Palestine was, in any case, a very small and unsettled one as compared with the vast, self-contained peninsula of India and the isolated and compact islands of Japan. It was on a trade route between Assyria and Egypt, the scene of constant conflict between the great empires of the ancient world, a buffer state in which there was no security. The religion was not therefore helped by geographical facts, and its history is all the more remarkable on that account. It is only since the final dispersion that the Jews have formally ceased to make converts. Once they were zealous missionaries, and their religion was by no means inherited as a right by birth. It was a creed which had to be sincerely believed by the individual, and it was offered to anyone who could receive it. The Jews still believe that they have the universal truth. Thus in one of the liturgies for the New Year there is a prayer for the ultimate conversion of mankind.

The teachings of Judaism are easier to understand than those of the Hindus or the Shintoists. This is partly because we are familiar with the main outlines, from the Jewish writings in the Old Testament, which is still read in our churches, and which forms a foundation to Christianity. But it is also because the outstanding doctrine is a simple, uncompromising belief in One God only, a single-hearted monotheism. The Jewish God, Yahweh, or Jehovah (the word is really the same—the first spelling giving the correct pronunciation), has much of that quality which we call *personality*. He is not only a great, indeed the supreme, Being, but He is also emphatically, and always, a *Person*. The Scriptures are often put into His mouth, and actions recorded of Him in a way which does not exist elsewhere in the literature of world religions. The Bible was held by the Jews to be verbally " inspired " (as also by Christians, at any rate until recently); it was the " Word of God," and had to be accepted in its entirety. Thus, by reading the Bible, we can discover the teaching and precepts of Judaism, set forth in fairly simple language.

The early history of the Jews is obscure. They were a branch of Semitic people who probably wandered into Palestine from the banks of the Euphrates in Chaldea, searching for fresh pasture lands, some time between the fifteenth and twelfth centuries B.C. At first they were merely nomadic tribes, and they only became a kingdom under David about 1000 B.C. What is astonishing from the religious point of view is that they came to form a unity of faith and way of living amid surrounding conditions of crude barbarism; a unity which persisted, despite the most adverse circumstances, and which finally emerged as a world-faith, giving birth to Christianity and forming a background to the religious life of Europe today. The word " Judah " comes from Jacob's fourth son, and originally applied to the southern half of Palestine when the country was split up into the two kingdoms of Judah and Israel. Gradually the term " Judaism " came to mean the faith and way of living of all those who combined in allegiance to Yahweh (or Jehovah).

We are mainly dependent on the biblical stories for an account as to how all this came about and, though it is difficult to detach history from legend, the Bible is the best guide to the development of the Jewish religion.

The Bible story tells us that Abraham reached by thought and revelation the conclusion that One God ruled the world and that idols were of no account. He left his kindred, who remained pagans, and went about preaching his faith, finally dying in exile. Abraham is commonly accepted as the pioneer of Judaism, and it is probable that he was a historical character. Thereafter, we are told, his followers were carefully sifted. Birth alone did not ensure adherence to the monotheistic community. Lot, for instance, the nephew of Abraham, gave up the calling of a wandering preacher and left his uncle. So elaborate was the sifting process that the phrase the " survival of the remnant " became a Jewish axiom. This meant that a few would continue to adhere to the pure doctrine, which was imperishable, but did not imply that the faith was arbitrarily bestowed by God on a favoured nation; it had to be earned by discipline, and defended by martyrdom if necessary, but was open to anyone who cared to pay the price. The Jews were capable of great self-sacrifice. When, in the days of Nehemiah, intermarriage threatened to re-engulf Judaism into idolatry and barbarism, the Jews sacrificed their homes and left their wives in order to save their faith. It was only later, when the monotheistic doctrine was firmly established, that the Jews began to look upon themselves as the " Chosen People " and to claim their religion as a right by birth.

Doubts have been cast upon the authenticity of Abraham as a historical character, but few upon Moses, the great law-giver of Israel. We may take it that Moses really existed and that he founded the system of Judaism as we know it. If the original monotheistic inspiration came from Abraham, it was Moses who inaugurated the religious way of life. Judaism thereafter was much more than a belief in One God; it was not only a creed, but a discipline which covered many activities of daily existence, such as the use of property, agriculture, business, health, diet, and even dress. According to the biblical narrative, Moses went to the Mount of Sinai (or Horeb in some versions) and stayed there forty days. He received, as an inspiration from God, the Ten Commandments, which are still read in our churches and which we know so well. These Commandments set forth, first, the principle of monotheism as against idolatry (forbidding the making of graven images), then the keeping of the Sabbath Day and the honouring of parents. From these follow prohibitions against murder, theft, sexual infidelity, perjury, and finally against covetousness. These later Commandments are based on the same principles of good ethics that are found in other religions. After the Ten Commandments, Moses is said to have received instruction about matters relating to daily life, and it is this whole body of teaching, some of it written down and some of it traditional, which forms the Torah (or Law), the backbone of the Jewish religious life. By reason of its minute detail, the Jews became more and more separate from the people round them, and later from all other religious communities. Other races have arrived at the conception of One God and have laid down the foundation of morality, but it was the distinctive way of life, combined with a vigorous and passionate devotion to the personal Yahweh which gave the Jewish religion its extraordinary power of survival and prevented it from being absorbed into other cults, despite continual disruptions, upheavals, and the final dispersion of its adherents. It was the Mosaic Law which concentrated monotheistic idealism into a racial religion.

After the time of Moses we read in the Bible of a long line of prophets whose teaching and deeds are recorded and who carried on in various ways the religion of the Jews. The Old Testament Scriptures are very unequal. They were written by many different people and at widely varying dates, and there are innumerable alterations and interpolations by later scribes. History and legend become inextricably confused, and sometimes there are conflicting accounts of the same events. But at their highest level the Jewish Scriptures contain some of the finest religious utterances in the world. When the line of the Prophets came to an end, the work was carried on by Rabbis, or Wise Men, one branch being the Pharisees, of whom we hear so much in the New Testament. These undertook to expound and to interpret the law of Moses. As is usual in this stage of elaboration and interpretation which is common to all religions, much attention was given to the " letter," and in some cases there was doubtless over-formality and the kind of mechanization which was condemned by Christ. But it is unfair to use the word Pharisee, in a general sense, as if it were synonymous with hypocrite. On the whole, the Pharisees were good and upright men, loyal and self-sacrificing, and it was largely their work which made it possible for the Jewish religion to be preserved when, in A.D. 70, the Temple was destroyed and the Jews were dispersed into foreign lands and left without a sanctuary.

The gradual evolution of the monotheistic principle can be followed, step by step, in the Old Testament. At first Jehovah, or Yahweh, was a tribal God, associated with the hills and with fighting. He was a "jealous" God, who, while admitting,

seemingly, the existence of rivals, grudged them worship. Many
of the deeds ascribed to Him at that time seem to us erratic and
unjust, even cruel. But it must be remembered that men can
only attribute those qualities to their gods, of which they have
already had experience in themselves. At first Divinity was associated mainly with the idea of *power*, for it was power that man,
weak as he found himself among the forces of Nature, desired
more than anything else. It was power that he both feared and
envied, and indeed wished to share, and, so long as his god was
powerful, anything else that he might do was regarded as beyond
criticism. All happenings, good or bad, had in any case to be
ascribed to Jehovah, and it was only later, when the idea of
righteousness became better established, that Satan, as a fallen
angel, was introduced to explain evil. Gradually " might "
ceased to be " right," and the great virtues, at first perhaps
justice and last mercy, came to be an integral part of the idea of
Divinity. The omnipotence and majesty of Jehovah increased
correspondingly until He passed from His limited position as
local deity and was worshipped as Lord over all the earth, both
transcendant and immanent. His rivals ceased to have any
reality at all. It will be noticed that the God of the Jews, though
at first represented as vindictive and capricious, had always one
form of what we may call moral integrity—a very important one
in the days when gross orgies were common. He was never
associated with licence or self-indulgence, nor were stories told
of him suggesting the free and easy ways of the Greek or
Roman gods, or the less creditable escapades of the Indian
Vishnu, when incarnate as Krishna. If, in the early stages, He
was frankly anthropomorphic—that is, made in the image of a
man—and a harsh man sometimes at that, He was at all times
austere, and this quality undoubtedly distinguished Him among
barbarous and primitive tribes. Later He became supreme, not
only in power, but also in righteousness.

One factor which emerges in the study of the Old Testament
is the belief that a Messiah would one day come and lead Israel.
This was supported by many prophecies and allusions. The
Jews, after the return from exile, suffered from the sense of
oppression under foreign rule, and the idea of a deliverance crept
into the re-edited Scriptures. The Messiah was thought of as
partly political and partly religious. When Jesus Christ came,

his followers saw in him the fulfilment of the prophecies, but the orthodox Jews did not accept this interpretation, and regarded the Christians as a heretical sect. When the Jews were finally dispersed, Christianity separated itself altogether and formed a world-religion of its own, but originally the basis of disagreement was mainly whether or not Jesus was the Messiah. For a while the Christians attended the Synagogue, and were regarded simply as a Jewish sect.

So great was the interest of the Jew in the fate of his nation that little stress seems to have been laid on the question of a future life, with its rewards and punishments. There are not many passages in the Old Testament dealing with this, and where these occur, scholars are inclined to disagree as to the precise meaning of the text. At first there seems to have been a shadowy abode of the dead, known as Sheol or Paradise, where all departed souls went, good or bad. Later the moral implications became clearer, and in the book of Daniel the doctrine of the resurrection of the just to eternal life, with a corresponding punishment for the wicked, was put forward. The Jews for the most part (with the exception of the Sadducees) seem to have accepted this, but the view was most firmly held by the Pharisees, and by the time of Christ it was fairly general. But it never aroused that concentrated enthusiasm and interest which has been shown in other religions, as, for instance, Christianity and Muhammadanism, especially the latter, which makes the promise of excessive joy for the righteous in the world to come a central feature and a leading motive for good conduct. The Jews were, and still are, disinclined to regard this world as a " vale of tears ", despite their turbulent history; the " Judgment " in the Old Testament was associated in their minds with life on this earth, security and fruitfulness being the alternative to national calamity. They have probably been less concerned with individual salvation than correspondingly religious persons belonging to most other faiths. Their aim was to form a theocracy—that is, a State ruled by God and responsible to Him only. Before the Exile there were kings of Israel and Judah who took upon themselves the functions of priests. After the return of the Jews from Babylon the country was ruled by priests only. There was no separation between religious and political life : the rule of the nation and the service of Yahweh were one and the same thing. This meant concentration on the perfecting of life in this world, an aim and a viewpoint which has always been characteristic of Judaism.

Judaism has not been without its sects, and there were many at the time of Christ's coming. There were the politically minded Sadducees, the fiery Zealots, the mystical Essenes, and various forms of Pharisaism. For the most part these faded out in the great catastrophe of A.D. 70. Only Pharisaism remained, and has preserved Judaism up to the present day. There is less tendency to split up into sects in Judaism, however, than in most of the other great religions. In modern times there have been reformed Jewish Churches where various rules have been relaxed and an effort has been made to bring the religion more into line with modern ideas. But for the most part the Jews are satisfied with their religion as it stands; they have amazing tenacity and great confidence in the righteousness and purity of their faith.

Modern Jews, where they practise their religion, still keep the great Jewish observances, such as the Day of Atonement (a day of fasting and prayer), the Feast of the Passover (a symbolic meal), and as much of the Mosaic Law as is possible under the conditions of the countries in which they live. They have great qualities, which include a high estimate of family life, of the importance of marriage, and of the charity due to their own people. They show little of that tendency towards asceticism which is so marked a feature of many other religions. A Rabbi, it is held, ought to have a wife, for marriage is the first injunction in the Bible. The world is not inherently evil and there is no need to abandon it in any sense. Neither is there any need for a mediator; man has direct access to God, and can achieve his own redemption by penitence and prayer. God is absolutely without rivals or incarnations and needs no representation. The worship of Jesus as the Son of God is to the Jew a form of blasphemy. The only other spiritual beings are ministering angels and devils, with Satan as the primal tempter.

One can sum up by saying that Judaism is the leading example of ethical monotheism. It recognizes God as a Person, incorporeal and holy, and asserts that the happiness of the human race depends on service to Him. Transcendence ranks perhaps above Immanence, though this, too, has its place. If a little withdrawn from the world that He has made, Yahweh is none the less the Primal Cause. The whole universe depends on Him.

Verses from the Scriptures

ABBREVIATIONS TO REFERENCES

A.	= Apocrypha	*Isa.*	= Isaiah
B.	= Bible	*Lev.*	= Leviticus
Deut.	= Deuteronomy	*Num.*	= Numbers
Eccl.	= Ecclesiastes and	*Prov.*	= Proverbs of Solomon
	Ecclesiasticus	*Ps.*	= Psalms of David
Ex.	= Exodus	*T.*	= Talmud
Gen.	= Genesis	*W. of S.*	= Wisdom of Solomon

He that is slow to **anger** is better than the mighty; and he that ruleth his spirit than he that taketh a city. *B. Prov.* 16, 32.

A soft **answer** turneth away wrath : but grievous words stir up anger. *B. Prov.* 15, 1.

Go to the **ant**, thou sluggard; consider her ways, and be wise; which having no guide, overseer, or ruler, provideth her meat in the summer, and gathereth her food in the harvest. How long wilt thou sleep, O sluggard? when wilt thou arise out of thy sleep? Yet a little sleep, a little slumber, a little folding of the hands to sleep : so shall thy poverty come as one that travelleth, and thy want as an armed man. *B. Prov.* 6, 6–11.

We generally reproach others with **blemishes** similar to our own. *T.*

The Lord **bless** thee, and keep thee : the Lord make his face to shine upon thee, and be gracious unto thee : the Lord lift up his countenance upon thee, and give thee peace. *B. Num.* 6, 24–6.

Behold, how good and joyful a thing it is, **brethren**, to dwell together in unity. *B. Ps.* 133, 1.

Thou shalt not hate thy **brother** in thine heart. . . . Thou shalt not avenge, nor bear any grudge . . . but thou shalt love thy neighbour as thyself. *B. Lev.* 19, 17–18.

Except the Lord **build** the house, they labour in vain that build it : except the Lord keep the city, the watchman waketh but in vain. It is vain for you to rise up early, to sit up late, to eat the bread of sorrows : for so he giveth his beloved sleep. *B. Ps.* 127, 1–2.

Cast thy **burden** upon the Lord, and he shall sustain thee. *B. Ps.* 55, 22.

My son, keep thy father's **commandment,** and forsake not the law of thy mother; bind them continually upon thine heart, and tie them about thy neck. When thou goest, it shall lead thee; when thou sleepest, it shall keep thee; and when thou awakest, it shall talk with thee. *B. Prov.* 6. 20.

The **fear** of the Lord is the beginning of wisdom; and the knowledge of the holy is understanding. *B. Prov.* 9, 10.

In every place where you find the imprint of men's **feet** there am I. *T.*

The most beautiful of all things man can do is to **forgive** wrong. *Rokeach.*

The best preacher is the **heart**; the best teacher is time; the best book is the world; the best friend is God. *T.*

If I ascend up into **heaven,** thou art there. If I make my bed in hell, behold, thou art there. If I take the wings of the morning, and dwell in the uttermost parts of the sea, even there shall thy hand lead me, and thy right hand shall hold me. *B. Ps.* 139, 8–10.

A wicked **inclination** is at first a guest. If thou grant it hospitality it will soon make itself master of the house. *T.*

My son, gather **instruction** from thy youth up : so shalt thou find wisdom till thine old age. *A. Eccl.* 6, 18.

He who adds not to his **learning** diminishes it. *T.*

The penalty of the **liar** is that he is not believed even when he speaks the truth. *T.*

Rest in the **Lord** and wait patiently for him : fret not thyself because of him who prospereth in his way. *B. Ps.* 36, 7.

And what doth the **Lord** require of thee, but to do justly, and to love mercy, and to walk humbly with thy God ? *B. Micah* 6, 8.

Trust in the **Lord** with all thine heart; and lean not unto thine own understanding. In all thy ways acknowledge him, and he shall direct thy paths. *B. Prov.* 3, 5–6.

But I say unto you : deeds of **love** are worth as much as all the commandments of the law. *T.*

Love him who reproves thee, that thou mayest add wisdom to thy wisdom; hate him who praises thee, that thy wisdom may not be diminished. *T.*

Love is the beginning and end of the Torah. *T.*

When I consider thy heavens, the work of thy fingers, the moon and the stars, which thou hast ordained; what is **man**, that thou art mindful of him? and the son of man that thou visitest him? for thou hast made him a little lower than the angels, and hast crowned him with glory and honour. *B. Ps.* 8, 3–5.

To bear patiently with bad **manners** is the test of good ones. *Gebirol.*

For I desired **mercy**, and not sacrifice, and the knowledge of God more than burnt-offerings. *B. Hosea* 6. 6.

But thou shalt love thy **neighbour** as thyself. *B. Lev.* 19, 18.

Judge not thy **neighbour** till thou art in his place. *T.*

The **pious** among all nations will have a share in the life to come. *T.*

Let your house be open wide and let the **poor** be the members of your household. *T.*

Give me neither **poverty** nor riches; feed me with food convenient for me. *B. Prov.* 30, 8.

Let another man **praise** thee, and not thine own mouth; a stranger and not thine own lips. *B. Prov.* 27, 2.

Who is first silent in a **quarrel** springs from a good family. *T.*

For I know that my **redeemer** liveth, and that he shall stand at the latter day upon the earth, and though after my skin worms destroy this body, yet in my flesh shall I see God. *B. Job* 19, 25–6.

God is our **refuge** and strength, a very present help in trouble. Therefore will not we fear, though the earth be removed and though the mountains be carried into the midst of the sea. *B. Ps.* 46, 1–2.

Without **religion** there can be no true morality; without morality there can be no true religion. *T.*

What doth the Lord thy God **require** of thee, but to fear the Lord thy God, to walk in all his ways, and to love him, and to serve the Lord thy God with all thy heart and with all thy soul. *B. Deut.* 10, 12.

But the souls of the **righteous** are in the hand of God, and there shall no torment touch them. In the sight of the unwise they seemed to die; and their departure is taken for misery. And their going from us to be utter destruction; but they are in peace. For though they be punished in the sight of men, yet is their hope full of immortality. And having been a little chastised, they shall be greatly rewarded : for God proved them, and found them worthy for himself. *A., W. of S.* 3, 1–5.

Come now, and let us reason together . . . though your **sins** be as scarlet, they shall be as white as snow : though they be red like crimson, they shall be as wool. *B. Isa.* 1, 18.

What is hurtful to yourself do not to your fellow man. That is the whole of the **Torah** and the remainder is but commentary. Go learn it. *T.*

But he was wounded for our **transgressions**, he was bruised for our iniquities : the chastisement of our peace was upon him; and with his stripes we are healed. All we like sheep have gone astray; we have turned every one to his own way; and the Lord hath laid on him the iniquity of us all. *B. Isa.* 53, 5–6.

Be willing to hear every godly discourse; and let not the parables of **understanding** escape thee. If thou seest a man of understanding, get thee betimes unto him, and let thy foot wear the steps of his door. *A. Eccl.* 6, 35–6.

Readings from the Scriptures

And Jacob went out from Beer-sheba, and went toward Haran. And he lighted upon a certain place, and tarried there all night, because the sun was set; and he took of the stones of that place, and put them for his pillows, and lay down in that place to sleep. And he dreamed, and behold a ladder set up on the earth, and the top of it reached to heaven : and behold the angels of God ascending and descending on it. And, behold, the Lord stood above it, and said, I am the Lord God of Abraham thy father, and the God of Isaac : the land whereon thou liest, to thee will I give it, and to thy seed; and thy seed shall be as the dust of the earth, and thou shalt spread abroad to the west, and to the east, and to the north, and to the south : and in thee and in thy seed shall all the families of the earth be blessed. And behold, I am with thee, and will keep thee in all places whither thou goest, and will bring thee again into this land; for I will not leave thee, until I have done that which I have spoken to thee of. And Jacob awaked out of his sleep, and he said, Surely the Lord is in this place; and I knew it not. And he was afraid, and said, How dreadful is this place! this is none other but the house of God, and this is the gate of heaven. And Jacob rose up early in the morning, and took the stone that he had put for his pillows, and set it up for a pillar, and poured oil upon the top of it. And he called the name of that place Beth-el : but the name of that city was called Luz at the first. *B. Gen.* 28, 10–19.

The Ten Commandments

1. I am the Lord thy God, which have brought thee out of the land of Egypt, out of the house of bondage.

2. Thou shalt have no other gods before me. Thou shalt not make unto thee any graven image, or any likeness of any thing that is in heaven above, or that is in the earth beneath, or that is in the water under the earth : thou shalt not bow down thyself to them, nor serve them : for I the Lord thy God am a jealous God, visiting the iniquity of the fathers upon the children unto the third and fourth generation of them that hate me; and shewing mercy unto thousands of them that love me and keep my commandments.

3. Thou shalt not take the name of the Lord thy God in vain; for the Lord will not hold him guiltless that taketh his name in vain.

4. Remember the sabbath-day, to keep it holy. Six days shalt thou labour, and do all thy work; but the seventh day is the sabbath of the Lord thy God; in it thou shalt not do any work, thou, nor thy son, nor thy daughter, thy man-servant, nor thy maid-servant, nor thy cattle, nor thy stranger that is within thy gates : for in six days the Lord made heaven and earth, the sea, and all that in them is, and rested the seventh day; wherefore the Lord blessed the sabbath-day and hallowed it.

5. Honour thy father and thy mother; that thy days may be long upon the land which the Lord thy God giveth thee.

6. Thou shalt not kill.

7. Thou shalt not commit adultery.

8. Thou shalt not steal.

9. Thou shalt not bear false witness against thy neighbour.

10. Thou shalt not covet thy neighbour's house, thou shalt not covet thy neighbour's wife, nor his man-servant, nor his maid-servant, nor his ox, nor his ass, nor any thing that is thy neighbour's. *B. Ex.* 20, 2–17 and *Deut.* 5, 6–21.

Thou shalt not avenge, nor bear any grudge against the children of thy people, but thou shalt love thy neighbour as thyself : I am the Lord. . . . Ye shall have one manner of law, as well for the stranger, as for one of your own country : for I am the Lord your God. . . . And if thy brother be waxen poor, and fallen in decay with thee; then thou shalt relieve him : yea, though he be a stranger, or a sojourner; that he may live with thee. Take thou no usury of him, or increase; but fear thy God; that thy brother may live with thee. Thou shalt not give him thy money upon usury, nor lend him thy victuals for increase. *B. Lev.* 19, 18; 24, 22; 25, 35–7.

Then the Lord answered Job out of the whirlwind, and said : Who is this that darkeneth counsel by words without knowledge ? . . . Where wast thou when I laid the foundations of the earth ? Declare if thou hast understanding. Who hath laid the measures thereof, if thou knowest ? Or who hath stretched the line upon it ? Whereupon are the foundations thereof fastened ? Or who laid the corner stone thereof ? When the morning stars sang together, and all the sons of God shouted for joy ? Or who shut up the sea with doors, when it brake forth, as if it had issued out of the womb ? When I made the cloud the garment thereof, and thick darkness a swaddling band for it, and brake up for it my decreed place, and set bars and doors, and said, Hitherto shalt thou come, but no further, and here shall thy proud waves be stayed ? Hast thou commanded the morning since thy days, and caused the dayspring to know his place ? . . . Knowest thou the ordinances of heaven ? Canst thou set the dominion thereof in the earth ? Canst thou lift up thy voice to the clouds, that abundance of waters may cover thee ? Canst thou send lightnings, that they may go, and say unto thee, Here we are ? Who hath put wisdom in the inward parts ? Or who hath given understanding to the heart ? . . . Shall he that contendeth with the Almighty instruct Him ? He that reproveth God, let

him answer it.   Then Job answered the Lord, and said, Behold
I am vile; what shall I answer thee ?   I will lay mine hand upon
my mouth.   *B. Job* 38, 1–2, 4–12, 33–6, and 40, 2–4.

O Lord our Lord, how excellent is thy name in all the earth!
who hast set thy glory above the heavens.   Out of the mouth of
babes and sucklings hast thou ordained strength because of thine
enemies, that thou mightest still the enemy and the avenger.
When I consider thy heavens, the work of thy fingers; the moon
and the stars, which thou hast ordained; what is man, that thou
are mindful of him ? and the son of man, that thou visitest him ?
For thou hast made him a little lower than the angels, and hast
crowned him with glory and honour.   Thou madest him to have
dominion over the works of thy hands, thou hast put all things
under his feet : all sheep and oxen, yea, and the beasts of the
field; the fowl of the air, and the fish of the sea, and whatsoever
passeth through the paths of the seas.   O Lord our Lord, how
excellent is thy name in all the earth!   *B. Ps.* 8.

The heavens declare the glory of God, and the firmament
sheweth his handiwork.ˑ Day unto day uttereth speech, and night
unto night sheweth knowledge.   There is no speech nor language,
where their voice is not heard.   Their line is gone out through
all the earth, and their words to the end of the world.   In them
hath he set a tabernacle for the sun.   Which is as a bridegroom
coming out of his chamber, and rejoiceth as a strong man to run
a race.   His going forth is from the end of the heaven, and his
circuit unto the ends of it : and there is nothing hid from the
heat thereof.   The law of the Lord is perfect, converting the
soul : the testimony of the Lord is sure, making wise the simple.
The statutes of the Lord are right, rejoicing the heart : the
commandment of the Lord is pure, enlightening the eyes.   The
fear of the Lord is clean, enduring for ever : the judgements of
the Lord are true and righteous altogether.   More to be desired
are they than gold, yea, than much fine gold : sweeter also than
honey and the honeycomb.   Moreover, by them is thy servant
warned; and in keeping of them there is great reward.   Who
can understand his errors ? cleanse thou me from secret faults.
Keep back thy servant also from presumptuous sins; let them not
have dominion over me : then shall I be upright, and I shall be
innocent from the great transgression.   Let the words of my

mouth, and the meditation of my heart, be acceptable in thy sight, O Lord, my strength, and my redeemer. *B. Ps.* 19.

The Lord is my shepherd; I shall not want. He maketh me to lie down in green pastures : he leadeth me beside the still waters. He restoreth my soul : he leadeth me in the paths of righteousness for his name's sake. Yea, though I walk through the valley of the shadow of death, I will fear no evil : for thou art with me; thy rod and thy staff they comfort me. Thou preparest a table before me in the presence of mine enemies : thou anointest my head with oil : my cup runneth over. Surely goodness and mercy shall follow me all the days of my life : and I will dwell in the house of the Lord for ever. *B. Ps.* 23.

Lord, who shall abide in thy tabernacle ? who shall dwell in thy holy hill ? He that walketh uprightly, and worketh righteousness, and speaketh the truth in his heart. He that backbiteth not with his tongue, nor doeth evil to his neighbour, nor taketh up a reproach against his neighbour. In whose eyes a vile person is contemned; but he honoureth them that fear the Lord. He that sweareth to his own hurt, and changeth not. He that putteth not out his money to usury, nor taketh reward against the innocent. He that doeth these things shall never be moved. *B. Ps.* 15.

I will lift up mine eyes unto the hills, from whence cometh my help. My help cometh from the Lord, which made heaven and earth. He will not suffer thy foot to be moved : he that keepeth thee will not slumber. Behold, he that keepeth Israel shall neither slumber nor sleep. The Lord is thy keeper : the Lord is thy shade upon thy right hand. The sun shall not smite thee by day, nor the moon by night. The Lord shall preserve thee from all evil; he shall preserve thy soul. The Lord shall preserve thy going out and thy coming in from this time forth, and even for evermore. *B. Ps.* 121.

The Lord is my light and my salvation; whom shall I fear ? the Lord is the strength of my life; of whom shall I be afraid ? When the wicked, even mine enemies and my foes, came upon me to eat up my flesh, they stumbled and fell. Though an host should encamp against me, my heart shall not fear : though war should rise against me, in this will I be confident. One thing have I desired of the Lord, that will I seek after; that I may dwell in the house of the Lord all the days of my life, to behold the beauty of the Lord, and to inquire in his temple. For in the time of trouble he shall hide me in his pavilion : in the secret of his tabernacle shall he hide me; he shall set me up upon a rock. And now shall mine head be lifted up above mine enemies round about me : therefore will I offer in his tabernacle sacrifices of joy; I will sing, yea, I will sing praises unto the Lord. Hear, O Lord, when I cry with my voice : have mercy also upon me, and answer me. When thou saidst, Seek ye my face : my heart said unto thee, Thy face, Lord, will I seek. Hide not thy face far from me; put not thy servant away in anger; thou hast been my help; leave me not, neither forsake me, O God of my salvation. When my father and my mother forsake me, then the Lord will take me up. Teach me thy way, O Lord, and lead me in a plain path, because of mine enemies. Deliver me not over unto the will of mine enemies : for false witnesses are risen up against me, and such as breathe out cruelty. I had fainted, unless I had believed to see the goodness of the Lord in the land of the living. Wait on the Lord : be of good courage, and he shall strengthen thine heart : wait, I say, on the Lord. *B. Ps.* 27.

Praise ye the Lord. Praise God in his sanctuary; praise him in the firmament of his power. Praise him for his mighty acts : praise him according to his excellent greatness. Praise him with the sound of the trumpet : praise him with the psaltery and harp. Praise him with the timbrel and dance; praise him with stringed instruments and organs. Praise him upon the loud cymbals : praise him upon the high sounding cymbals. Let everything that hath breath praise the Lord. Praise ye the Lord. *B. Ps.* 140.

He sendeth the springs into the valleys, which run among the hills. They give drink to every beast of the field : the wild asses quench their thirst. By them shall the fowls of the heaven have their habitation, which sing among the branches. He watereth the hills from his chambers : the earth is satisfied with the fruit of thy works. He causeth the grass to grow for the cattle, and herb for the service of man : that he may bring forth food out of the earth. And wine that maketh glad the heart of man, and oil to make his face to shine, and bread which strengtheneth man's heart. The trees of the Lord are full of sap; the cedars of Lebanon, which he hath planted; where the birds make their nests: as for the stork, the fir trees are her house. The high hills are a refuge for the wild goats; and the rocks for the conies. He appointed the moon for seasons; the sun knoweth his going down. Thou makest darkness, and it is night: wherein all the beasts of the forest do creep forth. The young lions roar after their prey, and seek their meat from God. The sun ariseth, they gather themselves together, and lay them down in their dens. Man goeth forth unto his work and to his labour until the evening. O Lord, how manifold are thy works! In wisdom hast thou made them all: the earth is full of thy riches. So is this great and wide sea, wherein are things creeping innumerable, both small and great beasts. . . . These wait all upon thee; that thou mayest give them their meat in due season. That thou givest them they gather: thou openest thine hand, they are filled with good. Thou hidest thy face, they are troubled: thou takest away their breath, they die, and return to their dust. *B. Ps.* 104, 10–25, 27–9.

He that dwelleth in the secret place of the most High shall abide under the shadow of the Almighty. I will say of the Lord, He is my refuge and my fortress: my God; in him will I trust. Surely he shall deliver thee from the snare of the fowler, and from the noisome pestilence. He shall cover thee with his feathers, and under his wings shalt thou trust; his truth shall be thy shield and buckler. Thou shalt not be afraid for the terror by night; nor for the arrow that flieth by day; nor for the pestilence that walketh in darkness; nor for the destruction that wasteth at noonday. A thousand shall fall at thy side, and ten thousand at thy right hand, but it shall not come nigh thee. Only with thine eyes shalt thou behold and see the reward of the wicked. Because thou hast made the Lord, which is my refuge, even the most High, thy habitation; there shall no evil befall thee, neither shall any plague come nigh thy dwelling. For he shall give his angels charge over thee, to keep thee in all thy ways. They shall bear thee up in their hands, lest thou dash thy foot against a stone. Thou shalt tread upon the lion and adder: the young lion and the dragon shalt thou trample underfeet. Because he hath set his love upon me, therefore will I deliver him: I will set him on high, because he hath known my name. He shall call upon me, and I will answer him : I will be with him in trouble; I will deliver him, and honour him. With long life will I satisfy him, and shew him my salvation. *B. Ps.* 91.

O come, let us sing unto the Lord : let us make a joyful noise to the rock of our salvation. Let us come before his presence with thanksgiving, and make a joyful noise unto him with psalms. For the Lord is a great God, and a great King above all gods. In his hand are the deep places of the earth : the strength of the hills is his also. The sea is his, and he made it : and his hands formed the dry land. O come, let us worship and bow down : let us kneel before the Lord our maker; For he is our God; and we are the people of his pasture, and the sheep of his hand. To-day, if ye will hear his voice, harden not your heart, as in the provocation, and as in the day of temptation in the wilderness. When your fathers tempted me, proved me, and saw my work. Forty years long was I grieved with this generation, and said, it is a people that do err in their heart, and they have not known my ways : unto whom I swear in my wrath that they should not enter into my rest. *B. Ps.* 95.

Bless the Lord, O my soul : and all that is within me, bless his holy name. Bless the Lord, O my soul, and forget not all his benefits : who forgiveth all thine iniquities; who healeth all thy diseases; who redeemeth thy life from destruction; who crowneth thee with lovingkindness and tender mercies; who satisfieth thy mouth with good things; so that thy youth is renewed like the eagle's. The Lord executeth righteousness and judgment for all that are oppressed. He made known his ways unto Moses, his acts unto the children of Israel. The Lord is merciful and gracious, slow to anger, and plenteous in mercy. He will not always chide : neither will he keep his anger for ever. He hath not dealt with us after our sins; nor rewarded us according to our iniquities. For as the heaven is high above the earth, so great is his mercy toward them that fear him. As far as the east is from the west, so far hath he removed our transgressions from us. Like as a father pitieth his children, so the Lord pitieth them that fear him. For he knoweth our frame; he remembereth that we are dust. As for man, his days are as grass : as a flower of the field, so he flourisheth. For the wind passeth

over it, and it is gone; and the place thereof shall know it no
more. But the mercy of the Lord is from everlasting to everlasting upon them that fear him, and his righteousness unto
children's children; to such as keep his covenant, and to those
that remember his commandments to do them. The Lord hath
prepared his throne in the heavens: and his kingdom ruleth over
all. Bless the Lord, ye his angels, that excel in strength, that do
his commandments, hearkening unto the voice of his word.
Bless ye the Lord, all ye his hosts; ye ministers of his, that do
his pleasure. Bless the Lord, all his works in all places of his
dominion: bless the Lord, O my soul. *B. Ps.* 103.

Who can find a virtuous woman? for her price is far above
rubies. The heart of her husband doth safely trust in her, so
that he shall have no need of spoil. She will do him good and
not evil all the days of her life. She seeketh wool, and flax, and
worketh willingly with her hands. She is like the merchants'
ships; she bringeth her food from afar. She riseth also while
it is yet night, and giveth meat to her household, and a portion
to her maidens. She considereth a field, and buyeth it: with the
fruit of her hands she planteth a vineyard. She girdeth her loins
with strength, and strengtheneth her arms. She perceiveth that
her merchandise is good: her candle goeth not out by night.
She layeth her hands to the spindle, and her hands hold the distaff.
She stretcheth out her hand to the poor; yea, she reacheth forth
her hands to the needy. She is not afraid of the snow for her
household: for all her household are clothed with scarlet. She
maketh herself coverings of tapestry; her clothing is silk and
purple. Her husband is known in the gates, when he sitteth
among the elders of the land. She maketh fine linen, and selleth
it; and delivereth girdles unto the merchant. Strength and
honour are her clothing; and she shall rejoice in time to come.
She openeth her mouth with wisdom; and in her tongue is the
law of kindness. She looketh well to the ways of her household,
and eateth not the bread of idleness. Her children arise up, and
call her blessed; her husband also, and he praiseth her. Many
daughters have done virtuously, but thou excellest them all.
Favour is deceitful, and beauty is vain: but a woman that feareth
the Lord, she shall be praised. Give her the fruit of her hands;
and let her own works praise her in the gates. *B. Prov.* 31, 10–31.

To every thing there is a season, and a time to every purpose under the heaven. A time to be born, and a time to die; a time to plant, and a time to pluck up that which is planted; a time to kill, and a time to heal; a time to break down, and a time to build up; a time to weep, and a time to laugh; a time to mourn, and a time to dance; a time to cast away stones, and a time to gather stones together; a time to embrace, and a time to refrain from embracing; a time to get, and a time to lose; a time to keep, and a time to cast away; a time to rend, and a time to sew; a time to keep silence, and a time to speak; a time to love, and a time to hate; a time of war, and a time of peace. What profit hath he that worketh in that wherein he laboureth ? . . . Wherefore I perceive that there is nothing better than that a man should rejoice in his own works; for that is his portion; for who shall bring him to see what shall be after him ? *B. Eccl.* 3, 1–9 and 22.

Remember now thy Creator in the days of thy youth, while the evil days come not, nor the years draw nigh, when thou shalt say, I have no pleasure in them; while the sun, or the light, or the moon, or the stars, be not darkened, nor the clouds return after rain : in the day when the keepers of the house shall tremble, and the strong men shall bow themselves, and the grinders cease because they are few, and those that look out of the windows be darkened. And the doors shall be shut in the streets, when the sound of the grinding is low, and he shall rise up at the voice of the bird, and all the daughters of musick shall be brought low; also when they shall be afraid of that which is high, and fears shall be in the way, and the almond tree shall flourish, and the grasshopper shall be a burden, and desire shall fail : because man goeth to his long home, and the mourners go about the streets : or ever the silver cord be loosed, or the golden bowl be broken, or the pitcher be broken at the fountain, or the wheel broken at the cistern. Then shall the dust return to the earth as it was : and the spirit shall return unto God who gave it. Vanity of vanities, saith the preacher; all is vanity. *B. Eccl.* 12, 1–8.

The people that walked in darkness have seen a great light : they that dwell in the land of the shadow of death, upon them hath the light shined. Thou hast multiplied the nation, and not increased the joy : they joy before thee according to the joy in harvest, and as men rejoice when they divide the spoil. For

thou hast broken the yoke of his burden, and the staff of his
shoulder, the rod of his oppressor, as in the day of Midian.   For
every battle of the warrior is with confused noise, and garments
rolled in blood; but this shall be with burning and fuel of fire.
For unto us a child is born, unto us a son is given : and the government shall be upon his shoulder : and his name shall be called
Wonderful, Counsellor, The mighty God, The Everlasting Father,
The Prince of Peace.   Of the increase of his government and
peace there shall be no end, upon the throne of David, and upon
his kingdom, to order it, and to establish it with judgement and
with justice from henceforth even for ever.   The zeal of the Lord
of hosts will perform this.   *B. Isa.* 9, 2–7.

And there shall come forth a rod out of the stem of Jesse, and
a Branch shall grow out of his roots : and the spirit of the Lord
shall rest upon him, the spirit of wisdom and understanding, the
spirit of counsel and might, the spirit of knowledge and of the
fear of the Lord; and shall make him of quick understanding in
the fear of the Lord; and he shall not judge after the sight of his
eyes, neither reprove after the hearing of his ears : but with
righteousness shall he judge the poor, and reprove with equity
for the meek of the earth : and he shall smite the earth with the
rod of his mouth, and with the breath of his lips shall he slay the
wicked.   And righteousness shall be the girdle of his loins, and
faithfulness the girdle of his reins.   The wolf also shall dwell
with the lamb, and the leopard shall lie down with the kid; and
the calf and the young lion and the fatling together; and a little
child shall lead them.   And the cow and the bear shall feed;
their young ones shall lie down together : and the lion shall eat
straw like the ox.   And the sucking child shall play on the hole
of the asp, and the weaned child shall put his hand on the cocka-
trice' den.   They shall not hurt nor destroy in all my holy
mountain : for the earth shall be full of the knowledge of the
Lord, as the waters cover the sea.   And in that day there shall
be a root of Jesse, which shall stand for an ensign of the people;
to it shall the Gentiles seek : and his rest shall be glorious.
B. Isa. 11, 1–10.

The eyes of the blind shall be opened, and the ears of the deaf
shall be unstopped.   Then shall the lame man leap as an hart,
and the tongue of the dumb sing : for in the wilderness shall

waters break out, and streams in the desert. And the parched ground shall become a pool and the thirsty land springs of water; in the habitations of dragons, where each lay, shall be grass with reeds and rushes. And an highway shall be there, and a way, and it shall be called, the way of holiness; the unclean shall not pass over it; but it shall be for those : the way-faring men, though fools, shall not err therein. No lion shall be there, nor any ravenous beast shall go up thereon, it shall not be found there; but the redeemed shall walk there. And the ransomed of the Lord shall return, and come to Zion with songs and ever-lasting joy upon their heads : they shall obtain joy and gladness, and sorrow and sighing shall flee away. *B. Isa.* 35, 5–10.

The voice of him that crieth in the wilderness, Prepare ye the way of the Lord, make straight in the desert a highway for our God. Every valley shall be exalted, and every mountain and hill shall be made low : and the crooked shall be made straight, and the rough places plain. And the glory of the Lord shall be revealed, and all flesh shall see it together : for the mouth of the Lord hath spoken it. The voice said, Cry. And he said, What shall I cry ? All flesh is grass, and all the goodliness thereof is as the flower of the field. The grass withereth, the flower fadeth : because the spirit of the Lord bloweth upon it : surely the people is grass. The grass withereth, the flower fadeth : but the word of our God shall stand for ever. *B. Isa.* 40, 3–8.

Ho, every one that thirsteth, come ye to the waters, and he that hath no money; come ye, buy, and eat; yea, come, buy wine and milk without money and without price. Wherefore do ye spend money for that which is not bread ? and your labour for that which satisfieth not ? hearken diligently unto me, and eat ye that which is good, and let your soul delight itself in fatness. Incline your ear, and come unto me : hear, and your soul shall live; and I will make an everlasting covenant with you, even the sure mercies of David. Behold, I have given him for a witness to the people, a leader and commander to the people. Behold, thou shalt call a nation that thou knowest not, and nations that knew not thee shall run unto thee because of the Lord thy God, and for the Holy One of Israel; for he hath glorified thee. Seek ye the Lord while he may be found, call ye upon him while he is near : let the wicked forsake his way, and the unrighteous man

his thoughts : and let him return unto the Lord, and he will
have mercy upon him; and to our God, for he will abundantly
pardon. For my thoughts are not your thoughts, neither are
your ways my ways, saith the Lord. For as the heavens are
higher than the earth, so are my ways higher than your ways, and
my thoughts than your thoughts. For as the rain cometh down,
and the snow from heaven, and returneth not thither, but watereth
the earth, and maketh it bring forth and bud, that it may give seed
to the sower, and bread to the eater : so shall my word be that
goeth forth out of my mouth : it shall not return unto me void,
but it shall accomplish that which I please, and it shall prosper
in the thing whereto I sent it. For ye shall go out with joy, and
be led forth with peace : the mountains and the hills shall break
forth before you into singing, and all the trees of the field shall
clap their hands. Instead of the thorn shall come up the fir tree,
and instead of the brier shall come up the myrtle tree : and it shall
be to the Lord for a name, for an everlasting sign that shall not be
cut off. *B. Isa.* 55, 1–13.

But in the last days it shall come to pass, that the mountain of
the house of the Lord shall be established in the top of the
mountains, and it shall be exalted above the hills; and people
shall flow unto it. And many nations shall come, and say, Come,
and let us go up to the mountain of the Lord, and to the house of
the God of Jacob; and he will teach us of his ways, and we will
walk in his paths : for the law shall go forth of Zion, and the
word of the Lord from Jerusalem. And he shall judge among
many people, and rebuke strong nations afar off; and they shall
beat their swords into plowshares, and their spears into pruning-
hooks : nation shall not lift up a sword against nation, neither
shall they learn war any more. But they shall sit every man
under his vine and under his fig tree; and none shall make them
afraid : for the mouth of the Lord of hosts hath spoken it. For
all people will walk every one in the name of his God, and we
will walk in the name of the Lord our God for ever and ever. In
that day, saith the Lord, will I assemble her that halteth, and I
will gather her that is driven out, and her that I have afflicted;
And I will make her that halted a remnant, and her that was cast
far off a strong nation : and the Lord shall reign over them in
mount Zion from henceforth, even for ever. *B. Micah* 4, 1–7.

Prayer of Manasses, King of Judah

O Lord, Almighty God of our fathers, Abraham, Isaac, and Jacob, and of their righteous seed; who hast made heaven and earth, with all the ornament thereof; who hast bound the sea by the word of thy commandment; who hast shut up the deep, and sealed it by thy terrible and glorious name; whom all men fear, and tremble before thy power; for the majesty of thy glory cannot be borne, and thine angry threatening toward sinners is importable : but thy merciful promise is unmeasurable and unsearchable; for thou art the most high Lord, of great compassion, longsuffering, very merciful, and repentest of the evils of men. Thou, O Lord, according to thy great goodness hast promised repentance and forgiveness to them that have sinned against thee : and of thine infinite mercies hast appointed repentance unto sinners, that they may be saved. Thou therefore, O Lord, that art the God of the just, hast not appointed repentance to the just, as to Abraham, and Isaac, and Jacob, which have not sinned against thee; but thou hast appointed repentance unto me that am a sinner; for I have sinned above the number of the sands of the sea. My transgressions, O Lord, are multiplied : my transgressions are multiplied, and I am not worthy to behold and see the height of heaven for the multitude of mine iniquities. I am bowed down with many iron bands, that I cannot lift up mine head, neither have any release : for I have provoked thy wrath, and done evil before thee : I did not thy will neither kept I thy commandments : I have set up abominations, and have multiplied offences. Now therefore I bow the knee of mine heart, beseeching thee of grace. I have sinned, O Lord, I have sinned, and I acknowledge mine iniquities : wherefore, I humbly beseech thee, forgive me, O Lord, forgive me, and destroy me not with mine iniquities. Be not angry with me for ever, by reserving evil for me; neither condemn me into the lower parts of the earth. For thou art the God, even the God of them that repent; and in me thou wilt shew all thy goodness : for thou wilt save me, that am unworthy, according to thy great mercy. Therefore I will praise thee for ever all the days of my life : for all the powers of the heavens do praise thee, and thine is the glory for ever and ever. Amen. *A.*

My son, be mindful of the Lord our God all thy days, and let not thy will be set to sin, or to transgress his commandments : do uprightly all thy life long, and follow not the ways of unrighteousness. For if thou deal truly, thy doings shall prosperously succeed to thee, and to all them that live justly. Give alms of thy substance; and when thou givest alms, let not thine eye be envious, neither turn thy face from any poor, and the face of God shall not be turned away from thee. If thou hast abundance, give alms accordingly; if thou have but a little, be not afraid to give according to that little : for thou layest up a good treasure for thyself against the day of necessity. Because that alms do deliver from death, and suffereth not to come into darkness. For alms is a good gift unto all that give it in the sight of the most High. . . . Do that to no man which thou hatest : drink not wine to make thee drunken : neither let drunkenness go with thee in thy journey. Give of thy bread to the hungry, and of thy garments to them that are naked; and according to thine abundance give alms; and let not thine eye be envious, when thou givest alms. Pour out thy bread on the burial of the just, but give nothing to the wicked. Ask counsel of all that are wise, and despise not any counsel that is profitable. *A. Tobit* 4, 5–11, 15–18.

Wisdom is . . . easily seen of them that love her, and found of such as seek her. She preventeth them that desire her, in making herself first known unto them. Whoso seeketh her early shall have no great travail : for he shall find her sitting at his doors. To think therefore upon her is perfection of wisdom : and whoso watcheth for her shall quickly be without care. For she goeth about seeking such as are worthy of her, sheweth herself favourably unto them in the ways, and meeteth them in every thought. For the very true beginning of her is the desire of discipline; and the care of discipline is love; and love is the keeping of her laws; and the giving heed unto her laws is the assurance of incorruption. *A., W. of S.* 6, 12–18.

My son, if thou come to serve the Lord, prepare thy soul for temptation. Set thy heart aright, and constantly endure, and make not haste in time of trouble. Cleave unto him, and depart not away, that thou mayest be increased at thy last end. Whatsoever is brought upon thee take cheerfully, and be patient when thou art changed to a low estate. For gold is tried in the fire, and acceptable men in the furnace of adversity. Believe in him, and he will help thee; order thy way aright, and trust in him. Ye that fear the Lord, wait for his mercy; and go not aside, lest ye fall. Ye that fear the Lord, believe him; and your reward shall not fail. Ye that fear the Lord, hope for good, and for everlasting joy and mercy. Look at the generations of old, and see; did ever any trust in the Lord, and was confounded? or did any abide in his fear, and was forsaken? or whom did he ever despise, that called upon him? For the Lord is full of compassion and mercy, longsuffering, and very pitiful, and forgiveth sins, and saveth in time of affliction. Woe be to fearful hearts, and faint hands, and the sinner that goeth two ways! Woe unto him that is faint-hearted! for he believeth not; therefore shall he not be defended. Woe unto you that have lost patience! and what will ye do when the Lord shall visit you? They that fear the Lord will not disobey his word; and they that love him will keep his ways. They that fear the Lord will seek that which is wellpleasing unto him; and they that love him shall be filled with the law. They that fear the Lord will prepare their hearts, and humble their souls in his sight, saying, We will fall into the hands of the Lord, and not into the hands of men: for as his majesty is, so is his mercy. *A. Eccl.* 2, 1–18.

For the Lord hath given the father honour over the children, and hath confirmed the authority of the mother over the sons. Whoso honoureth his father maketh an atonement for his sins: and he that honoureth his mother is as one that layeth up treasure. Whoso honoureth his father shall have joy of his own children; and when he maketh his prayer, he shall be heard. He that honoureth his father shall have a long life; and he that is obedient unto the Lord shall be a comfort to his mother. He that feareth the Lord will honour his father, and will do service unto his parents, as to his masters. Honour thy father and mother both in word and deed, that a blessing may come upon thee from them. For the blessing of the father establisheth the houses of children; but the curse of the mother rooteth out foundations. *A. Eccl.* 3, 1–9.

My son, defraud not the poor of his living, and make not the needy eyes to wait long. Make not an hungry soul sorrowful;

neither provoke a man in his distress. Add not more trouble to an heart that is vexed; and defer not to give to him that is in need. Reject not the supplication of the afflicted; neither turn away thy face from a poor man. Turn not away thine eye from the needy, and give him none occasion to curse thee: for if he curse thee in the bitterness of his soul, his prayer shall be heard of him that made him. Get thyself the love of the congregation, and bow thy head to a great man. Let it not grieve thee to bow down thine ear to the poor, and give him a friendly answer with meekness. Deliver him that suffereth wrong from the hand of the oppressor; and be not fainthearted when thou sittest in judgement. Be as a father unto the fatherless, and instead of an husband unto their mother: so shalt thou be as the son of the most High, and he shall love thee more than thy mother doth. Wisdom exalteth her children, and layeth hold of them that seek her. He that loveth her loveth life; and they that seek to her early shall be filled with joy. *A. Eccl.* 4, 1–12.

Accept no person against thy soul, and let not the reverence of any man cause thee to fall. And refrain not to speak, when there is occasion to do good, and hide not thy wisdom in her beauty. For by speech wisdom shall be known: and learning by the word of the tongue. In no wise speak against the truth; but be abashed of the error of thine ignorance. Be not ashamed to confess thy sins; and force not the course of the river. Make not thyself an underling to a foolish man; neither accept the person of the mighty. Strive for the truth unto death, and the Lord shall fight for thee. Be not hasty in thy tongue, and in thy deeds slack and remiss. Be not as a lion in thy house, nor frantick among thy servants. Let not thine hand be stretched out to receive, and shut when thou shouldst repay. *A. Eccl.* 4, 22–31.

Set not thine heart upon goods unjustly gotten; for they shall not profit thee in the day of calamity. Winnow not with every wind, and go not into every way: for so doth the sinner that hath a double tongue. Be stedfast in thy understanding; and let thy word be the same. Be swift to hear; and let thy life be sincere; and with patience give answer. If thou hast understanding, answer thy neighbour; if not, lay thy hand upon thy mouth. Honour and shame is in talk: and the tongue of man is

his fall. Be not called a whisperer, and lie not in wait with thy
tongue : for a foul shame is upon the thief, and an evil condemnation upon the double tongue. Be not ignorant of any
thing in a great matter or a small. *A. Eccl.* 5, 8–15.

The weed growing upon every water and bank of a river shall
be pulled up before all grass. Bountifulness is as a most fruitful
garden, and mercifulness endureth for ever. To labour, and to
be content with that a man hath, is a sweet life : but he that
findeth a treasure is above them both. Children and the building
of a city continue a man's name : but a blameless wife is counted
above them both. Wine and musick rejoice the heart : but the
love of wisdom is above them both. The pipe and the psaltery
make sweet melody : but a pleasant tongue is above them both.
Thine eye desireth favour and beauty : but more than both corn
while it is green. A friend and companion never meet amiss :
but above both is a wife with her husband. *A. Eccl.* 40, 16–23.

Let us now praise famous men, and our fathers that begat us.
The Lord hath wrought great glory by them through his great
power from the beginning. Such as did bear rule in their kingdoms, men renowned for their power, giving counsel by their
understanding, and declaring prophecies : leaders of the people
by their counsels, and by their knowledge of learning meet for
the people, wise and eloquent in their instructions : such as
found out musical tunes, and recited verses in writing : rich men
furnished with ability, living peaceably in their habitations :
all these were honoured in their generations, and were the glory
of their times. There be of them, that have left a name behind
them, that their praises might be reported. And some there be,
which have no memorial; who are perished, as though they had
never been; and are become as though they had never been
born; and their children after them. But these were merciful
men, whose righteousness hath not been forgotten. With their
seed shall continually remain a good inheritance, and their
children are within the covenant. Their seed standeth fast, and
their children for their sakes. Their seed shall remain for ever,
and their glory shall not be blotted out. Their bodies are buried
in peace; but their name liveth for evermore. *A. Eccl.* 44, 1–14.

The pride of the height, the clear firmament, the beauty of
heaven, with his glorious shew; the sun when it appeareth,

declaring at his rising a marvellous instrument, the work of the most High : at noon it parcheth the country, and who can abide the burning heat thereof ? A man blowing a furnace is in works of heat, but the sun burneth the mountains three times more; breathing out fiery vapours, and sending forth bright beams, it dimmeth the eyes. Great is the Lord that made it; and at his commandment it runneth hastily. He made the moon also to serve in her season for a declaration of times, and a sign of the world. From the moon is the sign of feasts, a light that decreaseth in her perfection. The month is called after her name, increasing wonderfully in her changing, being an instrument of the armies above, shining in the firmament of heaven; the beauty of heaven, the glory of the stars, an ornament giving light in the highest places of the Lord. At the commandment of the Holy One they will stand in their order, and never faint in their watches. Look upon the rainbow, and praise him that made it; very beautiful it is in the brightness thereof. It compasseth the heaven about with a glorious circle, and the hands of the most High have bended it. By his commandment he maketh the snow to fall apace, and sendeth swiftly the lightnings of his judgement. Through this the treasures are opened : and clouds fly forth as fowls. By his great power he maketh the clouds firm, and the hailstones are broken small. At his sight the mountains are shaken, and at his will the south wind bloweth. The noise of the thunder maketh the earth to tremble : so doth the northern storm and the whirl-wind; as birds flying he scattereth the snow, and the falling down thereof is as the lighting of grasshoppers. The eye marvelleth at the beauty of the whiteness thereof, and the heart is astonished at the raining of it. The hoarfrost also as salt he poureth on the earth, and being congealed, it lieth on the top of sharp stakes. When the cold north wind bloweth, and the water is congealed into ice, it abideth upon every gathering together of water, and clotheth the water as with a breastplate. It devoureth the mountains, and burneth the wilderness, and consumeth the grass as fire. A present remedy of all is a mist coming speedily : a dew coming after heat refresheth. By his counsel he appeaseth the deep, and planteth islands therein. They that sail on the sea tell of the danger thereof; and when we hear it with our ears, we marvel thereat. For therein be strange and wondrous works, variety of all kinds of beasts and whales created. *A. Eccl.* 43, 1–25.

Honour a physician with the honour due unto him for the uses which ye may have of him : for the Lord hath created him. For of the most High cometh healing, and he shall receive honour of the king. The skill of the physician shall lift up his head : and in the sight of great men he shall be in admiration. The Lord hath created medicines out of the earth; and he that is wise will not abhor them. Was not the water made sweet with wood, that the virtue thereof might be known ? And he hath given men skill, that he might be honoured in his marvellous works. With such doth he heal (men), and taketh away their pains. Of such doth the apothecary make a confection; and of his works there is no end ; and from him is peace over all the earth. My son, in thy sickness be not negligent : but pray unto the Lord, and he will make thee whole. Leave off from sin, and order thine hands aright, and cleanse thy heart from all wickedness. Give a sweet savour, and a memorial of fine flour; and make a fat offering, as not being. Then give place to the physician, for the Lord hath created him : let him not go from thee, for thou hast need of him. There is a time when in their hands there is good success. For they shall also pray unto the Lord, that he would prosper that, which they give for ease and remedy to prolong life. He that sinneth before his Maker, let him fall into the hand of the physician. My son, let tears fall down over the dead, and begin to lament, as if thou hadst suffered great harm thyself; and then cover his body according to the custom, and neglect not his burial. Weep bitterly, and make great moan, and use lamentation, as he is worthy, and that a day or two, lest thou be evil spoken of : and then comfort thyself for thy heaviness. For of heaviness cometh death, and the heaviness of the heart breaketh strength. In affliction also sorrow remaineth : and the life of the poor is the curse of the heart. Take no heaviness to heart : drive it away, and remember the last end. Forget it not, for there is no turning again : thou shalt not do him good, but hurt thyself. Remember my judgement : for thine also shall be so; yesterday for me, and to day for thee. When the dead is at rest, let his remembrance rest; and be comforted for him, when his spirit is departed from him. The wisdom of a learned man cometh by opportunity of leisure : and he that hath little business shall become wise. How can he get wisdom that holdeth the plough, and that glorieth in the goad, that driveth oxen, and is occupied in their labours, and whose talk is of bullocks? He giveth his mind to make furrows; and is diligent to give the kine fodder. So every carpenter and workmaster, that laboureth night and day: and they that cut and grave seals, and are diligent to make great variety, and give themselves to counterfeit imagery, and watch to finish a work: the smith also sitting by the anvil, and considering the iron work, the vapour of the fire wasteth his flesh, and he fighteth with the heat of the furnace: the noise of the hammer and the anvil is ever in his ears, and his eyes look still upon the pattern of the thing that he maketh; he setteth his mind to finish his work, and watcheth to polish it perfectly: so doth the potter sitting at his work, and turning the wheel about with his feet, who is alway carefully set at his work, and maketh all his work by number; he fashioneth the clay with his arm, and boweth down his strength before his feet; he applieth himself to lead it over; and he is diligent to make clean the furnace: all these trust to their hands: and every one is wise in his work. Without these cannot a city be inhabited: and they shall not dwell where they will, nor go up and down: they shall not be sought for in publick counsel, nor sit high in the congregation: they shall not sit on the judges' seat, nor understand the sentence of judgement; they cannot declare justice and judgement; and they shall not be found where parables are spoken. But they will maintain the state of the world, and all their desire is in the work of their craft. *A. Eccl.* 38.

5

ZOROASTRIANISM
(Parseeism)

IT may surprise many people to learn that the religion of Zoroaster (the word is a corruption of the Persian form *Zarathustra*) was at one time the most important in the world. It was the religion of the great Persian Empire, which stretched from Egypt to India during the two hundred years 521 to 321 B.C.

After a period of decline it was revived by the Emperor Artaxerxes (Ashdir), who called a great assembly to discuss the restoration of the creed in its original purity. It is said that sixty thousand people attended this meeting, and that when agreement seemed impossible the truth was received by one of the priests in a miraculous vision. This is probably a way of saying that one man found the significant answer; at any rate, it is a fact that the religion was revived about two hundred years after Christ and maintained until the seventh century, when it was ruthlessly stamped out by the Muhammadans. These conquerors swept over the whole of the Near East, and they did not spare "the infidels." Enormous numbers were killed, but a large band fled to India, where they became known as Parsees, from the word "Persians." Despite their small number, as compared with the vast population of India, these Parsees, largely owing to their standards of honesty and straightforward dealing, have made themselves indispensable as bankers, financiers, and business men in and around Bombay. In Persia, now known as Iran, only a few thousand Zoroastrians survive : they are to be found mostly in Kerman and Yezd or in scattered societies. The total number of Zoroastrians (including the Parsees) in the world today has been estimated at about one hundred and twenty-five thousand.

The importance of the religion must not, however, be judged by the small number of present-day adherents, but rather by the immense influence which it has had in the past, and which still shows itself in the theology of other religions. For instance, its doctrines percolated into Judaism, and thence to Christianity. The concept of Satan as the personification of evil, the idea of guardian angels, and the existence of spirit-forms, both of the living and of the dead, are of Persian origin. The background of the religion is of great antiquity. Similarity of ideas, as well as of names, to those used by the Brahmans suggest that these date back to a time when migrating Aryans had not yet penetrated into India and were still one people with the Iranians (Persians). This would be before the Vedas (described in the first chapter) were composed, some fifteen or sixteen hundred years before Christ. But there are also great diversities, showing that Iranian religion had developed a long way on its own account before the appearance of Zoroaster. Zoroaster himself was a reformer rather than an originator. Authorities differ greatly as to the date of his birth: some, indeed, have gone so far as to assert that he never lived at all, and others that there were two of him! There is little doubt, however, that he was a real person and that he lived about the seventh century before Christ, though as early as 1000 B.C. has also been suggested. It was he who synchronized and formulated Persian religious ideas, purifying them from accretions, and, above all, giving them an ethical basis. He may thus be said to be the founder of the religion in its completed, and also in its practical, form. He made of it, not only a metaphysical theory, but a life that could be lived.

Of Zoroaster himself we know very little. He seems to have lived in the eastern part of the territory occupied by the Iranian tribes in ancient times, somewhere in Afghanistan or Russian Turkistan. The name of his father, Pourushashpa, and that of his clan, Spitama, occur frequently in the sacred writings. Some poems mention his wife, H'vovi, who was a member of a noble family at the Court of King Hystaspes: this would suggest that Zoroaster was also of noble birth. Sons and daughters are also mentioned. Zoroaster seems to have succeeded in winning for his faith the ruler Hystaspes (Vishtaspa), the last of a long line of kings. This greatly increased his influence, and when the expanding Persian Empire spread over the district, swallowing up the small kingdom, the new version of the Persian religion was strong enough to be accepted and to become the official religion of the emperors. It is said that the Prophet met his death by violence.

The facts of his life are, however, extremely obscure, and it is his doctrines which are of the chief importance.

As is often the case with religious reformation, corruptions arose after the reformer's death, and elements were introduced which he himself had been at pains to condemn. As he left it, the religion of Zoroaster was, in many ways, one of the purest in the history of the world, and it is in this form that we shall first consider it. Historians of the time note with admiration that the Persians had no temples or altars and looked with contempt on those who built them. Even more remarkable, perhaps, was the doctrine, so new in those days, of individual responsibility, with the necessary corollary of free will. Morality was for Zoroaster something fundamental and eternal. It was no mere passing convention: man was free to make the vital choice between right and wrong. Both these were absolutely real and final. Here, then, was a fearless dualism. In the beginning there were two Spirits, both of whom possessed creative power, one acting positively and the other negatively. Ormuzd (the word is a corruption of Ahura Mazda—the " wise Lord ") is Light and Life and the source of all good, while whatever is false, destructive, immoral, dark, and ugly is the work of Ahriman (a corruption of the words Angra Mainyu), the Evil One. It was to the glory of man to ally himself with the Good Spirit, and so help to secure the triumph of good over evil. Zoroaster did not doubt that the great majority of mankind would throw in their lot with the Good. But after death a strict judgment would take place. All thoughts, words, and deeds would be entered in the Book of Life, and if the evil outbalanced the good, the soul would pass into the hands of the Evil One and suffer the pains of Hell. Only righteousness could ensure salvation. Later Zoroastrianism admitted the confession of sins to a priest, who could substitute a temporal penalty for eternal punishment for those who were truly penitent. Every family came to possess a confessor, who was paid for his services, and who cared for the spiritual welfare of the family as a whole. Young people were under his charge until the age of fifteen, when by a rite, somewhat similar to the Christian Service of Confirmation, they were admitted to the adult privileges of religion.

It will be seen that under Zoroastrianism the responsibility of man was very great. First he had to distinguish between the good and the bad, the bad being designated by one general term, *The Lie*. In order to assert this responsibility before anything else, one doctrine, which is regarded as essential in most theistic religions, was abandoned. That was the singleness and all-powerfulness of the Good God. Zoroaster was willing that the Good Spirit should share, as it were, authority over the universe, rather than that the existence of evil should in any way lose its reality or be attributed to divine creation. The Good Spirit had created, was responsible for, and dwelt within, only those things which were harmonious and righteous; the evil one reigned over, and had produced all else. Zoroastrianism was thus released from the difficulty of explaining how a good God could permit sin and suffering—a problem which has always presented a difficulty, especially perhaps in Christianity. Christianity inherited the character of Satan from Persia, through Judaism, but, here, in order to retain the omnipotence of God, he becomes a fallen angel—also originally a creation of the sinless One. Thus the problem is put farther back : how, it may still be asked, did God, in Whom there was no fault, create a Being who became the source of all evil and the ruin of the human creation ? Whence did the thought of evil arise ? Zoroastrianism removed all responsibility from the good God; but in doing so the power of that God was necessarily limited. He ruled only over part of the universe. This theory of two primary causes we now call Dualism, and of this the Persian religion is a fearless and logical example.

While the power of the Good Spirit is thus limited, that of man is increased, for he can actually, by his own endeavour, help to bring about the triumph of right over wrong. The battlefield of the two forces is the world, and every time man resists *The Lie*, he is helping in the final victory of Ormuzd over Ahriman.

The Dualism of Zoroastrianism is the leading feature of its metaphysic, yet there have been some attempts to resolve this into a Unity. Thus it has been asserted that Ormuzd and Ahriman were originally twin brothers, born of the same nameless Force, in order to work out the world's destiny, and, again, that Ahriman will finally be reconciled to the Good One, and will be received by him into a place of bliss. But such theories were generally regarded as heresies, and for all practical purposes the separation of the two forces was assumed to be fundamental.

There are many likenesses between Zoroastrianism and Christianity as taught by the Churches. The personality of Satan, the description of him as a Serpent, the emphasis on choice and free-will, the judgment and separation of the righteous from the evil ones after death, punishment in Hell or bliss in Heaven, a single earth-life and the existence of guardian angels and spiritual beings, are common to both religions. Later Zoroastrianism taught also the resurrection of the body, and there were prophesies as to the coming of a kind of Saviour called Saoshyant, who would assist in the final judgment. All this differs strikingly from the philosophy of India described in Chapter II, with its fundamental Monism, its emphasis on Reincarnation, and the doctrine of final absorption into the All-of-Being. In Zoroastrianism it is the importance of each man's soul which counts most; the soul exists eternally, and an irrevocable choice has to be made in the one earth-life.

Zoroastrian Scriptures contain directions for a ceremonial Baptism and a Sacred Meal. These appear in the Avesta, a collection of books of varying dates, all of which are accepted by the orthodox as the Word of Ahura Mazda (Ormuzd). Much of the original has been lost, however (two-thirds according to some scholars), either by the fanaticism of the Moslem conquerors during the seventh century or in the burning of buildings by Alexander the Great in 330 B.C. Within the Avesta, the Gathas alone represent the actual words of the Prophet, survivals from the discourses which he gave at the Court of King Hystaspes (Vishtaspa). These fine poems, or hymns, are in the form of dialogues between Zoroaster and Ahura Mazda (Ormuzd) or archangels whom he invokes as witnesses to the truth of his assertions. They contain general admonitions and solemn prophecies, and show the immense sense of responsibility felt by the Prophet. Zoroaster believed that God had appointed him to restore religion, and he shows the greatest earnestness, and even anxiety, to be adequate to his task. At the time of the revival of the religion under Artaxerxes (Ashdir) the Scriptures were collected, codified, and translated into Pahlavi, the language then in current use in Persia. Thus they became available to the people. This translation, which includes comments on the subject-matter, is called *Zend*, hence the whole body of the Scriptures is sometimes referred to as the Zend-Avesta—i.e., the

Avesta, as translated, and with its commentary. The *Gathas*—the words of Zoroaster himself—are for the most part in the *Yasna*, the chief prayer book of the Zoroastrians.

That part of the Avesta which is of later date shows a return to many of the ideas which were ignored or repudiated by Zoroaster himself. Thus in the *Yashts* there are poems glorifying gods who belonged to the original Pantheon, and dating back to the old polytheistic days when the deities represented the forces of Nature. At the same time there is a tendency to exalt the person of the Prophet, and stories are told of miracles such as his virgin birth and of his semi-divine nature. Observances are advocated, and one sacred book, called the Vendidad, consists almost entirely of codes of laws and regulations. The priests, known as the Magi, or wise men, had increased in importance, and an idea which they had widely developed was that of the Fravashi, or guardian angels of the faithful. The rituals advocated were, however, more concerned with hygiene than with religious doctrine as such; they include instructions as to ceremonial washings, the treatment of vermin and of corpses, and, on the positive side, the care of the cow and of all animals useful to man. The worship of the Zoroastrian Church remained comparatively simple. The essential symbol was the Divine Fire, which was kept burning in the altars and never allowed to go out. The fire-altars developed into fire-temples, where a kind of Mass or sacred meal was celebrated, consecrated milk, bread, and water being used. The priests performed the sacrifices, educated the young clergy, imposed penalties, carried out ceremonial purifications, and looked after the welfare of the layman.

The symbol of the Fire which was never allowed to go out was connected with the idea of Truth. In one of the *Yashts* the ancient Sun-God, Mithra, is represented as being paired with Ahura Mazda (Ormuzd) as the Lord of Truth. Truthfulness was the great Zoroastrian virtue. It is the light which will finally burn up *The Lie*. Thus the fire-symbol, though doubtless a survival of ancient worship of the forces of Nature, had, under the new religion, acquired a profound spiritual significance. Honour was paid to the rising sun as the source of the undying fire.

The Zoroastrian Scriptures are difficult to read, partly because of obscurity of language (especially in translation) and partly because of a certain allusiveness, hard for Europeans to follow. The injunctions as to the care of animals seem to us queer and fantastic. But it has to be remembered that the whole scene of man's life, according to this religion, was a struggle to assist the Good Spirit against the Evil One. Thus all that was unclean, harmful, and inharmonious must be destroyed, and all that was helpful, fertile, and life-giving encouraged. Man had at all times, on every plane and in every way, to help Ormuzd against Ahriman. He must care for the cow—so important to pastoral settlers : this was a religious duty. Animal life was not in itself sacred (as in some religions farther east), but only that part of it which was created by Ormuzd. What was harmful and filthy must be ruthlessly destroyed. This Dualism, running through-out the whole creation, forms the background of the Scriptures, and with this fact in mind they will be better understood. The great virtues of truthfulness, loyalty, and honesty are stressed in the moral teaching throughout.

Zoroastrianism survives as a living religion in the Parseeism of today. The Parsees, as followers of the ancient faith, are conspicuous for their uprightness and truthfulness and for their high standard of morality generally. They combine the work of good business men with high principles, which include charity and generosity. This is entirely consistent with the spirit of the faith. The visible world is held to be real and important, and the use and enjoyment of good things is helpful to Ahura Mazda. No severe asceticism or " renunciation of the world " is required. There are two main sects [1] and a number of observances and customs. Honour is still paid to the rising sun, and the ancient custom of neither burying nor burning the dead, but of exposing them to the vultures on the " Towers of Silence " is retained. There are only two distinct classes, the priests and the people, the office of priest being hereditary. The last ten days of a Parsee's year should be spent in doing deeds of charity.

It is said that the modern Parsee is a monotheist and that the original Dualism has largely disappeared. This may be true, yet the special sense of personal responsibility remains, and shows itself in the two great virtues of honesty and benevolence. The idea of helping Ahura Mazda in his work is fundamental, even though Ahriman may have sunk to an inferior position and is no

[1] The Shahanshahis and the Kadmis.

longer regarded as the serious rival that he was. In that case the
Evil One probably approximates more nearly to the conception
of Satan as held by the stricter Christian Churches.

Verses from the Scriptures

ABBREVIATIONS TO REFERENCES

Aog.	= Aogemadaecha	*Mkh.*	= Menog-i Khrad
Dd.	= Dadistan-i dinik	*Shnsh.*	= Shayast-na-shayast
Fragm. Darm.	= Fragments Darme-steter	*Vd.*	= Vendidad
		Y.	= Yasna
Fragm. West.	= Fragments Wester-gaard	*Yt.*	= Yasht

I was lovely, and thou madest me still lovelier; I was fair and
thou madest me still fairer; I was desirable and thou madest me
still more desirable; I was sitting in a forward place and thou
madest me sit in the foremost place, through this good thought,
through this good speech, through this good deed of thine; and
so henceforth men worship me for my having long sacrificed unto
and conversed with **Ahura Mazda.** *Hadokht 2, 30-2.*

Let no thought of **Angra Mainyu** (the devil) ever infect thee,
so that thou shouldst indulge in evil lusts, make derision and
idolatry, and shut to the poor the door of thy house. *Vishtasp Yt.*
37.

O ye mortals! Mark these **commandments,** which the Wise
Lord has given for happiness and for pain; long punishment for
the evil-doer, bliss for the follower of truth, joy of salvation ever
afterwards for the righteous! *Y.* 30, 11.

I **created** the stars, the moon, the sun, and the red burning
fire, the dogs, the birds, and the five kinds of animals; but, better
and greater than all, I created the righteous man who has truly
received from me the praise of Asha in the good religion. *Aog.*
30.

The **dead** shall rise up, life shall come back to the bodies and
they shall keep the breath. *Fragm. West.* 4, 3.

Thou shouldst not become presumptuous through great connections and race; for in the end thy trust is on thine own
deeds. *Mkh.* 2, 108.

Form no covetous **desire**, so that the demon of greediness may not deceive thee, and the treasure of the world may not be tasteless to thee, and that of the spirit, unperceived. *Mkh.* 2, 13–15.

Thou shouldst be **diligent** and moderate, and eat of thine own regular industry, and provide the share of the sacred beings and the good; and thus, the practice of this, in thy occupation is the greatest good work. *Mkh.* 2, 42.

The first perfection is **good thoughts**, the second good words, and the third good deeds. *Zad Sparam* 21, 15.

If several **healers** offer themselves together, namely, one who heals with the knife, one who heals with herbs, and one who heals with the holy word, it is this one who will best drive away sickness from the body of the faithful. *Vd.* 7, 44.

Holiness is the best of all good. Happy, happy the man who is holy with perfect holiness. . . . The will of the Lord is the law of holiness; the riches of Vohu-manô (the Spirit of Goodness) shall be given to him who works in this world for Mazda, and wields according to the will of Ahura the power he gave to him to relieve the poor. *Vd.* 19, 22.

Whoever wishes to **love** Ahura Mazda, in the world, should love the righteous man. . . . Since the righteous man is the counterpart of Ahura Mazda the Lord. *Shnsh.* 15, 7–8.

That **nature** only is good when it shall not do unto another whatever is not good for its own self.—Do not unto others all that which is not well for oneself. *Dd.* 94, 5 and *Shnsh.* 13, 29.

May **obedience** conquer disobedience within this house, and may peace triumph over discord here, and generous giving over avarice, reverence over contempt, speech with truthful words over lying utterance, may the righteous order gain the victory over the demon of the lie. *Y.* 60, 5.

All good thoughts, all good words, all good deeds will reach **paradise**. All evil thoughts, all evil words, all evil deeds will reach hell. And all good thoughts, all good words, all good deeds are the badge of the righteous for paradise. *Fragm. West.* 3, 2.

For every man of **piety** is a wise citizen in accordance with the holy Order, and so are all who are in truth within Thy Realm, O Lord! *Gathas* 49, 5.

Every good work which thou art able to do to-day do not **postpone** for to-morrow, and accomplish with thine own hand the counsel of thine own soul . . . for there have been many people whose remaining life was one day, and they have been taken away in the presence of fifty years' work. *Sad Dar* 81, 10–12.

Poverty which is through honesty is better than opulence which is from the treasure of others. *Mkh.* 15, 4.

Any one in the world here below can win **purity** for himself, namely, when he cleanses himself with good thoughts, words and deeds. *Vd.* 10, 19.

One is to become a friend of everyone, and this is thy nature; also, bring them on into goodness, and this is thy wisdom; also, consider them as thine own, and this is thy **religion**; also, through them it shall produce happiness, and this is thy soul. *Dd.* 94, 6.

These four habits are the principles of the **religion** of Zaratust; to exercise liberality in connection with the worthy; to do justice; to be friendly unto everyone; to be sincere and true and to keep falsehood far from themselves. *Sad Dar* 65, 7.

He has gained nothing who has not gained the **soul**. *Fragm. Darm.* 3.

He that does not restore a thing lent, when it is asked for back again, **steals** the thing; he robs the man. So he does every day, every night, as long as he keeps in his house his neighbour's property, as though it were his own. *Vd.* 4, 1.

Everyone is to practise **thanksgiving** continually, and it is requisite that he maintains it through good and bad. *Sad Dar* 65, 1.

Neither our **thoughts**, nor commands, nor our understandings, nor our beliefs, nor our deeds, nor our consciences, nor our souls, are at one. *Gathas* 45, 2.

One **truthful** man is better than the whole world speaking falsehood. *Sad Dar* 62, 5.

It is knowledge, of which no one knows a superfluity. It is learning and skill, which no one is able to deprive one of. It is understanding and intellect, which it is not possible to buy at a price. It is wisdom, with which every one and one's own self are untroubled and satisfied. . . . **Wisdom** is better than the wealth of every kind which is in the world. *Mkh.* 40, 19–22 and 47, 6.

Readings from the Scriptures

I announce and I will complete my Yasna to Ahura Mazda, the Creator, the radiant and glorious, the greatest and the best, the most beautiful, the most firm, the wisest, and the one of all whose body is the most perfect, who attains His ends the most infallibly, because of His Righteous Order, to Him who disposes our minds aright, who sends His Joy-creating grace afar; who made us, and has fashioned us, and who has nourished and protected us, who is the most bounteous Spirit! I announce and I will complete my Yasna to the Good Mind, and to Righteousness the Best, and to the Sovereignty which is to be desired, and to Piety the Bountiful, and to the two, the Universal Weal and Immortality (to the body of the Kine, and to the Kine's Soul) and to the Fire of Ahura Mazda, that one who more than all the Bountiful Immortals has made most effort for our succour. *Y.* 1, 1–2.

If I have offended thee, whether by thought, or word, or deed, whether by act of will, or without intent or wish, I earnestly make up the deficiency of this in praise to thee. If I have caused decrease in that which is Thy Yasna, and Thy homage, I announce and celebrate to thee the more for this! Yea, all ye lords, the greatest ones, holy lords of the ritual order, if I have offended you by thought, or word, or deed, whether with my will, or without intending error, I praise you now the more for this, I announce to you the more if I have caused decrease in this which is your Yasna, and your praise. *Y.* 1, 21–2.

May'st Thou, O Ahura Mazda! reign at Thy will, and with a saving rule over Thine own creatures, and render Ye the holy man also a sovereign at his will over matters, and over plants, and over all the clean and sacred creatures which contain the seed of Righteousness. Strip ye the wicked of all power! . . . I pray for the freedom and glory of the entire existence of the holy man while I bless it, and I pray for the repression and shame of the entire existence of the wicked. *Y.* 8, 5, 8.

This first blessing I beseech of thee, O Haoma, sacred plant, thou that drivest death afar! I beseech of thee for heaven, the best life of the saints, the radiant, all glorious. This second blessing I beseech of thee, O Haoma, thou that drivest death afar! this body's health before that blest life is attained. This third blessing I beseech of thee, O Haoma, thou that drivest death afar! the long vitality of life. This fourth blessing, I beseech of thee, O Haoma, thou that drivest death afar! that I may stand forth on this earth with desires gained, and powerful, receiving satisfaction, overwhelming the assaults of hate, and conquering the lie. This fifth blessing, O Haoma, I beseech of thee, thou that drivest death afar! that I may stand victorious on earth, conquering in battles, overwhelming the assaults of hate, and conquering the lie. This sixth blessing I ask of thee, O Haoma, thou that drivest death afar! that we may get good warning of the thief, good warning of the murderer, see first the bludgeon-bearer, get first sight of the wolf. May no one which-soever get first the sight of us. In the strife with each may we be they who get the first alarm. *Y.* 9, 19–21.

I celebrate my praises for good thoughts, good words, and good deeds for my thoughts, my speeches, and my actions. With chanting praises I present all good thoughts, good words, and good deeds, and with rejection I repudiate all evil thoughts, and words, and deeds. Here I give to you, O ye Bountiful Immortals! sacrifice and homage with the mind, with words, deeds, and my entire person; yea, I offer to you the flesh of my very body as your own. And I praise Righteousness. A blessing is Righteousness called the Best. *Y.* 11, 17–18.

And we worship the former religions of the world devoted to Righteousness which were instituted at the creation, the holy religions of the Creator Ahura Mazda, the resplendent and glorious. . . . Yea, we worship the Creator Ahura Mazda and the Fire, Ahura Mazda's son, and the good waters which are Mazda-made and holy, and the resplendent sun of the swift horses, and the moon with the seed of cattle in his beams; and we worship the star Tistrya, the lustrous and glorious; and we worship the soul of the Kine of blessed endowment, and its Creator Ahura Mazda; and we worship Mithra of the wide pastures, and Sraosha (Obedience) the blessed, and Rashnu the most just, and the good, heroic, bountiful Fravashis of the saints, and the Blow-of-victory Ahura-given as it is. . . . And we worship the two, the milk-offering and the libation, the two which cause the waters to flow forth, and the plants to flourish. . . . And we worship all waters and all plants, and all good men, and all good women. And we worship all these Yazads, higher beings, heavenly and earthly, who are beneficent and holy. And we worship thee our dwelling-place who art the earth, and Thee, O Ahura Mazda, O holy Lord of this abode! which is the home of healthy herds and healthy men, and of those who are both endowed with health and lovers of the ritual right. *Y.* 16, 3-4, 8-10.

And now in these Thy dispensations, O Ahura Mazda! do Thou wisely act for us, and with abundance with Thy bounty and Thy tenderness as touching us; and grant that reward which Thou hast appointed to our souls, O Ahura Mazda! Of this do Thou Thyself bestow upon us for this world and the spiritual; and now as part thereof do Thou grant that we may attain to fellowship with Thee, and Thy Righteousness for all duration. And do Thou grant us, O Ahura! men who are righteous, and both lovers and producers of the Right as well. And give us trained beasts for the pastures, broken in for riding, and for bearing, that they may be in helpful companionship with us, and as a source of long enduring vigour, and a means of rejoicing grace to us for this. So let there be a kinsman lord for us, with the labourers of the village, and so likewise let there be the clients or the peers. And by the help of those may we arise. So may we be to You, O Mazda Ahura! holy and true, and with free giving of our gifts. *Y.* 40, 1-4.

This I ask thee, tell me truly, Ahura—as to prayer, how it should be to one of you. O Mazda, might one like thee teach it to his friend such as I am, and through friendly right give us support, that good thought may come unto us. This I ask thee, tell me truly Ahura—whether at the beginning of the best existence the recompenses shall bring blessedness to him that meets with them. Surely he, O Right, the holy one, who watched in his spirit the transgression of all, is himself the benefactor unto all that lives, O Mazda. This I ask thee, tell me truly, Ahura. Who is by generation the father of right, at the first? Who determined the path of sun and stars? Who is it by whom the moon waxes and wanes again : This, O Mazda, and yet more, I am fain to know. This I ask thee, tell me truly, Ahura. Who upheld the earth beneath and the firmament from falling ? Who the waters and the plants ? Who yoked swiftness to winds and clouds ? Who is, O Mazda, creator of good thought ? This I ask thee, tell me truly, Ahura. What artist made light and darkness ? What artist made sleep and waking ? Who made morning, noon, and night, that call the understanding man to his duty ? *Y.* 44, 1-5.

I pray with benedictions for a benefit, and for the good, even for the entire creation of the holy and the clean ; I beseech for them for the generation which is now alive, for that which is just coming into life, and for that which shall be hereafter. And I pray for that sanctity which leads to prosperity, and which has long afforded shelter, which goes on hand in hand with it, which joins it in its walk, and of itself becoming its close companion as it delivers forth its precepts, bearing every form of healing virtue which comes to us in waters, appertains to cattle, or is found in plants, and overwhelming all the harmful malice of the Daevas, and their servants who might harm this dwelling and its lord, bringing good gifts, and better blessings, given very early, and later gifts, leading to successes, and for a long time giving shelter. And so the greatest, and the best, and most beautiful benefits of sanctity fall likewise to our lot for the sacrifice, homage, propitiation, and the praise of the Bountiful Immortals, for the bringing prosperity to this abode, and for the prosperity of the entire creation of the holy, and the clean, and as for this, so for the opposition of the entire evil creation. And I pray for this as I praise through Righteousness, I who am beneficent, those who are likewise of a better mind. *Y.* 42, 1-4.

And may the good and heroic and bountiful Fravashis of the saints come here, and may they go hand in hand with us with the healing virtues of their blessed gifts as widespread as the earth, as far-spread as the rivers, as high-reaching as the sun, for the furtherance of the better men, for the hindrance of the hostile, and for the abundant growth of riches and of glory. May Sraosha (Obedience) conquer disobedience within this house, and may peace triumph over discord here, and generous giving over avarice, reverence over contempt, speech with truthful

words over lying utterance. May the Righteous Order gain the
victory over the Demon of the Lie. *Y.* 60, 4-5.

Hear ye then with your ears; see ye the bright flames with the
eyes of the Better Mind. It is for a decision as to religions, man
and man, each individually for himself. Before the great effort
of the cause, awake ye all to our teaching! Thus are the primeval
spirits who as a pair combining their opposite strivings, and yet
each independent in his action, have been famed of old. They
are a better thing, they two, and a worse, as to thought, as to word,
and as to deed. And between these two let the wisely acting
choose aright. Choose ye not as the evil-doers! Yea when the
two spirits came together at the first to make life, and life's
absence, and to determine how the world at the last shall be
ordered, for the wicked Hell the worst life, for the holy Heaven
the Best Mental State. . . . Wherefore, O ye men! ye are learning thus these religious incitations which Ahura gave in our
happiness and our sorrow. And ye are also learning what is
the long wounding for the wicked, and the blessings which are
in store for the righteous. And when these shall have begun
their course, salvation shall be your portion! *Gathas* 30, 2-4, 11.

Yea, he will act with justice but with vengeance, for he who
does evil to the wicked by word, or with thought and plan, and
who therein does not dally, but toils labouring as with both the
hands, or he again who admonishes one for his good, such as these
are offering a gift to their religious faith in the love and with the
approving view of Ahura Mazda; they are offering to conscience.
. . . Let the man who is the best toward the righteous saint,
whether lord's kinsman, or as village labourer, with the allied peer
of the master, having light, and endowed with energy for the
cattle . . . let such an one be for us in the work-field of the
Righteous Order, in the pastures of Thy Good Mind. *Gathas*
33, 2-3.

O Ahura Mazda, most beneficent Spirit, Maker of the material
world, thou Holy One! What of the Holy Word is the strongest?
What is the most victorious? What is the most glorious? What
is the most effective? What is the most fiend-smiting? What
is the best-healing? What destroyeth best the malice of Daevas
and Men? What maketh the material world best come to the
fulfilment of its wishes? What freeth the material world best

from the anxieties of the heart ? Ahura Mazda answered : That is the strongest part of the Holy Word; that is the most victorious; that is the most glorious; that is the most effective; that is the most fiend-smiting; that is the best-healing; that destroyeth best the malice of Daevas and Men; that maketh the material world best come to the fulfilment of its wishes; that freeth the material world best from the anxieties of the heart. . . . Worship me, O Zarathustra, by day and by night, with offerings of libations well accepted. I will come unto thee for help and joy, I, Ahura Mazda; the waters, the plants, and the Fravashis of the holy ones will come unto thee for help and joy. If thou wantest, O Zarathustra, to destroy the malice of Daevas and Men, of the oppressors, of the blind and of the deaf, of the two-legged ruffians, of the two-legged heretics, of the four-legged wolves; and of the hordes with the wide front, with the many spears, bearing the spear of havoc; then, recite thou these my names every day and every night. *Yasts and Sirozahs* 1, 1–4, 9–11.

Prayer is the greatest of spells, the best healing of all spells. One may heal with Holiness, one may heal with the Law, one may heal with the knife, one may heal with herbs, one may heal with the Holy Word : amongst all remedies this one is the healing one that heals with the Holy Word : this one it is that will best drive away sickness from the body of the faithful : for this one is the best-healing of all remedies. *Yt.* 3, 5–6.

When the sun rises up, purification comes upon the earth made by Ahura, purification unto the flowing waters, unto the waters of the wells, unto the water of the seas, unto the water that is standing. Purification comes unto the righteous creation, which is of the holy spirits. If indeed the sun were not to rise, then the demons would kill all things that are in the seven regions. He who offers up a sacrifice unto the undying, shining, swift-horsed Sun—to withstand darkness, to withstand the Daevas born of darkness, to withstand the robbers and bandits . . . to withstand death that creeps in unseen—offers it up to Ahura Mazda . . . offers it up to his own soul. . . . I bless the sacrifice and the invocation, and the strength and vigour of the undying, shining, swift-horsed Sun. *Yt.* 6, 2–4, 7.

We worship the piety and the Fravashi of the holy Zarathustra; who first thought what is good, who first spoke what is good, who first did what is good; who was the first Priest, the first Warrior, the first Plougher of the ground; who first knew and first taught; who first possessed and first took possession of the Bull, of Holiness, of the Word, the obedience to the Word, and dominion, and all the good things made by Mazda, that are the offspring of the good Principle. *Yt.* 13, 88.

O thou youth of good thoughts, good words, and good deeds, of good religion, I am thy own conscience! Everybody did love thee for that greatness, goodness, fairness, and freedom from sorrow, in which thou dost appear to me. . . . I was lovely and thou madest me still lovelier; I was fair and thou madest me still fairer; I was desirable and thou madest me still more desirable; I was sitting in a forward place and thou madest me sit in the foremost place, through this good thought, through this good speech, through this good deed of thine; and so henceforth men worship me for my having long sacrificed unto and conversed with Ahura Mazda. The first step that the soul of the faithful man made, placed him in the Good-Thought Paradise; the second step that the soul of the faithful man made, placed him in the Good-Word Paradise; the third step that the soul of the faithful man made, placed him in the Good-Deed Paradise; the fourth step that the soul of the faithful man made, placed him in the Endless Lights. *Yt.* 22, 11, 14–15.

Proclaim thou ever unto the poor : " Ever mayest thou wait here for the refuse that is brought unto thee, brought by those who have profusion of wealth! " Thus the Drug (Lie) will not fall upon thee and throw thee away; thou wilt wield kingly power there. The Law of Mazda will not deliver thee unto pain. Thou art entreated for charity by the whole of the living world, and she is ever standing at thy door in the person of thy brethren in the faith : beggars are ever standing at the door of the stranger, amongst those who beg for bread. Ever will that bread be burning coal upon thy head. . . . Let no thought of Angra Mainyu ever infect thee, so that thou shouldst indulge in evil lusts, make derision and idolatry, and shut to the poor the door of thy house. *Yt.* 24, 35–7.

Upon the material world the fatal winters are going to fall, that shall bring the fierce, foul frost; upon the material world the fatal winters are going to fall, that shall make snow-flakes fall thick, even an aredvî deep on the highest tops of mountains. And all the three sorts of beasts shall perish, those that live in the wilderness, and those that live on the tops of the mountains, and those that live in the bosom of the dale, under the shelter of stables. Before that winter, those fields would bear plenty of grass for cattle : now with floods that stream, with snows that melt, it will seem a happy land in the world, the land wherein footprints even of sheep may still be seen. Therefore make thee a Vara (enclosure) long as a riding-ground on every side of the square, and thither bring the seeds of sheep and oxen, of men, of dogs, of birds, and of red blazing fires. Therefore make thee a Vara, long as a riding-ground on every side of the square, to be an abode for men; a Vara, long as a riding-ground on every side of the square, to be a fold for flocks. There thou shalt make waters flow in a bed a hâthra long; there thou shalt settle birds, by the ever-green banks that bear never-failing food. There thou shalt establish dwelling places, consisting of a house with a balcony, a courtyard, and a gallery. Thither thou shalt bring the seeds of men and women, of the greatest, best, and finest kinds on this earth. Thither thou shalt bring the seeds of every kind of cattle, of the greatest, best, and finest kinds on this earth; thither thou shalt bring the seeds of every kind of tree fruit. . . . All those seeds shalt thou bring, two of every kind, to be kept inexhaustible there, so long as those men shall stay in the Vara. There shall be no humpbacked, none bulged forward there; no impotent, no lunatic; no poverty, no lying; no meanness, no jealousy; no decayed tooth, no leprous to be confined; nor any of the brands wherewith Angra Mainyu stamps the bodies of mortals. In the largest part of the place thou shalt make nine streets, six in the middle part, three in the smallest. To the streets of the largest part thou shalt bring a thousand seeds of men and women; to the streets of the middle part, six hundred; to the streets of the smallest part, three hundred. That Vara thou shalt seal up with the golden ring, and thou shalt make a door, and a window self-shining within. *Vd.* 2, 22–30.

The second place where the earth feels most happy is the place whereon one of the faithful erects a house, with a priest within; with cattle, with a wife, with children and good herds within;

and wherein afterwards the cattle go on thriving, holiness, fodder, the dog, the wife, the child, the fire and every blessing of life is thriving.—The third place where the earth feels most happy is where one of the faithful cultivates most corn, grass and fruit, where he waters ground that is dry, or dries ground that is too wet.—The fourth place where the earth feels most happy is where there is most increase of flocks and herds. Who is the fifth that rejoice the earth with greatest joy? . . . It is he who tilling the earth, kindly and piously gives to one of the faithful.—Who dost not till me, the earth, with the left arm and the right, with the right arm and the left, ever shalt thou stand at the door of the stranger, among those who beg for bread; ever shalt thou wait there for the refuse that is brought unto thee, brought by those who have profusion of wealth.—No one who does not eat has strength to do works of holiness, strength to do works of husbandry, strength to beget children. By eating, every material creature lives, by not eating, it dies away. *Vd.* 3, 2–6, 28, 33.

He who sows corn, sows holiness : he makes the law of Mazda grow higher and higher : he makes the law of Mazda as fat as he can with a hundred acts of adoration, a thousand oblations, ten thousand sacrifices. When barley is coming forth, the Daevas start up; when the corn is growing rank, then faint the Daevas' hearts; when the corn is being ground, the Daevas groan, when wheat is coming forth, the Daevas are destroyed. In that house they can no longer stay, from that house they are beaten away, wherein wheat is thus coming forth. It is as though red hot iron were turned about in their throats, when there is plenty of corn. *Vd.* 3, 31–2.

The law of Mazda indeed, takes away from him who confesses it the bonds of his sin; it takes away the sin of breach of trust; it takes away the sin of murdering one of the faithful; it takes away the sin of burying a corpse; it takes away the sin of deeds for which there is no atonement; it takes away the heaviest penalties of sin; it takes away any sin that may be sinned. In the same way the law of Mazda cleanses the faithful from every evil thought, word, and deed, as a swift-rushing mighty wind cleanses the plain. So let all the deeds thou doest be henceforth good; a full atonement for thy sin is effected by means of the law of Mazda. *Vd.* 3, 41–2.

Purity is for man, next to life, the greatest good, that purity that is procured by the law of Mazda to him who cleanses his own self with good thoughts, words, and deeds. . . . As much as a great stream flows swifter than a slender rivulet, so much above all other utterances in greatness, goodness, and fairness is this law, this fiend-destroying law of Zarathustra. As high as the great tree stands above the small plants it overshadows, so high above all other utterances in greatness, goodness, and fairness is this law, this fiend-destroying law of Zarathustra. *Vd.* 5, 21, 24.

O Ahura Mazda! most beneficent spirit, Maker of the material world, thou Holy One! How shall I cleanse the house? How the fire? how the water? how the earth? how the cow? how the tree? how the faithful man and the faithful woman? how the stars? how the moon? how the sun? how the boundless light? how all good things, made by Mazda, the offspring of the holy principle? Ahura Mazda answered: Thou shalt chant the cleansing words, and the house shall be clean; clean shall be the fire, clean the water, clean the earth, clean the cow, clean the tree, clean the faithful man and the faithful woman, clean the stars, clean the moon, clean the sun, clean the boundless light, clean all good things, made by Mazda, the offspring of the holy principle. So thou shalt say these fiend-smiting and most-healing words; thou shalt chant the Ahura-Vairya (personification of prayer) five times: " The will of the Lord is the law of holiness." . . . If thou wantest to cleanse the water, say these words aloud: " Waters we worship, the waters in the tree, the waters in the stream, the waters in the rain." . . . If thou wantest to cleanse the cow, say these words aloud: " For the cow we order thee to do these most excellent deeds, that she may have a resting place and fodder." *Vd.* 11, 1–3, 5, 6.

He who sleeps on throughout the night, who does not perform the Yasna nor chant the hymns, who does not worship by word or by deed, who does neither learn nor teach, with a longing for everlasting life, he lies when he says, " I am an Athravan (fire priest)," do not call him an Athravan. Him thou shalt call an Athravan, who throughout the night sits up and demands of the holy Wisdom, which makes man free from anxiety, with dilated heart, and cheerful at the head of the Kinvat bridge, and which makes him reach that world, that holy world, that excellent world, the world of paradise. Therefore demand of me, thou upright one! of me, who am the Maker, the best of all beings, the most knowing, the most pleased in answering what is asked of me; demand of me, that thou mayst be the better, that thou mayest be the happier. O Maker of the material world, thou Holy One! What is it that makes the unseen power of Death increase? It is the man that teaches a wrong law; it is the man who continues for three years without wearing the sacred girdle, without chanting the Gathas, without worshipping the good waters. *Vd.* 18, 5–9.

Who was he who first of the healthful, the wise, the happy, the wealthy, the glorious, the strong men of yore, drove back sickness to sickness, drove back death to death, and first turned away the point of the poniard and the fire of fever from the bodies of mortals. Thrita it was who first of the healthful, the wise, the happy, the wealthy, the glorious, the strong man of yore, drove back sickness to sickness, drove back death to death, and first turned away the point of the poniard and the fire of fever from the bodies of mortals. He asked for a source of remedies; he obtained it from Khshathra-Vairya, to withstand sickness and to withstand death, to withstand pain and fever, to withstand the disease, rottenness and infection which Angra Mainyu had created by his witchcraft against the bodies of mortals. And I Ahura Mazda brought down the healing plants that, by many hundreds, by many thousands, by many myriads, grow up all around the one Gaokerena (King of healing plants). All this health do we call by our blessing-spells, by our prayers, by our praises, upon the bodies of mortals. To thee, O Sickness, I say avaunt! to thee, O Death, I say avaunt! to thee, O Pain, I say avaunt! to thee, O Fever, I say avaunt! to thee, O Disease, I say avaunt! By their might may we smite down the Drug! May they give to us strength and power, O Ahura! I drive away sickness, death, pain and fever, the disease, rottenness, and infection which Angra Mainyu has created by his witchcraft against the bodies of mortals. I drive away all manner of diseases and deaths. . . . May the much-desired bestower of good come here, for the men and women of Zarathustra to rejoice, for the faithful to rejoice; with the desirable reward that is won by means of the law, and with that boon for holiness that is vouchsafed by Ahura! *Vd.* 20, 1–11.

All good thoughts, and all good words, and all good deeds are thought, and spoken, and done with intelligence; and all evil thoughts, and words, and deeds are thought, and spoken, and done with folly. And let the men who think, and speak, and do all good thoughts, and words, and deeds inhabit Heaven as their home. And let those who think, and speak, and do evil thoughts, and words, and deeds abide in Hell. For to all who think good thoughts, speak good words, and do good deeds, Heaven, the best world, belongs. *Zend-Avesta, Miscellaneous Fragments* 3.

Thou shouldst not become presumptuous through any happiness of the world; for the happiness of the world is such-like as a cloud that comes on a rainy day, which one does not ward off by any hill. Thou shouldst not become presumptuous through much treasure and wealth; for in the end it is necessary for thee to leave all. . . . Thou shouldst not become presumptuous through great connections and race; for in the end thy trust is on thine own deeds. Thou shouldst not become presumptuous through life; for death comes upon thee at last, and the perishable part falls to the ground. *Mkh.* 2.

With enemies fight with equity. With a friend proceed with the approval of friends. With a malicious man carry on no conflict, and do not molest him in any way whatever. With a greedy man thou shouldst not be a partner, and do not trust him with the leadership. With a slanderous man do not go to the door of kings. With an ill-famed man form no connection. With an ignorant man thou shouldst not become a confederate and associate. With a foolish man make no dispute. With a drunken man do not walk on the road. From an ill-natured man take no loan.—Him who is less than thee consider an equal, and an equal as a superior, and a greater than him as a chieftain and a chieftain as a ruler. *Mkh.* 2, 3.

These are the people it is necessary to consider as rich :—one is he who is perfect in wisdom; the second whose body is healthy, and he lives fearlessly; the third, who is content with that which has come; the fourth, he whose destiny is a helper in virtue; the fifth, who is well-famed in the eyes of the sacred beings, and by the tongues of the good; the sixth, whose trust is on this one, pure, good religion of the Mazda-worshippers; and the seventh, whose wealth is from honesty. And these are the people to be considered as poor:—one is he with whom there is no wisdom; the second, whose body is not healthy; the third, who lives in his fear, terror, and falsehood; the fourth, who is not ruling in his own body; the fifth, whose destiny is no helper; the sixth, who is infamous in the eyes of the sacred beings, and on the tongues of the good; and the seventh, who is old, and no child and kindred exist. *Mkh.* 35, 3–18.

The rule is this, that thou shouldst not consider even anyone hopeless of heaven, and they should not set their minds steadfastly on hell; thereby much sinfulness for which there is a desire would be undesirable, because there is nothing which is a sin in my religion for which there is no retribution. . . . Through how many ways and motives of good works do people arrive first at heaven? The first good work is liberality. The second, truth. The third, thankfulness. The fourth, contentment. The fifth, wanting to produce welfare for the good, and becoming a friend to everyone. *Shnsh.* 12, 28 and *Mkh.* 37, 2–8.

Give me, O Atar, son of Ahura Mazda! lively welfare, lively maintenance, lively living; fulness of welfare, fulness of maintenance, fulness of life; knowledge, sagacity; quickness of tongue; holiness of soul; a good memory; and then the understanding that goes on growing and the one that is not acquired through learning; and then the manly courage, firm-rooted, unsleeping, sleeping only for a third part of the day and of the night, quick to rise up from bed, ever awake; and a protecting, virtuous offspring, able to rule countries and assemblies of men, well growing up, good, freeing us from the pangs of hell, endowed with a good intellect, that may increase my house, my borough, my town, my country, my empire. . . . May herds of oxen grow for thee, and increase of sons; may thy mind be master of its vow, may thy soul be master of its vow, and mayest thou live on in the joy of the soul all the nights of thy life. *Nyayis* 5, 10–11, 16.

Seek ye for a store of good deeds, men and women! for a store of good deeds is full of salvation. For the ox turns to dust, the horse turns to dust; silver and gold turn to dust, the valiant strong man turns to dust; the bodies of all men mingle with the dust. What do not mingle with the dust are the confessions which a man recites in this world and his almsgiving to the holy and righteous. For they shall partake of the vision of the Best Life who most give alms to the righteous and most care for them. He that gives to a lover of the Lie despises Righteousness by his giving. Understand fully, my son, what is well done and not well done, and do not to others all that which is not well for thyself. *Aog.* 83, 4.

6

TAOISM

THIS is now the fifth of the eleven religions, and it may be interesting, perhaps, to run over the ground. We first considered India, and found the Hindus (who have been described as the most religious people in the world) still carrying on traditions which have been handed down to them from the earliest times. Their culture had not spread to other countries and, with the exception of some spheres of Muhammadanism, which we shall be considering later, the religious life of the nation was unaffected by foreign influence. We then went to Japan, and found there another national and non-proselytizing religion—Shintoism. This word, however, is derived, not from the people, but from the central feature of belief : it means The Way of the Gods. In Palestine we found yet another religion peculiar to a race and, as in the case of the Hindus, named after them. This was Judaism, but the Jews, instead of remaining in their own country, like the Hindus and the Japanese, had spread all over the world. Despite this wide dispersion, however, the religion remained national and racial; indeed, it became increasingly so, for although in early times the Jews had made converts, after the loss of their country they ceased to do so. Judaism and the Jews came to belong exclusively to one another. These first three religions are therefore racial and non-proselytizing, and none of them is the religion of a founder. In the Zoroastrianism of Persia, the fourth religion, we met for the first time the claims of a founder, from whose name the title is derived. But Zoroastrianism, which once aspired to universality, survives today only as Parseeism, where once more the name of a people (Parsee means Persian) appears, and the Parseeism of today is again non-proselytizing. Coming in this, the sixth chapter, to China, we find, once more, a non-proselytizing religion belonging to a special people. Taoism, like Shintoism, does not incorporate the name of that people in its title, but expresses the central feature of doctrine. *Tao* comes from the term *Way* ; a term used in China from very early times. Nevertheless, Taoism does claim a founder, known as Lao-Tze, who is generally accepted as having developed the vague concept of the Tao into a religion. The actual existence of Lao-Tze has been disputed, but it is most probable that he was a real person and that he lived, like Zoroaster, in the sixth century B.C. The sixth century B.C. was in fact a remarkable period. Not only Lao-Tze and Zoroaster, but also two other religious founders, both of whom influenced China, Confucius and Gautama Buddha, were born in that century. There are, in fact, three religions in China. Taoism will first be considered because of the extreme antiquity of its leading concept, but most people will probably associate Chinese religion pre-eminently with the name of Confucius. Confucianism will be dealt with in the following chapter, and Buddhism, which was of foreign origin and not indigenous to China, in Chapter 9. Lao-Tze is supposed to have been born about fifty years before Confucius, so in any case he comes first. The two great men are said to have met, and the story suggests that Confucius was reproved by Lao-Tze and told " to put aside his proud air and ungoverned will." Confucius was, however, much impressed, and compared Lao-Tze to a " dragon who could mount on the wind through the clouds and rise to Heaven."

The word " Tao " has been variously rendered into English. It has been translated as God, Universal Supreme Reason, the Logos, the Way, the Great Way of the World, and by other terms. In very early times it was associated with the revolution or " Way of the Heavens " about the earth, this movement being regarded as the cause of all earthly happenings. Later, Tao came to be regarded as the source of energy lying *behind* the visible order of Nature. This energy was impersonal, eternal, and omnipresent : in the world it worked out spontaneously for the good of all beings. The Tao was said to have originally produced the Yin and the Yang, the positive and the negative, or male and female, forces of Nature. These, in their turn, gave birth to Heaven and Earth and to all human beings. The Tao thus became an undefined principle which can hardly be represented by any single word in English. Indeed, in the opening passage of the Tao-Te-Ching (the Bible of the Taoists) we read :

" The Tao that can be expressed is not the Unchanging Tao :
The Name that can be named is not the Unchanging Name."

We must be content, then, to leave the word Tao as meaning
something like unconditioned Being, or First Cause.

The traditional story of the life of Lao-Tze, which is very
slender, is as follows :

Lao-Tze's personal name was Li-poh-yang, Lao-Tze being a
title of respect given to him by his followers. This means either
" Old Master" or " Old Boy," and we must remember that in
China " old " is a complimentary term, used neither with conde-
scension nor with pity. He is said to have been a Keeper of the
Royal Archives or Treasury of the Court of Chou, and from this
post he retired in his old age. The story of his meeting with
Confucius has already been told. There is another legend concerning the end of his life which is very pleasing. On his retire-
ment, it is said, he went on a journey to the west and reached a
pass in the mountains in the north-west boundary of China.
There the Warden of the Gate refused to let him pass until he had
written down the results of his accumulated wisdom. He there-
upon composed the book, known as the Tao-Te-Ching, of which
the opening lines have already been quoted. This book, which has
been translated, it is said, more times than any book in the world
except the Bible, is now generally assigned by scholars to a later
date, possibly the third instead of the sixth century B.C. This is
all that even legend has to say of the life of Lao-Tze. The
arrangement of the book, the Tao-Te-Ching (Te means virtue
and Ching, or King, means book or Canon), is somewhat confused, and so also are many of the characters which go to make up
the Chinese writing, with the result that versions differ a good
deal. Nevertheless, the main teaching is quite clear, and we do
find here the kernel of Taoism. The aim of a man's life is to
find, accept and live in union with the mysterious Tao, which is
something that cannot be defined or named, yet which is the
only Reality. The doctrine is thus mystical, and can be compared to the esoteric teaching of the Brahmans. Yet—and here
is the difference—Taoism was a religion for everybody. It
taught that man must try to go back, as it were, not forward, in
order to live as spontaneously as possible, in close contact with
Nature. People should be simple, frugal, and attached to the

soil. They should not strive to become "educated"; they should remain, not so much ignorant as *innocent*. Thus they would be happy, because they would be true to themselves, just as flowers and birds are. They would then be content with little and enjoy what they had. Politically the small village State was the ideal, and all centralized government was undesirable. Indeed, the less government of any kind the better : men should not even be aware that they were being ruled. The best governor, it was said, was he of whose existence no one even knew! All ambition, striving, force, and legal restraints were to be avoided, and, above all, war. Taoism was strictly pacifist. Even virtues— and here perhaps is the strangest part of the teaching of Lao-Tze —even virtues, such as justice, were not to be sought, because these create their opposites and therefore a state of tension. They imply striving and the clash of contraries. The realization of the Tao could only come about by complete acceptance of everything, by non-resistance, quietism, and nearness to the spontaneous life of Nature. The Tao is constantly compared to water, which is so gentle that it finds always the lowest place and resists nothing, yet so strong that it is capable of overflowing all things. Thus the later schemes for education, proposed by Confucius, his doctrines of acquired order and the pursuit of virtue were all opposed to the Taoist School.

The greatest disciple of Lao-Tze was Chuang-Tze, who lived and wrote in the fourth and third centuries B.C., some two hundred years later than the Master himself. He, with another writer, Lieh-Tze, who preceded him, cover the whole field of Taoism as understood by the early devotees, and "The Book of Chuang-Tze" gives details about Confucius as well as of Lao-Tze and other sages. Chuang-Tze's writings are full of allegory, anecdote, and imaginary conversations. He wished to induce the Chinese to accept Lao-Tze rather than Confucius as their teacher, and the latter sometimes appears at a disadvantage, or even as himself expounding the Taoist doctrine. Chuang-Tze developed Taoism into a more definite philosophy. As in the Tao-Te-Ching, the Tao is the basis of all things, yet it is not itself a *thing*. It is even more abstract than non-existence, which is made definite by its opposition to existence, so it has been called "non-existing non-existence"! Yet Tao is the only Reality, and it is upon Tao that both the individual man and the social structure must be founded. The writings of this great apostle of Taoism show profound insight combined with great beauty of poetic imagination. They have also at times a quaint humour, which is even more noticeable in Chuang-Tze's predecessor, Lieh-Tze.

The later development of Taoism was associated with the practice of magic, alchemy, divination, and many forms of wonder-working. This " degeneration " has been severely condemned by Western scholars, yet it is easy to see how it came about. Since the Tao was believed to be the underlying universal power, it was thought that, by seeking it, it might be possible to escape the limitations of time and place, and so transcend the physical plane. Thus spiritual union would be accompanied by physical emancipation. Something of the same idea had prevailed among the Brahmans of India. They had claimed that by the practice of special forms of breathing, accompanied by meditation and ascetic self-discipline (Yoga), they could contact the divine life, and that, in the process, special powers would be obtained over the forces of physical nature. But there was this difference between the religious life of India and that of China. The Hindus had a system of caste, which implied the principle of *function*, brought about by Reincarnation and the working of Karma (Works). Thus only men born to it, so to speak, could enter into the mystical way. The priestly caste, the Brahmans, had the key to all religious understanding; the lower castes (the people) were not even allowed to read the Scriptures. Thus there was some safeguard against the popularization of practices designed to bestow supernatural powers. To the genuine Yogi spiritual awareness was the aim : any supernormal control came about incidentally. The early Taoist mystics undoubtedly practised meditation, abstention from food, and breath control with the same sincere desire to obtain awareness of the Tao, but the wish to use superhuman powers spread too easily to the people in general. They became obsessed with the idea of magic and the attempt to discover an elixir of life which would render them immortal. A reigning emperor sent a fully equipped expedition over the sea to search for the Islands of the Blest, where men would be found who lived for ever and who were never ill. Everything associated with magic became a passion : astrology, fortune-telling, alchemy, and wonder-working. Professor Soothill, writing in 1923, says of the relapse of Taoism into a system of magic :

> " A charge cannot be laid at the door of Laocius [a Latinized form of the name of Lao-Tze], and it is a pity that the lofty moral teachings of Laocius and Chuang-Tze proved to be beyond the capacity of their successors. Even in Chuang-Tze we find elements of the bizarre, men who could walk through the solid rock, leap down terrifying precipices unharmed, walk through fire unsinged, travel thousands of miles through the air, absenting themselves for many days, men who did not die, but were translated and so on. . . . Taoist devotees today walk up ladders of swords, pass through blazing fire, push long needles through their cheeks. . . . They are called upon to clear the haunted house, expel demons, rid a town of cholera spirits, pour magical curses on the thief, and undertake incantations for rain." [1]

The man who was responsible for organizing Taoism with all these elements into a Church was Chang-Liang (Tao-Ling)— said to have been born in A.D. 34. He made of himself a kind of pope, the first of a long line of celestial preceptors who have continued up to the present day and who have had considerable political influence. Chang-Liang, with a band of followers, set up a miniature State, based on Taoist principles, in a remote district, and his work was carried on in different parts of China by other members of his family. He was supposed to have possessed miraculous powers, and one of his descendants is credited with having discovered the elixir of life and become an immortal. The sacred office was handed on from father to son, and in course of time the Emperor granted a kind of Papal State in Kiangsi, which is still the centre of the Taoist Church.

The later history of Taoism is thus one of ever-increasing complexity and accretion. The arrival in China of Buddhism during the first century of our era was a further complication, and resulted in imitation, adaptation, and absorption of many ideas which originally came from India. Temples, convents, and monasteries were set up; saints and deities, often even national heroes, came to be worshipped. Finally a Taoist Trinity emerged with the title of the " Three Pure Ones," which consisted of Lao-

[1] *The Three Religions of China*, W. E. Soothill. Oxford University Press.

Tze himself, the Jade Emperor (a mythical figure symbolizing the Supreme Ruler of the Universe), and an ancient primal deity—Chaos or the Demi-urge. A Power, known as the " original first principle, venerated of Heaven," is sometimes worshipped by the more mystical-minded as the source of all these three.

Before leaving the subject of Taoism we must note that the religions of Buddhism, Confucianism (which will be dealt with later), and Taoism are not mutually exclusive. It would be unthinkable in the West that a man should describe himself as a Roman Catholic and also a Methodist. Yet a Chinese might quite easily say that he was a Confucianist, a Buddhist, and a Taoist—that, in fact, he belonged to all the three religions at the same time. Buddhist priests are often in charge of Taoist temples, Confucius himself is represented in the writings of Chuang-Tze as expounding the theories of Taoism : some Taoists even adore Confucius as a god. The combining of the three religions is amusingly illustrated by Dr. Carpenter in his book " The Panorama of Religions."

> " As early as the sixth century a famous Buddhist scholar was asked by the Emperor if he was a Buddhist and he pointed to his Taoist cap. ' Are you a Taoist ? ' he showed his Confucian shoes. ' Are you a Confucian ? ' he wore a Buddhist scarf."

There has been some mutual opposition between these three religions, especially as we saw in the rival theories of Lao-Tze and Confucius, yet adaptation has been more general, for the Chinese have the " gift of acceptance," and a marked feature of all three religions is tolerance. We can, if we like, put it in another way. It is possible that each religion gives something that the others lack. Confucius taught the rules of good order and right behaviour for everyday life. Taoism has been said to supply " the missing elements of beauty, mystery, romance, and colour," while Buddhism brought the organized religious life with devotion, worship, temples, and orders of monks and nuns.

Taoism may be regarded as the most ancient of the faiths, the background and foundation, perhaps, of both the others. Its leading idea is of such great antiquity that it has been said that it is the only real religion of China. It is Taoism which has made the Chinese pre-eminently sensitive to beauty, and, unless corrupted by Western ideas, contented with little for the enjoyment of life. More than any other nation they have in the past understood how to make the most of what is given, however little that may be. This must not be confused with asceticism; rather is it the reverse : the power to enjoy without the continual urge to " improve " one's circumstances. The harm done by association with magic and wizardry should not be exaggerated, and indeed some useful discoveries have incidentally been made in the spheres of chemistry, physics, and medicine. In any case, such practices, though popular and sensational, do not necessarily invalidate a spiritual philosophy which has underlain the life of a nation from earliest times. It is always easy to point to the degeneration of religions other than one's own, and particularly, perhaps, is this the case with Taoism. To describe its later developments, however, as " animistic, polytheistic and a mass of superstitious magic " is to give only part of the truth. Where an enormous number of people in all stages of development are associated with a doctrine, crude and false elements will inevitably rise to the surface : it is to the underlying levels that we should look, to the writings of the Scriptures, and to the effect on the character of the people as a whole. Those who wish to appreciate Taoism in its pure form should become familiar with the Tao-Te-Ching, and the book of Chuang-Tze, and, further, with early Chinese painting and other works of art which have been so largely inspired by the teachings of Lao-Tze.

Verses from the Scriptures

ABBREVIATIONS TO REFERENCES

C.T. = Chuang Tzŭ   T.T.C. = Tao Tê Ching
K.Y.P. = T'ao Shang Kan Ying P'ien   L.T. = Lieh Tzŭ

There is no guilt greater than to sanction ambition; no calamity greater than to be discontented with one's lot; no fault greater than the wish to be getting. Therefore the sufficiency of **contentment** is an enduring and unchanging sufficiency. *T.T.C.* 46.

The simplicity of the nameless Tao brings about an absence of desire, the absence of **desire** gives tranquillity. *T.T.C.* 37.

Do not call attention to the **faults** of others; nor boast of your own excellence. Stay evil, and promote goodness. Renounce much; accept little. *K.Y.P.*

A man who knows that he is a **fool** is not a great fool.   A man who knows his error is not greatly in error.   *C.T.* 12.

The **future** is not to be waited for; the past is not to be sought again.   *C.T.* 4.

Extend your help without seeking reward.   **Give** to others and do not regret or begrudge your liberality.   Those who are thus are good.   *K.Y.P.*

To the **good** I would be good.   To the not-good I would also be good, in order to make them good.   *T.T.C.* 49.

Blessed is the man who speaketh what is **good**, who thinketh what is good, who practiseth what is good.   *K.Y.P.*

If the **government** is tolerant, the people will be without guile.   If the government is meddling, there will be constant infraction of the law.   *T.T.C.* 75.

Perfect **happiness** is the absence of happiness.   *C.T.* 18.

He that **humbles** himself shall be preserved entire.   He that bends shall be made straight.   He that is empty shall be filled. He that is worn out shall be renewed.   He who has little shall succeed.   He who has much shall go astray.   *T.T.C.* 22.

For we can only **know** that we know nothing, and a little knowledge is a dangerous thing.   *C.T.* 33.

To **know** when one does not know is best.   To think one knows when one does not know is a dire disease   Only he who recognizes this disease as a disease can cure himself of the disease.   *T.T.C.* 71.

He who **knows** other men is discerning; he who knows himself is intelligent.   He who overcomes others is strong; he who overcomes himself is mighty.   He who is satisfied with his lot is rich.   *T.T.C.* 33.

There has been such a thing as **letting mankind alone**; there has never been such a thing as governing mankind with success. Letting alone springs from fear lest men's natural dispositions be perverted and their virtue laid aside.   But if their natural dispositions be not perverted nor their virtue laid aside, what room is there left for government.   *C.T.* 11.

Men of this world all rejoice in others being **like themselves**, and object to others not being like themselves.   *C.T.* 11.

For **love** is victorious in attack, and invulnerable in defence. Heaven arms with love those it would not see destroyed. *T.T.C.* 67.

When **merit** has been achieved, do not take it to yourself; for if you do not take it to yourself, it shall never be taken from you. *T.T.C.* 2.

Regard your **neighbour's gain** as your own gain; and regard your neighbour's loss as your own loss. *K.Y.P.*

Strive to keep the world to its own **original simplicity**. And as the wind bloweth where it listeth, so let virtue establish itself. *C.T.* 14.

Do not swerve from the **path of virtue**; do not bring about your own good deeds,—lest your labour be lost. Do not make for wealth; do not aim at success,—lest you cast away that which links you to God. *C.T.* 29.

When no man hurts one hair, and no one benefits the world, all below heaven will be at **peace**. *Yang Chu.*

The **perfect man** ignores self; the divine man ignores action; the true sage ignores reputation. *C.T.* 1.

The art of **preserving life** consists in being able to keep all in one, to lose nothing, to estimate good and evil without divination, to know when to stop, and how much is enough, to leave others alone and attend to oneself, to be without cares and without knowledge,—to be in fact as a child. *C.T.* 23.

Recompense injury with kindness. *T.T.C.* 63.

Verily God does not **reward** man for what he does, but for what he is. *C.T.* 32.

Nothing, in the ordering of this world, is either at all times **right** or at all times wrong. What formerly passed current may nowadays be rejected; what is now rejected may by and by come into use again. *L.T.* 8.

The **sage** does not accumulate for himself. The more that he expends for others, the more does he possess of his own; the more that he gives to others, the more does he have himself. *T.T.C.* 81.

The **sage** does not show himself; therefore he is seen everywhere. He does not define himself, therefore he is distinct.

He does not boast of what he will do, therefore he succeeds. He is not proud of his work, and therefore it endures. He does not contend, and for that very reason no one under heaven can contend with him. So then we see that the ancient saying " To remain whole be twisted! " was no idle word. *T.T.C. 22.*

The misery I suffer comes from over-attention to my own **self**, and the troubles of the empire from over-regulation in everything. *L.T. 2.*

He who raises himself on tip-toe cannot **stand** firm; he who stretches his legs wide apart cannot walk. He who is self-approving does not shine; he who boasts has no merit; he who exalts himself does not rise high. *T.T.C. 24.*

In **striving for others**, avoid fame. In striving for self, avoid disgrace. Pursue a middle course. Thus you will keep a sound body, and a sound mind, fulfil your duties, and work out your allotted span. *C.T. 3.*

He who, conscious of being **strong**, is content to be weak,—he shall be a cynosure of men. *T.T.C. 28.*

What man is there that can take of his own super-abundance and give it to mankind? Only he who possesses **Tao**. *T.T.C. 77.*

Tao acts without action, does without doing, finds flavour in what is flavourless, can make the small great and the few many, requites injuries with good deeds, deals with the hard while it is still easy, with the great while it is still small. In the government of empire everything difficult must be dealt with while it is still easy, everything great must be dealt with while it is still small. Therefore the sage never has to deal with the great; and so achieves greatness. *T.T.C. 63.*

Nature cannot be changed. Destiny cannot be altered. Time cannot stop. **Tao** cannot be obstructed. Once attain to Tao, and there is nothing which you cannot accomplish. Without it, there is nothing which you can accomplish. *C.T. 14.*

Tao is the sanctuary where all things find refuge, the good man's priceless treasure, the guardian and saviour of him who is not good. *T.T.C. 62.*

I have **three precious things** which I hold fast and prize. The first is gentleness; the second is frugality; the third is humility, which keeps me from putting myself before others. Be gentle, and you can be bold; be frugal, and you can be liberal; avoid putting yourself before others, and you can become a leader among men. *T.T.C.* 67.

The skilful **traveller** leaves no tracks; the skilful speaker makes no blunders; the skilful reckoner uses no tallies. He who knows how to shut uses no bolts—yet you cannot open. He who knows how to bind uses no cords—yet you cannot undo. *T.T.C.* 27.

A **victory** should be celebrated with the Funeral Rite. *T.T.C.* 31.

The **way** is like an empty vessel that yet may be drawn from without even needing to be filled. It is bottomless; the very progenitor of all things in the world. In it all sharpness is blunted, all tangles untied, all glare tempered, all dust smoothed. It is like a deep pool that never dries. (Dust is the Taoist symbol for the noise and fuss of everyday life.) *T.T.C.* 4.

The great **way** is very smooth, but the people love the bypaths. *T.T.C.* 53.

Without going out of doors one may know the whole **world**; without looking out of the window one may see the Way of heaven. The further one travels, the less one may know. Thus it is that without moving you shall know; without looking you shall see; without doing you shall achieve. *T.T.C.* 47.

Readings from the Scriptures

The Tao that can be expressed is not the eternal Tao;
The name that can be defined is not the unchanging name.
Non-existence is called the antecedent of heaven and earth;
Existence is the mother of all things.
From eternal non-existence, therefore, we serenely observe the mysterious beginning of the universe;
From eternal existence we clearly see the apparent distinctions.
These two are the same in source and become different when manifested.
This sameness is called profundity. Infinite profundity is the gate whence comes the beginning of all parts of the universe. *T.T.C.* 1.

It is because every one under Heaven recognizes beauty as beauty, that the idea of ugliness exists. And equally if every one recognized virtue as virtue, this would merely create fresh conceptions of wickedness. For truly Being and Not-being grow out of one another; difficult and easy complete one another. Long and short test one another. High and low determine one another. The sounds of instrument and voice give harmony to one another. Front and back give sequence to one another. Therefore the Sage relies on actionless activity, carries on wordless teaching, but the myriad creatures are worked upon by him; he does not disown them. He rears them, but does not lay claim to them, controls them, but does not lean upon them, achieves his aim, but does not call attention to what he does; and for the very reason that he does not call attention to what he does he is not ejected from fruition of what he has done. *T.T.C.* 2.

Not exalting the worthy keeps the people from emulation.

Not valuing rare things keeps them from theft. Not showing what is desirable keeps their hearts from confusion.

Therefore the sage rules by emptying their hearts,

Filling their stomachs, weakening their ambitions,

And strengthening their bones.

He always keeps them from knowing what is evil and desiring what is good; thus he gives the crafty ones no chance to act. He governs by non-action; consequently there is nothing ungoverned. *T.T.C.* 3.

The highest goodness is like water. Water is beneficient to all things but does not contend. It stays in places which others despise. Therefore it is near Tao.

In dwelling, think it a good place to live;

In feeling, make the heart deep;

In friendship, keep on good terms with men;

In words, have confidence;

In ruling, abide by good order;

In business, take things easy;

In motion, make use of the opportunity.

Since there is no contention, there is no blame. *T.T.C.* 8.

Thirty spokes unite in one nave; the utility of the cart depends on the hollow centre in which the axle turns. Clay is moulded into a vessel; the utility of the vessel depends on its hollow interior. Doors and windows are cut out in order to make a house : the utility of the house depends on the empty spaces. Thus, while the existence of things may be good, it is the non-existent in them which makes them serviceable. The five colours will blind a man's sight. The five sounds will deaden a man's hearing. The five tastes will spoil a man's palate. Chasing and hunting will drive a man wild. Things hard to get will do harm to a man's conduct. Therefore the Sage makes provision for the inner self and not for the eye. He rejects the latter and chooses the former. *T.T.C.* 11–12.

Do away with learning, and grief will not be known.

Do away with sageness and eject wisdom, and the people will be more benefited a hundred times.

Do away with benevolence and eject righteousness, and the people will return to filial duty and parental love.

Do away with artifice and eject gains, and there will be no robbers and thieves.

These four, if we consider them as culture, are not sufficient.

Therefore let there be what the people can resort to :

Appear in plainness and hold to simplicity;

Restrain selfishness and curtail desires.   *T.T.C.* 19.

Be humble, and you will remain entire.

Be bent, and you will remain straight.

Be vacant, and you will remain full.

Be worn, and you will remain new.

He who has little will receive.

He who has much will be embarrassed.

Therefore the sage keeps to One and becomes the standard for the world.

He does not display himself; therefore he shines.

He does not approve himself; therefore he is noted.

He does not praise himself; therefore he has merit.

He does not glory in himself; therefore he excels.

And because he does not compete; therefore no one in the world can compete with him.   *T.T.C.* 22.

He who knows others is wise;

He who knows himself is enlightened.

He who conquers others is strong;
He who conquers himself is mighty.
He who knows contentment is rich.
He who keeps on his course with energy has will.
He who does not deviate from his proper place will long endure.
He who may die but not perish has longevity. *T.T.C.* 33.

What is most perfect seems to have something missing; yet its use is unimpaired. What is most full seems empty; yet its use will never fail. What is most straight seems crooked; the greatest skill seems like clumsiness, the greatest eloquence like stuttering. Movement overcomes cold; but staying still overcomes heat. So he (the Sage) by his limpid calm puts right everything under heaven. *T.T.C.* 45.

The way (Tao) out into the light often looks dark, the way that goes ahead often looks as if it went back. The way that is least hilly often looks as if it went up and down, the " power " that is really loftiest looks like an abyss, what is sheerest white looks blurred. The " power " that is most sufficing looks inadequate, the " power " that stands firmest looks flimsy. What is in its natural, pure state looks faded; the largest square has no corners, the greatest vessel takes the longest to finish, great music has the faintest notes, the Great Form is without shape. For Tao alone supports all things and brings them to fulfilment. *T.T.C.* 41.

Those who know do not speak; those who speak do not know. Block the passages, shut the doors, let all sharpness be blunted, all tangles untied, all glare tempered. All dust smoothed. This is called the mysterious levelling. He who has achieved it cannot either be drawn into friendship or repelled, cannot be benefited, cannot be harmed, cannot either be raised or humbled, and for that very reason is highest of all creatures under heaven. Use directness in ruling a state, indirectness in waging war; practise non-interference in order to win the empire. As restrictions and prohibitions are multiplied in the empire, the people grow poorer and poorer. When the people are subjected to overmuch government, the land is thrown into confusion. When the people are skilled in many cunning arts, strange are the objects of luxury that appear. The greater the number of laws and enactments, the more thieves and robbers there will be. Therefore the Sage says : " So long as I do nothing, the people will work out their own reformation. So long as I love calm, the people will right themselves. If only I keep from meddling, the people will grow rich. If only I am free from desire, the people will come naturally back to simplicity." *T.T.C.* 56–7.

That which is at rest is easily kept hold of; before a thing has given indications of its presence, it is easy to take measures against it; that which is brittle is easily broken; that which is very small is easily dispersed. Action should be taken before a thing has made its appearance; order should be secured before disorder has begun. The tree which fills the arms grew from the tiniest sprout; the tower of nine stories rose from a small heap of earth; the journey of a thousand *li* commenced with a single step. He who acts, destroys; he who grasps, loses. Therefore the Sage does not act, and so does not destroy; he does not grasp, and so he does not lose. . . . Heed the end no less than the beginning, and your work will not be spoiled. *T.T.C.* 64.

I have three treasures, which I hold and keep safe :
The first is called love; the second is called moderation;
The third is called not venturing to go ahead of the world.
Being loving, one can be brave; being moderate, one can be ample;
Not venturing to go ahead of the world, one can be the chief of all officials.
Instead of love, one has only bravery; instead of moderation, one has only amplitude;
Instead of keeping behind, one goes ahead :
These lead to nothing but death.
For he who fights with love will win the battle; he who defends with love will be secure.
Heaven will save him, and protect him with love. *T.T.C.* 67.

Viewed from the standpoint of Tao, a beam and a pillar are identical. So are ugliness and beauty, greatness, wickedness, perverseness, and strangeness. Separation is the same as construction : construction is the same as destruction. Nothing is subject either to construction or to destruction, for these conditions are brought together into ONE. Only the truly intelligent understand this principle of the identity of all things. . . . If there was a beginning, then there was a time before that beginning. And a time before the time which was before the time of that beginning. If there is existence, there must have been non-existence. And if there was a time when nothing existed, then there must have been a time before that—when even nothing did not exist. Suddenly, when nothing came into existence, could one really say whether it belonged to the category of existence or of non-existence? Even the very words I have just now uttered, —I cannot say whether they have really been uttered or not. . . . Perfect Tao does not declare itself. Nor does perfect argument express itself in words. Nor does perfect charity show itself in acts. Nor is perfect honesty absolutely incorruptible. Nor is perfect courage absolutely unyielding. For the Tao which shines forth is not Tao. Speech which argues falls short of its aim. Charity which has fixed points loses its scope. Honesty which is absolute is wanting in credit. Courage which is absolute misses its object. These five are, as it were, round, with a strong bias towards squareness. Therefore that knowledge which stops at what it does not know, is the highest knowledge. . . . I heard Confucius say, " The true sage pays no heed to mundane affairs. He neither seeks gain nor avoids injury. He asks nothing at the hands of man. He adheres, without questioning, to Tao. Without speaking, he can speak; and he can speak and yet say nothing." C.T. 2.

The feet can walk; let them walk. The hands can hold; let them hold. Hear what is heard by your ears; see what is seen by your eyes. Let your knowledge stop at what you do not know; let your ability stop at what you cannot do. Use what is naturally useful; do what you spontaneously can do, act according to your will within the limit of your nature, but have nothing to do with what is beyond it. This is the most easy matter of non-action. . . . There exists two sources of safety. One is destiny: the other is duty. A child's love for its parents is destiny. It is inseparable from the child's life. A subject's allegiance to his sovereign is duty. Beneath the canopy of heaven there is no place to which he can escape from it. These two sources of safety may be explained as follows. To serve one's parents without reference to place but only to the service, is the acme of filial piety. To serve one's prince without reference to the act but only to the service, is the perfection of a subject's loyalty. To serve one's own heart so as to permit neither joy nor sorrow within, but to cultivate resignation to the inevitable,—this is the climax of Virtue. . . . The honours of this world are light as feathers, yet none estimate them at their true value. The misfortunes of this life are weighty as the earth itself, yet none can keep out of their reach. No more, no more, seek to influence by virtue. . . . Hills suffer from the trees they produce. Fat burns by its own combustibility. Cinnamon trees furnish food : therefore they are cut down. The lacquer tree is felled for use. All men know the use of useful things; but they do not know the use of useless things. *C.T.* 4.

Life and Death, existence and non-existence, success and non-success, poverty and wealth, virtue and vice, good and evil report, hunger and thirst, warmth and cold,—these all revolve upon the changing wheel of Destiny. Day and night they follow one upon the other, and no man can say where each one begins. Therefore they cannot be allowed to disturb the harmony of the organism, nor enter into the soul's domain. Swim however with the tide, so as not to offend others. Do this day by day without break, and live in peace with mankind. Thus you will be ready for all contingencies, and may be said to have your talents perfect. *C.T.* 5.

The pure men of old acted without calculation, not seeking to secure results. They laid no plans. Therefore, failing, they had no cause for regret; succeeding, no cause for congratulation. And thus they could scale heights without fear; enter water without becoming wet; fire, without feeling hot. So far had their wisdom advanced towards Tao. The pure men of old slept without dreams, and waked without anxiety. They ate without discrimination, breathing deep breaths. For pure men draw breath from their uttermost depths; the vulgar only from their throats. Out of the crooked, words are retched up like vomit. If men's passions are deep, their divinity is shallow. The pure men of old did not know what it was to love life or to hate death. They did not rejoice in birth, nor strive to put off dissolution. Quickly come, and quickly go;—no more. They did not forget whence it was they had sprung, neither did they seek to hasten their return thither. Cheerfully they played their allotted parts, waiting patiently for the end. This is what is called not to lead the heart astray from Tao. . . . Tao has its laws, and its evidences. It is devoid both of action and of form. It may be transmitted, but cannot be received. It may be obtained, but cannot be seen. Before heaven and earth were, Tao was. It has existed without change from all time. Spiritual beings drew their spirituality therefrom, while the universe became what we can see it now. To Tao, the zenith is not high, nor the nadir low; no point in time is long ago, nor by lapse of ages has it grown old. *C.T.* 6.

Away then with wisdom and knowledge, and great robbers will disappear! Discard jade and destroy pearls, and petty thieves will cease to exist. Burn tallies and break signets, and the people will revert to their natural integrity. Split measures and smash scales, and the people will not fight over quantities. Utterly abolish all the restrictions of Sages, and the people will begin to be fit for the reception of Tao. . . . Feed then your people with your heart. Rest in inaction, and the world will be good of itself. Cast your slough. Spit forth intelligence. Ignore all differences. Become one with the infinite. Release your mind. Free your soul. Be vacuous. Be Nothing! Let all things revert to their original constitution. If they do this, without knowledge, the result will be a simple purity which they will never lose; but knowledge will bring with it a divergence therefrom. Seek not the names nor the relations of things, and all things will flourish of themselves. *C.T.* 10–11.

To act by means of inaction is God. To speak by means of inaction is exemplification of Tao. To love men and care for things is charity. To recognize the unlike as the like is breadth of view. To make no distinctions is liberal. To possess variety is wealth. And so, to hold fast to virtue is strength. To complete virtue is establishment. To follow Tao is to be prepared. And not to run counter to the natural bias of things is to be perfect. He who fully realizes these ten points, by storing them within enlarges his heart, and with this enlargement brings all creation to himself. Such a man will bury gold on the hillside and cast pearls into the sea. He will not struggle for wealth, nor strive for fame. He will not rejoice at old age, nor grieve over early death. He will find no pleasure in success, no chagrin in failure. He will not account a throne as his own private gain, nor the empire of the world as glory personal to himself. His glory is to know that all things are one, and that life and death are but phases of the same existence! *C.T.* 12.

Repose, tranquillity, stillness, inaction,—these were the levels of the universe, the ultimate perfection of Tao. Therefore wise rulers and Sages rest therein. Resting therein they reach the unconditioned, from which springs the conditioned; and with the conditioned comes order. Again, from the unconditioned comes repose, and from repose comes movement, and from movement comes attainment. Further, from repose comes inaction, and from inaction comes potentiality of action. And inaction is happiness; and where there is happiness no cares can abide, and life is long. . . Therefore, those of old who apprehended Tao, first apprehended God. Tao came next, and then charity and duty to one's neighbour, and then the functions of public life, and then forms and names, and then employment according to capacity, and then distinctions of good and bad, and then discrimination between right and wrong, and then rewards and punishments. Thus wise men and fools met with their dues; the exalted and the humble occupied their proper places. And the virtuous and the worthless being each guided by their own natural instincts, it was necessary to distinguish capabilities, and to adopt a corresponding nomenclature, in order to serve the ruler, nourish the ruled, administer things generally, and elevate self. Where knowledge and plans are of no avail, one must fall back upon the natural. This is perfect peace, the acme of good government. Therefore it has been written, "Wherever there is form, there is also its name." Forms and names indeed the ancients had, but did not give precedence to them. *C.T.* 13.

Were Tao something which could be presented, there is no man but would present it to his sovereign, or to his parents. Could it be imparted or given, there is no man but would impart it to his brother or give it to his child. But this is impossible for the following reason. Unless there is a suitable endowment within, Tao will not abide. Unless there is outward correctness, Tao will not operate. The external being unfitted for the impression of the internal, the true Sage does not seek to imprint.

The internal being unfitted for the reception of the external, the true Sage does not seek to receive. *C.T.* 14.

Birth is not a beginning; death is not an end. There is existence without limitation; there is continuity without a starting-point. Existence without limitation is Space. Continuity without a starting-point is Time. There is birth, there is death, there is issuing forth, there is entering in. That through which one passes in and out without seeing its form, that is the Portal of God. The Portal of God is Non-Existence. All things sprang from Non-Existence. Existence could not make existence existence. It must have proceeded from Non-Existence, and Non-Existence and Nothing are one. . . . Perfect politeness is not artificial; perfect duty to one's neighbour is not a matter of calculation; perfect wisdom takes no thought; perfect charity recognizes no ties; perfect trust requires no pledges. Discard the stimuli of purpose. Free the mind from disturbances. Get rid of entanglements to virtue. Pierce the obstructions to Tao. Honours, wealth, distinction, power, fame, gain,—these six stimulate purpose. Mien, carriage, beauty, arguments, influence, opinions,—these six disturb the mind. Hate, ambition, joy, anger, sorrow, pleasure,—these six are entanglements to virtue. Rejecting, adopting, receiving, giving, knowledge, ability, —these six are obstructions to Tao. The key to which is inaction. *C.T.* 23.

The lust of the eye is for beauty. The lust of the ear is for music. The lust of the palate is for flavour. The lust of ambition is for gratification. Man's greatest age is one hundred years. A medium old age is eighty years. The lowest estimate is sixty years. Take away from this the hours of sickness, disease, death, mourning, sorrow, and trouble, and there will not remain more than four or five days a month upon which a man may open his mouth to laugh. Heaven and Earth are everlasting. Sooner or later every man has to die. *C.T.* 29.

The heart of man is more dangerous than mountains and rivers, more difficult to understand than Heaven itself. Heaven has its periods of spring, summer, autumn, winter, day-time and night. Man has an impenetrable exterior, and his motives are inscrutable. Thus some men appear to be retiring when they are really forward. Others have abilities, yet appear to be worthless. Others are compliant, yet gain their ends. Others take a firm stand, yet yield the point. Others go slow, yet advance quickly. Those who fly to duty towards their neighbour as though thirsting after it, drop it as though something hot. Thus the loyalty of the superior man is tested by employing him at a distance, his respectfulness by employing him near at hand, his ability, by troublesome missions. His trustworthiness, by specification of time limits. His integrity by entrusting him with money. His fidelity, by dangerous tasks. His decorum, by filling him with wine. His knowledge, by unexpected questions. His morality, by placing him in disreputable surroundings. Under the application of these nine tests, the inferior man stands revealed. *C.T.* 32.

Adopt no absolute position. Let externals take care of themselves. In motion, be like water. At rest, like a mirror. Respond, like the echo. Be subtle, as though non-existent. Be still, as though pure. Regard uniformity as peace. Look on gain as loss. Do not precede others. Follow them. He who is conscious of being strong, is content to be weak,—he shall be a cynosure of men. He who conscious of purity, puts up with disgrace,—he shall be the cynosure of mankind. He who when others strive to be first, contents himself with the lowest place, is said to accept the contumely of the world. He who when others strive for the substantial, contents himself with the unsubstantial, stores up nothing and therefore has abundance. There he is in the midst of his abundance which comes to him without effort on his part. He does nothing, and laughs at the artifices of others. He who when others strive for happiness is content with security, is said to aim at avoiding evil. He who makes depth of fundamental importance and moderation his rule of life, is said to crush that which is hard within him and temper that which is sharp. To be in liberal sympathy with all creation, and not to be aggressive towards one's fellow-men,—this may be called perfection. *C.T.* 33.

The Tao of God operates ceaselessly; and all things are produced. The Tao of the sovereign operates ceaselessly; and the empire rallies around him. The Tao of the sage operates ceaselessly; and all within the limit of surrounding ocean acknowledge his sway. He who apprehends God, who is in relation with the sage, and who recognizes the radiating virtue of the sovereign,—his actions will be to him unconscious, the actions of repose. The repose of the sage is not what the world calls repose. His repose is the result of his mental attitude. All creation could not disturb his equilibrium; hence his repose. When water is still it is like a mirror, reflecting the beard and the eyebrows. It gives the accuracy of the water-level, and the philosopher makes it his model. And if water thus derives lucidity from stillness, how much more the faculties of the mind? The mind of the sage being in repose becomes the mirror of the universe, the speculum of all creation. Repose, tranquillity, stillness, inaction,—these were the levels of the universe, the ultimate perfection of Tao. Therefore wise rulers and sages rest therein. Repose, tranquillity, stillness, inaction,—these were the source of all things. Keep to this when coming forward to pacify a troubled world, and your merit shall be great and your name illustrious, and the empire united into one. In your repose you will be wise; in your movements, powerful. By inaction you will gain honour; and by confining yourself to the pure and simple, you will hinder the whole world from struggling with you for show. *C.T.* 13.

7

CONFUCIANISM

IN order to understand Confucianism (and indeed the Taoism of the previous chapter more fully) it is necessary to go back to a period far earlier than that in which Confucius and Lao-Tze lived. In the General Introduction, and also in the chapter on Hinduism, we saw how the idea of a Supreme Deity emerged from primitive Polytheism, with its host of gods, godlings, demons, and spirits of all kinds. One god tended to become more powerful than the others and was gradually recognized as the King of the Pantheon. As time went on, he began to acquire abstract qualities, such as power, wisdom, and the like. The lesser gods withdrew more and more to the position of vassals, until at last the King-God stood alone as Ruler, and thus the conception of one God (monotheism) became established. This is a late stage in the development of religion, but it was reached very early in China, and we can read about it on the very first pages of recorded history. The Shu-King[1] is an extremely ancient book, dating from many hundreds of years before Christ, and it purports to deal with a period some fourteen hundred years earlier still. There we read how the Emperor, Shun (traditional date 2357 B.C.), sacrificed to the Supreme Deity, Shang-Ti, and the accounts suggest that this was then no new practice. The Emperor Shun was probably a mythical personage, but there is no doubt that the culture associated with him existed at some very remote period. Shang-Ti is described as the Creator of All Things. His will is glorious and may be known; He can be honoured and served, and must be obeyed. His favour depends on the righteousness of the worshipper; He warns and punishes evil-doers. Not only do we find this supreme God, who can be compared to the great monotheistic deities of later religions, but also a correspondingly advanced moral and ethical code. The Emperor Yao, for instance, is said to have been " reverent, wise, cultured, thought-

---

[1] Also spelt " Ching " (see page 133 onwards).

126

ful, and withal sincerely modest": the "light of his goodness shone to the four corners of the Empire, extending from the highest to the lowest." The Emperor Shun is recorded as saying when he appointed a teacher, " Teach our sons so that they may be straight and yet gentle, magnanimous yet dignified, strong yet not harsh, decided yet not overbearing." These ethics represent the end-product of a high stage of religious culture; they are as fine as any which appear in later religions.

There is another word in these ancient writings which seems almost interchangeable with Shang-Ti; this is the word T'sien, which is usually translated " Heaven." T'sien is credited with all the qualities of Shang-Ti and with some others as well; it seems to be an impersonal form of the Supreme Deity, more approachable by the people, perhaps, for only the Emperor could sacrifice to Shang-Ti. T'sien is the word almost always used by Confucius himself, and may perhaps be held to correspond with our term " Divine Providence."

About 550 B.C., when Confucius was born, China was in a very disturbed state. The feudal system was breaking down, rulers were ignored, and there was continual intrigue and fighting. Reading the old chronicles, it seemed to him that the solution lay in a return to the Ancients, and he began to try to find out all that he could about them. There existed a vast mass of literature, history, poetry, and so on, but it was in a disjointed and confused state. Confucius therefore embarked on the task of collecting and editing, choosing what was most worth while and making this available in several great volumes. These books came to be known as the Five King (King=volume) and were gradually accepted as the Canon of the Chinese Classics. The names of these volumes are :

The Yi-King (Book of Changes).
The Shu-King (Book of History).
The Shih-King (Book of Poetry).
The Li-King (Book of Ritual).
The Ch'un Ch'iu or Spring and Autumn Annals.

When we speak of Confucianism we thus mean all these ancient writings, as well as the books dating from the time of the Master himself and later. Confucius said, " I am a transmitter not a creator. . . . I have transmitted what was taught to me without making up anything of my own. I have been faithful to and loved the Ancients." The later Confucian books are four in number :

> The Great Learning (attributed to Confucius himself).
>
> The Doctrine of the Mean (attributed to a grandson of Confucius).
>
> The Confucian Analects (sayings of the Master by various disciples).
>
> The Book of Mencius (a work by a disciple who lived about a hundred years after Confucius).

To these we shall return later.

Confucius was, then, in the first place, what we may call a great editor. Possibly he did not do all the work that is attributed to him, but he certainly did a great deal of it, for we know from the story of his life that he spent many years in study and teaching and that he consistently directed men's minds back to the ancients. His life was simple. He was no martyr or miracle-worker, but a tireless student, writer, and teacher, and he held various public offices. He was born about 550 B.C. in the State of Lu, which is now part of the Shang-Tung province. His clan name was K'ung, and Confucius was merely the latinized form (given by early Roman Catholic missionaries) of K'ung Fu'tze, meaning philosopher, or master, K'ung. For a time he left the State of Lu, following the banished ruler, but returned when he was unable to find an outlet for his work. Later he spent some thirteen years wandering from State to State trying to induce rulers to put themselves under his guidance. When he returned to Lu the second time he was in his sixties, and he spent the last years of his life on further editing and teaching. His death occurred in 478 B.C., when he was probably in his seventy-third year. He was buried with honour, and many of his disciples built huts near his grave and lived there for several years as a sign of veneration.

Confucius himself felt that he had failed in his mission because he had not been able to find a ruler who would consistently put his ideas into practice. That the example of a ruler was essential was a doctrine he had inherited from the earliest times, for the Emperor Shun is recorded in the Shu-King as saying : " If the sovereign can realize the arduous responsibility of the sovereignty and each minister of his ministry, government will be well ordered and the people sedulous after virtue."

The subsequent history of Confucianism is free from many of the elements that are associated with other religions. There is no deification of the Master, there are no stories of miracles performed by him or occurring at his birth. Nevertheless the honour paid to him has been greater (short of worship) than that given to any other single man in history, and this steadily increased until the twentieth century. In A.D. 1 the Sage was canonized as " Duke Ni, the All-Complete and Illustrious," and in A.D. 57 sacrifices were ordered to be offered to him. In 609 a temple was erected in his honour at every centre of learning. In 657 he was styled K'ung, the Ancient Teacher, the Perfect Sage, which remains his title until the present day. In 1907 he was raised to the highest rank of those beings who are entitled to have sacrifices in their honour. His name became synonymous with Chinese civilization. The classics came to be regarded as the foundation of all education, and knowledge of them as essential for all public examinations. Hundreds of students have learnt to repeat every sentence in the classical books, and the masses of the people have scores of the maxims in their minds.

Nevertheless, Confucianism had its enemies. In 212 B.C. Ch'in Shih Huang, who has been called the Napoleon of China, sought out and destroyed all the Confucian books he could find and buried alive hundreds of scholars who swore by the name of Confucius. This " burning of the books " did not, however, destroy the culture. Too much was known by heart, and many writings were saved. In 195 B.C. the Emperor of the next dynasty, Kao Ti, sacrificed at the tomb of Confucius and did his best to restore the books. Taoism, the religion which was considered in the preceding chapter, was also opposed to Confucianism. But the Chinese genius for compromise prevailed, and a way was found by which a man might even describe himself as belonging to both religions. The same applies to the opposition which came from Buddhism, a religion which was introduced later into China, and which will be considered in Chapter 9. Here again the Chinese power of adaptation enabled a man to say that he was both a Buddhist and a Confucian, and often he would proclaim himself a Taoist as well!

For over two thousand years, then, Confucianism was the State system of China. In 1912, with the establishment of the Republic, it ceased to be the State religion and suffered a decline.

It remained, however, as a kind of Church, and is now gradually being revived as one of the principal cults. Actually it has never lost its hold on the hearts of the people, and China's four hundred millions are still Confucian at heart.

Of the books which date from the time of Confucius or later, far the best known is the Analects. This is a roughly arranged volume made up of contributions from different groups of disciples. They tell us a good deal about the teacher himself and also about his personal teaching and special directions on the right way to live. The leading ideas set forth in the Analects may be summed up as (1) the natural perfectibility of man, (2) the evolution of the special or Princely Man, (3) the importance of the individual, (4) what may be described as " human-heartedness."

With regard to (1), the perfectibility of man, it has been said that no one has honoured virtue more sincerely for its own sake than Confucius. He offered no rewards or punishments, and never pointed to possible consequences in a future life. He believed that man was naturally good and would return to virtue, once a good example was set up by the upper and ruling classes.

Closely connected with the theory of the essential goodness of humanity is the idea of the Special Man who shows rare superiority of character and behaviour. Various translations have been given of the Chinese term used; for instance, " superior man," " wise man," " man of honour," " princely man," " higher man," and even, as an English translation, our own word " gentleman." Actually, although the Chinese term involves more, our code of the gentleman is covered in the Analects in a remarkable way. The superior man, the " gentleman," must have both a good manner and good manners. He will be free from brusqueness and violence, frank and sincere, and his speech and deportment will accord with the best traditions of his time. He will never boast or push himself forward, talk too much, or exalt himself by the indirect means of disparaging others (a marked method of " small " men). He will not be puffed up by success or soured by failure, and will make friends only with men of his own sort. He will never be lonely, for he will be recognized as a brother by all other " gentlemen." His training will be of a moral type, the emphasis being always on character and the production of a noble nature, rather than of a person who merely studies what is " useful." The " gentleman " will never become a "tool." He will take no side in politics (here our conception is exceeded), but will always support the right wherever he finds it.

According to the Analects, few people can attain to the complete ideal of the " gentleman " or superior man (even Confucius did not claim to have done this), but all can develop the fundamental virtues. Thus the Master laid great stress on the person; indeed, it has been said that the importance of the self-conscious, moral individual amounts to a discovery. His answers to questions show how intensely interested he was in the actual people with whom he came into contact. The virtue which must be cultivated, above all, by the individual may be translated as *human-heartedness*, which implies an understanding consideration for all other individuals; " the treatment which you would not have for yourself, do not mete out to other people." An individual can thus only become truly himself by allowing others to do the same. These are the leading ideas set forth in the Analects, but there are many others almost as notable. One is the importance of a balanced view, as, for example, between thought and learning. " If a man learns, but does not think, then he is nothing. If he thinks and does not learn, then he is in a dangerous state." The relationship between man and man comes first. Be a good son, a good brother, and a good friend, and " if you have any energy left after attending to conduct, then study books." The five virtues are kindness, rectitude, decorum, wisdom, and sincerity. There is little in the Analects about the divine life, which, however, is always presumed to be present. Prayer is an attitude of mind, but vain without virtue : " the man who sins against heaven has nowhere he can pray." God is the ultimate Judge; " if the way is to prevail, it is the will of Heaven. If it is to be discarded, it is the will of Heaven."

Of the other Confucian books only a few words can be said. The Great Learning is of uncertain authorship, though parts of it, at least, are thought to be by the Master himself. It is essentially a text-book, composed with a view to being learnt by heart, and it deals with such Confucian doctrines as the dependance of political government on personal virtue. The Doctrine of the Mean is attributed to a grandson of Confucius and develops the idea of the Middle Way, personal responsibility, sincerity in man, and human-heartedness. The Book of Mencius is supposed to have been written by the philosopher Meng, who lived about a hundred years after Confucius and was the greatest of all the disciples. The plan of the book is much the same as that of the Analects. The essential goodness of man's nature is strongly stressed and, more than the Master, perhaps, Mencius championed the cause of the weak against the strong, insisting that a ruler's first duty is to improve the lot of the common people.

A few words should perhaps be added on what is called Ancestor-worship. In Western minds, this cult has been largely associated with Chinese religion, but its importance as a distinctive feature may well be exaggerated. So-called Ancestor-worship is best thought of as forming part of the high honour in which the family is held at all times, filial piety being among the greatest of the social virtues. It must be remembered, too, that the Imperial House was usually believed to have descended from some ancient deity, and it was these semi-divine ancestors who were first worshipped, the practice being extended to private families later on. For instance, in the Book of Odes and in the Shu-King we read of sacrifices being offered to the dead of the Imperial House, while in the later Li-Ki we find these also made by private persons to their own ancestors. Here we are told that a boy, clad in white, would represent the departed person, while the eldest son made a sacrifice, usually of some animal. Later ancestral tablets took the place of impersonations. The spirit of the East has been, at least until quite lately, intensely conservative. The tendency has been to look back rather than forward, to assume that the old is better than the new, age than youth, the fundamental root than the blossoms of the tree. With this spirit, so different from that of the West, Confucius was in whole-hearted agreement, and, without stressing them particularly, he took for granted the ritual observances in honour of ancestors that belonged to his time.

To sum up. Confucianism may perhaps be described as the Religion of Books. More than any other it is associated with a literature which has become the classics of a nation. Confucius was a founder, chiefly in the sense that he was a collector and editor of that vast store of ancient wisdom. His personal teaching, though valuable, would not have stood alone. Confucianism may thus, with these reservations, be regarded as a religion of a founder, whose name is, of course, incorporated in the title.

Though Confucian ideas spread in a general sense to Japan, they really belong to the Chinese, and thus Confucianism is another religion of a special people and seeks no converts.

Verses from the Scriptures

ABBREVIATIONS TO REFERENCES

An. = Analects
D. = Douglas, R.K., *Confucianism and Taoism.*

D.M. = Doctrine of the Mean
G.L. = The Great Learning
Menc. = Mencius

Looking at small **advantages** prevents great affairs from being accomplished. *An.* 13, 17.

In **ascending** high you begin from where it is low, and in travelling far you begin from where it is near. *Shu Ching* 4, 5.

In giving heed to the **beginning** think of the end; the end will then be without distress. *Shu Ching* 5, 17.

To be in one's inmost heart in kindly sympathy with all things; to love all men; to allow no selfish thoughts;—this is the nature of **benevolence** and righteousness. Saying of Confucius. *Chuang Tzu*, 13.

Never has a man who has **bent** himself been able to make others straight. *Menc.* 3, 2, 1.

To go **beyond** the mark is as bad as to come short of it. *An.* 11, 15.

Calamity and happiness in all cases are men's own seeking. *Menc.* 2, 3.

Heaven-sent **calamities** you may stand up against, but you cannot survive those brought on by yourself. *Shu Ching*, 4, 5.

I have heard it said that **contentions** do not arise in great things, neither are they founded in small things, but in adaptability or non-adaptability, and in the perfection or imperfection of self-effort. *Shu Ching* 4, 2.

A man must first **despise** himself, and then others will despise him. A family must first destroy itself, and then others will destroy it. A kingdom must first smite itself, and then others will smite it. *Menc.* 4, 8.

The **disease** of men is this : that they neglect their own fields and go to weed the fields of others, and that what they require from others is great, while what they lay upon themselves is light. *Menc.* 7, 2, 32.

What a man **dislikes** in his superiors, let him not display in the treatment of his inferiors; what he dislikes in inferiors, let him not display in the service of his superiors. *G.L.* 10, 2.

The path of **duty** lies in what is near, and men seek for it in what is remote. The work of duty lies in what is easy, and men seek for it in what is difficult. *Menc.* 4, 1, 11.

The **evil** of men is that they like to be teachers of others. *Menc.* 4, 1, 23.

I daily **examine** myself on three points—In planning for others have I failed in conscientiousness? In intercourse with friends have I been insincere? and have I failed to practise what I have been taught? *An.* 1, 4.

From the loving example of one **family** a whole state becomes loving, and from its courtesies, the whole state becomes courteous. *G.L.* 9, 3.

The inferior type of man always tries to gloss over his **faults**. *An.* 19, 8.

Pardon inadvertent **faults**, however great; and punish purposed crimes, however small. *Shu Ching* 2, 2.

A house may be burned by smouldering **fire**, when a fierce flame would have shown itself and have been easily extinguished. *Inscription in the Hall of Light.*

Friendship with a man is friendship with his virtue, and does not admit of assumptions of superiority. *Menc.* 5, 2, 3.

The chase of **gain** is rich in hate. *An.* 4, 12.

A **gem** is not polished without rubbing, nor a man perfected without trials. *Inscription in the Temple of Everlasting Harmony.*

A **gentleman** blames himself, while a common man blames others. *An.* 15, 20.

Wheresoever you **go**, employ all your heart. *Shu Ching* 5, 9.

What **goes** out from thee comes back to thee again. *Menc.* 1, 2, 12.

All are **good** at first, but few prove themselves to be so at the last. *Shih Ching* 3, 1.

The **good** in you I will not dare to keep concealed; and for the evil in me I will not dare to forgive myself. *Shu Ching* 4, 3.

When you see a **good man** think of emulating him, when you see a bad man, examine your own heart. *An.* 4, 17.

The small man thinks that small acts of **goodness** are no benefit, and does not do them; and that small deeds of evil do no harm, and does not abstain from them. Hence his wickedness becomes great till it cannot be covered, and his guilt becomes great till it cannot be pardoned. *I Ching*, Appendix 3, 2, 5, 38.

Holding himself good, one loses his **goodness**; esteeming himself capable, one is bereft of his merit. *Shu Ching* 3, 13.

True **goodness** is loving your fellow men. True wisdom is knowing your fellow men. *An.* 12, 22.

The **great man** is he who does not lose his child's heart. *Menc.* 4, 2, 12.

To nourish the **heart** there is nothing better than to make the desires few. *Menc.* 7, 35.

He who offends against **heaven** has none to whom he can pray. *An.* 3, 13.

The less **indulgence** one has for oneself, the more one may have for others. *Inscription in Examination Hall of Canton.*

Recompense **injury** with justice and recompense kindness with kindness. *An.* 14, 36.

Those who are born with the possession of **knowledge** are the highest class of men. Those who learn, and so readily get possession of knowledge, are the next. Those who are dull and stupid, and yet succeed in learning, are another class next to these. While those who are dull and stupid and yet do not learn, are the lowest of the people. *Lun Yu* 16, 9.

To keep old **knowledge** warm and get new, makes the teacher. *An.* 2, 11.

Rule by **love.** *Menc.* 1, 2, 12.

The ways are two: **love** and want of love. That is all. *Menc.* 4, 1, 2.

Love makes a spot beautiful; who chooses not to dwell in love, has he got wisdom? Love is the high nobility of Heaven, the peaceful home of man. To lack love, when nothing hinders us, is to lack wisdom. Lack of love and wisdom lead to lack of courtesy and right, and without these man is a slave. *Menc.* 2, 1, 7.

If you **love** men, and they are unfriendly, look into your love; if you rule men, and they are unruly, look into your wisdom; if you are courteous to them, and they do not respond, look into your respect. If what you do is vain, always seek within. *Menc.* 4, 1, 4.

Do not be ashamed of **mistakes**, and go on to make them crimes. *Shu Ching* 4, 8.

He who requires **much** from himself, and little from others will be secure from hatred. *An.* 15, 14.

Instead of being concerned that you have no **office**, be concerned to think how you may fit yourself for office. Instead of being concerned that you are not known, seek to be worthy of being known. *An.* 4, 14.

Tzu Kung asked saying: Is there any one maxim which ought to be acted upon throughout one's whole life? The Master replied: Surely the maxim of **reciprocity** is such:—Do not unto others what you would not they should do unto you. *An.* 15, 23.

Do not be over-anxious for **relaxation** or repose, he who is so will achieve neither. *Inscription in the Hall of Light.*

If you can one day **renovate** yourself, do so from day to day. *Inscription on the bathing-tub of the Emperor T'ang.* G.L. 2, 1.

Better than one who knows what is **right** is one who is fond of what is right; and better than one who is fond of what is right is one who delights in what is right. *An.* 6, 18.

In the way of the superior man there are four things, to none of which have I as yet attained—To **serve** my father as I would require my son to serve me; to serve my prince as I would require my minister to serve me; to serve my elder brother as I would require my younger brother to serve me; and to offer first to friends what one requires of them. *Chung Yung* 13, 4.

There are many **services** but the service of parents is the root of all others. There are many charges, but the charge of oneself is the root of all others. *Menc.* 4, 19.

Sincerity is the way of Heaven. To think how to be sincere is the way of man. Never has there been one possessed of complete sincerity who did not move others. Never has there been one without sincerity who was able to move others. *Menc.* 4, 1, 12.

Fight thine own **sins**, not the sins of others; will not evil be mended? *An.* 12, 21.

The **sovereign** without the people has none whom he can employ; and the people without the sovereign have none whom they can serve. Do not consider yourself so large as to deem others small. *Shu Ching* 6, 4.

The ancients were guarded in their **speech**, and like them we should avoid loquacity. Many words invite many defeats. Avoid also engaging in many businesses, for many businesses create many difficulties. *Inscription on statue in the ancestral Temple of Lô.*

Do not glory in your **strength**, there is always a stronger. *Inscription in the Hall of Light.*

Study without thought is vain; thought without study is perilous. *An.* 2, 15.

When you find a person worthy to **talk** to and fail to talk to him, you have missed your man. When you find a man unworthy to talk to and you talk to him, you have missed (i.e., wasted) your words. A wise man neither misses his man nor misses his words. *An.* 7.

If I am walking with two other men, each of them will serve as my **teacher**. I will pick out the good points of the one and imitate them, and the bad points of the other and correct them in myself. *An.* 7, 21.

Teaching is the half of learning. *Shu Ching* 4, 8.

The union of many **threads** makes an unbreakable cord. *Inscription in the Hall of Light.*

To ride with the **tide** is better than to be wise or clever; to wait on the seasons is better than fields of loam. *Menc.* 2, 1, 1.

Truth does not depart from human nature. If what is regarded as truth departs from human nature, it may not be regarded as truth. *Li Chi.*

Only **virtue** can compel Heaven, and there is no distance to which it cannot reach. Fulness is predisposed to reduction, while humility receives increase. *Shu Ching* 1, 3.

Virtue cannot live in solitude : neighbours are sure to grow up around it. *An.* 4, 25.

A man of inward **virtue** will have virtuous words on his lips, but a man of virtuous words is not always a virtuous man. The man of perfect goodness is sure to possess courage, but the courageous man is not necessarily good. *An.* 14, 5.

The man of moral **virtue**, wishing to stand firm himself, will lend firmness unto others; wishing himself to be enlightened, he will enlighten others. To be able to do to others as we would be done by—this is the true domain of moral virtue. *An.* 6, 28.

To learn and never be filled, is **wisdom**; to teach and never be weary is love. *Menc.* 2, 1, 2.

The **wise**, through not thinking, become foolish; and the foolish, by thinking, become wise. *Shu Ching* 5, 18.

Heed **words** as well as acts; thoughts also; and remember even when alone that the Divine is everywhere. *Inscription in the Hall of Light.*

Readings from the Scriptures

The Master said : " Fine words and an insinuating appearance are seldom associated with true virtue." The Master said : " A youth, when at home, should be filial, and, abroad, respectful to his elders. He should be earnest and truthful. He should overflow in love to all, and cultivate the friendship of the good. When he has time and opportunity, after the performance of these things, he should employ them in polite studies. If the Scholar be not grave, he will not call forth any veneration, and his learning will not be solid. Hold faithfulness and sincerity as first principles. Have no friends not equal to yourself. When you have faults, do not fear to abandon them." *An.* 1, 3, 4, 6, 8.

Yen Yüan inquired as to the meaning of true goodness. The Master said : " The subdual of self, and reversion to the natural laws governing conduct—this is true goodness. If a man can for the space of one day subdue his selfishness and revert to natural laws, the whole world will call him good. True goodness springs from a man's own heart. How can it depend on other men ? Do not use your eyes, your ears, your power of speech or your faculty of movement without obeying the inner law of self-control. Chung Kung inquired as to the meaning of true goodness." The Master said : " When out of doors, behave as though you were entertaining a distinguished guest; in ruling the people, behave as though you were officiating at a solemn sacrifice; what you would not wish done to yourself, do not unto others. Then in public as in private life you will excite no ill-will." *An.* 12, 1–2.

> It was the lesson of our great ancestor :—
> The people should be cherished;
> They should not be down-trodden :
> The people are the root of a country;
> The root firm, the country is tranquil.
> When I look throughout the empire,
> Of the simple men and simple women,
> Any one may surpass me.
> If I, the one man, err repeatedly ;—
> Should dissatisfaction be waited for till it appears ?
> Before it is seen, it should be guarded against.
> In my relation to the millions of the people,
> I should feel as much anxiety as if I were driving six horses
with rotten reins. *Shu Ching* 1, 4–5.

The ancients who wished to illustrate illustrious virtue throughout the empire, first ordered well their own States. Wishing to order well their States, they first regulated their families, wishing to regulate their families, they first cultivated their persons. Wishing to cultivate their persons, they first rectified their hearts. Wishing to rectify their hearts, they first sought to be sincere in their thoughts. Wishing to be sincere in their thoughts, they first extended to the utmost their knowledge. Such extension of knowledge lay in the investigation of things. Things being investigated, knowledge became complete. Their knowledge being complete, their thoughts were sincere. Their thoughts being sincere, their hearts were then rectified. Their hearts being rectified, their persons were cultivated. Their persons being cultivated, their families were regulated. Their families being regulated, their States were rightly governed. Their States being rightly governed, the whole empire was made tranquil and happy. *G.L., D.*

What is meant by "making the thoughts sincere" is the allowing no self-deception, as when we hate a bad smell, and as when we love what is beautiful. This is called self-enjoyment. Therefore, the superior man must be watchful over himself when he is alone. There is no evil to which the mean man, dwelling retired, will not proceed, but when he sees a superior man, he instantly tries to disguise himself, concealing his evil, and displaying what is good. The other beholds him, as if he saw his heart and reins :—of what use is his disguise ? This is an instance of the saying—" What truly is within will be manifested without." Therefore, the superior man must be watchful over himself when he is alone. *G.L., D.*

What heaven has conferred is called the nature; an accordance with this nature is called the path of duty; the regulation of this path is called instruction. The path may not be left for an instant. If it could be left, it would not be the path. On this account, the superior man does not wait till he sees things, to be cautious, nor till he hears things, to be apprehensive. There is nothing more visible than what is secret, and nothing more manifest than what is minute. Therefore the superior man is watchful over himself, when he is alone. While there are no stirrings of pleasure, anger, sorrow, or joy, the mind may be said to be in the state of equilibrium. When those feelings have been stirred, and they act in their due degree, there ensues what may be called the state of harmony. This equilibrium is the great root from which grow all the human actings in the world, and this harmony is the universal path which they all should pursue. *D.M.* 1.

To be fond of learning is to be near to knowledge. To practise with vigour is to be near to magnanimity. To possess the feeling of shame is to be near to energy. He who knows these three things, knows how to cultivate his own character. Knowing how to cultivate his own character, he knows how to govern other men. Knowing how to govern other men, he knows how to govern the empire with all its States and families. . . . Self-adjustment and purification, with careful regulation of his dress, and the not making a movement contrary to the rules of propriety :—this is the way for the ruler to cultivate his person. Discarding slanders, and keeping himself from the seductions of beauty; making light of riches, and giving honour to virtue :—this is the way for him to encourage men of worth and talents. Giving them places of honour and large emolument, and sharing with them in their likes and dislikes :—this is the way for him to encourage his relatives to love him. Giving them numerous officers to discharge their orders and commissions :—this is the way for him to encourage the great ministers. According to them a generous confidence, and making their emoluments large :—this is the way to encourage the body of officers. Employing them only at the proper times, and making the imposts light :—this is the way to encourage the people. By daily examinations and monthly trials, and by making their rations in accordance with their labours :—this is the way to encourage the classes of artisans. To escort them on their departure and meet them on their coming; to commend the good among them, and show compassion to the incompetent :—this is the way to treat indulgently men from a distance. To restore families whose line of succession has been broken, and to revive States that have been extinguished; to reduce to order States that are in confusion, and support those which are in peril; to have fixed times for their own reception at court, and the reception of their envoys; to send them away after liberal treatment, and welcome their coming with small contributions :—this is the way to cherish the princes of the States. *D.M.* 20.

1. Esteem most highly filial piety and brotherly submission, in order to give due prominence to the social relations.

2. Behave with generosity to the branches of your kindred, in order to illustrate harmony and benignity.

3. Cultivate peace and concord in your neighbourhoods, in order to prevent quarrels and litigations.

4. Recognize the importance of husbandry and the culture of the mulberry-tree, in order to ensure a sufficiency of clothing and food.

5. Show that you prize moderation and economy, in order to prevent the lavish waste of your means.

6. Make much of the colleges and seminaries, in order to make correct the practice of the scholars.

7. Discountenance and banish strange doctrines, in order to exalt the correct doctrine.

8. Describe and explain the laws, in order to warn the ignorant and obstinate.

9. Exhibit clearly propriety and yielding courtesy, in order to make manners and customs good.

10. Labour diligently at your proper callings, in order to give settlement to the aims of the people.

11. Instruct sons and younger brothers, in order to prevent them from doing what is wrong.

12. Put a stop to false accusations, in order to protect the honest and the good.

13. Warn against sheltering deserters, in order to avoid being involved in their punishments.

14. Promptly and fully pay your taxes, in order to avoid the urgent requisition of your quota.

15. Combine in hundreds and tithings, in order to put an end to thefts and robbery.

16. Study to remove resentments and angry feelings, in order to show the importance due to the person and life.

Sixteen Maxims issued by the Emperor K'ang-he. Imperial Confucianism, Lecture 1.

How should a sovereign act in order that he may govern properly? Confucius replied: Let him honour the five excellent, and banish the four bad things. . . . The five good things are :—

1. When the person in authority is beneficent without great expenditure; that is, when he makes more beneficial to his people the things from which they naturally derive benefit :

2. When he lays tasks on the people without their repining; that is, when he chooses the labours which are proper, and employs them on them :

3. When he pursues what he desires without being covetous; that is, when his desires are set on benevolent government and he realizes it :

4. When he maintains a dignified ease without being proud; that is, whether he has to do with many people or with few, or

with great things or with small; he does not dare to show any disrespect :

5. When he is majestic without being fierce; that is, when he adjusts his clothes and cap, and throws a dignity into his looks, so that, thus dignified, he is looked at with awe.

The four bad things are :—

1. To put the people to death without having instructed them; —this is called cruelty.

2. To require from them suddenly the full tale of work without having given them warning;—this is called oppression.

3. To issue orders as if without urgency, at first, and when the time comes, to insist upon them with severity;—this is called injury.

4. And, generally speaking, to give pay or rewards to men, and yet to do it in a stingy way;—this is called acting the part of a mere official. *Lun Yu.* 20, 2.

I say that every man has a heart that pities others, for the heart of every man is moved by fear and horror, tenderness and mercy, if he suddenly sees a child about to fall into a well. . . . No man is without a merciful, tender heart, no man is without a heart for shame and hatred, no man is without a heart to give away and yield, no man is without a heart for right and wrong. A merciful, tender heart is the seed of love; a heart for shame and hatred is the seed of right; a heart to give way and yield is the seed of courtesy; a heart for right and wrong is the seed of wisdom. Man has these four seeds in him as he has four limbs. And having these four seeds in him, if he says of himself " I cannot ", he robs himself; and if he says of his Lord " He cannot ", he robs his Lord. *Menc.* 3, 6.

There is a way to win all below heaven : win the people and all below heaven is won. There is a way to win the people : win their hearts and the people are won. There is a way to win their hearts : gather for them and give them what they wish, do not do to them the things they hate. The people turn to love as water flows down or beasts haunt the graves. Thus, the otter drives the fish to the deep, the hawk drives the birds to the thicket. *Menc.* 7, 9.

I hate a semblance which is not the reality. I hate the darnel, lest it be confounded with the corn. I hate glib-tonguedness, lest it be confounded with righteousness.　I hate sharpness of tongue, lest it be confounded with sincerity.　I hate the music of Ch'ing, lest it be confounded with the true music.　I hate the reddish blue, lest it be confounded with vermilion.　I hate your good careful men of the villages, lest they be confounded with the truly virtuous.　*Menc.* 7, 37.

8

JAINISM

WHILE Confucius was teaching and working on the ancient Scriptures in China, two great men had arisen in India who were evolving religious systems which have lasted to the present day. One of these was Gautama, afterwards called the Buddha (lit., the Enlightened One), and the other was Vardhamana, afterwards called Mahavira (from Maha = great; Vira, a hero). The system of Gautama is known as Buddhism, from the name Buddha, and that of Vardhamana as Jainism, which comes from the word *Jina*, a conqueror. Buddhism became one of the major religions of the world, for although it was later expelled from India, the land of its birth, it swept over a vast portion of Asia. Jainism, on the other hand, has the fewest adherents of any existing religion except Parseeism; it is confined to about one and a half millions, almost all of whom are in India.

It used to be thought that Jainism was an offshoot of Buddhism; but this is an error: the two systems are quite distinct, and Jainism is the older. Indeed, it may be regarded as prehistoric. Vardhamana, or Mahavira—to give him his religious title—was the twenty-fourth and last of a long line of Tirthankaras, or saints, from whom the Jains profess to derive their doctrines. Tirthankara comes from the word *Tirtha*, a ford or crossing over, and therefore means one who can lead mankind across the troubled world to a state of bliss. The first Tirthankara, known as Rishabha Deva (Deva = pure soul), is a prehistoric person, who is supposed to have laid down the Jain doctrines. The last but one, named Parasvanath, is, with Mahavira himself, usually accepted as a historical character.[1] Thus it will be seen that the origins of Jainism are extremely ancient. Mahavira reformed, synthesized, and completed the system, and to that extent only he may be regarded as the founder. Buddhism and Jainism have, however, much in common. Both Buddha and Mahavira sprang

---

[1] All the Tirthankaras are entitled to the name of "Conqueror," Jina, but this is notably given to the first and to Mahavira himself.

from the warrior caste, and thus asserted the right of the laity as against the powerful Brahman priesthood. Both emphasized the sanctity of all life, thereby condemning Hindu sacrifices : both denied the authority of the Vedas and protested, in theory at any rate, against the caste system which, as we saw in the chapter on Hinduism, was the pillar of the Brahmanical scheme. On the other hand, both religions, being Hindu in origin, assumed the truth of many of the Hindu doctrines; such, for instance, as the law of Karma (i.e., Works), and the transmigration, in some form or another, of the human soul. But whereas Buddhism modified the doctrine of the reincarnation of the individual in a special way which we shall consider in the next chapter, Jainism strengthened it. Individual souls, according to Mahavira, are eternally separate; they remain distinct, even when perfected, and are not absorbed, as taught by the Brahmans, into the Being of God.

Just as Jainism is sometimes wrongly described as an offshoot of Buddhism, so again it is often assumed to be a sect of the Hindus. Owing to the small numbers, the locality in India and the adoption of Indian terms and ideas, this is natural enough, yet it cannot really be justified. The question arises here, perhaps, as to what exactly is a sect. A sect is a sub-division of some larger religion which reveres the same teachers and uses the same scriptures, albeit with a different interpretation. The Jains possess sacred writings entirely their own : they have their special rules, observances, temples, priests, and line of prophets. Their doctrine of the way of salvation and the nature of the human soul is neither Buddhist nor Hindu. They remain a distinct community, and their religion must therefore be regarded as a self-sufficient system.

We do not know much of the life of Mahavira, but he was certainly a historical person, whose existence can be established by records. The date of his birth is usually given as 599 B.C., so that if the date, 550 B.C., given for Confucius in the preceding chapter be correct, Mahavira would be the older contemporary by about forty-nine years. If, again, the date for Gautama Buddha be 563 B.C., Mahavira would have been the elder by thirty-six years. Dates must, however, be received with caution : the point here is that all these three great men were contemporaries.

Mahavira was born at Vaishali, twenty-seven miles north of Patna. He belonged to an aristocratic family of the warrior caste, and was brought up as a strict Jain. He married and had a daughter, but when he was thirty years old his parents died, and he then adopted the life of an ascetic. For twelve years he either wandered about or sat in the squatting position, with joined heels and head bowed in deep meditation. At the end of this time he arrived, we are told, at a state of omniscience : he knew all that was happening and the reason for all things. So great a power had he acquired over the human body that he no longer needed even to sleep. Eighteen characteristics were required of a Tirthankara, and at the end of his twelve years' meditation it is said that Mahavira had acquired them all. As a leader, teacher, and perfected man, he then arose and went forth to preach. This he did, so the story goes, for another thirty years, after which he died at the age of seventy-two, and is then said to have entered into Nirvana.

When Mahavira became a Tirthankara he realized the full implications of the Jain religion, the foundations of which had been laid down by his twenty-three predecessors. He gave the final form which continues until this day. The leading doctrine was *Ahimsa*, non-injury to all living things : *Non-injury is religion*, says one of the Scriptures. Thus the Jains hold that all life is sacred and must not be harmed by deed, word, or thought. Nevertheless, life can be classified according to the number of " senses " it possesses, and certain " one-sensed " life may be used for food : nuts, fruit, and some vegetables. All flesh, fowl, and fish are forbidden, also eggs and honey, and strict Jains do not eat root vegetables, since these are held to contain " one-sensed " life in large quantities. Even " one-sensed " life must be spared as much as possible, and, for that reason again, wine and spirits are forbidden, destruction being assumed to be present in the process of fermentation. Jains may not engage in any business that involves killing : they may not be butchers, fishmongers, gunmakers, or brewers. The greatest gift which one living being can make to another is, so the Jains hold, the gift of *safety*. To refrain from taking life is, then, the Jain's first duty and constitutes his first vow. The second is to refrain from telling lies or divulging the secrets of another. The third is to refrain from theft, which includes such forms of dishonesty as receiving stolen goods, smuggling, using false weights and measures or counterfeit coin. The fourth is to control sex passion, even in marriage, and, apart from this, to practise chastity. The fifth is to limit the desire for possessions to what is actually required. These five vows are binding on laymen and monks alike, but the Jain monk or ascetic must apply them much more strictly. He must watch every step, for fear of killing a creature, he must strain the water he drinks, and he must not light a fire. He must maintain absolute celibacy, and he must possess no property whatsoever. He must accept only what is given him : he must have no home, but wander continually from place to place. For a monk these vows are the five great vows. For a layman there are five lesser ones. In addition, there are another seven vows which must be taken by a monk and may also be taken by a layman who wishes to make spiritual progress. These involve fasts, retreats, and various other forms of discipline—Jainism is essentially a monastic religion, the monk leads the way, he is in close touch with the laity, who consult him in their difficulties and regard his as the ideal life. For ordinary people there are also thirty-five rules, most of which, it may be said, form the basis of good social living anywhere. Here are some of them. A Jain should engage in some kind of business, trade, or profession which does not involve the destruction of life. He should marry unless—which is better—he can remain truly celibate; he may not gamble or indulge in any excess. He should conform to established customs, keep the laws of his country, and seek the company of good people. He should read the Scriptures every day and try to resolve the doubts of other people. That the rules have been well kept is shown by the fact that the Jain community has a high standard of morality, and it has been said that a criminal Jain is hardly ever known.

The great enemies of the soul, according to Jain teaching, are the passions. The major passions are anger, pride, deceitfulness, and greed. Worry, fear, disgust, and sex-indulgence are also passions. These must be removed by mental and moral discipline, for, it should be noticed, the soul is naturally good, and the passions are " unnatural " accretions.

The teaching as regards the soul differs fundamentally from that taught by surrounding Hinduism. Each soul is individual and eternal and alone. It will not be fused with other souls, nor will it, as the Brahmans taught, be absorbed into the Universal Soul or divine life when it is perfected. It was neither created nor evolved. It always was, and it remains, distinct during the whole of its beginningless and endless existence. The soul reincarnates according to its deserts, as in Hinduism, but it takes away a kind of bodily substance with it at death. Thus it remains embodied even in Heaven or Hell, and the four kinds of embodied existence are Animal, Human, Hell, Heaven. Souls are thus a combination of matter and spirit : by removing the matter the soul becomes "pure." Pure souls reach a state of bliss, knowledge, and immortality, never again to return to any kind of embodied existence. A state of purity can be attained only by right belief, right knowledge, and right conduct. These are the three Jewels of Jainism. The pure state is the " natural " one, and the individual has to free himself. All living things are divided into two classes, embodied and liberated, but freedom can be obtained only after the human stage has been reached. The universe is without beginning and without end, and there is no personal and cosmic ruler from whom help may be sought. The Jain Deity is the Tirthankara, but it is as the perfected human being, the liberated man, that he is worshipped. In theory, at any rate, anyone may attain to this state, anyone may become a " pure " soul—i.e., God. God may, indeed, be thought of as all liberated souls taken together, who, however, are not merged into one another. Their pure, unfettered spirituality is known as Jiva. It is, however, difficult to be sure what the Jains today really think about God. A Jain saint, Vijaha Dharma Guri, who died some years ago, preached a sermon before the Maharajah of Benares in which he asserted that Jains believe in Paramatman, the World-Self. Probably the spiritually advanced man does so, while popular worship is given to the Tirthankara. The leading doctrine of the religion is, however, that a man can free himself, that he can throw off accretions and become divine in his own right. The emphasis is on individual effort, and whether or not there is a World-Soul or some other ultimate principle becomes irrelevant. More perhaps than any other religion in the world, Jainism honours the soul of each man as its own saviour and eternally distinct. Devout Jains repeat after their evening reading of the holy books :

" The Soul is the maker and the non-maker. Itself makes happiness and misery, is its own friend and its own foe, decides its own condition, good or evil, is its own river Veyarana [Veyarana is a river in Hell]."

Beyond this the metaphysics of Jainism are extremely elaborate, and are worked out in the minutest detail. There is a vast literature, but little of this has been published : the books are guarded with the greatest care, and some may even be concealed. Jainism, as will have been seen, has a strong leaning towards asceticism, the rules for monks being very strict, including, for instance, only three hours' sleep, while a Tirthankara is said not to sleep at all! Suicide is a sin, but ascetics and laymen may hasten death by starvation, though for the latter this is permissible only in old age. In the days when the religion was flourishing, thousands of devotees starved themselves to death in such sacred places as Sravana and Belgole.

Mahavira was succeeded by patriarchs, but since there were two lines of these, Jainism split up very early into two main sects. These are known as the Digambaras, the sky-clad, and the Swetambaras, the white-robed. The name of the Digambaras arises from the belief that in theory no clothes should be worn, lest vermin be destroyed in the folds. In practice, they had to conform to custom, while the Swetambaras, who are less strict, wore white. The Digambaras deny that a woman can enter Nirvana : to do this she must be reincarnate as a man. Adherents of both sects are found in most Indian cities, and they are important in Marwar, Bombay, and Mysore : a few are in Burma. The Digambaras are strongest in the south. The Jains in general are more important than their numbers suggest, as they are generally traders of some sort and are prosperous and reliable. They have the highest standard of literacy of any Indian community.

Apart from sacred books, the Jains have a considerable secular literature, and their skill in the art of carving is world-famous. Indeed, they brought the art of carving in stone to the highest point, and Satrunjaya has been described as one of the loveliest temple-cities in the world. They are the only Indian community to represent the human form entirely unclothed in religious statuary. Some of their temples in honour of Mahavira or other Tirthankaras were destroyed under Brahman influence : in order to save others from destruction by Muhammadans, miniatures of Muhammadan tombs were sometimes placed in them and Moghul features incorporated. Buddhist models were adopted in some of the cave-temples.

In the social sphere the Jains have given practical expression to the tenderness for life by establishing hospitals for old and sick animals.

To sum up, the Jains are small in numbers but strong in influence. They have a voluminous literature both sacred and secular, and have excelled in sculpture and architecture. Their doctrine of each soul as eternally distinct is foreign to the spirit of the East as a whole and more akin to the Western emphasis on the individual. Tender towards life in others, they are severe towards themselves, for while organizing hospitals for sick animals on the one hand, on the other they may, as we have seen, starve to death to secure spiritual emancipation. Their moral standard and their mental ability are high.

Verses from the Scriptures

ABBREVIATIONS TO REFERENCES

DV.	= Dasha-vaikalika-sutra	*RS.*	= Ratna-Karanda-Shravaka-Achara
J.	= Jaina, *Outlines of Jainism.*		
MS.	= Magadhi Shloka	*SK.*	= Sutrakritanga
N.	= Naladiyar	*SS.*	= Samadhi Shataka
NP.	= Nirgrantha-Pravachana	*SSh.*	= Sanskrit Shloka
PA.	= Purushartha Siddhyupaya	*TS.*	= Tattvartha-sutra, also called Tattvarthadhigama-sutra
PP.	= Paramatma-prakasha		
PR.	= Pravacana-sara	*US.*	= Uttaradhyayana-sutra
PS.	= Panchastikaya-sara	*W.*	= Warren, *Jainism*
		YS.	= Yogashastra

Difficult to **conquer** is oneself. But when that is conquered everything is conquered. *US.* 9, 36.

Though a man should **conquer** thousands and thousands of valiant foes, greater will be his victory if he conquers nobody but himself. Fight with yourself; why fight with external foes? He who conquers himself through himself will obtain happiness. *US.* 9, 34–5.

One who identifies himself with his soul regards bodily transmigration of his soul at **death** fearlessly, like changing one cloth for another. *SS.* 77.

One who has identified his own self with the body in which it is encased, is extremely afraid of **death**, seeing therein his own destruction and separation from friends. *SS.* 76.

By doing **evil** the self becomes a rogue, an animal or inhabitant of hell; and always beset by thousands of pains, it strays incessantly. *PR.* 1, 12.

Subdue wrath by **forgiveness**, conquer vanity by humbleness, fraud by straightforwardness, and vanquish greed through contentment. *DV.* 8, 39.

One must worship the **God**, serve the Guru (teacher), study the scriptures, control the senses, perform austerities, and give alms. *SSh.*

Every **good deed** will bear its fruit to men; there is no escape from the effect of one's actions. Through riches and the highest pleasures my soul has the reward for its virtues. *US.* 13, 10.

Master of his senses and avoiding wrong, one should do no **harm** to any living being, neither by thoughts nor words nor acts. *SK.* 1, 11, 12.

The essence of right conduct is not to **injure** anyone; one should know only this, that non-injury is religion. *N.* 14, 15.

In happiness and suffering, in joy and grief, regard all creatures as you regard your own self, and do not **injure** others with that which would injure yourself. *YS.* 2, 20.

Do not **kill** living beings in any of the three ways, by mind, word or deed. *NP.* 14, 11.

Viler than unbelievers are those cruel ones who make the law that teaches **killing**. *YS.* 2, 37.

Right belief, right knowledge, right conduct, these together constitute the path to **liberation** (moksha). *TS.* 1, 1.

That which is free from birth, old age, disease, death, grief, pain and fear, is eternal, blissful, and of the nature of pure delight, is called **Nirvana**. *RS.* 131.

Non-injury is the highest religion. *W.* p. 6.

Forgiveness, humility, straightforwardness, truth, contentment, restraint, austerities, charity, non-attachment and chastity are the ten **observances** to be followed. *PA.* 204.

Religious observances : these are five, viz. :
1. Walking carefully so as not to hurt any living being.
2. Speaking reverently and without hurting anyone's feelings.
3. Taking only pure food not specially prepared for the saint.
4. Careful handling of the few things, such as water-bowl, brush, and scriptures which ascetics may keep.
5. Great care as to where to answer the calls of nature. *PA.* 203.

Self is the one invincible foe when acting with the four cardinal passions : anger, pride, deceitfulness, and greed. *US.* 23, 38.

The **soul** is the maker and non-maker, and itself makes happiness and misery, is its own friend and its own foe, decides its own condition good or evil, is its own river Veyarana (the river in which hell-beings are tormented and drowned.) *MS.*

Soul (jiva) is the only conscious or knowing substance, the remaining five substances are without consciousness, viz., matter, space, time, dharma (fulcrum of motion), adharma (fulcrum of stationariness) are different from soul. *PP.* 143.

The **soul** is without shape (it takes the shape of its body, ant, man, elephant), taste, tangibility, smell, or colour; it consists of knowledge which can in one moment know the whole universe; it has supreme felicity, being free from attachment, aversion, desires and passions; it is also imperishable and pure. *PP.* 143.

A man should wander about **treating** all creatures as he himself would be treated. *SK.* 1, 11, 33.

In this world of misery, disease, old age, and death, there is no other protection, refuge or help than our own practice of the **truth.** Others are powerless; as we sow we reap. *W.* 123.

The observance of the five lesser vows, non-injury, truthfulness, non-stealing, chastity, and limitation of possessions, and refraining from the use of wine, flesh, and honey are the eight fundamental **virtues of a householder.** *RS.* 66.

Readings from the Scriptures

Oh soul! thou art always afraid of pain, and desirous of pleasure. Therefore I also offer thee the object of thy desire, which tends to give pleasure and remove pain. If perchance, in this advice, there be something which though sweet at fruition, is yet unpalatable, be thou not afraid of that, just as a sick person is not afraid of bitter medicine. Persons, who are vain and full of talk, and clouds which thunder but give no rain, are easy to find. But it is difficult to find those kind-hearted persons who desire to uplift the world, just as it is difficult to find clouds, full of rain and beneficial to the world. . . . Perfect knowledge of the scripture; pure conduct; inclination to persuade others to the right path; keen interest in the propagation of the right path of liberation; obeisance to the learned; pride-less-ness; knowledge of the world; gentleness; desire-less-ness; whoever possesses these and other qualities of the leader of ascetics, be he the Teacher of worthy people. . . . Demerit produces pain, happiness follows Truth (Dharma). All men desire the early attainment of true happiness; it arises from the destruction of all Karman. This destruction of the Karmas results from right conduct; that right conduct depends upon right knowledge. And that right knowledge is acquired from the Scriptures. . . . The tranquillity, knowledge, vows, and austerities of a person is of the value of a stone. But it becomes adorable, like a great jewel if accompanied by right belief. . . . Whether happy or miserable in this world, thou must exercise piety; if happy to increase thy happiness; and if miserable, to remove thy misery. The pleasures derived from all senses-objects are fruits of the trees of the garden of piety. Therefore preserve thou the trees, and pluck the fruits by all means. Piety is the cause of happiness. The cause cannot oppose its own effect. Therefore for fear of being deprived of present sense-pleasures, thou shouldst not be indifferent to piety (Dharma). The person who in consequence of piety has acquired prosperity may have enjoyments while preserving piety, like the peasant who gets corn from the seed, but preserves the seed of that corn. . . . So long as piety abides well in the heart, the man does not slay even his slayer. When that religion goes away, the father and the son are found killing each other. Therefore the protection of this world depends verily upon Dharma only. There is no demerit in enjoying pleasures; but there is demerit in doing what tends to destroy their source. Indigestion is not caused by sweet food, but by eating it beyond its limit. . . . Acquire merit. Even an unheard of calamity does not affect the doer of meritorious deeds. Indeed it does him good. See the sun, which oppresses the whole world with its heat, gives a lovely bloom to lotuses. . . . Being moved with the desire of getting Kingship, which is only a small bit of pleasure, the father often tries to cheat his son, and the son the father. It is strange that this foolish world, which is fallen between the jaws of birth and death, does not see yonder Death indefatigably snatching away the body. . . . It is a great pity that thou shouldst out of ignorance make thyself miserable so

long in the world by ploughing and sowing the land, by serving
kings in many ways, and by wandering about in jungles and on
the seas, in pursuit of pleasure. Thou wishest to get oil from
sand; thou wishest to live on poison. Dost thou not know that
thy happiness lies in subduing the demon of desires? . . . The
wealth of even good men is not increased by pious income; as the
seas can never be filled with fresh water only. Happiness is that,
where there is no unhappiness, knowledge is that, where there is
no ignorance. Being entangled in enjoyments, and therefore
thoughtless, thou art again and again made miserable by occupation, etc., to obtain wealth and other objects of this world. If
thou under-goest the same trouble even once, intending to obtain
liberation, then certainly thou wouldst never experience the pain
of being born again and again. Ignorant of the true nature of
things, considering some to be desirable and others undesirable,
why dost thou waste thy time, being often attached to external
things again and again. Attain to internal peace of mind before
you are reduced to ashes in the cruel and approaching Death's
abdominal fire. Oh friend! dependent upon external things and
floating in the river of desire, thou hast come down from a long
long distance. Dost thou not know that thou thyself art quite
capable of crossing this river easily? be independent, and thou
shalt reach the shore very soon, otherwise, thou shalt founder in
the ocean of existence, which is terrible on account of the deep
and wide-open mouth of the unvanquishable crocodile of death.
Thou desirest now, without any revulsion to pick up again, as
if thou hadst never tasted before, what has been discarded by
the sensualists, after the satiety of enjoyment. Oh soul! canst
thou gain peace so long as thou dost not conquer this desire-evil
which is the victory banner of the forces of your powerful enemy,
the host of sins. . . . That same day which appears as to-morrow
for one, becomes yesterday for him. Nothing can be called stable.
This world is being uprooted by the wind of time. . . . Fire
burns when fed with fuel, and goes out for want of it. But it is
a wonder that the terrible fire of delusion blazes strongly in both
the ways on getting the objects of desire and also on not getting
them. . . . The poor are discontented for not obtaining wealth,
and the rich too are so for want of contentment. Alas! all are
in trouble. Only an ascetic is happy. Happiness, dependent
upon others leads to pain. Only independent happiness is com-

mendable. Else how could the ascetics be called happy ? . . .
Live in a way as though you felt, " Nothing is mine " and thou
wilt be lord over the three worlds. . . . Tell me, if there be any
other laudable means except asceticism, of attaining liberation. . . .
Such a passage of meditation would lead an ascetic to the desired
goal, without any mishaps, where knowledge is the guide, modesty
a companion, austerities the provision, right conduct a palanquin,
heavens the halting places, merits guards, the way straight, with
abundance of the water of tranquillity of mind, compassion a
shade, and meditation a chariot. . . . Birth is, the mother; death,
father; mental and physical sufferings, brothers; and decrepi-
tude is the friend of this living being in the last stage. And yet
there is love for the body. . . . A remedy should be sought, so
long as a thing is remediable. And for those who are incurable,
the only remedy is to be indifferent. Whose object is not lost
by operation of anger. . . . Formerly, on this earth were born
persons, who had truth in their word, knowledge of the scriptures
in their intellect, compassion in their heart, bravery and fortitude
in the arm, wealth for large charity to needy persons, and who
trod in the path free from worldly attachments. Even such great
persons have been described in the scriptures to have been free
from pride. It is a great wonder, that now-a-days those who do
not possess even slight virtues, are found to be over-bearing.
How then can a man entertain pride, when there are greater ones
than himself in this world ? . . . Fate is the Karma, good or
bad, acquired by an embodied being in past life. By their
operation, the ensuing pleasure or pain is experienced. He,
who performs good deeds only is praise-worthy. But he who
for extirpating both good and bad Karmas renounces all undertakings, possessions, deserves to be adored by the good. In this
world pleasure and pain arise out of the fruition of past Karmas.
The sacred Books of the Jainas—*Atmanushasana*, 2–4, 6, 8–9,
15, 18–21, 26–7, 31, 34, 42, 45–50, 52, 56, 65–6, 110, 113, 125,
201, 207, 216, 218–19, 262–3.

Again, one must, by all possible means, first attain right belief;
because only on the acquisition thereof do knowledge and conduct
become right. . . . One should ever cherish feelings of deep
affection for religion, which brings about the treasure of spiritual
happiness, and for the principle of non-injury, and also for co-

religionists. One should ever make his own self radiant by the light of the three jewels, and should add to the glory of Jainism by exceptional charity, austerity, worship of Jina, the Conqueror, and by learning. . . . Any injury whatsoever to the material or conscious vitalities caused through passionate activity of mind, body or speech is Himsa, assuredly. . . . The want of abstinence from Himsa, and indulgence in Himsa, both constitute Himsa; and thus whenever there is careless activity of mind, body, or speech, there always is injury to vitalities. . . . One who does not actually commit Himsa, becomes responsible for the consequences of Himsa; and another who actually commits Himsa, would not be liable for the fruit of Himsa. To one, trifling Himsa brings in time serious result; to another grievous Himsa at time of fruition causes small consequence. . . . Himsa is committed by one, and there are many who suffer the consequences; many commit Himsa, and only one suffers the consequence for Himsa. . . . Those who desire avoiding Himsa, should, first of all take care to renounce wine, flesh, honey, and the five Udumbar fruits. . . . Flesh cannot be procured without causing destruction of life; one who uses flesh, therefore commits Himsa, unavoidably. . . . He who eats, or touches, a raw, or a cooked piece of flesh, certainly kills a group of spontaneously-born living beings constantly gathering together. Even the smallest drop of honey in the world very often represents the death of bees; the fool who uses honey is a great destroyer. . . . Never entertain the wrong idea that religion flourishes through gods, and that therefore everything may be offered to them. Do not kill embodied beings, under such perverted judgment. . . . Beings which kill others should not be killed in the belief that the destruction of one of them leads to the protection of many others. . . . One should never think of hunting, victory, defeat, battle, adultery, theft, etc., because they only lead to sin. Sinful advice should never be given to persons living upon art, trade, writing, agriculture, arts and crafts, service, and industry. One should not without reason dig ground, uproot trees, trample lawns, sprinkle water, etc., nor pluck leaves, fruit, and flowers. One should be careful not to give instruments of Himsa, such as knife, poison, fire, plough, sword, bow, etc. One may not listen to, accept, or teach such bad stories as increase attachment, etc., and are full of absurdities. Renounce gambling from a distance.

It is the first of all evils, the destroyer of contentment, the home of deceit, and the abode of theft and falsehood. He who deliberately renounces all other unnecessary sins, leads his Ahimsa vow ceaselessly up to admirable victory. . . . Having due regard to his own powers, the wise should even renounce those objects of enjoyment, which are not prohibited; and in respect of those even which he cannot renounce, he should limit the enjoyment by day or night. Again having regard to one's capacity at the time, a further limit to the limits already set, should be made every day. He who being thus contented with a few limited enjoyments, renounces the vast majority of them, observes Ahimsa par-excellence because of abstention from considerable Himsa. . . . The qualifications of a donor are, disregard of worldly benefit, forbearance, sincerity, joy, absence of jealousy, sorrow, and pride. Only such things should be given as food as help in the prosecution of studies, and the due observance of austerities, and which do not bring about fondness, disgust, incontinence, intoxication, pain, fear, etc. The recipients are of three classes, according to their respective possession of qualities leading to Moksha. They are true believers without vows, with partial vows, and with full vows. In making a gift one gets over greed, which is a form of Himsa, and hence gifts made to a worthy recipient amount to a renunciation of Himsa. Why should one not be called greedy if he does not offer food to a saint who visits his home, is well-qualified and who, acting like a honey-bee, accepts gifts without causing any injury to others. (A saint similarly takes a meagre meal out of food prepared by a householder for himself, without making any special arrangements for a saint.) . . . Fasting, reduced diet, sleeping and resting in lonely places, renouncing the Rasas (milk, curd, ghee, oil sweet, and salt), bodily suffering, mental vow to accept food under undisclosed conditions, are external austerities and should be practised. Respect, service, expiation, renunciation, study and concentration are the internal austerities which should be observed. . . . Equanimity, praising, bowing, repentance and renunciation, and giving up attachment for the body are the six daily duties, which should be observed. One should carefully observe the three controls, proper control of body, proper control of speech, and proper control of mind. Careful movement, careful speech, careful eating, careful placing and removal of things, careful evacuation of excrement, are the five Samitis to be observed. Forgiveness, humility, straight-forwardness, truth, contentment, restraint, austerities, charity, non-attachment, and chastity are the ten observances to be followed. Transitoriness, helplessness, mundaneness, loneliness, separateness, impurity, inflow, stoppage and shedding of Karmas, universe, variety of right path, and nature of Right path, these twelve meditations should be contemplated continuously. . . . Hunger, thirst, cold, heat, insect bite, nudity, ennui, women, walking, sitting, resting, abuse, beating, begging, non-obtaining, disease, contact with thorny shrubs, etc., dirt, respect and disrespect, conceit of knowledge, lack of knowledge, slack belief, are twenty-two sufferings. These should be ever endured without any feeling of vexation, by one who desires to get rid of all cause for pain. Ratna-Traya the three Jewels (right belief, knowledge and conduct) should be followed, even partially, every moment of time without cessation by a householder desirous of everlasting liberation. . . . Right belief is conviction in one's own Self, Knowledge is a knowledge of one's own Self; conduct is absorption in one's own Self. How can there be Bondage by these. The Sacred Book of the Jainas, Vol. 4, *PA*. 21, 29–30, 43, 48, 51–2, 55, 61, 65, 68–9, 80, 83, 141–7, 164–6, 169–73, 198–9, 201–5, 208–9, 216.

Right faith consists in believing in the true ideal, scriptures and teacher. Such right faith is free from three follies, has eight members, and no pride. The three follies are :

1. Worshipping, with the desire of obtaining the favour of deities whose minds are full of personal likes and dislikes, is called the folly of devotion to false divinity.

2. Bathing in so-called sacred rivers and oceans, setting up heaps of sand and stones as objects of worship, immolating oneself by falling from a precipice, or by being burnt up in fire.

3. Worshipping false ascetics who have not renounced worldly goods, occupations, or causing injury to others. . . . The eight members are :

1. Freedom from doubt.

2. Freedom from desire for worldly comforts.

3. Freedom from aversion to or regard for the body, etc.

4. Freedom from inclination for the wrong path.

5. Redeeming the defects of ineffective believers.

6. Sustaining souls in right conviction.
7. Loving regard for pious persons.
8. Publishing the greatness of Jaina doctrines. *J.* p. 108.

Dharmastikaya or dharma conditions the motion of things that can move, matter and life, itself being unaffected by movement. Just as water, being itself indifferent or neutral, is the condition for the movement of fishes, so dharma, itself non-motive, is the *sine qua non* of the motion of living beings and material things. It is a real substance, is devoid of the qualities of taste, colour, smell, sound, and touch. It pervades the loka (inhabited part of space), it is continuous because of the inseparability of its parts, and has extension because of its coextensiveness with the loka. The nature of Adharmastikaya or Adharma is essentially similar to that of Dharma. But it is, like the earth, which is the resting place of things, the *sine qua non* of rest for things not in motion, both animate and inanimate. . . . Know that the substance called Adharma is of the same kind as the substance Dharma. It, like the earth, is the essential condition of things not in motion. *PS.* 90–3 and *J.* p. 85.

9

BUDDHISM

WE now come to one of the major religions of the world, a religion which has been mentioned in several of the previous chapters—the religion of Buddhism. We may perhaps say *the* major religion. For it claims the greatest number of adherents, about 520,000,000.[1] It is difficult, however, to be quite sure of figures, for in large parts of Asia a man may profess Buddhism and some other religion as well. This seems strange to us, for no Westerner would proclaim himself a Christian and also a member of some other religion, yet in the East, a dual, or even a treble, allegiance is quite possible. Figures have therefore been variously given, and it is possible that the number of Buddhists may be even greater than that stated. In any case, it probably exceeds that of all the Christian Churches taken together, and may represent one in every three of the human race. Geographically a huge part of Asia is involved—China, Japan, Tibet, Manchuria, Korea, Mongolia, Siam (Thailand), and Ceylon. There are some Buddhists in India, some in southern Siberia, and a number among the Tartars round the Caspian basin. There are also Buddhists in Western countries, and there is a Buddhist Society in London. We have now reached, then, the religion which has probably more adherents than any other in the world.

In some ways Buddhism contrasts sharply with Jainism, which was systematized at about the same time and in the same part of India. In Buddhism the Founder offers something entirely new, and does not claim to be the last of a long line of predecessors. He puts forward a universal solution to the problems of mankind. The religions of Judaism, Hinduism, and Shintoism were, as we saw in previous chapters, racial cults; Buddhism purports to be *the* Truth, final and complete in itself, available for all men everywhere. It is thus on the same plane as the two other world religions, Christianity and Muhammadanism (or Islam), which will be considered next. Buddhism is more difficult for us to

---

[1] See Distribution Table, page 331.

understand than Christianity and Muhammadanism, for the terms and ideas that go with it are less familiar. The Buddha was born a Hindu, and he assumed the validity of certain Hindu doctrines, such as that of Karma (Works) and Reincarnation, which were considered in the chapter on Hinduism. A little knowledge of the background will, however, make the approach easier.

In the process of spreading, world religions inevitably adapt themselves to the needs of many types of men and many nationalities. Buddhism has therefore taken on widely different forms, just as Christianity has done. The observances of Llamanism in Tibet differ, for instance, from simpler forms of Buddhism as completely, perhaps, as a High Mass differs from a Quaker meeting. It is the Buddhism of the early Scriptures that will be described here.

The date of the birth of the Buddha is variously given, but is most generally agreed to be somewhere about 563 B.C. At that time there was an Aryan tribe called the Sakyas living on the banks of the river Rohina, about 100 miles north-east of the city of Benares. This clan occupied a territory of about 900 square miles, partly on the slopes of the Himalayas and partly on the plains below. The rice fields of the clan were watered by streams from the mountains, whose glorious snow-clad peaks were seen all the year round. The principal town of the territory was Kapila-vastu, a place which has now disappeared, and it was near here that the Buddha was born. His father's name was Suddhodana, which means " Pure Rice "; the family name was Gautama, and it was by this name that the future Buddha was first known. It is said that the father was a king, which means the Rajah of a small Principality, and he belonged to the Kshatriya, or warrior caste. The family were wealthy according to the standards of the time, for we are told that the Buddha had three homes, one for winter, one for summer, and one for the rainy season.

The story goes that Suddhodana had married two sisters, both of whom were childless, and that therefore there were special rejoicings when it was found that, at the age of forty-five, the elder sister was about to give birth to a baby. In accordance with custom, she set off to be delivered at her parents' house, but on the way the child was prematurely born under the satin trees of a delightful grove, called Lumbini. Mother and child were taken back to the Rajah's palace, and there the mother died seven days later.

The boy was named Siddhartha, which means " desire accomplished," and he was brought up by his aunt. We do not know much about his childhood, except that he is said to have excelled in archery. At a very early age (as is customary in India) he was married to his cousin Yasodhara, a beautiful princess, daughter of the Rajah of Koli. The King, Suddhodana, did all he could to make the pair happy and they were surrounded with luxury and comfort. It is said that a Brahman warned the King that if the young Prince saw the " Four Signs " he would leave the world, so every care was taken that the sad side of life should be kept from him. This proved to be impossible, for there came a day when Gautama drove in his chariot into the surrounding country and met, one by one, the Four Signs : first an old man, then a very sick man, then a corpse, and lastly a hermit dwelling apart in contemplation. In other words, he realized for the first time the grim realities of old age, disease, and death, and he saw that men were trying to escape from the desolation of heart caused by these. In vain the King tried to distract his son's sad thoughts by plays and amusements : the young Prince no longer cared for such things; he only saw in sharp contrast the life of luxury and the misery which existed in the world. About that time a son was born to him, and Gautama, hearing the news as he walked in a beautiful garden by a river, cried out, " A Fetter is born." He realized that this new tie would make it harder to renounce his life at the palace, and the child was thereafter called *Rahula*— which means Impediment. That night, we are told, Gautama decided to leave at once. He rose from his bed, and called to his Charioteer, Channa, who had been with him when he saw the Four Signs, to saddle him a horse. His favourite animal, Kanthaka, was prepared, and then Gautama went to say farewell to his son. The mother was sleeping on a bed strewn with jasmine and other flowers, with her hand on her son's head. Lest he should wake her and find it impossible to go, the Prince turned away from the threshold, saying : " When I have become enlightened I will return and see my son." He then rode forth with Channa till he reached the river Anoma. There he crossed the water, cut off his hair, and sent the faithful charioteer back with his horse. He had renounced everything—home, wealth, power, his young wife, and his only child—and now he was a penniless wanderer. This act the Buddhists call the Great Renunciation, and the story is probably true in essentials, for it belongs to the very earliest form of Buddhist belief. Gautama was now twenty-nine years of age, and he withdrew into the jungles of Uruvela, some fifty miles south of Patna, and began to practise severe forms of self-mortification. He attached himself to various Brahman teachers and studied the Vedas and the accumulated wisdom of the priests and philosophers of Hinduism. His two chief instructors, Alara Kalama and Udraka Ramaputra, offered forms of mystical ecstasy as the means of emancipation, and so rapidly did Gautama advance that he himself was invited to become a teacher. This offer and similar ones he refused, and went on to struggle alone—increasing the severity of his penances. So severe, indeed, was his self-mortification that he was reduced almost to a skeleton and, in his own reported words, his ribs " stuck out as beams of an old shed " and the bones of his spine were " like a row of spindles." He is said finally to have eaten only one grain of rice a day, and he came near to the point of death. But he was still without enlightenment. He began to realize that there was no value in self-mortification and that the truth was no more to be found that way than in a life of luxury. He cried out for food, whereupon the five mendicants who were with him forsook him, believing that his resolution had broken down. He was now entirely alone, and at this stage, we are told, he was tempted by Mara, the Evil One, to give up his quest. The various forms of temptation are described in the Scriptures as being accompanied by violent upheavals of nature, but Gautama remained unmoved. He then sat down under a tree—a pipal or peepul tree, later called the Bo, or Bohdi tree, the Tree of Wisdom. There he remained in deep meditation. We do not know how long he waited, but one of the Scriptures tells us that it was in the last watch of the night that victory came. Then he saw all things clearly : the meaning of existence, the cause of sorrow, and the way in which release might be achieved. He had no longer any doubts ; he had attained Enlightenment and become a Buddha (Enlightened One) : he had entered Nirvana.

Buddhist poets have rivalled one another in attempting to do honour to this supreme triumph. We are told that " 10,000 worlds were made glorious " by it ; " the 8,000 league-long hells were flooded with radiance; " " the ocean became sweet to the taste "; that the blind, the deaf, and cripples were cured, and prisoners set free. But the reported words of Gautama himself are the most significant.

" When this knowledge, this insight had arisen within me, my heart was set free from intoxication of lusts, set free from the intoxication of becomings, set free from the intoxication of ignorance. In me, thus emancipated, there arose the certainty of that emancipation. And I came to know : ' Rebirth is at an end. The higher life has been fulfilled. What had to be done has been accomplished. After this present life there will be no beyond.' This last insight did I attain to in the last watch of the night. Ignorance was beaten down, insight arose, darkness was destroyed, the light came, inasmuch as I was there strenuous, aglow, master of myself." [1]

The records tell us that after his enlightenment the Buddha remained in the forest for four times seven days, and that for the first seven he " enjoyed the bliss of emancipation." Then he was again visited by Mara, the Devil, who tried to persuade him to pass away out of the world, since men would never understand his doctrine. This he refused to do, saying that the " wonderworking truth " must be proclaimed among men. A haughty Brahman then came and questioned him, and the Buddha explained that his system involved the renunciation of the idea of self. There then occurred, we are told, a period of real hesitation. Gautama wondered whether, indeed, it would be of any use to try to teach the world, sunk in darkness, a doctrine which was difficult to grasp and very unwelcome in its demands. For he was asking men to give up, not homes, families, and comforts (this they would have understood), but the strenuous life of asceticism associated with religious progress in India at that time and, more than this, all their previous conceptions about gods, ritual, and the development of the soul; they were, in fact, to give up the idea of soul and selfhood altogether. They were to rid themselves of the concept " I am." Could he make them understand a doctrine at once so simple and yet apparently so lacking in appeal ? Would they understand why they had to do this ?

[1] Maha-saccaka Sutta, from *Early Buddhism*, T. W. Rhys Davids.

Surely it were better, now that his own great struggle was at an end, to retain what he had won and rest in his own joy and peace. The early Buddhist Church attaches great importance to this period of hesitation. It is said, for instance, that Brahma himself appeared to the Buddha and implored him to go forth into the world, because there would be some people, at least, who would understand. Eventually Gautama agreed, out of love and pity, it is said, for suffering mankind, and the pious Buddhist regards this decision with great gratitude and joy.

Gautama first intended to return to his old teachers, Alara and Udraka, but, hearing that they were dead, he decided to walk the one hundred miles to Benares, whither the five disciples who had left him had gone. He found them in the cool of the evening in the old deer-park, about three miles north of the city. They received him coldly, and when he told them that he had found the Truth, they asked how they could believe this, since he had failed in his final effort at physical endurance. Only one, the aged Knodanna, trusted him, and this man was afterwards known as " the Knodanna who understood."

The Buddha then preached his first sermon, the title of which is best translated as *The Foundation of the Kingdom of Righteous- ness*. It is strange, after nearly two thousand five hundred years, to think of that little group in the deer-park in the cool of an Indian evening. Anyone passing by would have seen six men, one apparently talking volubly, and would never have guessed that here was the inception of a world religion which would today still claim more adherents than any other in the world.

The sermon began by emphasizing the importance of the Middle Way. Neither devotion to the world, the Buddha said, nor asceticism, can save a man, but only complete detachment. There are four great truths which concern suffering. The first is that life is full of pain : there are disease, decay, and death, separation from the pleasant, and, most of all, unsatisfied desire. The second truth is that this pain is caused by craving of some kind, either for things of this world or for happiness in a future life. The third truth asserts that this craving can be got rid of; and the fourth lays down a Way by which this can be done. The Way is the Noble Eightfold Path, and its stages are Right Views, Right Desires, Right Speech, Right Conduct, Right Mode of Livelihood, Right Effort, Right Mindfulness, and Right Rapture. The

sermon is said to have taken some days to deliver, but it is only
briefly summarized in the Scriptures, though there are elaborate
commentaries.   At first the disciples found it very hard to give up
their belief in ascetic practices, which seemed to them the only
alternative to a worldly life, but eventually they were convinced
that there was a Middle Way, by which men could live in the
world and yet become detached from it.   The Tathagata—or
Newly Come, as Gautama was now called (a name by which he
always referred to himself)—then preached another sermon,
which was on the impermanence of all things.   He showed that
the schoolboy is not the same as the baby in the cradle or as the
mature man, and that we must realize that we are all changing
from moment to moment.   Change does not belong only to the
body—it is characteristic of the whole man.   Thus there is
no complete and continuing self,—no ego, or *atman*, as the
Brahmans called the soul, and the sense of " I am " is therefore
a delusion.   What holds us together, as it were, and gives us a
false sense of individuality is a compound of five forms of cling-
ing, called the five aggregates.   These are the *Skandhas*, and
they continue to exist after a man dies, unless, that is, he can
destroy them by losing the sense of craving.   When they continue
to exist they go on together and enter into a new body.   This is
the only form in which the Buddha taught the current Indian
doctrine of Reincarnation.   Once in a new body, the *Skandhas*
work out a series of results, according to the law of Karma.
Karma, as we saw in the chapter on Hinduism, means literally
Works : it is that which causes a man to be born again in order
to reap the fruit of his actions—whether this be good or bad.
But whereas in Hinduism it is a soul, or *atman*, that reincarnates,
in Buddhism there was no soul, but only this group of attributes,
known as the *Skandhas*.   In both cases Karma can be destroyed
and prevented from being built up again : for both Buddha and
the Brahmans assumed that human existence implied suffering
and that the perfected state was that which no longer required
rebirth.   In Hinduism the soul is then free to enter into the
divine life of the World-Soul; in Buddhism man is delivered
even from this.   For he is delivered from the delusion of self-
hood altogether.

This doctrine of the composite nature of a human being is a
very difficult one, yet it is the cardinal teaching of Buddhism, as

originally taught, and is associated with the idea of Impermanence. Realization of this is essential to entry into the Path, the first stage of which is *Right Views*. The three Heresies were later defined as :—

(*a*) The Heresy of Individuality.
(*b*) Doubt.
(*c*) Reliance on ritual and ceremonies.

These must all be discarded before Right Views can be attained.

Certain other Indian teachers had expounded the doctrine of Impermanence, but none had taught that the idea of the soul itself must be renounced as the prelude to the good life. It was a hard teaching, yet we read that all the five disciples now became Arahats—that is, fully initiated and able to teach the new doctrine themselves. Arahat means the state of one who is worthy. Large numbers of people of all castes, both men and women, came to hear the teachers, were converted, and many went out in their turn to preach, for Buddhism was from the first a missionary religion. The Buddha himself spent the rest of his long life [1] going about Northern India making converts : his success was amazing. There is a touching story told of his return to his old home, where his family, at first hostile, became converted.

At first Gautama's methods were similar to those of other Indian teachers of the day. There were no means of printing, so that the only way of publishing was through the minds of hearers. *They* were the books. A group of disciples would be gathered together and taught, and when they understood, the doctrines would be *learnt by heart*. This learning by heart had become a fine art, so that when, much later on, the Scriptures came to be written down, they may be taken to be an accurate account of the teaching as first delivered. There are large numbers of categories, such as, for instance, the Five Hindrances, the Ten Bonds, the Four Intoxications, the Ten Sins, the Four Sublime Conditions, the Three Heresies, and so on. Later, Gautama instituted orders of monks, who were to lead simple lives but to refrain from all forms of self-torture. They were strictly forbidden to perform any miracle whatever. At first they were wandering preachers, but later monasteries were built where they could be found and consulted. The monks shaved

---

[1] According to tradition he lived to be over eighty.

their heads, wore orange robes, and carried a small begging-bowl with which to beg their food.   They were all celibates, and their rule of life was stricter than that laid down for the laity.   Later, orders for women were also founded by Gautama.   The Buddha lived to be over eighty, and was thus able to elaborate his doctrines and organize the details of his method.

The Way of the Buddha is the Noble Eightfold Path, and much study could be given to each stage.   It will only be possible here to comment on matters about which there is most often misunderstanding.   It is said, for instance, that Buddhism is inhuman, in that it requires men to repress all aspiration.   Under the second stage of the Path (Right Desires) the Scriptures make it clear that one should desire all good things, but that these should be for other people rather than for the self.   The Three Sublime conditions are stated as Joy in the Joy of others, Sorrow for the Grief of others, and Equanimity in one's own joy or sorrow. One must cultivate love for all men and, leading on from this, refuse to injure any living thing.   Thus, strictly speaking, Buddhists are vegetarians as well as pacifists.   Right Effort, the sixth stage, includes constant intellectual awareness, for, of the three cardinal sins in Buddhism—sensuality, ill-will, and dullness (or torpor)—the last is the worst.   Under Right Conduct we find, again, that Love and Joy are to be the guiding motives : but, as before, they must be directed towards others.   We read :

> " Let a man cultivate towards the whole world a heart of love unstinted. . . . This state of heart is the best in the world."

And again :

> " All the means that can be used for doing right are not worth the sixteenth part of the emancipation of the heart through love."

These and many other verses show that Buddhism is by no means a religion of coldness and isolation.   What it does ask is that a man shall renounce, not love as such, but *love for himself*. He must give up all *personal* craving, not only for the things of this world, but also for advantages in any other : he must even give up belief in his own sense of " I."   Thus Buddhism teaches selflessness more fully and more logically than any other religion in the world.

And what is the end of the Path? The end of the Path is Nirvana, the state attained by Gautama under the Bo-tree. The word means literally "blowing-out," and it used to be thought that this blowing out meant annihilation, but as more has become known about Buddhism, it has become increasingly clear that the extinction means the getting rid of the flames of ill-will and sensuality, and that what then remains is a state of bliss, absolute peace, complete certainty. The fact that Nirvana can be attained in this life, and that it was so attained by the Buddha, is proof that it cannot mean extinction. Beyond this we can say nothing positive, because words fail before conditions which are outside ordinary experience. Only those who reach the end of the Path and attain Nirvana will know what it really is.

A man has to save himself—no gods or rituals can help him. Discussions as to the origin and end of the world, Eternity, Infinity, and the like, were resolutely barred by Gautama as irrelevant. They were called the Indeterminates—talk about which could only lead to fruitless speculation. Buddhism, thus, puts practice first. The renunciation of self and the living stage by stage in the Noble Path must be the prelude to that knowledge which will be the climax of experience. Nirvana is the end, just as renunciation of self-hood is the beginning.

At first Buddhism met with little opposition from the Brahmans. It appeared to be only the teaching of one of the many sects that grew up in the forests and afterwards spread to a wider circle. But gradually its denunciation of caste, its opposition to ritual, and contempt of priestly power began to excite hostility. But there is no evidence of actual persecution till after the reign of the Emperor Asoka, who lived from 264 to 227 B.C. and who, himself a convert, made Buddhism the official religion, sent missionaries to Ceylon, and gave great gifts of lands and money to the Church. Although wealth brought political power, or perhaps because of this, Buddhism thereafter began to decline, being partly absorbed and partly stamped out by the Brahmans. It lingered on till the thirteenth century of our era, but became mixed up with all kinds of extraneous elements, and finally died out altogether as an organized faith in India. The number of Buddhists there is now negligible. Outside India, however, Buddhism continued on its triumphant progress. About the first century A.D. it passed into Kashmir, then into Nepal, Tibet, China, Japan,

Burma, and Siam (Thailand) and Ceylon. Siam (Thailand), Burma and Ceylon belong to the Southern group; Nepal, Tibet, China, and Japan, to the Northern, and the teaching and practice of these two schools [1] vary considerably. Although Buddhism is essentially a missionary religion, it has always carried on its propaganda by peaceful means. Its method has been gradual permeation—never violence.

The earliest Scriptures were written in Pali—the spoken language of the people—and the three principal divisions are known as the three " basketfuls " (Pitakas). Later the writings were in Sanskrit, the more formal language of cultured people. Sanskrit is to Pali as Latin is to Italian. Some confusion is caused to students by the fact that words and names are sometimes given in Pali and sometimes in Sanskrit. The Sanskrit version is used here.

Buddhism has inevitably undergone wide modifications in the course of spreading and with the lapse of time. The Buddha himself came to be worshipped, and not only he, but large numbers of lesser Buddhas and saints. Doctrines and observances foreign to the original tradition have crept in, yet the guiding inspiration remains, and the voluminous Scriptures are still the support of countless millions. It is notable that wars and persecutions have never disfigured the history of Buddhism.

Verses from the Scriptures

ABBREVIATIONS TO REFERENCES

As. Ed.	= Asoka's Edicts	*Digha Mah.*	
B.	= Beal's Dhammapada	*Par. Sut.*	= Digha, Maha-Parinib-
Carus G.B.	= Carus (Paul) *The*		bana Suttanta
	Gospel of Buddha	*F.S.H.T.K.*	= Fo-Sho-Hing-Tsan-
Dham.	= Dhammapada		King
		S.N.	= Sutta-Nipata
		Vin. Mah.	= Vinaya, Mahavagga

People are in **bondage**, because they have not yet removed the idea of " I." *Carus G.B.* 9, 4.

Everything is **burning**. . . . The eye is burning; what the eye sees is burning. . . . It is burning with the fire of lust, the fire of anger, with the fire of ignorance; it is burning with the sorrows of birth, decay, death, grief, lamentation, suffering,

[1] Called the Hinayana and the Mahayana respectively.

dejection and despair. Buddha's Fire Sermon—*Vin. Mah.* 1, 21, 2.

Neither the flesh of fish, nor fasting, nor nakedness, nor tonsure, nor matted hair, nor dirt, nor rough skins, nor the worshipping of the fire, nor the many immortal penances in the world, nor hymns, nor oblations, nor sacrifice, nor observance of the seasons, purify a mortal who has not **conquered his doubt.** *S.N.* 248.

Go then through every country, **convert** those not yet converted; throughout the world that lies burnt up with sorrow, teach everywhere; instruct those lacking right instruction. Go, therefore! each one travelling by himself, filled with compassion, go! rescue and receive. *F.S.H.T.K.* 1299–1300.

Craving is the hankering after pleasure, or existence, or success. It is the germ from which springs all human misery; birth, old age, and suffering. *Vin. Mah.* 16, 20.

" **Decay** is inherent in all component things! Work out your salvation with diligence! " This was the last word of the Tathâgata! *Digha Maha. Par. Sut.* 6, 10.

Go ye now, O monks, and wander, for the benefit of the many, for the welfare of mankind, out of compassion for the world. Preach the **dhamma** (doctrine) which is glorious in the beginning, glorious in the middle, and glorious in the end, in the spirit as well as in the letter. There are beings whose eyes are scarcely covered with dust, but if the doctrine is not preached to them they cannot attain salvation. Proclaim to them a life of holiness. They will understand the doctrine and accept it. *Vin. Mah.* 1, 11, 1.

The sacred **Eightfold path** or middle way—right views, right resolve, right speech, right action, right living, right effort, right attention, right meditation. . . which leads to the extinction of suffering and Nirvana. Buddha's First Sermon. *Vin. Mah.* 1, 6, 18.

To see another's **fault** is easy; to see one's own is hard. Men winnow the faults of others like chaff; their own they hide as a crafty gambler hides a losing throw. *Dham.* 252.

Conquer your **foe** by force, you increase his enmity. Conquer by love, and you will reap no after-sorrow. *F.S.H.T.K.* 2241.

Practise then the art of " **giving up** " all search, for " giving up " desire is the joy of perfect rest (Nirvana). Know then! that age, disease, and death, these are the great sorrows of the world. *F.S.H.T.K.* 1442.

Let no man think lightly of **good**, saying in his heart, it will not come nigh unto me. Even by the falling of water-drops a water-pot is filled; the wise man becomes full of good, even if he gather it little by little. *Dham.* 22.

Good people walk on whatever befall. *Dham.* 83.

For **hatred** does not cease by hatred at any time : hatred ceases by love, this is an old rule. The world does not know that we must all come to an end here;—but those who know it, their quarrels cease at once. *Dham.* 5–6.

Hurt none by word or deed, be consistent in well-doing, be moderate in food, dwell in solitude, and give yourself to meditation—this is the advice of Buddhas. *Dham.* 185.

Earnestness is the path of **immortality** (Nirvana), thoughtlessness the path of death. Those who are in earnest do not die, those who are thoughtless are as if dead already. *Dham.* 21.

The taking of life, killing, cutting, binding, stealing, lying, fraud and deception . . . this is **impurity**, but not the eating of flesh. Neither the flesh of fish, nor fasting, nor the tonsure, matted hair, dirt, or rough skins, nor even the many immortal penances in the world, the hymns, oblations, sacrifices, and worship of the seasons, purify a mortal who has not overcome his doubts. *S.N.* 2, 2, 4, 11.

It is the **iron's** own rust that destroys it : it is the sinner's own acts that bring him to hell. *Dham.* 240.

Judge not thy neighbour. *Siamese Buddhist Maxim.*

Be ye **lamps** unto yourselves. Be ye a refuge to yourselves. Betake yourselves to no external refuge. Hold fast to the truth as a lamp, hold fast as a refuge to the truth. Look not for refuge to anyone besides yourselves. *Digha Mah. Par. Sut.* 2, 33.

Laziness is the ruin of homes, idleness is the ruin of beauty, negligence is the ruin of the watcher. Unchastity is a stain on a woman, miserliness is a stain on the donor, to do evil is a stain in this and other worlds. But greater than all these stains, ignorance is the worst of all. *Dham.* 241–3.

Let him not destroy, or cause to be destroyed, any **life** at all, or sanction the acts of those who do so. Let him refrain from even hurting any creature, both those that are strong and those that tremble in the world. *S.N.* 393.

Full of **love** for all things in the world, practising virtue, in order to benefit others, this man alone is happy. *Dham.* 39.

If a man lives a hundred years, and engages the whole of his time and attention in religious offerings to the gods, sacrificing elephants and horses and other things, all this is not equal to one act of pure **love** in saving life. *Dham.* 7, 2.

As a **mother**, even at the risk of her own life, protects her son, her only son : so let him that has recognized the truth cultivate good will without measure among all beings. *S.N.* 148.

The **odour of flowers** travels not against the wind, nor that of sandal, nor the fragrant powder of frankincense or jasmine; but the sweet odour of good men travels with the wind and against it. *Dham.* 54.

Hurt not **others** with that which pains yourself. *Udanavarga* 5, 18.

As rain does not break through a well-thatched house, **passion** will not break through a well-reflecting mind. *Dham.* 14.

I would be a **protector** of the unprotected, a guide of wayfarers, a ship, a dyke, and a bridge for them who seek the further shore : a lamp for them who need a lamp, a bed for them who need a bed, a slave for them who need a slave. *Santi-deva's Bodhicharyavatara, "* The Path of Light."

He who takes **refuge** with Buddha, the Law, and the Church; he who, with clear understanding, sees the four holy truths :— viz : pain, the origin of pain, the destruction of pain, and the eightfold holy way that leads to the quieting of pain :—that is the safe refuge, that is the best refuge; having gone to that refuge, a man is delivered from all pain. *Dham.* 190–2.

Wherein does **religion** consist ? It consists in doing as little harm as possible, in doing good in abundance, in the practise of love, of compassion, of truthfulness and purity, in all the walks of life. *As. Ed.*

Never think or say that your own **religion** is the best. Never denounce the religion of others. *As. Ed.*

Do not decry other **sects**, do not depreciate others, but rather honour whatever in them is worthy of honour. *As. Ed.*

When thou seest that thine own **self** is at ease and thy fellow in distress, that thou art in high estate and he is brought low, that thou art at rest and he is at labour, then make thine own self lose its pleasure and bear the sorrow of thy fellows. *Santi-deva's Bodhicharyavatara.* " The Path of Light."

If one were to conquer a thousand thousand in battle he who conquers **self** is the greatest warrior. *Dham.* 103.

To make an end of **self-seeking**, that is blessedness. *Udana-varga* 30, 26.

It is nature's rule, that as we **sow**, we shall reap, she recognizes no good intentions, and pardons no errors. *Ta-chwang-Yan-King-Lun Sermon* 57.

If a man make himself as he teaches others to be, then, being himself well-**subdued**, he may subdue others; one's own self is indeed difficult to subdue. Self is the lord of self, who else could be the lord ? With self well-subdued, a man finds a lord such as few can find. *Dham.* 159–160.

This is the noble truth of the origin of **suffering**; it is the thirst for being which leads from birth to birth, together with lust and desire, which finds gratification here and there : the thirst for pleasure, the thirst for being, the thirst for power. Buddha's First Sermon—2nd Truth. *Vin. Mah.* 1, 6, 20.

This is the noble truth of the extinction of **suffering**; the extinction of this thirst by complete annihilation of desire, letting it go, expelling it, separating oneself from it, giving it no room. Buddha's First Sermon—3rd Truth. *Vin. Mah.* 1, 61, 21.

All that we are is the result of what we have **thought**; it is founded on our thoughts; it is made up of our thoughts. If a man speaks or acts with an evil thought pain follows him as the wheel follows the foot of the ox that draws the carriage, but if a man speaks or acts with a pure thought happiness follows him like a shadow that never leaves him. *Dham.* 1–2.

To the **virtuous** all is pure. *Tripitaka.*

Faith is **wealth**! Obedience is wealth! Modesty also is wealth! Hearing is wealth, and so is Charity! Wisdom is sevenfold riches. *Dham.* 4, 2.

I consider the **welfare** of all people as something for which I must work. *As. Ed.*

Stars, darkness, a lamp, a phantom, dew, a bubble. A dream, a flash of lightning, and a cloud—thus we should look upon the **world**. *The Vagrakkhedika* 32.

Look upon the **world** as a bubble, look upon it as a mirage; the king of death does not see him who thus looks down upon the world. . . . He whose evil deeds are covered by good deeds, brightens up this world, like the moon when freed from clouds. . . . Better than sovereignty over the earth, better than going to heaven, better than lordship over all worlds, is the reward of the first step in holiness. *Dham.* 170, 173, 178.

Readings from the Scriptures

The Buddha's Discourse with the wandering ascetic Vacchagotta.

Vaccha, the view that the world is eternal is a jungle, a wilderness, a theatrical show, a perversion, a fetter . . . and does not tend to aversion, absence of passion, cessation, tranquillity, supernatural faculty, perfect knowledge, Nirvana. . . . Considering it disadvantageous I have accordingly adopted none of these views. . . . The Tathāgata, Vaccha, is free from views. . . . With the destruction of, and indifference towards, and the ceasing and abandonment of all imaginings, all agitations, all false views of the self or of anything belonging to a self . . . the Tathāgata is liberated, thus I say. . . . Deep is this doctrine, difficult to be seen and comprehended, good, excellent, beyond the sphere of reasoning, subtle, intelligible only to the wise. . . . The Tathāgata, who is released from what is called form, is deep, immeasurable, hard to fathom and like a great ocean. It does not fit the case to say that he is born again, to say that he is not born again, to say that he is both born again and not born again, or to say he is neither born again nor not born again. *The Questions of Vacchagotta Majjhima-Nikāya Sutta Pitaka.*

The fletcher carves and adjusts the horn of which his bow is made; the pilot manages his ship; the architect hews his beams;

the wise man governs his body himself. For as, by way of simile, the solid rock is unshaken by the wind, so the wise man, grave of thought, quails not whether praised or blamed : just as a deep lake is not easily stirred but remains tranquil and still, so the wise man hearing the Law (way), his heart is quiet and at rest. The great man is entirely free from covetous desire—he dwells in a place of light himself enlightened. Although perchance he meet with sorrow, he rejoices, without ostentation, he exhibits his wisdom. The wise man (Bhadra) concerns himself with no worldly business; he desires neither wealth, children, or possessions (land), always carefully observing the precepts, and walking in the way of supreme wisdom, he hankers not after strange doctrine or wealth or honour. The wise man, knowing the character of instability, as a tree in the midst of sand, uses every effort to change his friend whose mind is unfixed, and to bring him back from impurity to virtue (purity). *B. Dham.* 14, 1–2.

The teaching of the wise is this, that by wisdom we preserve ourselves. The foolish ridicule it—they see, and yet do wickedly; and so by their wicked deeds they reap misfortune, as he who sows the noxious plant (reaps the same). The wicked man in his own person accumulates (receives the fruit of his) guilt; the good man reaps good fruit (merit) in his own person; and so each one for himself prepares the harvest for himself. The concerns of another do not effect one's case—doing good, then we reap good, just as one who sows that which is sweet enjoys the same. *B. Dham.* 20, 2.

Truly men seek through fear many a refuge; they resort to mountains and valleys, and spirits residing in trees; they erect images as gods, and pay religious worship to them, seeking happiness (merit). But such refuge as this is neither fortunate nor best; not one of them is able to save thee from sorrow or accumulated pain. But he who takes refuge in Buddha, the Law, and the Church, and with clear insight penetrates the meaning of the four truths, he will certainly attain (see) supreme wisdom. He who seeks personal refuge in these three, finds the most fortunate and the best. In these only, without other refuge, a man may find deliverance from all sorrow. *B. Dham.* 22, 2.

From love or lust comes sorrow, from lust comes fear; where there is no lust or, no ground for lust, what sorrow, what fear can there be? From pleasure comes sorrow, from pleasure comes fear; where there is no ground for pleasure, what grief or fear can there be? From covetousness (greed) comes sorrow, from greed comes fear; where one is free from covetousness, there can be no sorrow or fear. But to be greedy to fulfil perfectly the requirements (moral rules) of the Law—to be truthful in everything or, to be perfectly truthful, to be modest in everything, to conduct his own business (to order himself) according to what is right—this is to lay a foundation of love from all. The idea of pleasure not yet produced, his thoughts and words composed, his mind unaffected by any bewilderment of love, he indeed shall mount above or cut off the Stream. *B. Dham.* 24, 1.

Amongst men there is no one who is not blamed, from old time till now. Since they blame the man of many words, they blame the patient and quiet man; they also blame the man who seeks the happy medium; there is always blame in the world. Those who desire to find fault with the righteous (holy) man are never able to discriminate with impartiality (take a middle course); they blame him entirely or they praise him entirely, but it is all done from some false idea of profit or fame. But he whom the enlightened and wise praise, and whom they consider and call upright and good, a man of true wisdom and innocent life, without any ground for censure in himself, as a Rahat for purity, there is no blame for him—such an one the gods themselves must admire, even Brahma and Sakra must praise such an one. *B. Dham.* 25, 1.

Absence of daily prayer is the disease of daily conversation (words). Want of diligence is the disease of a household. Want of becoming dignity is the disease of manner (outward appearance). Carelessness is the disease of business. Stinginess is the disease of charity. Vice is the disease of daily conduct. Both now and hereafter an evil Rule of Life (Law) is an everlasting disease (taint). But the disease of all diseases, than which none is worse, is ignorance. *B. Dham.* 26, 1.

As a tree, as long as its root is firm and safe, although cut down, still survives and produces fruit; so, unless the remnants of lust are destroyed and uprooted, a man must return again and again to receive sorrow. The monkey, away from the tree, first of all enjoys release, and then returns again to its bondage, such is the

case with men, they escape from hell and then return to it. Longing thoughts are like the ever-flowing waters of a river; giving
way to the free enjoyment of indolence and luxury, the mind like
a savage dog seeks for continued indulgence, and the man himself
becomes clouded and unable to see the truth. Every thought
flowing in the same channel, then lusts bind a man as with strong
ratten bonds. The wise man alone is able rightly to distinguish
the truth, he is able to cut off the very root and source of his lustful
thoughts. A man by self-indulgence becomes sleek and shining,
his thoughts increase like the sprouting tendril, the depth of lust
cannot be fathomed; from this proceeds the ever-increasing
succession of old age and continual death. *B. Dham.* 32, 1.

As a fletcher makes straight his arrow, a wise man makes
straight his trembling and unsteady thought, which is difficult
to guard, difficult to hold back. As a fish taken from his watery
home and thrown on the dry ground, our thought trembles all
over in order to escape the dominion of Mâra (the tempter). It
is good to tame the mind, which is difficult to hold in and flighty,
rushing wherever it listeth; a tamed mind brings happiness. . . .
Whatever a hater may do to a hater, or an enemy, a wrongly-
directed mind will do us greater mischief. Not a mother, not a
father will do so much, nor any other relative; a well-directed
mind will do us greater service. *Dham.* 33–5, 42–3.

Stem the stream and pass over, without desire as a Brahman!
Understanding the end of all that is made or, of all modes of
conduct, this is truly named the life of a Brahmachârin. In or,
by means of the two laws of nothingness, pure and spotless passing
over the gulf, casting off all the bonds of desire, this is to be a
Brahmachârin indeed. It is not by his clan, or his plaited hair,
that a man is called a Brahman, but he who walks truthfully and
righteously, he is indeed rightly called a good man (Bhadra).
What avails the plaited hair, O fool! the garment of grass, what
good? Within there is no quittance of desire, then what advantage the outward denial of self? Put away lust, hatred, delusion,
sloth and all its evil consequences, as the snake puts off its skin,
this is to be a Brahmachârin indeed. Separate yourself from all
worldly associations—let the mouth speak no foul words—
thoroughly investigate the eight paths (Ashtânga mârga), this
is to be a Brahmachârin indeed. To have cast off all thoughts

of family affection, to have given up all desire after home, and all the bonds of personal preference loosed, this is to be a Brahma-chârin indeed. He who has given up all thoughts about this world or the next, and places no reliance on either—this man is a Brahmachârin indeed. He who understands his own previous history, and has come to an end of all future chance of birth or death, him I call a Brahmachârin. He who is perfect in knowledge is a Brahmachârin. *B. Dham.* 35, 1.

What is life but the flower or the fruit which falls, when ripe, but yet which ever fears the untimely frost ? Once born there is nought but sorrow; for who is there can escape death ? From the first moment of conception in the womb, the result of passion-ate love and desire, there is nought but the bodily form, transitory as the lightning flash. It is difficult to dam up the daily flow of the waters of life. The body is but a thing destined to perish. There is no certain form given to the spirit conceived with the body. Once dead it is again born—the connections of sin and of merit cannot be overreached. It is not a matter of one life, or one death, but from the act of renewed conception proceeds all the consequences of former deeds, resulting in joy or misery; the body dies but the spirit is not entombed! . . . It is the mind alone (spirit) that determines the character of life in the three worlds. Just as the life has been virtuous or the contrary, is the subsequent career of the individual. Living in the dark, dark-ness will follow; the consequent birth is as the echo from the cavern, immersed in carnal desires, there cannot be any thing but carnal appetite; all things result from previous conduct, as the traces follow the elephant-step, or the shadow the substance. *B. Dham.* 37, 1.

He who has faith, and delights in the true Law, this man is fortunate above all others. He who looks for good luck neither from gods or sacrifices to spirits but from himself is truly fortunate. A friend of the virtuous, and holding with the righteous, always making the consideration of virtue his first aim, keeping his body in strict obedience to the rules of propriety, this man is fortunate indeed! Avoiding bad people and following the good, giving up wine, and using strict moderation in all personal gratification, not lusting after female beauty, this man is indeed a fortunate one. Ever anxious to listen to the rules of right conduct, persevering in the study of the Law and Rules of Discipline (Dharma and Vinaya), self-restrained and without offence, this man is fortunate above all. If a householder, then caring for his father and mother, and looking after the welfare of his house, and properly fostering his wife and child, not occupying himself in vain and useless avocations, this man is indeed fortunate. Not giving way to idleness or self-honour, knowing the character of moderation as to himself, and thoughtful of his friends, at proper times reading the Scriptures and practising himself in them, this man is truly fortunate. Patiently continuing in the way of duty of what he hears he ought to do, rejoicing to see a religious person (Shaman), and ever inviting such an one to instruct him in religion, this man is happy. Observing the religious seasons (fasts), and during such seasons using strict self-abstinence, always desiring to see the virtuous and holy man, placing his confidence in the instruction of the enlightened, this man is fortunate. Once convinced of the happiness of religion (Bodhi), then with upright heart never swerving from his faith, desiring above all things to escape the three evil ways of birth, this man is truly happy. With equal mind, devoting himself to charity, honouring all the wise alike, and paying respect to the Divine Spirits, this man is indeed happy. Always anxious to get rid of sensual desires and covetousness, to escape from delusive thoughts, ignorance, and anger, ever constant in the pursuit of true wisdom, this man is indeed fortunate. Even in discarding the evil using no extraordinary appearance of effort, but steadily persevering in the practise of what is right, always acting as he ought to act, this man is fortunate indeed. Full of love for all things in the world, practising virtue in order to benefit others, this man alone is happy. The wise man dwelling in the world, pursuing this line of fortunate behaviour with constancy, ever pressing onwards to complete what knowledge he has gained, this is a happy man indeed. *B. Dham.* 39, 1.

Long is the night to him who is awake; long is a mile to him who is tired; long is life to the foolish who do not know the true law. If a traveller does not meet with one who is his better, or his equal, let him firmly keep to his solitary journey; there is no companionship with a fool. "These sons belong to me, and this wealth belongs to me," with such thoughts a fool is tormented.

He himself does not belong to himself; how much less sons and wealth? The fool who knows his foolishness, is wise at least so far. But a fool who thinks himself wise, he is called a fool indeed. If a fool be associated with a wise man even all his life, he will perceive the truth as little as a spoon perceives the taste of soup. . . . As long as the evil deed done does not bear fruit, the fool thinks it is like honey; but when it ripens, then the fool suffers grief. . . . And when the evil deed, after it has become known, brings sorrow to the fool, then it destroys his bright lot, nay, it cleaves his head. . . . One is the road that leads to wealth, another the road that leads to Nirvana; if the Bhikshu, the disciple of Buddha, has learnt this, he will not yearn for honour, he will strive after separation from the world. *Dham.* 60–4, 69, 72, 75.

Even though a speech be a thousand of words, but made up of senseless words, one word of sense is better, which if a man hears, he becomes quiet. Even though a Gâthâ (poem) be a thousand of words, but made up of senseless words, one word of a Gâthâ is better, which if a man hears, he becomes quiet. Though a man recite a hundred Gâthâs made up of senseless words, one word of the law is better, which if a man hears, he becomes quiet. If one man conquer in battle a thousand times thousand men, and if another conquer himself, he is the greatest of conquerors. One's own self conquered is better than all other people; not even a god, a Gandharva, not Mâra with Brahman could change into defeat the victory of a man who has vanquished himself, and always lives under restraint. . . . And he who lives a hundred years, ignorant and unrestrained, a life of one day is better if a man is wise and reflecting. And he who lives a hundred years, idle and weak, a life of one day is better if a man has attained firm strength. And he who lives a hundred years, not seeing beginning and end, a life of one day is better if a man sees beginning and end. And he who lives a hundred years, not seeing the immortal place, a life of one day is better if a man sees the immortal place. *Dham.* 100–5, 111–14.

If a man commits a sin, let him not do it again; let him not delight in sin: pain is the outcome of evil. If a man does what is good, let him do it again; let him delight in it: happiness is the outcome of good. Even an evil-doer sees happiness as long as his evil deed has not ripened; but when his evil deed has

ripened, then does the evil-doer see evil. Even a good man sees
evil days, as long as his good deed has not ripened; but when his
good deed has ripened, then does the good man see happy days.
Let no man think lightly of evil, saying in his heart, It will not come
nigh unto me. Even by the falling of water-drops a water-pot is
filled; the fool becomes full of evil, even if he gather it little by
little. Let no man think lightly of good, saying in his heart, It
will not come nigh unto me. Even by the falling of water-drops
a water-pot is filled; the wise man becomes full of good, even if
he gather it little by little. . . . He who has no wound on his
hand, may touch poison with his hand; poison does not affect
one who has no wound; nor is there evil for one who does not
commit evil. . . . Some people are born again; evil-doers go
to hell, righteous people go to heaven; those who are free from all
worldly desires attain Nirvana. Not in the sky, not in the midst
of the sea, not if we enter into the clefts of the mountains, is there
known a spot in the whole world where a man might be freed
from an evil deed. *Dham.* 117–22, 124, 126–7.

The best of ways is the eightfold; the best of truths the four
words; the best of virtues passionlessness; the best of men he
who has eyes to see. This is the way, there is no other that
leads to the purifying of intelligence; Go on this way! Everything else is the deceit of Mâra (the tempter). If you go on this
way, you will make an end of pain! The way was preached by
me, when I had understood the removal of the thorns in the
flesh. You yourself must make an effort. The Tathâgatas
(Buddhas) are only preachers. The thoughtful who enter the
way are freed from the bondage of Mâra. All created things
perish, he who knows and sees this becomes passive in pain;
this is the way to purity. All created things are grief and pain,
he who knows and sees this becomes passive in pain; this is the
way that leads to purity. . . . So long as the love of man towards
women, even the smallest, is not destroyed, so long is his mind
in bondage, as the calf that drinks milk is to its mother. Cut out
the love of self, like an autumn lotus, with thy hand! Cherish
the road of peace. Nirvana has been shown by Buddha. *Dham.*
273–8, 284–5.

Restraint in the eye is good, good is restraint in the ear, in the
nose restraint is good, good is restraint in the tongue. In the

body restraint is good, good is restraint in speech, in thought restraint is good, good is restraint in all things. A Bhikshu, restrained in all things, is freed from all pain. He who controls his hand, he who controls his feet, he who controls his speech, he who is well controlled, he who delights inwardly, who is collected, who is solitary and content, him they call Bhikshu. The Bhikshu who controls his mouth, who speaks wisely and calmly, who teaches the meaning and the Law, his word is sweet. He who dwells in the Law, delights in the Law, meditates on the Law, follows the Law, that Bhikshu will never fall away from the true Law. Let him not despise what he has received, nor ever envy others : a mendicant who envies others does not obtain peace of mind. A Bhikshu who, though he receives little, does not despise what he has received, even the gods will praise him, if his life is pure, and if he is not slothful. He who never identifies himself with his body and soul, and does not grieve over what is no more, he indeed is called a Bhikshu. The Bhikshu who acts with kindness, who is calm in the doctrine of Buddha, will reach the quiet place (Nirvana), cessation of natural desires, and happiness. O Bhikshu, empty the boat! if emptied, it will go quickly; having cut off passion and hatred, thou wilt go to Nirvana. Cut off the five senses, leave the five, rise above the five. The Bhikshu whose body and tongue and mind are quieted, who is collected, and has rejected the baits of the world, he is called Quiet. Rouse thyself by thyself, examine thyself by thyself. Thus self-protected and attentive wilt thou live happily, O Bhikshu ! For self is the lord of self, self is the refuge of self; therefore curb thyself as the merchant curbs a good horse. The Bhikshu, full of delight, who is calm in the doctrine of Buddha, will reach the quiet place Nirvana, cessation of natural desires, and happiness. He who, even as a young Bhikshu, applies himself to the doctrine of Buddha, brightens up this world, like the moon when free from clouds. *Dham.* 360–82.

Earnest among the heedless;
Wide awake among the sleepers;
The wise makes progress, leaving those behind
As the swift steed the horse who has no strength. . . .
It is good to tame the mind,
Difficult to hold in, and flighty;

Rushing where'er it listeth;
A tamed mind is the bringer of bliss. . . .
Whatever an enemy may do to an enemy,
Or an angry man to an angry man,
A mind intent on what is wrong
Works evil worse. . . .
As the bee—injuring not
The flower, its colour, or scent—
Flies away, taking the nectar;
So let the wise man dwell upon the earth. . . .
Not where others fail, or do or leave undone,
The wise should notice what himself has done or left undone. . . .
Like a beautiful flower full of colour, without scent,
The fine words of him who does not act accordingly are fruit-
less.
Like a beautiful flower full of colour and full of scent,
The fine words of him who acts accordingly are full of fruit. . . .
As long as the sin bears no fruit,
The fool, he thinks it honey;
But when the sin ripens,
Then, indeed, he goes down into sorrow. . . .
One may conquer a thousand thousand men in battle,
But he who conquers himself alone is the greatest victor. . . .
Let no man think lightly of sin, saying in his heart, " It cannot
overtake me."
As the waterpot fills by even drops of water falling,
The fool gets full of sin, ever gathering little by little. . . .
How is there laughter ? How is there joy ?
While the fire of passion, and hatred, and ignorance is always
burning,
Ye, surrounded by darkness,
Why seek ye not a light ? . . .
Let a man make himself what he preaches to others;
The well-subdued may subdue others; one's self, indeed, is
hard to tame. . . .
He who formerly was heedless, and afterwards becomes
earnest,
Lights up this world, like the moon escaped from a cloud. . . .
The man who has transgressed one law, and speaks lies,
And scoffs at the next world, there is no evil he will not do. . . .

Let us live happily, then, not hating those who hate us!
Let us live free from hatred among men who hate!
Let us live happily, then, free from ailments among the ailing!
Let us dwell free from afflictions among men who are sick at heart!

Let us live happily, then, free from care among the busy!
Let us dwell free from yearning among men who are anxious!
Let us live happily, then, though we call nothing our own!
We shall become like the bright gods who feed on happiness!
Victory breeds hatred, for the conquered is ill at ease.
The tranquil live well at ease, careless of victory and defeat. . . .
He who holds back rising anger as one might a rolling chariot,
Him, indeed, I call a driver : others only hold the reins.
Let a man overcome anger by kindness, evil by good;
Let him conquer the stingy by a gift, the liar by truth.
Let him speak the truth; let him not yield to anger;
Let him give when asked, even from the little he has!
By these three things he will enter the presence of the gods. . . .
What ought to be done is neglected; what ought not to be done
is done.

Those who are proud and slothful their asavas (delusions)
increase . . .

The gift of the Law exceeds all gifts,
The sweetness of the Law exceeds all sweetness;
The delight of the Law exceeds all delight;
The extinction of thirst overcomes all grief. *Dham.* 29, 35, 42,
49–50, 52, 61, 103, 121, 146, 159, 172, 176, 197–201, 222–4, 292,
354.

I do not call a man a Brâhmana because of his origin or of his
mother. He is indeed arrogant, and he is wealthy : but the poor,
who is free from all attachments, him I call indeed a Brâhmana.
Him I call indeed a Brâhmana who has cut all fetters, who never
trembles, is independent and unshackled. Him I call indeed a
Brâhmana who has cut the strap and the thong, the chain with all
that pertains to it, who has burst the bar, and is awakened. Him
I call indeed a Brâhmana who, though he has committed no
offence, endures reproach, bonds, and stripes, who has endurance
for his force, and strength for his army. Him I call indeed a
Brâhmana who is free from anger, dutiful, virtuous, without

appetite, who is subdued, and has received his last body. . . .
Him I call indeed a Brâhmana who finds no fault with other
beings, whether feeble or strong, and does not kill nor cause
slaughter. Him I call indeed a Brâhmana, who is tolerant with
the intolerant, mild with fault-finders, and free from passion
among the passionate. Him I call indeed a Brâhmana from whom
anger and hatred, pride and envy have dropt like a mustard seed
from the point of a needle. . . . Him I call indeed a Brâhmana,
the manly, the noble, the hero, the great sage, the conqueror,
the impassable, the accomplished, the awakened. Him I call indeed a Brâhmana who knows his former abodes, who sees heaven
and hell, has reached the end of births, is perfect in knowledge,
a sage, and whose perfections are all perfect. *Dham.* 396–400,
405–7, 422–3.

Faith is the seed I sow, and good works are as the rain that
fertilizes it; wisdom and modesty are the parts of the plough,
and my mind is the guiding rein. I lay hold of the handle of the
Law; earnestness is the goad I use; and diligence is my draught
ox. Thus the ploughing is ploughed, destroying the weeds of
delusion. The harvest that it yields is the ambrosia fruit of
Nirvana, and by this ploughing all sorrow ends. *S.N.* 76.

The man who is angry and bears hatred, who is wicked and
hypocritical, who has embraced wrong views, who is deceitful,
let one know him as an outcast. Whosoever in this world harms
living beings, whether once or twice born, and in whom there is
no compassion for living beings. Whosoever destroys or lays
siege to villages and towns, and is known as an enemy. . . .
Whosoever being rich does not support mother or father when
old and past their youth. . . . Whosoever having gone to
another's house and partaken of his good food, does not in return
honour him when he comes. . . . Whosoever exalts himself and
despises others, being mean by his pride, let one know him as an
outcast. *S.N.* 115–17, 123, 127, 131.

Faith is in this world the best property for a man ; Dhamma,
well observed, conveys happiness; truth indeed is the sweetest
of things; and that life they call the best which is lived with
understanding. . . . By faith one crosses the stream, by zeal the
sea, by exertion one conquers pain, by understanding one is

purified. . . . He who does what is proper, who takes the yoke
upon him and exerts himself, will acquire wealth, by truth he
will obtain fame, and being charitable he will bind friends to
himself.   He who is faithful and leads the life of a householder,
and possesses the following four Dhammas (virtues), truth,
justice (dhamma), firmness, and liberality,—such a one indeed
does not grieve when passing away.   *S.N.* 181, 183, 186–7.

> Many gods and men
> Have held various things blessings,
> When they were yearning for happiness.
> Do thou declare to us the chief good.
>
> Not to serve the foolish,
> But to serve the wise;
> To honour those worthy of honour :
> This is the greatest blessing.
>
> To dwell in a pleasant land,
> Good works done in a former birth,
> Right desires in the heart :
> This is the greatest blessing.
>
> Much insight and education,
> Self-control and pleasant speech,
> And whatever word be well-spoken :
> This is the greatest blessing.
>
> To support father and mother,
> To cherish wife and child,
> To follow a peaceful calling :
> This is the greatest blessing.
>
> To bestow alms and live righteously,
> To give help to kindred,
> Deeds which cannot be blamed :
> These are the greatest blessing.
>
> To abhor, and cease from sin,
> Abstinence from strong drink,
> Not to be weary in well-doing,
> These are the greatest blessing.

Reverence and lowliness,
Contentment and gratitude,
The hearing of the law at due seasons,
This is the greatest blessing.

To be long-suffering and meek,
To associate with the tranquil (i.e., Buddhist monks),
Religious talk at due seasons,
This is the greatest blessing.

Self-restraint and purity,
The knowledge of the Noble Truths,
The realization of Nirvana,
This is the greatest blessing.

Beneath the stroke of life's changes,
The mind that shaketh not,
Without grief or passion, and secure,
This is the greatest blessing.

On every side are invincible,
They who do acts like these,
On every side they walk in safety,
And theirs is the greatest blessing.
                    (Buddhist Beatitudes.)   *S.N.* 257–68.

Let the Bhikkhu subdue his passion for human and divine pleasures, then after conquering existence and understanding the Dhamma, such a one will wander rightly in the world. Let the Bhikkhu, after casting behind him slander and anger, abandon avarice and be free from compliance and opposition, then such a one will wander rightly in the world. He who having left behind both what is agreeable and what is disagreeable, not seizing upon anything, is independent in every respect and liberated from bonds, such a one will wander rightly in the world. . . . He who is not opposed to any one in word, thought or deed, who, after having understood the Dhamma perfectly, longs for the state of Nibbâna, such a one will wander rightly in the world. . . . The Bhikkhu who, after leaving behind covetousness and existence, is disgusted with cutting and binding others, he who has overcome doubt, and is without pain, such a one will wander rightly in the world. . . . He to whom there are no affections whatsoever, whose sins are extirpated from the root, he free from desire and not longing for anything, such a one will wander rightly in the world. He whose passions have been destroyed, who is free from pride, who has overcome all the path of passion, is subdued, perfectly happy, and of a firm mind, such a one will wander rightly in the world. *S.N.* 360–2, 364, 366, 368–9.

Do not ask about descent, but ask about conduct; from wood, it is true, fire is born; likewise a firm Muni, although belonging to a low family, may become noble, when restrained from sinning by humility. . . . He in whom there lives no deceit, no arrogance, he who is free from cupidity, free from selfishness, free from desire, who has banished anger, who is calm, the Brahmâna who has removed the taint of grief, Tathâgata deserves the oblation. He who has banished every resting-place of the mind, he for whom there is no grasping, he who covets nothing either in this world or in the other, Tathâgata deserves the oblation. . . . He who does not measure himself by himself, who is composed, upright, firm, without desire, free from harshness, free from doubt, Tathâgata deserves the oblation. *S.N.* 462, 469–70, 477.

The real treasure is that laid up by man or woman
Through charity and piety, temperance and self-control,
In the sacred shrine, or the Buddhis Order,
In individual man, in the stranger and sojourner,
In his father and mother, and elder brother.
The treasure thus hid is secure, and passes not away;
Though he leave the fleeting riches of this world, this a man takes with him—
A treasure that no wrong of others, and no thief, can steal.
Let the wise man do good deeds—the treasure that follows of itself. *Nidhikanda Sutta.*

It is through not understanding and grasping four Noble Truths, O brethren, that we have had to run so long, to wander so long in this weary path of transmigration, both you and I. . . . The noble truth about sorrow; the noble truth about the cause of sorrow; the noble truth about the cessation of sorrow; and the noble truth about the path that leads to that cessation. But when these noble truths are grasped and known the craving for existence is rooted out, that which leads to renewed existence is destroyed, and then there is no more birth! . . . By not seeing the four Noble Truths as they really are, long is the path that is traversed through many a birth; when these are grasped, the cause of birth is then removed, the root of sorrow rooted out, and there is no more birth. *Mahâ-Parinibbâna-Sutta* 2, 2–3.

Be ye lamps unto yourselves. Be ye a refuge to yourselves. Betake yourselves to no external refuge. Hold fast to the truth as a lamp. Hold fast as a refuge to the truth. Look not for refuge to any one besides yourselves. And how, Ânanda, is a brother to be a lamp unto himself, a refuge to himself, betaking himself to no external refuge, holding fast to the truth as a lamp, holding fast as a refuge to the truth, looking not for refuge to any one besides himself? *Mahâ-Parinibbâna-Sutta* 2, 33.

There is a middle path, O Bhikkhus, avoiding these two extremes, discovered by the Tathâgata—a path which opens the eyes, and bestows understanding, which leads to peace of mind, to the higher wisdom, to full enlightenment, to Nirvana! . . . It is this noble eightfold path; that is to say :

>Right views;
>Right aspirations;
>Right speech;
>Right conduct;
>Right livelihood;
>Right effort;
>Right mindfulness; and
>Right contemplation.

This, O Bhikkhus, is that middle path, avoiding these two extremes, discovered by the Tathâgata—that path which opens the eyes, and bestows understanding, which leads to peace of mind, to the higher wisdom, to full enlightenment, to Nirvana! Now, this, O Bhikkhus, is the Noble Truth concerning suffering. Birth is attended with pain, decay is painful, disease is painful, death is painful. Union with the unpleasant is painful, painful is separation from the pleasant; and any craving that is unsatisfied, that too is painful. In brief, the five aggregates which spring from attachment (the conditions of individuality and their cause) are painful. Now this, O Bhikkhus, is the Noble Truth concerning the origin of suffering. Verily, it is that thirst or craving, causing the renewal of existence, accompanied by sensual delight, seeking satisfaction now here, now there—that is to say, the craving for the gratification of the passions, or the craving for a future life, or the craving for success in this present life. Now this, O Bhikkhus, is the noble truth concerning the destruction of suffering. Verily, it is the destruction, in which no passion remains, of this very thirst; the laying aside of, the getting rid of, the being free from, the harbouring no longer of this thirst. *Dhamma-Kakka-Ppavattana-Sutta* 3–7.

Deer are lured to their destruction by songs, insects for the sake of the brightness fly into the fire, the fish greedy for the flesh swallows the iron hook,—therefore worldly objects produce misery as their end. As for the common opinion, " pleasures are enjoyments," none of them when examined is worthy of being enjoyed; fine garments and the rest are only the accessories of things,—they are to be regarded as merely the remedies for pain. Water is desired for allaying thirst; food in the same way for removing hunger; a house for keeping off the wind, the heat of the sun, and the rain; and dress for keeping off the cold and to cover one's nakedness. So too a bed is for removing drowsiness; a carriage for remedying the fatigue of a journey; a seat for alleviating the pain of standing; so bathing as a means of washing, health, and strength. . . . Since variableness is found in all pleasures, I cannot apply to them the name of enjoyment; the very conditions which mark pleasure, bring also in its turn pain. Heavy garments and fragrant aloe-wood are pleasant in the cold, but an annoyance in the heat; and the moonbeams and sandal-wood are pleasant in the heat, but a pain in the cold. . . . When I see how the nature of pleasure and pain are mixed, I consider royalty and slavery as the same; a king does not always smile, nor is a slave always in pain. . . . And since after even conquering the whole earth, one city only can serve as a dwelling-place, and even there only one house can be inhabited, is not royalty mere labour for others? And even in royal clothing one pair of garments is all he needs, and just enough food to keep off hunger; so only one bed, and only one seat; all a king's other distinctions are only for pride. And if all these fruits are desired for the sake of satisfaction, I can be satisfied without a kingdom;

and if a man is once satisfied in this world, are not all distinctions indistinguishable? *Buddha-Karita of Asvaghosha* 11, 35-8, 41-2, 44, 47-9.

Everything, brethren, is on fire.   How, brethren, is everything on fire?   The eye, brethren, is on fire, visible objects are on fire, the faculty of the eye is on fire, the sense of the eye is on fire, and also the sensation, whether pleasant or unpleasant or both, which arises from the sense of sight, is on fire.   With what is it on fire? With the fire of passion, of hate, of illusion is it on fire, with birth, old age, death, grief, lamentation, suffering, sorrow, and despair. Thus I declare.   The ear is on fire, sounds are on fire (etc.). . . . The nose is on fire, scents are on fire, the tongue is on fire, tastes are on fire, the body is on fire, objects of touch are on fire, the mind is on fire, mental objects are on fire, the faculty of the mind is on fire, the perception of the mind is on fire, the sensation, whether pleasant or unpleasant or both, which arises from the inner sense is on fire.   With what is it on fire?   With the fire of passion, of hate, or illusion is it on fire, with birth, old age, death, grief, lamentation, suffering, sorrow, and despair.   Thus I declare. The wise and noble disciple, brethren, perceiving this, is indifferent to the eyes, indifferent to visible objects, indifferent to the faculty of the eye, indifferent to sensation, whether pleasant or unpleasant or both, which arises from the sense of sight.   He is indifferent to the ear, indifferent to sounds, indifferent to the nose, indifferent to scents, indifferent to the tongue, indifferent to tastes, indifferent to the body, indifferent to objects of touch, indifferent to the mind, indifferent to mental objects, indifferent to the faculty of the mind, indifferent to the perception of the mind, indifferent to the sensation, whether pleasant or unpleasant or both, which arises from the inner sense.   And being indifferent he becomes free from passion, by absence of passion is he liberated, and when he is liberated the knowledge " I am liberated " arises. Re-birth is destroyed, a religious life is lived, duty is done, and he knows there is nothing more for him in this state. *Vin. Mah.* I, 21.

The Three Refuges

I go for Refuge to the Buddha,
I go for Refuge to the Law (Dhamma),
I go for Refuge to the Order.

The Ten Commandments

These ten are binding upon members of the order. (These members may at any time return unquestioned to lay life.) The laity are bound by the first five and on fast days keep them all except the last.

1. Not to destroy life.
2. Not to take what is not given.
3. To abstain from unchastity.
4. Not to lie or deceive.
5. To abstain from intoxicants.
6. To eat temperately and not after noon.
7. Not to behold dancing, singing, or plays.
8. Not to wear garlands, perfumes, or adornments.
9. Not to use high or luxurious beds.
10. Not to accept gold or silver.

Vin. Mah. 1, 56.

10

CHRISTIANITY

W E come now to the second major religion of the contemporary world, a religion about five and a half centuries younger than Buddhism and with fewer adherents (if statistics can be trusted)—some 500,000,000 as against 520,000,000 Buddhists. This is the religion of Christianity. All attempts to give numbers must, however, be received with great caution. It may be questioned, for instance, whether Russia should be included without qualification in the list of Christian countries, while in the East multiple allegiance makes it hard to say whether a man is, or is not, a Buddhist. It is certain, however, that each of these religions claims a wider adherence than any other, and that, taken together, they represent the greater part of the religious consciousness of mankind. Their importance, moreover, is not due to numbers alone. Both have spread over wide tracts of the globe, Buddhism in the eastern, and Christianity in the western, hemisphere, and both have become absorbed in the culture of widely differing nationalities. They are thus religions aiming at universality, and are in an entirely different category from national cults, such as Confucianism (which claims some 400,000,000 Chinese) or Hinduism (with some 300,000,000 Hindus). The only other existing religion that can compare with Buddhism and Christianity is Muhammadanism, the third major religion, which will be considered in the next chapter.

Although its numbers may be rather fewer, Christianity has had a world-influence greater than Buddhism. It has been the religion of " progressive " countries, and has therefore been associated with Western civilization and the advance of science and modern education. Wherever in Buddhist countries there have been corresponding developments, these have been in imitation of European models rather than along the lines of their own culture. Christianity and material progress have thus advanced together, but they do not necessarily belong to one another. Indeed, to some extent there has been a conflict between them, which has resulted in later times in scepticism and the attitudes known as agnosticism (the doctrine that nothing can be known about God) and materialism (the doctrine that nothing exists but matter). A way of adaptation has, however, generally been found; the Christian ethic has survived periods of great change and is even able, in modern times, to use such discoveries as rapid printing and broadcasting in order to strengthen its own culture, whereas Buddhism remains remote. Again, Christianity has covered a wider geographical sphere. Arising in the Middle East, it passed north and west and, having spread over Europe, accompanied the discoverers to the Americas, large parts of Africa, Australia, and New Zealand. Buddhism has never been involved in discovery or large-scale annexation of new lands; its method was that of gradual permeation throughout Asia. It is thus, with negligible exceptions, confined to one continent, whereas Christianity took possession of three, besides a wide dispersion elsewhere. It can therefore fairly be stated that although its numbers are fewer than those of its great rival, Buddhism, it has had the greater influence on history, and is still the most influential faith in the world.

Christianity is the religion of this country, and in this chapter we reach what must be, for most of us, the radiating centre, as it were, for our personal reactions to the religious question. A complete detachment will therefore be difficult; and in any case it will be impossible to consider the many varied angles of approach. The most that can be done in a short introduction is to attempt some kind of simplification; the briefest statement as to how Christianity compares with other religions.

The word " Christian " is used in a number of different senses. This is only to be expected, in view of the innumerable phases and processes of adaptation through which it has passed, but this is particularly noticeable at the present time, when there is a good deal of confusion in the world and rival " Ideologies " are being put forward. For some people " Christian " means little more than a humanitarian outlook, the underlying principles of which have been taught in other religions (though this takes a more active form in the West). For others it implies the dogmas and observances of various churches, or again, it may mean adherence to the ethical teaching, or to the Person, of Christ, irrespective of any particular form of worship. To a large majority it implies an enlightened social order, and we are all familiar with the ideal of the Christian gentleman, the upright man who behaves honourably towards women, who is kind to the weak, and who keeps his word. The improved position of women, it may be said in passing, is one of the features most readily associated with a Christian society. There are also " good works," which may be linked up with particular churches or based on a generally diffused application of humane principles.

The co-ordinating factor lying behind these various, and often rather vague, interpretations of the word " Christian " is the *Person of Christ*. More than any other religion Christianity relies upon a *Person*, upon a life actually lived : indeed, so much has this been the case that it has been said that more attention has been paid to the teaching *about* Jesus of Nazareth than to the teaching *by* him.

In the religions of Founders—and Christianity is, of course, one of these—there are always two things : the Man and his Teaching. In the first place these are intimately connected. The doctrine does not stand alone : it is delivered by a *Person*, who speaks from his own heart and special experience. This was the case with Buddhism : it is the case with Christianity, but in Christianity the personality of the Founder is even more important in relation to his teaching than it is in Buddhism. There are several reasons for this.

The Buddha had a long life, and was therefore able to elaborate his religion and to leave to his disciples an already well-developed system. The ministry of Jesus was very short—three years, perhaps (though some authorities give as little as one to one and a half)—so that it was only possible to initiate a small band of disciples and to enunciate his doctrines in fundamental and general terms. On the other hand, he left them with an example of a perfect life, one in which no blemish could be found, and which ended with a willing martyrdom. More even than this : it ended with his reported resurrection from the dead and his " Ascension into Heaven " with his physical body. The life of Gautama Buddha had been less perfect, viewed as a whole ; before he attained his enlightenment under the Bo-tree he had experienced two opposed kinds of life, both of which had failed. It was never suggested, moreover, that he had made a physical conquest over death, though many of the later stories of his infancy, youth, and ministry resemble those of the Christian gospels. For instance, there was an angelic visitation to his father, he was virgin-born, and angels sang at his birth. A Buddhist Simeon, Asita, held the child in his arms and predicted his future greatness. He fasted forty-nine days, and was tempted by the spirit of Evil to acquire worldly power. He had a disciple who tried to walk on the water but sank, and also a band of twelve followers. He was transfigured and made a triumphal entry into a city. His greatest sermon, the Fire Sermon, was preached from a mountain, and he is also said to have descended into Hell, where he preached to the souls imprisoned there. But he is never reported to have risen from the dead—that is, as having immortalized the physical body, nor, indeed, is this recorded of any other founder or prophet in the history of religion. Thus the life of Christ stands out with unique significance, and the interest taken in his Person was reinforced by the claims which he made for himself as reported in the Scriptures. He spoke of his intimate relationship with God, and admitted his identity with the Messiah (Anointed One), a deliverer whom the Jews had long expected and whose coming had been foretold. He claimed the power to forgive sins and in many other ways assumed authority. There is another point which is significant when making a comparison with Buddhism. The Indian doctrine of Reincarnation has a bearing on the earth-life of each individual. Though that doctrine was greatly modified by Gautama, it remained in the background, while in the popular mind the belief gained prevalence that the Buddha himself had been incarnate many times and that he would return again and again in human flesh. When a series of future earth-lives is predicted for the Founder of the Faith, as well as for all other men, a single life-history fails to stand out, perhaps, with the same stark significance. The Eastern doctrine of a plurality of lives was not unknown to the Jews, as some scripture passages show, but it had not appreciably coloured their thought, and Jesus himself did not teach it. Thus Christianity is pre-eminently a religion arising from, and centred in, a single life-pattern : and it thus raises the life-history of every person to a position of importance correspondingly greater than that in any other religion.

The word " Christianity " incorporates the title bestowed on the Founder, just as the word Buddhism does. " Christ " comes from Christos, the Greek word for the Hebrew Messiah, or Anointed One, and the name Christian, we are told in the Acts of the Apostles (xi. 6), was first given to the followers of Jesus of Nazareth at Antioch in Syria. This origin is important, because it reminds us that Christianity arose out of Judaism and that the first Christians were Jews by birth and training, who for a time continued to conform to the Jewish observances and attend the Synagogues. There was, at first, no definite break with tradition.

The story of the life of the Founder may now be briefly told. Jesus was born in Palestine before the end of the reign of Herod the Great, the Jewish Governor who ruled that district under the authority of the Roman Emperor. Paradoxically the date of birth has to be stated as B.C. 4 at the latest, because it is known that Herod died in that year and that as he was alive at the same time as Jesus, the original calculation upon which our calendar is based is at fault. The birthplace is said to have been a stable near the small village of Bethlehem, but the home of Jesus was in Nazareth, much farther north, in the province of Galilee. There he lived with his mother Mary and Joseph, her husband, who was assumed to be his father. The records state, however, that he was miraculously born of a virgin. Joseph was a carpenter, and it may be assumed that Jesus worked in his shop until, at the age of about thirty, he became a public teacher. He then went about the country, preaching, gathering disciples, and performing miracles, especially miracles of healing. His ministry may have lasted only a year : more probably it was about two and a half years, from the winter of A.D. 26 to the spring of A.D. 29. He then came into conflict with the religious authorities, was betrayed by Judas, one of his own disciples, arrested on a charge of having blasphemously stated that he was the " Messiah," the Son of the Living God, found guilty on his own confession, and sentenced to the cruel death of crucifixion, despite the efforts of the Roman judge, Pontius Pilate, to find some way to save him. Two thieves were executed with him. This appeared to be the end, but actually it was only the beginning. The body, which was taken away from the cross by disciples, disappeared from the tomb, and during the forty days which followed, Jesus, we are told, made a number of appearances to his followers. In all 539 persons are reported as having seen him. At the final appearance he is said to have vanished into the air while " two men in white apparel " told the disciples that he had " ascended into Heaven." The Resurrection turned the sorrow of the disciples into joy. Christ had now completed the triumph of his Personality, and thenceforth their main attention was concentrated on this immense fact.

The teaching given by Jesus during his ministry was very simple, yet so exalted that it has been claimed that it has never yet been put into practice. He laid great emphasis on the Fatherhood of God, a conception which is, of course, found in the Old Testament and also in other religions, but he gave it an insistence, a directness, and simplicity which were new. He wanted his disciples to realize that if they could accept God as a Father in absolute sincerity, rest, happiness, and a sense of security would follow. For a father loves each child individually and is inspired by love rather than by law. Thus the Prodigal Son is received with honour directly he returns to his father, and the virtuous son, who protests against this seeming injustice, is reproved. The labourers, who were hired late, received the same pay as those " who had borne the heat of the day," and the protests of the latter were rejected, for love is greater than justice. The sun rises on the good and on the evil and the rain falls on the just and the unjust. The value of each person is paramount, and as all receive the same overshadowing love of the Father, so all should give to others love which knows no limitations. " If a man compel thee to go with him one mile, go with him twain . . . if he ask of thee thy cloak give him thy coat also." Love must be unconditional, it can have no reservations, and it must embrace enemies as well as friends.

Jesus spoke often, too, of the Kingdom of Heaven. At the time of the birth of Christ, the Jews had been expecting a Kingdom to be established by the power of a Messiah (Anointed One). This was chiefly thought of as a worldly kingdom, the political triumph of Israel, who would be freed from bondage to the Roman Emperor. Jesus took the current idea but gave it a new meaning. The Kingdom of Heaven was a spiritual state, ever near at hand, yet hard to enter. A change of heart was first needed—the kind of repentance that would bring about trustfulness and humility. " Except ye become as little children ye shall in no wise enter into the Kingdom of Heaven." Riches of any kind were a hindrance. " How hardly shall he that hath riches enter into the Kingdom of Heaven! " Yet the Kingdom was very real : it existed potentially in the world, and was open to any who could repent and replace their anxious self-seeking by complete trust in the Fatherhood of God and the experience of a love for others which has thrown off all reservations. There is, thus, in the teaching of Christ, a perfect blending of simplicity and profundity.

The greatest sermon of Jesus was preached from a mountain, more probably a little hill. He also spoke in the synagogues, in private houses, by the lakeside—anywhere, in fact, where crowds assembled to hear him. He used the simple, ordinary language of the people, and the homely imagery of the parable or story.

There is little in the recorded teaching of Christ about what we call theology—that is, direct instruction about the nature of God. There was no need for this, since God is our Father in an intimate loving sense. Neither is much laid down as to ways of worship. Jesus confirmed the traditions of the Jews, that God is single, holy, all-powerful, and compassionate : he himself worshipped in the Temple and Synagogues, kept the Jewish observances, and quoted the Jewish Scriptures. He took what was already there, but gave it a new depth and significance. He condemned the Scribes and Pharisees, not because they followed Jewish traditions, but because they put the letter above the spirit. He did, however, make unique claims for himself and for his own mission, and it is impossible to read the New Testament without recognizing these. He "knew the Father," "he had been sent by Him." When faced with the direct question at his trial, "Art thou the Messiah, the Son of the living God ? " he replied, " I am." The attempt to separate the ethical teaching of Christ from his personal claim to authority (an attempt which is largely of modern origin) cannot be justified; the two are inseparably bound up together in the Scriptures.

The fact that Christ's teaching was accompanied by miracles is of less importance than this claim to divine authority. Miracles were by no means unexpected in the East, as we saw when Gautama Buddha expressly forbade his disciples to perform these. They are recorded in the Old Testament and in the Scriptures of other religions, and St. Paul, of whom we shall speak shortly, claimed to have worked " signs " and to have shared this power with the other Apostles. Miracles have been well defined as " the supremacy of the spiritual forces of the world to an extraordinary degree over the material." The miracles in the Gospels were not as a rule used to prove any doctrine : they seem rather to have been spontaneous acts overflowing from the personal love and compassion of Jesus. They were, however, often associated with his power to forgive sins : and the important point is here, as elsewhere, his claim to authority. There are passages asserting that he would come again to judge the world, and this Second Coming was expected at any moment by the early Church.

The account of the life and teaching of Jesus has come down to us in writings called the four Gospels, attributed to Matthew, Mark, Luke, and John, who were all disciples of the Lord in his life-time. Though there are some discrepancies, their agreement is more remarkable when we consider that they were not written down until long after the events which they describe. This is especially true of the first three, which are therefore called the Synoptic Gospels, because they make a synopsis of the facts then generally accepted. The Fourth Gospel, attributed to St. John, differs in style, and is much later than the others, being usually dated by scholars as not earlier than A.D. 100. The date for St. Matthew is usually given as about A.D. 70, St. Mark a few years earlier, and St. Luke about A.D. 83. We have, however, much earlier documents than these : the letters of St. Paul, which were written between A.D. 52 and 65, the latter being the traditional date of Paul's martyrdom in Rome.

Paul was, in one sense, the greatest of all the disciples, though he was not one of the original band, and had never seen Jesus. He was a very different kind of man from the simple fishermen who had been the first followers. He was a Roman citizen, and had been educated under Greek influences. But he was also a Jew by birth and upbringing, and was trained in the doctrines of the Pharisees. He thus brought a remarkable blend of thought to the new religion, which he began by persecuting. We read that his conversion was brought about by a vision of Christ, who appeared to him when he was on the road to Damascus. Thereafter he gave all his energy to spreading the Christian doctrines, until he was finally beheaded under the Emperor Nero.

It is to St. Paul that we owe the foundation of the doctrine of the Atonement. The death of Christ now becomes not only the martyred end of a perfect life, but a sacrifice offered for the sins of the world. St. Paul was accustomed to the idea of the sacrifice, which he had found in other religions, and it seemed to him that some means of reconciliation was necessary between God and sinful men. But as no offering could be perfect, by reason of our fallen state, God Himself had at last supplied the willing victim, His own Son. Such a perfect sacrifice could avail perfectly and once for all—those who shared in it and trusted in Christ could win salvation and eternal life—not only spiritually, but in some sense also in the physical body. The entire interest of Paul was centred in Jesus, and he broke away from the Jewish–Christian standpoint and carried the mystical doctrine of redemption to the Gentiles. He was the first great missionary, and he travelled about Asia Minor and the eastern parts of Europe, and finally to Rome. It has been said that Paul so transformed Christianity as to make of it a new religion, but this view may easily be an exaggerated one. No protests were made by those who had earlier been disciples, except doubts as to whether the Gentiles should be admitted, and Paul's developments proceeded along lines already accepted.

The teaching of St. Paul continued to be developed and it laid the foundation for the doctrine of the Trinity. The idea of Father, Son, and Spirit had been foreshadowed in the Jewish Scriptures, and now seemed to express perfectly the three aspects of the Godhead. God was the Father, the Creator, the Absolute Source; as Son, He was Incarnate in Jesus; and as Spirit He dwells in our hearts and in all creation. The doctrine of a Trinity within the Godhead, which had been foreshadowed in other religions, now became the foundation of the Christian Creed.

Christianity is thus the great Trinitarian religion. The subsequent history of the Faith is a long and complicated story of development upon this basis. The Jewish associations were never wholly lost, and the ancient Jewish Scriptures still form part of the Christian Sacred Book, the Bible. The main body of the Church grew into an elaborate organization, with its principal Bishop, who later became known as the Pope, at Rome. In the process of spreading, it took in a large number of elements, doctrines, and observances from other sources and incorporated, transformed, and absorbed these. It was not without difficulty and danger that this long process of elaboration and adaptation was worked out. There were constant disputes, heresies, schisms, wars, and even persecution, before the three creeds [1] were laid down and fully defined. Nor was the position ever felt to be quite safe. Despite the original teaching of Christ as to universal love and forbearance, Christianity has been a great fighting religion, and has defended its position with the greatest vigour and persistence and with all available means, not excluding violence. Paradoxically, intense devotion to Christ has led to many deeds being committed in his name which are directly opposed to his teaching.

While it is not possible to trace the turbulent history of Christianity here, a few words must be added about the two main divisions known to everyone, Catholic and Protestant. These are primarily two different ways of approach, for the fundamental doctrines are the same. The Church, as it developed, laid increasing emphasis on tradition. It claimed that while little was written down, more had been carried on by word of mouth, especially by the priests, who were the direct successors of the Apostles. The Church was thus the guardian of Truth as first revealed, and men could find salvation only by submitting to her authority. She was kept from error in her later developments by the Holy Spirit, whom Christ had promised to leave as a Divine Guide. One of the doctrines which became increasingly prominent was that of the Virgin Birth of Christ. This is not mentioned by St. Paul, but appears in the Gospels of St. Matthew and St. Luke, and as time went on increasing honour was paid to Mary, as Mother of God. Her statue was placed in churches, prayers were addressed to her, festivals were kept in her honour. When in the fifteenth century the movement arose called the Reformation, this was one of the developments which the Protestants (so called because they protested) wished to discard. Another was the supreme authority of the Pope of Rome, together with a large number of ritual observances and ceremonials. Protestantism, in its extreme form, asserts that a man must return to the Bible for his guidance, that he should accept no doctrine which he cannot find there, and that he has a right to use his private judgment. Protestantism developed very differently in different countries, and in many cases only reached its logical form gradually; at first it was mainly concerned with throwing off the rule of Rome, but it ended, as was only natural, by splitting the Christian Church into

[1] The Apostle's, Nicene, and Athanasian.

a large number of different sects. The effort to return to the simple Christianity of the primitive Church resulted in the destruction of many beautiful things and a barrenness, even an ugliness, in worship. In the east of Europe there had been other Christian bodies which had rejected the authority of Rome, long before the Reformation in this country : principally the Greek (Orthodox) Churches. But these had retained their magnificent ritual, their mysteries, powerful priesthood, and emphasis on tradition. The Mass—the Sacrament which was the principal service of the Catholic Church and which was the offering of the Body and Blood of Christ under the visible signs of bread and wine—still held the central place there also. Beyond certain somewhat obscure differences of doctrine, the methods were the same as those of Rome. The Anglo-Catholic party within the Church of England has in recent times taken up a similar position : the importance of tradition returns, and the main point at issue is the authority of the Pope. The broad divisions of Christendom may therefore be said to be Roman Catholic, Protestant and Eastern, while the Anglo-Catholics and certain other communities emphasize tradition and ceremonial but reject the Papal claims.

A few words must be added on the question of sin. Penitence is an essential feature of Christianity; sin is the great danger to the soul. Man has to make a supreme choice in a single earth-life, and he has been given free-will with which to choose. So important is this choice that nothing less than his eternal misery or eternal bliss may depend on it. Man has no inherent right to salvation, because by his fall in the Garden of Eden we are all sinners; he can, however, win this by identifying himself with the Sacrifice of Christ. According to some Protestant sects, faith alone will avail, however great a man's sinfulness : in the Catholic Church he cannot be saved if he die in mortal (that is, in serious and deliberate) sin without absolution, even if he is a believer. In both cases, however, he has the remedy at his disposal. The doctrine of Predestination, which has been held by some Protestant sects, and which teaches that certain souls are destined to be saved or lost, has never been a central feature of Christianity, where individual choice and free-will rank so highly. Belief in a final Hell has been a stumbling-block, not only because of the terrible alternative which it puts before men, but because it suggests a dualism in which evil will continue to exist side by side with good and so prevent the ultimate triumph of God. The Christian Churches have, however, fearlessly accepted this contradiction. It is not an article of faith to believe that anyone is damned, but the possibility of losing the chance of redemption forever emphasizes to the full the responsibility of choice. The stress in Christianity is thus on the individual and on his own power to make his fate. In modern times these doctrines have tended to recede into the background in favour of a more easygoing Christianity. The very word " salvation " means little to most people, and concentration is rather on this world than on the next. The result as seen in the general life of society is not altogether promising, and raises the question as to whether religions can survive without the background of their dogmas and with the elimination of their harder demands. There remains, none the less, a wide diffusion of Christian principles and an effort to hold to these, even where much of the dogmatic framework is discarded as " outworn." This shows itself in vigorous support of the rights of individual men, as against the doctrines of totalitarian ideologies. It may be said, in fact, that the latest stand of Christianity is the defence of the individual. Behind this defence there is ever the figure of Jesus of Nazareth, whose life, death, and teaching were the guiding inspiration and comfort of countless millions in the Ages of Faith, and which still, after some nineteen and a half centuries, have the power to attract and to show new forms of adaptation. Christianity is pre-eminently the religion of a Person and of Personality.

Verses from the Scriptures

ABBREVIATIONS TO REFERENCES

All quotations are from the Holy Bible.

Col.	= Colossians	*Rev.*	= Revelation
Eph.	= Ephesians	*Rom.*	= Romans
Gal.	= Galatians	*Thes.*	= Thessalonians
Heb.	= Hebrews	*Tim.*	= Timothy
Matt.	= St. Matthew		

If ye **abide** in me, and my words abide in you, ye shall ask what ye will, and it shall be done unto you. *John* 15, 7.

Set your **affection** on things above, not on things on the earth. *Col.* 3, 2.

He that is not with me is **against** me; and he that gathereth not with me scattereth abroad. *Matt.* 12, 30.

Sell that ye have, and give **alms**; provide yourselves bags which wax not old, a treasure in the heavens that faileth not, where no thief approacheth, neither moth corrupteth. For where your treasure is, there will your heart be also. *Luke* 12, 33–4.

Ask, and it shall be given you; seek, and ye shall find; knock, and it shall be opened unto you. For everyone that asketh receiveth; and he that seeketh findeth; and to him that knocketh it shall be opened. *Luke* 11, 9–10.

Ye have not, because ye **ask** not. Ye ask, and receive not, because ye ask amiss. *James* 4, 2–3.

Let all **bitterness**, and wrath, and anger, and clamour, and evil-speaking, be put away from you, with all malice. And be ye kind one to another, tender-hearted, forgiving one another, even as God for Christ's sake hath forgiven you. *Eph.* 4, 31–2.

God hath made of one **blood** all nations of men. *Acts* 17, 26.

There is one **body**, and one spirit . . . one Lord, one faith, one baptism, one God and father of all, who is above all, and through all, and in you all. *Eph.* 4, 4–6.

As the **branch** cannot bear fruit of itself, except it abide in the vine; no more can ye, except ye abide in me. I am the vine, ye are the branches : he that abideth in me, and I in him, the same bringeth forth much fruit : for without me ye can do nothing. *John* 15, 4–5.

It is written, that man shall not live by **bread** alone, but by every word of God. *Luke* 4, 4.

Or what man is there of you, whom if his son ask **bread**, will he give him a stone ? *Matt.* 7, 9.

Inasmuch as ye have done it unto one of the least of these my **brethren**, ye have done it unto me. *Matt.* 25, 40.

It is neither good to eat flesh, nor to drink wine, nor any thing whereby thy **brother stumbleth**, or is offended, or is made weak. *Rom.* 14, 21.

If thy **brother trespass** against thee, rebuke him; and if he repent, forgive him. And if he trespass against thee seven times in a day, and seven times in a day turn again to thee, saying I repent; thou shalt forgive him. *Luke* 17, 3–4.

Let **brotherly love** continue. Be not forgetful to entertain strangers; for thereby some have entertained angels unawares. Remember them that are in bonds, as bound with them; and them which suffer adversity, as being yourselves also in the body. *Heb.* 13, 1–3.

For many are **called**, but few are chosen. *Matt.* 22, 14.

It is easier for a **camel** to go through the eye of a needle, than for a rich man to enter into the kingdom of God. *Matt.* 19, 24.

For to be **carnally minded** is death; but to be spiritually minded is life and peace. For if ye live after the flesh ye shall die : but if ye through the spirit do mortify the deeds of the body, ye shall live. *Rom.* 8, 6, 13.

And above all things have fervent **charity** among yourselves : for charity shall cover the multitude of sins. Use hospitality one to another without grudging. *I Peter* 4, 8–9.

For whom the Lord loveth he **chasteneth**. *Heb.* 12, 6.

Suffer little **children**, and forbid them not, to come unto me, for of such is the kingdom of heaven. *Matt.* 19, 14; *Mark* 10, 14; *Luke* 18, 16.

Verily I say unto you, except ye become converted, and become as little **children**, ye shall not enter into the kingdom of heaven. Whosoever therefore shall humble himself as this little child, the same is greatest in the kingdom of heaven. And whoso shall receive one such little child in my name, receiveth me. But whoso shall offend one of these little ones which believe in me, it were better for him that a millstone were hanged about his neck, and that he were drowned in the depth of the sea. *Matt.* 18, 3–6.

I will not leave you **comfortless** : I will come to you. *John* 14, 18.

If ye love me keep my **commandments**. *John* 14, 15.

Mind not high things, but **condescend** to men of low estate. Be not wise in your own conceits. *Rom.* 12, 16.

I have learned in whatsover state I am, therewith to be **content**. *Phil.* 4, 11.

Be thou faithful unto **death**, and I will gi... life. *Rev.* 2, 10.

God will render to every man according to ... 2, 6.

And whatsoever ye **do**, do it heartily, as to ... unto men. *Col.* 3, 23.

All things whatsoever ye would that men should **do** to you, do ye even so to them : for this is the law and the prophets. *Matt.* 7, 12; *Luke* 6, 31.

Whether therefore ye **eat**, or drink, or whatsoever ye do, do all to the glory of God. *I Cor.* 10, 31.

Be not overcome of **evil**, but overcome evil with good. *Rom.* 12, 21.

See that none render **evil** for evil unto any man; but ever follow that which is good, both among yourselves, and to all men. Rejoice evermore. Pray without ceasing. In everything give thanks. . . . Prove all things; hold fast that which is good. Abstain from all appearance of evil, and the very God of Peace sanctify you wholly. *I Thess.* 5, 15–23.

And whosoever shall **exalt** himself shall be abased; and he that shall humble himself shall be exalted. *Matt.* 23, 12.

First cast out the beam out of thine own **eye**; and then shalt thou see clearly to cast out the mote out of thy brother's eye. *Matt.* 7, 5.

Eye hath not seen, nor ear heard, neither have entered into the heart of man, the things which God hath prepared for them that love him. *I Cor.* 2, 9.

What doth it profit my brethren though a man say he hath **faith**, and have not works ? Can faith save him ? Faith without works is dead. *James* 2, 26.

Faith is the substance of things hoped for, the evidence of things not seen. *Heb.* 11, 1.

Watch ye, stand fast in the **faith**, quit you like men, be strong. Let all your things be done with charity. *I Cor.* 16, 13–14.

He that is **faithful** in that which is least, is faithful also in much; and he that is unjust in the least, is unjust also in much. *Luke* 16, 10.

ware of **false prophets**, which come to you in sheep's
clothing, but inwardly they are ravening wolves. *Matt.* 7, 15.

For whosoever shall do the will of my **Father** which is in heaven,
the same is my brother, and sister, and mother. *Matt.* 12, 50.

Confess your **faults** one to another, and pray one for another,
that ye may be healed. The effectual fervent prayer of a righteous man availeth much. *James* 5, 16.

When thou makest a **feast** call the poor, the maimed, the lame,
the blind; and thou shalt be blessed; for they cannot recompense
thee. *Luke* 14, 13–14.

For where two or three are **gathered** together in my name,
there am I in the midst of them. *Matt.* 18, 20.

Give, and it shall be given unto you; good measure, pressed
down and shaken together, and running over, shall men give into
your bosom. For with the same measure that ye mete withal it
shall be measured to you again. *Luke* 6, 38.

Every man according as he purposeth in his heart, so let him
give; not grudgingly, or of necessity : for God loveth a cheerful
giver. *II Cor.* 9, 7.

It is more blessed to **give** than to receive. *Acts* 20, 35.

Give to every man that asketh of thee; and of him that taketh
away thy goods ask them not again. *Luke* 6, 30.

With **God** all things are possible. *Matt.* 19, 26; *Mark* 10, 27.

God is light, and in him is no darkness at all. *I John* 1, 5.

Of a truth I perceive that **God** is no respecter of persons : but
in every nation he that feareth him, and worketh righteousness, is
accepted with him. *Acts* 10, 34–5.

Godliness is great riches, if a man be content with that he
hath; for we brought nothing into the world, neither may we
carry any thing out. *I Tim.* 6, 6–7.

And we know that all things work together for **good** to them
that love God. *Rom.* 8, 28.

And if ye do **good** to them which do good to you, what thank
have ye ? for sinners also do even the same. *Luke* 6, 33.

Whosoever will be **great** among you, let him be your minister; and whosoever will be chief among you let him be your servant. *Matt.* 20, 26–7.

But he that is **greatest** among you shall be your servant. And whosoever shall exalt himself shall be abased; and he that shall humble himself shall be exalted. *Matt.* 23, 11–12.

We then that are strong ought to bear the **infirmities** of the weak, and not to please ourselves. *Rom.* 15, 1.

There is neither **Jew** nor Greek, there is neither bond nor free, there is neither male nor female : for ye are all one in Christ Jesus. *Gal.* 3, 28.

Judge not, and ye shall not be judged; condemn not, and ye shall not be condemned : forgive, and ye shall be forgiven. *Luke* 6, 37; *Matt.* 7, 1.

For wherein thou **judgest** another, thou condemnest thyself; for thou that judgest doest the same things. *Rom.* 2, 1.

Seek ye first the **Kingdom of God**, and his righteousness; and all these things shall be added unto you. *Matt.* 6, 33.

Come unto me all ye that **labour** and are heavy laden, and I will give you rest. *Matt.* 11, 28.

The **letter** killeth, but the spirit maketh alive. *II Cor.* 3, 6.

For whosoever will save his **life** shall lose it : and whosoever will lose his life for my sake, the same shall save it. For what is a man profited, if he shall gain the whole world and lose his own soul ? Or what shall a man give in exchange for his soul ? *Matt.* 16, 25–6; *Luke* 9, 24.

Take no thought for your **life**, what ye shall eat, or what ye shall drink; nor yet for your body, what ye shall put on. Is not the life more than meat, and the body than raiment ? *Matt.* 6, 25; *Luke* 12, 22.

Let your **light** so shine before men, that they may see your good works, and glorify your father which is in heaven. *Matt.* 5, 16.

And why take ye thought for raiment ? Consider the **lilies** of the field how they grow, they toil not neither do they spin : and yet I say unto you, that even Solomon in all his glory was not arrayed like one of these. *Matt.* 6, 28–9; *Luke* 12, 27.

God is **love**; and he that dwelleth in love dwelleth in God, and God in him. *I John* 4, 15.

There is no fear in **love** : but perfect love casteth out fear. *I John* 4, 18.

Greater **love** hath no man than this, that a man lay down his life for his friends. *John* 15, 13.

If ye **love** me, keep my commandments; and I will pray the father and he shall give you another comforter, that he may abide with you for ever. *John* 14, 15–16.

A new commandment I give unto you, that ye **love** one another, as I have loved you, that ye also love one another. By this shall all men know that ye are my disciples, if ye have love one to another. *John* 13, 34–5.

Thou shalt **love** the Lord thy God with all thy heart, and with all thy soul, and with all thy mind. This is the first and great commandment, and the second is like unto it, thou shalt love thy neighbour as thyself. On these two commandments, hang all the law and the prophets. *Matt.* 22, 37–40.

Love your enemies, do good to them that hate you, bless them that curse you, and pray for them which despitefully use you. And unto him that smiteth thee on the one cheek, offer also the other; and him that taketh away thy cloak forbid not to take thy coat also. *Luke* 6, 27–9; *Matt.* 5, 39–40.

He that **loveth** not knoweth not God; for God is love. *I John* 4, 8.

For the love of **money** is the root of all evil. *I Tim.* 6, 10.

Take therefore no thought for the **morrow**, for the morrow shall take thought for the things of itself. Sufficient unto the day is the evil thereof. *Matt.* 6, 34.

The **night** is far spent, the day is at hand : let us therefore cast off the works of darkness, and let us put on the armour of light. *Rom.* 13, 12.

All these things spake Jesus unto the multitude in **parables** : and without a parable spake he not unto them, that it might be fulfilled which was spoken by the prophet, saying, I will open my mouth in parables; I will utter things which have been kept secret from the foundation of the world. *Matt.* 13, 34-5.

Peace I leave with you, my peace I give unto you; not as the world giveth, give I unto you. Let not your heart be troubled, neither let it be afraid. *John* 14, 27.

The **peace of God** which passeth all understanding, shall keep your hearts and minds. *Phil.* 4, 7.

They that are whole need not a **physician**; but they that are sick. I came not to call the righteous, but sinners to repentance. *Luke* 5, 31-2; *Mark* 2, 17.

No man having put his hand to the **plough**, and looking back, is fit for the kingdom of God. *Luke* 9, 62.

And all things, whatsoever ye shall ask in **prayer**, believing, ye shall receive. *Matt.* 21, 22.

A **prophet** is not without honour, save in his own country, and in his own house. *Matt.* 13, 57.

These things have I (Jesus) spoken unto you in **proverbs** : but the time cometh when I shall no more speak unto you in proverbs. *John* 16, 25.

Unto the **pure** all things are pure. *Titus* 1, 15.

Pure **religion** and undefiled before God and the father is this, to visit the fatherless and widows in their affliction, and to keep himself unspotted from the world. *James* 1, 27.

I am the **resurrection**, and the life : he that believeth in me, though he were dead, yet shall he live. And whosoever liveth and believeth in me, shall never die. *John* 11, 25-6.

Be ye therefore wise as **serpents**, and harmless as doves. *Matt.* 10, 16.

Thou fool, that which thou **sowest** is not quickened, except it die. *I Cor.* 15, 36.

Be not deceived; God is not mocked; for whatsoever a man **soweth**, that shall he also reap. *Gal.* 6, 7.

Are not two **sparrows** sold for a farthing ? and one of them shall not fall on the ground without your father. But the very hairs of your head are all, numbered. *Matt.* 10, 29–30; *Luke* 12, 6.

Woe unto you, when all men shall **speak well** of you. *Luke* 6, 26.

Let nothing be done through **strife** or vainglory; but in lowliness of mind let each esteem others better than themselves. *Phil.* 2, 3.

Watch and pray that ye enter not into **temptation** : the spirit indeed is willing but the flesh is weak. *Matt.* 26, 41; *Mark* 14, 38.

Whatsoever things are **true**, whatsoever things are honest, whatsoever things are just, whatsoever things are pure, whatsoever things are lovely, whatsoever things are of good report; if there be any virtue, and if there be any praise, think on these things. *Phil.* 4, 8.

The **wisdom** of this world is foolishness with God. *I Cor.* 3, 19.

Readings from the Scriptures

The same day went Jesus out of the house, and sat by the sea side. And great multitudes were gathered together unto him, so that he went into a ship, and sat; and the whole multitude stood on the shore. And he spake many things unto them in parables, saying, Behold, a sower went forth to sow; and when he sowed, some seeds fell by the way side, and the fowls came and devoured them up; some fell upon stony places, where they had not much earth : and forthwith they sprung up, because they had no deepness of earth : and when the sun was up, they were scorched; and because they had no root, they withered away. And some fell among thorns; and the thorns sprung up, and choked them : but other fell into good ground, and brought forth fruit, some an hundredfold, some sixtyfold, some thirtyfold. Who hath ears to hear, let him hear. And the disciples came, and said unto him, Why speakest thou unto them in parables ? He answered and said unto them, Because it is given unto you to know the mysteries of the kingdom of heaven, but to them it is not given. For whosoever hath, to him shall be given, and he shall have more abundance : but whosoever hath not, from him shall be taken away even that he hath. Therefore speak I to them in parables : because they seeing see not; and hearing they hear not, neither do they understand. And in them is fulfilled the prophecy of Esaias, which saith, By hearing ye shall hear, and shall not understand; and seeing ye shall see, and shall not perceive : For this people's heart is waxed gross, and their ears are dull of hearing, and their eyes they have closed; lest at any time they should see with their eyes, and hear with their ears, and should understand with their heart, and should be converted, and I should heal them. But blessed are your eyes, for they see : and your ears, for they hear. For verily I say unto you, that many prophets and righteous men have desired to see those things which ye see, and have not seen them; and to hear those things which ye hear, and have not heard them.

Hear ye therefore the parable of the sower: When any one heareth the word of the kingdom, and understandeth it not, then cometh the wicked one, and catcheth away that which was sown in his heart. This is he which received seed by the way side. But he that received the seed into stony places, the same is he that heareth the word, and anon with joy receiveth it; yet hath he not root in himself, but dureth for a while : for when tribulation or persecution ariseth because of the word, by and by he is offended. He also that received seed among the thorns is he that heareth the word; and the care of this world, and the deceitfulness of riches, choke the word, and he becometh unfruitful. But he that received seed into the good ground is he that heareth the word, and understandeth it; which also beareth fruit, and bringeth forth, some an hundredfold, some sixty, some thirty.

Another parable put he forth unto them, saying, The kingdom of heaven is likened unto a man which sowed good seed in his field : but while men slept, his enemy came and sowed tares among the wheat, and went his way. But when the blade was sprung up, and brought forth fruit, then appeared the tares also. So the servants of the householder came and said unto him, Sir, didst not thou sow good seed in thy field ? from whence then hath it tares ? He said unto them, An enemy hath done this. The servants said unto him, Wilt thou then that we go and gather them up ? But he said, Nay; lest while ye gather up the tares, ye root up also the wheat with them. Let both grow together until the harvest : and in the time of harvest I will say to the reapers,

Gather ye together first the tares, and bind them in bundles to burn them : but gather the wheat into my barn.

Another parable put he forth unto them, saying, The kingdom of heaven is like to a grain of mustard seed, which a man took, and sowed in his field : which indeed is the least of all seeds : but when it is grown, it is the greatest among herbs, and becometh a tree, so that the birds of the air come and lodge in the branches thereof.

Another parable spake he unto them ; The kingdom of heaven is like unto leaven, which a woman took, and hid in three measures of meal till the whole was leavened. All these things spake Jesus unto the multitude in parables; and without a parable spake he not unto them : that it might be fulfilled which was spoken by the prophet, saying, I will open my mouth in parables; I will utter things which have been kept secret from the foundation of the world. Then Jesus sent the multitude away, and went into the house : and his disciples came unto him, saying, Declare unto us the parable of the tares of the field. He answered and said unto them, He that soweth the good seed is the Son of man; the field is the world; the good seed are the children of the kingdom; but the tares are the children of the wicked one; the enemy that sowed them is the devil; the harvest is the end of the world; and the reapers are the angels. As therefore the tares are gathered and burned in the fire; so shall it be in the end of this world. *Matt.* 13, 1–40.

And seeing the multitudes, he went up into a mountain : and when he was set, his disciples came unto him : and he opened his mouth, and taught them, saying,

Blessed are the poor in spirit : for theirs is the kingdom of heaven. Blessed are they that mourn : for they shall be comforted. Blessed are the meek : for they shall inherit the earth. Blessed are they which do hunger and thirst after righteousness : for they shall be filled. Blessed are the merciful, for they shall obtain mercy. Blessed are the pure in heart : for they shall see God. Blessed are the peacemakers : for they shall be called the children of God. Blessed are they which are persecuted for righteousness' sake : for theirs is the kingdom of heaven. Blessed are ye, when men shall revile you, and persecute you, and shall say all manner of evil against you falsely, for my sake. Rejoice and be exceeding glad : for great is your reward in heaven : for so persecuted they the prophets which were before you.

Ye are the salt of the earth : but if the salt have lost his savour, wherewith shall it be salted ? It is thenceforth good for nothing, but to be cast out, and to be trodden under foot of men. Ye are the light of the world. A city that is set on an hill cannot be hid. Neither do men light a candle, and put it under a bushel, but on a candlestick; and it giveth light unto all that are in the house. Let your light so shine before men, that they may see your good works, and glorify your Father which is in heaven. (The Beatitudes). *Matt.* 5, 1–16.

Think not that I am come to destroy the law, or the prophets : I am not come to destroy, but to fulfil. For verily I say unto you, Till heaven and earth pass, one jot or one tittle shall in no wise pass from the law, till all be fulfilled. Whosoever therefore shall break one of these least commandments, and shall teach men so, he shall be called the least in the kingdom of heaven : but whosoever shall do and teach them, the same shall be called great in the kingdom of heaven. For I say unto you, That except your righteousness shall exceed the righteousness of the scribes and Pharisees, ye shall in no case enter into the kingdom of heaven. Ye have heard that it was said by them of old time, Thou shalt not kill; and whosoever shall kill shall be in danger of the judgement. But I say unto you, That whosoever is angry with his brother without a cause shall be in danger of the judgement : and whosoever shall say to his brother, Raca, shall be in danger of the council : but whosoever shall say, Thou fool, shall be in danger of hell fire. Therefore if thou bring thy gift to the altar, and there rememberest that thy brother hath aught against thee; leave there thy gift before the altar, and go thy way : first be reconciled to thy brother, and then come and offer thy gift. Agree with thine adversary quickly, whiles thou art in the way with him; lest at any time the adversary deliver thee to the judge, and the judge deliver thee to the officer, and thou be cast into prison. Verily I say unto thee, Thou shalt by no means come out thence, till thou hast paid the uttermost farthing. Ye have heard that it was said by them of old time, Thou shalt not commit adultery. But I say unto you, That whosoever looketh on a woman to lust after her hath committed adultery with her already in his heart.

And if thy right eye offend thee, pluck it out, and cast it from thee : for it is profitable for thee that one of thy members should perish, and not that thy whole body should be cast into hell. And if thy right hand offend thee, cut it off, and cast it from thee : for it is profitable for thee that one of thy members should perish, and not that thy whole body should be cast into hell. It hath been said, Whosoever shall put away his wife, let him give her a writing of divorcement. But I say unto you, That whosoever shall put away his wife, saving for the cause of fornication, causeth her to commit adultery : and whosoever shall marry her that is divorced committeth adultery. Again, ye have heard that it hath been said by them of old time, Thou shalt not forswear thyself, but shalt perform unto the Lord thine oaths. But I say unto you, Swear not at all; neither by heaven; for it is God's throne; nor by the earth; for it is his footstool; neither by Jerusalem; for it is the city of the great King. Neither shalt thou swear by thy head, because thou canst not make one hair white or black. But let your communication be, Yea, yea; Nay, nay : for whatsoever is more than these cometh of evil. *Matt.* 5, 17–37.

Ye have heard that it hath been said, An eye for an eye, and a tooth for a tooth : But I say unto you, That ye resist not evil : but whosoever shall smite thee on thy right cheek, turn to him the other also. And if any man will sue thee at the law, and take away thy coat, let him have thy cloke also. And whosoever shall compel thee to go a mile, go with him twain. Give to him that asketh thee, and from him that would borrow of thee, turn not thou away. Ye have heard that it hath been said, Thou shalt love thy neighbour, and hate thine enemy. But I say unto you, Love your enemies, bless them that curse you, do good to them that hate you, and pray for them which despitefully use you, and persecute you; That ye may be the children of your Father which is in heaven : for he maketh his sun to rise on the evil and on the good, and sendeth rain on the just and on the unjust. For if ye love them which love you, what reward have ye ? do not even the publicans the same ? And if ye salute your brethren only, what do ye more than others ? do not even the publicans so ? Be ye therefore perfect, even as your Father which is in heaven is perfect. *Matt.* 5, 38–48.

Take heed that ye do not your alms before men, to be seen of them : otherwise ye have no reward of your Father, which is in heaven. Therefore when thou doest thine alms, do not sound a trumpet before thee, as the hypocrites do in the synagogues and in the streets, that they may have glory of men. Verily I say unto you, They have their reward. But when thou doest alms, let not thy left hand know what thy right hand doeth, that thine alms may be in secret : and thy Father which seeth in secret himself shall reward thee openly. And when thou prayest, thou shalt not be as the hypocrites are : for they love to pray standing in the synagogues and in the corners of the streets, that they may be seen of men. Verily I say unto you, They have their reward. But thou, when thou prayest, enter into thy closet, and when thou hast shut the door, pray to thy Father which is in secret; and thy Father which seeth in secret shall reward thee openly. But when ye pray, use not vain repetitions, as the heathen do : for they think that they shall be heard for their much speaking. Be not ye therefore like unto them, for your Father knoweth what things ye have need of, before ye ask him. After this manner therefore pray ye :

Our Father which art in heaven, hallowed be thy name. Thy kingdom come. Thy will be done in earth, as it is in heaven. Give us this day our daily bread. And forgive us our debts, as we forgive our debtors. And lead us not into temptation, but deliver us from evil : For thine is the kingdom, and the power, and the glory, for ever. Amen. For if ye forgive men their trespasses, your heavenly Father will also forgive you. But if ye forgive not men their trespasses, neither will your Father forgive your trespasses. *Matt.* 6, 1–15.

Lay not up for yourselves treasures upon earth, where moth and rust doth corrupt, and where thieves break through and steal. But lay up for yourselves treasures in heaven, where neither moth nor rust doth corrupt, and where thieves do not break through nor steal; for where your treasure is, there will your heart be also. The light of the body is the eye : if therefore thine eye be single, thy whole body shall be full of light. But if thine eye be evil, thy whole body shall be full of darkness. If therefore the light that is in thee be darkness, how great is that darkness. No man can serve two masters : for either he will hate the one, and love the other; or else he will hold to the one, and despise the other. Ye cannot serve God and mammon. *Matt.* 6, 19–24.

Judge not, that ye be not judged. For with what judgement ye judge, ye shall be judged : and with what measure ye mete, it shall be measured to you again. And why beholdest thou the mote that is in thy brother's eye, but considerest not the beam that is in thine own eye ? Or how wilt thou say to thy brother, Let me pull out the mote out of thine eye; and, behold, a beam is in thine own eye ? Thou hypocrite, first cast out the beam out of thine own eye; and then shalt thou see clearly to cast out the mote out of thy brother's eye. Give not that which is holy unto the dogs, neither cast ye your pearls before swine, lest they trample them under their feet, and turn again and rend you. Ask, and it shall be given you; seek and ye shall find; knock, and it shall be opened unto you. For every one that asketh receiveth; and he that seeketh findeth; and to him that knocketh it shall be opened. · Or what man is there of you, whom if his son ask bread, will he give him a stone ? Or if he ask a fish, will he give him a serpent ? If ye then, being evil, know how to give good gifts unto your children, how much more shall your Father which is in heaven give good things to them that ask him ? Therefore all things whatsoever ye would that men should do to you, do ye even so to them : for this is the law and the prophets. Enter ye in at the strait gate : for wide is the gate, and broad is the way, that leadeth to destruction, and many there be which go in thereat, because strait is the gate, and narrow is the way, which leadeth unto life, and few there be that find it. *Matt.* 7, 1–14.

Then said Jesus unto his disciples, If any man will come after me, let him deny himself, and take up his cross, and follow me. For whosoever will save his life shall lose it : and whosoever will lose his life for my sake shall find it. For what is a man profited, if he shall gain the whole world, and lose his own soul ? or what shall a man give in exchange for his soul ? For the Son of man shall come in the glory of his Father with his angels; and then he shall reward every man according to his works. Verily I say unto you, There be some standing here, which shall not taste of death, till they see the Son of man coming in his kingdom. *Matt.* 16, 24–8.

And as they were eating, Jesus took bread, and blessed it, and brake it, and gave it to the disciples, and said, Take, eat; this is my body. And he took the cup, and gave thanks, and gave it to them, saying, Drink ye all of it; For this is my blood of the new testament, which is shed for many for the remission of sins. *Matt.* 26, 26–8.

Then shall the kingdom of heaven be likened unto ten virgins, which took their lamps, and went forth to meet the bridegroom. And five of them were wise, and five were foolish. They that were foolish took their lamps, and took no oil with them. But the wise took oil in their vessels with their lamps. While the bridegroom tarried, they all slumbered and slept. And at midnight there was a cry made, Behold, the bridegroom cometh; go ye out to meet him. Then all those virgins arose, and trimmed their lamps. And the foolish said unto the wise, Give us of your oil; for our lamps are gone out. But the wise answered, saying, Not so; lest there be not enough for us and you : but go ye rather to them that sell, and buy for yourselves. And while they went to buy, the bridegroom came; and they that were ready went in with him to the marriage, and the door was shut. Afterward came also the other virgins, saying, Lord, Lord, open to us. But he answered and said, Verily I say unto you, I know you not. Watch therefore; for ye know neither the day nor the hour wherein the Son of man cometh. *Matt.* 25, 1–13.

And the apostles gathered themselves together unto Jesus, and told him all things, both what they had done, and what they had taught. And he said unto them, Come ye yourselves apart into a desert place, and rest awhile : for there were many coming and going, and they had no leisure so much as to eat. And they departed into a desert place by ship privately. And the people saw them departing, and many knew him, and ran afoot thither out of all cities, and outwent them, and came together unto him. And Jesus when he came out, saw much people, and was moved with compassion toward them, because they were as sheep not having a shepherd : and he began to teach them many things. And when the day was now far spent, his disciples came unto him, and said, This is a desert place, and now the time is far passed : send them away, that they may go into the country round about, and into the villages, and buy themselves bread : for they have nothing to eat. He answered and said unto them, Give ye them to eat. And they say unto him, Shall we go and buy two hundred penny-worth of bread, and give them to eat ? He saith unto them, How many loaves have ye ? go and see. And when they knew, they said, Five, and two fishes. And he commanded them to make all sit down by companies upon the green grass. And they sat down in ranks, by hundreds, and by fifties. And when he had taken the five loaves and the two fishes, he looked up to heaven, and blessed, and brake the loaves, and gave them to his disciples to set before them; and the two fishes divided he among them all. And they did all eat, and were filled. And they took up twelve baskets full of the fragments, and of the fishes. And they that did eat of the loaves, were about five thousand men. *Mark* 6, 30-44.

And they brought young children to him, that he should touch them; and his disciples rebuked those that brought them. But when Jesus saw it, he was much displeased, and said unto them, Suffer the little children to come unto me, and forbid them not; for of such is the kingdom of God. Verily I say unto you, Whosoever shall not receive the kingdom of God as a little child, he shall not enter therein. And he took them up in his arms, put his hands upon them, and blessed them. *Mark* 10, 13-16.

And one of the scribes came, and having heard them reasoning together, and perceiving that he had answered them well, asked him, Which is the first commandment of all ? And Jesus answered him, The first of all the commandments is, Hear, O Israel; The Lord our God is one Lord : and thou shalt love the Lord thy God with all thy heart, and with all thy soul, and with all thy mind, and with all thy strength : this is the first commandment. And the second is like, namely this, Thou shalt love thy neighbour as thyself. There is none other commandment greater than these. *Mark* 12, 28-31.

And Jesus being full of the Holy Ghost returned from Jordan, and was led by the Spirit into the wilderness, being forty days tempted of the devil. And in those days he did eat nothing : and when they were ended, he afterward hungered. And the devil said unto him, If thou be the Son of God, command this stone that it be made bread. And Jesus answered him, saying,

It is written, That man shall not live by bread alone, but by every word of God. And the devil, taking him up into a high mountain, showed unto him all the kingdoms of the world in a moment of time. And the devil said unto him, All this power will I give thee, and the glory of them : for that is delivered unto me; and to whomsoever I will I give it. If thou therefore wilt worship me, all shall be thine. And Jesus answered and said unto him, Get thee behind me, Satan : for it is written, Thou shalt worship the Lord thy God, and him only shalt thou serve. And he brought him to Jerusalem, and set him on a pinnacle of the temple, and said unto him, If thou be the Son of God, cast thyself down from hence, for it is written, He shall give his angels charge over thee, to keep thee, and in their hands they shall bear thee up, lest at any time thou dash thy foot against a stone. And Jesus answering said unto him, It is said, Thou shalt not tempt the Lord thy God. And when the devil had ended all the temptation, he departed from him for a season. *Luke* 4, 1–13.

And it came to pass, that, as the people pressed upon him to hear the word of God, he stood by the lake of Gennesaret, and saw two ships standing by the lake : but the fishermen were gone out of them, and were washing their nets. And he entered into one of the ships, which was Simon's, and prayed him that he would thrust out a little from the land. And he sat down, and taught the people out of the ship. Now when he had left speaking, he said unto Simon, Launch out into the deep, and let down your nets for a draught. And Simon answering said unto him, Master, we have toiled all the night, and have taken nothing : nevertheless at thy word I will let down the net. And when they had this done, they enclosed a great multitude of fishes : and their net brake. And they beckoned unto their partners, which were in the other ship, that they should come and help them. And they came, and filled both the ships, so that they began to sink. When Simon Peter saw it, he fell down at Jesus' knees, saying, Depart from me; for I am a sinful man, O Lord. For he was astonished, and all that were with him, at the draught of the fishes which they had taken. And so was also James, and John, the sons of Zebedee, which were partners with Simon. And Jesus said unto Simon, Fear not; from henceforth thou shalt catch men. And when they had brought their ships to land, they forsook all, and followed him. And it came to pass, when he was in a certain city, behold a man full of leprosy; who seeing Jesus fell on his face, and besought him, saying, Lord, if thou wilt, thou canst make me clean. And he put forth his hand, and touched him, saying, I will: be thou clean. And immediately the leprosy departed from him. And he charged him to tell no man : but go, and show thyself to the priest, and offer for thy cleansing, according as Moses commanded, for a testimony unto them. But so much the more went there a fame abroad of him: and great multitudes came together to hear, and to be healed by him of their infirmities. And he withdrew himself into the wilderness, and prayed. *Luke* 5, 1–16.

The angel Gabriel was sent from God unto a city of Galilee, named Nazareth, to a virgin espoused to a man whose name was Joseph, of the house of David; and the virgin's name was Mary. And the angel came in unto her, and said, Hail, thou that art highly favoured, the Lord is with thee : blessed art thou among women. And when she saw him, she was troubled at his saying, and cast in her mind what manner of salutation this should be. And the angel said unto her, Fear not, Mary : for thou hast found favour with God. And, behold, thou shalt conceive in thy womb, and bring forth a son, and shalt call his name **Jesus.** He shall be great, and shall be called the Son of the Highest; and the Lord God shall give unto him the throne of his father David : and he shall reign over the house of Jacob for ever; and of his kingdom there shall be no end. Then said Mary unto the angel, How shall this be, seeing I know not a man ? And the angel answered and said unto her, The Holy Ghost shall come upon thee, and the power of the Highest shall overshadow thee : therefore also that holy thing which shall be born of thee shall be called the Son of God. . . . And Mary said, Behold the handmaid of the Lord; be it unto me according to thy word. And the angel departed from her. *Luke* 1, 26–35 and 38.

And Mary said : My soul doth magnify the Lord, and my spirit hath rejoiced in God, my Saviour. For he hath regarded the lowly estate of his handmaiden; for, behold, from henceforth all generations shall call me blessed. For he that is mighty hath done to me great things; and holy is his name. And his mercy is on them that fear him, from generation to generation.

He hath shewed strength with his arm. He hath scattered the proud in the imagination of their hearts. He hath put down the mighty from their seats, and exalted them of low degree. He hath filled the hungry with good things, and the rich he hath sent empty away. He hath holpen his servant Israel, in remembrance of his mercy; as he spake to our fathers, to Abraham, and to his seed for ever. (The Magnificat.) *Luke* 1, 46–55.

Blessed be the Lord God of Israel; for he hath visited and redeemed his people, and hath raised up an horn of salvation for us in the house of his servant David; as he spake by the mouth of his holy prophets, which have been since the world began; that we should be saved from our enemies, and from the hand of all that hate us; to perform the mercy promised to our fathers, and to remember his holy covenant; the oath which he sware to our father Abraham, that he would grant unto us, that we being delivered out of the hand of our enemies might serve him without fear, in holiness and righteousness before him, all the days of our life. And thou, child, shalt be called the Prophet of the Highest: for thou shalt go before the face of the Lord to prepare his ways; to give knowledge of salvation unto his people by the remission of their sins, through the tender mercy of our God, whereby the day-spring from on high hath visited us, to give light to them that sit in darkness and in the shadow of death, to guide our feet into the way of peace. (The Benedictus.) *Luke* 1, 68–79.

And he said, A certain man had two sons: and the younger of them said to his father, Father, give me the portion of goods that falleth to me. And he divided unto them his living. And not many days after the younger son gathered all together, and took his journey into a far country, and there wasted his substance with riotous living. And when he had spent all, there arose a mighty famine in that land; and he began to be in want. And he went and joined himself to a citizen of that country; and he sent him into his fields to feed swine. And he would fain have filled his belly with the husks that the swine did eat: and no man gave unto him. And when he came to himself, he said, How many hired servants of my father's have bread enough and to spare, and I perish with hunger! I will arise and go to my father, and will say unto him, Father, I have sinned against heaven, and before thee, and am no more worthy to be called thy son : make me as one of thy hired servants. And he arose, and came to his father. But when he was yet a great way off, his father saw him, and had compassion, and ran, and fell on his neck, and kissed him. And the son said unto him, Father, I have sinned against heaven, and in thy sight, and am no more worthy to be called thy son. But the father said to his servants, Bring forth the best robe, and put it on him; and put a ring on his hand, and shoes on his feet : and bring hither the fatted calf, and kill it; and let us eat, and be merry : For this my son was dead, and is alive again; he was lost, and is found. And they began to be merry. Now his elder son was in the field : and as he came and drew nigh unto the house, he heard musick and dancing. And he called one of the servants, and asked what these things meant. And he said unto him, Thy brother is come; and thy father hath killed the fatted calf, because he hath received him safe and sound. And he was angry, and would not go in : therefore came his father out, and intreated him. And he answering said to his father, Lo, these many years do I serve thee, neither transgressed I at any time thy commandment : and yet thou never gavest me a kid, that I might make merry with my friends : But as soon as this thy son was come, which hath devoured thy living with harlots, thou hast killed for him the fatted calf. And he said unto him, Son, thou art ever with me, and all that I have is thine. It was meet that we should make merry, and be glad : for this thy brother was dead, and is alive again : and was lost and is found. *Luke* 15, 11–32.

And it came to pass in those days, that there went out a decree from Cæsar Augustus, that all the world should be taxed. (And this taxing was first made when Cyrenius was governor of Syria.) And all went to be taxed, every one into his own city. And Joseph also went up from Galilee, out of the city of Nazareth, into Judea, unto the city of David, which is called Bethlehem, (because he was of the house and lineage of David,) to be taxed with Mary his espoused wife, being great with child. And so it was, that, while they were there, the days were accomplished that she should be delivered. And she brought forth her firstborn son, and wrapped him in swaddling clothes, and laid him in a manger; because there was no room for them in the inn. And there were in the same country shepherds abiding in the field, keeping watch over their flock by night.   And, lo, the angel of the Lord came upon them, and the glory of the Lord shone round about them; and they were sore afraid.   And the angel said unto them, Fear not : for, behold, I bring you good tidings of great joy, which shall be to all people.   For unto you is born this day in the city of David a Saviour, which is Christ the Lord.   And this shall be a sign unto you; Ye shall find the babe wrapped in swaddling clothes, lying in a manger.   And suddenly there was with the angel a multitude of the heavenly host praising God, and saying, Glory to God in the highest, and on earth peace, good will toward men.   And it came to pass, as the angels were gone away from them into heaven, the shepherds said one to another, Let us now go even unto Bethlehem, and see this thing which is come to pass, which the Lord hath made known unto us.   And they came with haste, and found Mary and Joseph, and the babe lying in a manger.   And when they had seen it, they made known abroad the saying which was told them concerning this child.   And all they that heard it wondered at those things which were told them by the shepherds.   But Mary kept all these things, and pondered them in her heart.   And the shepherds returned, glorifying and praising God for all the things that they had heard and seen, as it was told unto them.   And when eight days were accomplished for the circumcising of the child, his name was called **Jesus,** which was so named of the angel before he was conceived in the womb.   *Luke* 2, 1–21.

And, behold, a certain lawyer stood up, and tempted him, saying, Master, what shall I do to inherit eternal life ? He said unto him, What is written in the law ? how readest thou ? And he answering said, Thou shalt love the Lord thy God with all thy heart, and with all thy soul, and with all thy strength, and with all thy mind; and thy neighbour as thyself.   And he said unto him, Thou hast answered right : this do and thou shalt live. But he, willing to justify himself, said unto Jesus, And who is my neighbour ? And Jesus answering said, A certain man went down from Jerusalem to Jericho, and fell among thieves, which stripped him of his raiment, and wounded him, and departed, leaving him half dead.   And by chance there came down a certain priest that way : and when he saw him, he passed by on the other side. And likewise a Levite, when he was at the place, came and looked on him, and passed by on the other side. But a certain Samaritan, as he journeyed, came where he was : and when he saw him, he had compassion on him, and went to him, and bound up his wounds, pouring in oil and wine, and set him on his own beast, and brought him to an inn, and took care of him. And on the morrow when he departed, he took out two pence, and gave them to the host, and said unto him, Take care of him; and whatsoever thou spendest more, when I come again, I will repay thee. Which now of these three, thinkest thou, was neighbour unto him that fell among the thieves ? And he said, He that shewed mercy on him. Then said Jesus unto him, Go, and do thou likewise. *Luke* 10, 25–37.

And he said unto his disciples, Therefore I say unto you, Take no thought for your life, what ye shall eat : neither for the body, what ye shall put on. The life is more than meat, and the body is more than raiment. Consider the ravens : for they neither sow nor reap; which neither have storehouse nor barn; and God feedeth them : how much more are ye better than the fowls ? And which of you with taking thought can add to his stature one cubit ? If ye then be not able to do that thing which is least, why take ye thought for the rest ? Consider the lilies how they grow : they toil not, they spin not; and yet I say unto you, that Solomon in all his glory was not arrayed like one of these. If then God so clothe the grass, which is to-day in the field, and to-morrow is cast into the oven; how much more will he clothe you, O ye of little faith ? And seek not ye what ye shall eat, or what ye shall drink, neither be ye of doubtful mind. For all these things do the nations of the world seek after : and your Father knoweth that ye have need of these things. But rather seek ye the Kingdom of God; and all these things shall be added unto you. *Luke* 12, 22–31.

These words spake Jesus, and lifted up his eyes to heaven, and said, Father, the hour is come; glorify thy Son, that thy Son may also glorify thee : As thou hast given him power over all flesh, that he should give eternal life to as many as thou hast given him. And this is life eternal, that they might know thee the only true God, and Jesus Christ, whom thou hast sent. I have glorified thee on the earth : I have finished the work which thou gavest me to do. And now, O Father, glorify thou me with thine own self with the glory which I had with thee before the world was. I have manifested thy name unto the men which thou gavest me out of the world : thine they were, and thou gavest them me; and they have kept thy word. Now they have known that all things whatsoever thou hast given me are of thee. For I have given unto them the words which thou gavest me; and they have received them, and have known surely that I came out from thee, and they have believed that thou didst send me. I pray for them : I pray not for the world, but for them which thou hast given me; for they are thine. And all mine are thine, and thine are mine; and I am glorified in them. And now I am no more in the world, but these are in the world, and I come to thee. Holy Father, keep through thine own name those whom thou hast given me, that they may be one, as we are. While I was with them in the world, I kept them in thy name : those that thou gavest me I have kept, and none of them is lost, but the son of perdition; that the scripture might be fulfilled. And now come I to thee; and these things I speak in the world, that they might have my joy fulfilled in themselves. I have given them thy word; and the world hath hated them, because they are not of the world, even as I am not of the world. I pray not that thou shouldst take them out of the world, but that thou shouldst keep them from the evil. They are not of the world, even as I am not of the world. Sanctify them through thy truth : thy word is truth. As thou hast sent me into the world, even so have I also sent them into the world. And for their sakes I sanctify myself, that they might also be sanctified through the truth. Neither pray I for these alone, but for them also which shall believe on me through their word; that they all may be one; as thou, Father, art in me, and I in thee, that they also may be one in us : that the world may believe that thou hast sent me. And the glory which thou gavest me I have given them; that they may be one, even as we are one. I in them, and thou in me, that they may be made perfect in one; and that the world may know that thou hast sent me, and hast loved them, as thou hast loved me. Father, I will that they also, whom thou hast given me, be with me where I am; that they may behold my glory, which thou hast given me : for thou lovedst me before the foundation of the world. O righteous Father, the world hath not known thee : but I have known thee, and these have known that thou hast sent me. And I have declared unto them thy name, and will declare it : that the love wherewith thou hast loved me may be in them, and I in them. *John* 17.

In the beginning was the Word, and the Word was with God, and the Word was God. The same was in the beginning with God. All things were made by him; and without him was not any thing made that was made. In him was life; and the life was the light of men. And the light shineth in darkness; and the darkness comprehended it not. There was a man sent from God, whose name was John. The same came for a witness, to bear witness of the Light, that all men through him might believe. He was not that light, but was sent to bear witness of that Light. That was the true light, which lighteth every man that cometh into the world. He was in the world, and the world was made by him, and the world knew him not. He came unto his own, and his own received him not. But as many as received him, to them gave he power to become the sons of God, even to them that believe on his name : Which were born, not of blood, nor of the will of the flesh, nor of the will of man, but of God. And the Word was made flesh, and dwelt among us, (and we beheld his glory, the glory as of the only begotten of the Father), full of grace and truth. *John* 1, 1–14.

There was a man of the Pharisees, named Nicodemus, a ruler of the Jews : the same came to Jesus by night, and said unto him, Rabbi, we know that thou art a teacher come from God : for no man can do these miracles that thou doest, except God be with him. Jesus answered and said unto him, Verily, verily, I say unto thee, Except a man be born again, he cannot see the Kingdom of God. Nicodemus saith unto him, How can a man be born when he is old ? can he enter the second time into his mother's womb, and be born ? Jesus answered, Verily, verily, I say unto thee, Except a man be born of water and of the Spirit, he cannot enter into the Kingdom of God. That which is born of the flesh is flesh; and that which is born of the Spirit is Spirit. Marvel not that I said unto thee, Ye must be born again. The wind bloweth where it listeth, and thou hearest the sound thereof, but canst not tell whence it cometh, and whither it goeth : so is every one that is born of the Spirit. Nicodemus answered and said unto him, How can these things be? Jesus answered and said unto him, Art thou a master of Israel, and knowest not these things? Verily, verily, I say unto thee, We speak that we do know, and testify that we have seen; and ye receive not our witness. If I have told you earthly things, and ye believe not, how shall ye believe, if I tell you of heavenly things? And no man hath ascended up to heaven, but he that came down from heaven, even the Son of man which is in heaven. *John* 3, 1–13.

And in that day ye shall ask me nothing. Verily, verily, I say unto you, Whatsoever ye shall ask the Father in my name, he will give it you. Hitherto have ye asked nothing in my name : ask, and ye shall receive, that your joy may be full. These things have I spoken unto you in proverbs : but the time cometh, when I shall no more speak unto you in proverbs, but I shall show you plainly of the Father. At that day ye shall ask in my name : and I say not unto you, that I will pray the Father for you : For the Father himself loveth you, because ye have loved me, and have believed that I came out from God. I came forth from the Father, and am come into the world : again, I leave the world, and go to the Father. His disciples said unto him, Lo, now speakest thou plainly, and speakest no proverb. Now are we sure that thou knowest all things, and needest not that any man should ask thee : by this we believe that thou camest forth from God. Jesus answered them, Do ye now believe? Behold, the hour cometh, yea, is now come, that ye shall be scattered, every man to his own, and. shall leave me alone : and yet I am not alone, because the Father is with me. These things I have spoken unto you, that in me ye might have peace. In the world ye shall have tribulation : but be of good cheer; I have overcome the world. *John* 16, 23–33.

Let not your heart be troubled : ye believe in God, believe also in me. In my Father's house are many mansions : if it were not so, I would have told you. I go to prepare a place for you. And if I go and prepare a place for you, I will come again, and receive you unto myself; that where I am, there ye may be also. And whither I go ye know, and the way ye know. Thomas saith unto him, Lord, we know not whither thou goest; and how can we know the way? Jesus saith unto him, I am the way, the truth, and the life : no man cometh unto the Father, but by me.

If ye had known me, ye should have known my Father also : and from henceforth ye know him, and have seen him. Philip saith unto him, Lord, shew us the Father, and it sufficeth us. Jesus saith unto him, Have I been so long time with you, and yet hast thou not known me, Philip ? he that hath seen me hath seen the Father; and how sayest thou then, Shew us the Father ? Believest thou not that I am in the Father, and the Father in me ? the words that I speak unto you I speak not of myself : but the Father that dwelleth in me, he doeth the works. Believe me that I am in the Father, and the Father in me : or else believe me for the very works' sake. Verily, verily, I say unto you, He that believeth on me, the works that I do shall he do also; and greater works than these shall he do; because I go unto my Father. And whatsoever ye shall ask in my name, that will I do, that the Father may be glorified in the Son. If ye shall ask any thing in my name, I will do it. If ye love me, keep my commandments. And I will pray the Father, and he shall give you another Comforter, that he may abide with you for ever; Even the Spirit of Truth; whom the world cannot receive, because it seeth him not, neither knoweth him : but ye know him; for he dwelleth with you, and shall be in you. I will not leave you comfortless : I will come to you. Yet a little while, and the world seeth me no more; but ye see me : because I live, ye shall live also. At that day ye shall know that I am in my Father, and ye in me, I in you. He that hath my commandments, and keepeth them, he it is that loveth me : and he that loveth me shall be loved of my Father, and I will love him, and will manifest myself to him. Judas saith unto him, (not Iscariot) Lord, how is it that thou wilt manifest thyself unto us, and not unto the world ? Jesus answered and saith unto him, If a man love me, he will keep my words : and my Father will love him, and we will come unto him, and make our abode with him. He that loveth me not keepeth not my sayings : and the word which ye hear is not mine, but the Father's which sent me. These things have I spoken unto you, being yet present with you. But the comforter, which is the Holy Ghost, whom the Father will send in my name, he shall teach you all things, and bring all things to your remembrance, whatsoever I have said unto you. Peace I leave with you, my peace I give unto you : not as the world giveth, give I unto you. Let not your heart be troubled, neither let it be afraid. Ye have heard how I said unto

you, I go away and come again unto you. If ye loved me, ye
would rejoice, because I said, I go unto the Father : for my
Father is greater than I. And now I have told you before it
come to pass, that, when it is come to pass, ye might believe.
Hereafter I will not talk much with you : for the prince of this
world cometh, and hath nothing in me. But that the world may
know that I love the Father; and as the Father gave me commandment, even so I do. Arise, let us go hence. *John* 14.

I am the good shepherd, and know my sheep, and am known of
mine. As the Father knoweth me, even so know I the Father :
and I lay down my life for the sheep. And other sheep I have,
which are not of this fold : them also I must bring, and they shall
hear my voice; and there shall be one fold, and one shepherd.
Therefore doth my Father love me, because I lay down my life,
that I might take it again. No man taketh it from me, but I lay
it down of myself. I have power to lay it down, and I have power
to take it again. This commandment have I received of my
Father. *John* 10, 14–18.

For God so loved the world, that he gave his only begotten
Son, that whosoever believeth in him should not perish, but have
everlasting life. For God sent not his Son into the world to
condemn the world; but that the world through him might be
saved. / He that believeth on him is not condemned : but he that
believeth not is condemned already, because he hath not believed
in the name of the only begotten Son of God. And this is the
condemnation, that light is come into the world, and men loved
darkness rather than light, because their deeds were evil. For
every one that doeth evil hateth the light, neither cometh to the
light, lest his deeds should be reproved. But he that doeth truth
cometh to the light, that his deeds may be made manifest, that
they are wrought in God. *John* 3, 16–21.

I am the true vine, and my Father is the husbandman. Every
branch in me that beareth not fruit he taketh away : and every
branch that beareth fruit, he purgeth it, that it may bring forth
more fruit. Now ye are clean through the word which I have
spoken unto you. Abide in me, and I in you. As the branch
cannot bear fruit of itself, except it abide in the vine; no more
can ye, except ye abide in me. I am the vine, ye are the branches :

He that abideth in me, and I in him, the same bringeth forth much fruit : for without me ye can do nothing. If a man abide not in me, he is cast forth as a branch, and is withered; and men gather them, and cast them into the fire, and they are burned. If ye abide in me, and my words abide in you, ye shall ask what ye will, and it shall be done unto you. Herein is my Father glorified, that ye bear much fruit; so shall ye be my disciples. As the Father hath loved me, so have I loved you : continue ye in my love. If ye keep my commandments, ye shall abide in my love; even as I have kept my Father's commandments, and abide in his love. These things have I spoken unto you, that my joy might remain in you, and that your joy might be full. This is my commandment, That ye love one another, as I have loved you. Greater love hath no man than this, that a man lay down his life for his friends. Ye are my friends, if ye do whatsoever I command you. Henceforth I call you not servants; for the servant knoweth not what his Lord doeth : but I have called you friends; for all things that I have heard of my Father I have made known unto you. Ye have not chosen me, but I have chosen you, and ordained you, that ye should go and bring forth fruit, and that your fruit should remain : that whatsoever ye shall ask of the Father in my name, he may give it you. These things I command you, that ye love one another. If the world hate you, ye know that it hated me before it hated you. If ye were of the world, the world would love his own : but because ye are not of the world, but I have chosen you out of the world, therefore the world hateth you. Remember the word that I said unto you, The servant is not greater than his lord. If they have persecuted me, they will also persecute you; if they have kept my saying, they will keep yours also. But all these things will they do unto you for my name's sake, because they know not him that sent me. If I had not come and spoken unto them, they had not had sin : but now they have no cloke for their sin. He that hateth me hateth my Father also. If I had not done among them the works which none other man did, they had not had sin : but now have they both seen and hated both me and my Father. But this cometh to pass, that the word might be fulfilled that is written in their law, They hated me without a cause. But when the Comforter is come, whom I will send unto you from the Father, even the Spirit of Truth, which proceedeth from the Father, he shall testify of me : And ye also shall bear witness, because ye have been with me from the beginning. *John* 15, 1–27.

Pilate then went out unto them, and said, What accusation bring ye against this man? They answered and said unto him, If he were not a malefactor, we would not have delivered him up unto thee. Then said Pilate unto them, Take ye him, and judge him according to your law. The Jews therefore said unto him, It is not lawful for us to put any man to death; that the saying of Jesus might be fulfilled, which he spake, signifying what death he should die. Then Pilate entered into the judgement hall again, and called Jesus, and said unto him, Art thou the King of the Jews? Jesus answered him, Sayest thou this thing of thyself, or did others tell it thee of me? Pilate answered, Am I a Jew? Thine own nation and the chief priests have delivered thee unto me: what hast thou done? Jesus answered, My kingdom is not of this world; if my kingdom were of this world, then would my servants fight, that I should not be delivered to the Jews: but now is my kingdom not from hence. Pilate therefore said unto him, Art thou a king then? Jesus answered, Thou sayest that I am a king. To this end was I born, and for this cause came I into the world, that I should bear witness unto the truth. Every one that is of the truth heareth my voice. Pilate saith unto him, What is truth? And when he had said this, he went out again unto the Jews, and saith unto them, I find in him no fault at all. But ye have a custom, that I should release unto you one at the passover: will ye therefore that I release unto you the King of the Jews? Then cried they all again, saying, Not this man, but Barabbas. Now Barabbas was a robber. *John* 18, 29–40.

Then Pilate therefore took Jesus, and scourged him. And the soldiers platted a crown of thorns, and put it on his head, and they put on him a purple robe, and said, Hail, King of the Jews! and they smote him with their hands. Pilate therefore went forth again, and saith unto them, Behold, I bring him forth to you, that ye may know that I find no fault in him. Then came Jesus forth, wearing the crown of thorns, and the purple robe. And Pilate saith unto them, Behold the man! When the chief priests therefore and officers saw him, they cried out, saying, Crucify him, crucify him. Pilate saith unto them, Take ye him, and crucify him : for I find no fault in him. The Jews answered him, We have a law, and by our law he ought to die, because he made himself the Son of God. When Pilate therefore heard that saying, he was the more afraid; and went again into the judgement hall, and saith unto Jesus, Whence art thou ? But Jesus gave him no answer. Then saith Pilate unto him, Speakest thou not unto me ? Knowest thou not that I have power to crucify thee, and have power to release thee ? Jesus answered, Thou couldest have no power at all against me, except it were given thee from above : therefore he that delivered me unto thee hath the greater sin. And from thenceforth Pilate sought to release him : but the Jews cried out, saying, If thou let this man go, thou art not Cæsar's friend : whosoever maketh himself a king speaketh against Cæsar. When Pilate therefore heard that saying, he brought Jesus forth, and sat down in the judgement seat in a place that is called the Pavement, but in the Hebrew, Gabbatha. And it was the preparation of the passover, and about the sixth hour : and he saith unto the Jews, Behold your King! But they cried out, Away with him, away with him, crucify him. Pilate saith unto them, Shall I crucify your King ? The chief priests answered, We have no King but Cæsar. Then delivered he him therefore unto them to be crucified. And they took Jesus, and led him away. . . . Then the soldiers, when they had crucified Jesus, took his garments, and made four parts, to every soldier a part; and also his coat; now the coat was without seam, woven from the top throughout. They said therefore among themselves, Let us not rend it, but cast lots for it, whose it shall be : that the Scripture might be fulfilled, which saith, They parted my raiment among them, and for my vesture they did cast lots. These things therefore the soldiers did. Now there stood by the cross of Jesus his mother, and his mother's sister, Mary the wife of Cleophas, and Mary Magdalene. When Jesus therefore saw his mother, and the disciple standing by, whom he loved, he saith unto his mother, Woman, behold thy son! Then saith he to the disciple, Behold thy mother! And from that hour that disciple took her unto his own home. *John* 19, 1–16, 23–7.

Now a certain man was sick, named Lazarus, of Bethany, the town of Mary and her sister Martha. (It was that Mary which anointed the Lord with ointment, and wiped his feet with her hair, whose brother Lazarus was sick.) Therefore his sisters sent unto him, saying, Lord, behold, he whom thou lovest is sick. When Jesus heard that, he said, This sickness is not unto death, but for the glory of God, that the Son of God might be glorified thereby. Now Jesus loved Martha, and her sister, and Lazarus. When he had heard therefore that he was sick, he abode two days still in the same place where he was. Then after that saith he to his disciples, Let us go into Judea again. His disciples say unto him, Master, the Jews of late sought to stone thee; and goest thou thither again ? Jesus answered, Are there not twelve hours in the day ? If any man walk in the day, he stumbleth not, because he seeth the light of this world. But if a man walk in the night, he stumbleth, because there is no light in him. These things said he : and after that he saith unto them, Our friend Lazarus sleepeth; but I go, that I may awake him out of sleep. Then said his disciples, Lord, if he sleep, he shall do well. Howbeit Jesus spake of his death : but they thought that he had spoken of taking of rest in sleep. Then said Jesus unto them plainly, Lazarus is dead. And I am glad for your sakes that I was not there, to the intent ye may believe; nevertheless let us go unto him. Then said Thomas, which is called Didymus, unto his fellow disciples, Let us also go, that we may die with him. Then when Jesus came, he found that he had lain in the grave four days already. Now Bethany was nigh unto Jerusalem, about fifteen furlongs off. And many of the Jews came to Martha and Mary, to comfort them concerning their brother. Then Martha, as soon as she heard that Jesus was coming, went and met him : but Mary sat still in the house. Then said Martha unto Jesus, Lord, if thou hadst been here, my brother had not died. But I know, that even now, whatsoever thou wilt ask of God, God will give it thee. Jesus saith unto her, Thy brother shall rise again. Martha saith unto him, I know that he shall rise again in the resurrection at the last day. Jesus said unto her, I am the resurrection, and the life : he that believeth in me, though he were dead, yet shall he live. And whosoever liveth and believeth in me shall never die. Believest thou this ? She saith unto him, Yea, Lord : I believe that thou art the Christ, the Son of God, which should come into the world. And when she had so said, she went her way, and called Mary her sister secretly, saying, The Master is come, and calleth for thee. As soon as she heard that, she arose quickly, and came unto him. Now Jesus was not yet come into the town, but was in that place where Martha met him. The Jews then which were with her in the house, and comforted her, when they saw Mary, that she rose up hastily and went out, followed her, saying, She goeth unto the grave to weep there. Then when Mary was come where Jesus was, and saw him, she fell down at his feet, saying unto him, Lord, if thou hadst been here, my brother had not died. When Jesus therefore saw her weeping, and the Jews also weeping which came with her, he groaned in the spirit, and was troubled, and said, Where have ye laid him? They say unto him, Lord, come and see. Jesus wept. Then said the Jews, Behold how he loved him! And some of them said, Could not this man, which opened the eyes of the blind, have caused that even this man should not have died? Jesus therefore again groaning in himself cometh to the grave. It was a cave, and a stone lay upon it. Jesus said, Take ye away the stone. Martha, the sister of him that was dead, saith unto him, Lord, by this time he stinketh : for he hath been dead four days. Jesus saith unto her, Said I not unto thee, that, if thou wouldest believe, thou shouldest see the glory of God? Then they took away the stone from the place where the dead was laid. And Jesus lifted up his eyes, and said, Father, I thank thee that thou hast heard me. And I knew that thou hearest me always, but because of the people which stand by I said it, that they may believe that thou hast sent me. And when he thus had spoken, he cried with a loud voice, Lazarus, come forth. And he that was dead came forth, bound hand and foot with grave-clothes; and his face was bound about with a napkin. Jesus saith unto them, Loose him, and let him go. Then many of the Jews which came to Mary, and had seen the things which Jesus did, believed on him. But some of them went their ways to the Pharisees, and told them what things Jesus had done. *John* 11, 1–46.

I am that bread of life. Your fathers did eat manna in the wilderness, and are dead. This is the bread which cometh down from heaven, that a man may eat thereof, and not die. I am the living bread which came down from heaven : if any man eat of this bread, he shall live for ever : and the bread that I will give is my flesh, which I will give for the life of the world. The Jews therefore strove among themselves, saying, How can this man give us his flesh to eat ? Then Jesus said unto them, Verily, verily, I say unto you, Except ye eat the flesh of the Son of man, and drink his blood, ye have no life in you. Whoso eateth my flesh, and drinketh my blood, hath eternal life; and I will raise him up at the last day. For my flesh is meat indeed, and my blood is drink indeed. He that eateth my flesh and drinketh my blood, dwelleth in me, and I in him. As the living Father hath sent me, and I live by the Father : so he that eateth me, even he shall live by me. This is that bread which came down from heaven : not as your fathers did eat manna, and are dead : he that eateth of this bread shall live for ever. *John* 6, 48–58.

Then spake Jesus again unto them, saying, I am the light of the world : he that followeth me shall not walk in darkness, but shall have the light of life. The Pharisees therefore said unto him, Thou bearest record of thyself; thy record is not true. Jesus answered and said unto them, Though I bear record of myself, yet my record is true : for I know whence I came, and whither I go. . . . Ye judge after the flesh; I judge no man. And yet if I judge, my judgement is true : for I am not alone, but I and the Father that sent me. It is also written in your law, that the testimony of two men is true. I am one that bear witness of myself, and the Father that sent me beareth witness of me. Then said they unto him, Where is thy Father ? Jesus answered, Ye neither know me, nor my Father : if ye had known me, ye should have known my Father also. These words spake Jesus in the treasury, as he taught in the temple : and no man laid hands on him; for his hour was not yet come. *John* 8, 12–20.

The first day of the week cometh Mary Magdalene early, when is was yet dark, unto the sepulchre, and seeth the stone taken away from the sepulchre. Then she runneth, and cometh to Simon Peter, and to the other disciple, whom Jesus loved, and saith unto them, They have taken away the Lord out of the sepulchre, and we know not where they have laid him. . . . Then cometh Simon Peter following him, and went into the sepulchre, and seeth the linen clothes lie, and the napkin, that was about his head, not lying with the linen clothes, but wrapped together in a place by itself. Then went in also that other disciple, which came first to the sepulchre, and he saw, and believed. For as yet they knew not the Scripture, that he must rise again from the dead. *John* 20, 1–2, 6–9.

And Saul, breathing out threatenings and slaughter against the disciples of the Lord, went unto the high priest, and desired of him letters to Damascus to the synagogues, that if he found any of this way, whether they were men or women, he might bring them bound unto Jerusalem. And as he journeyed, he came near Damascus : and suddenly there shined round about him a light from heaven. And he fell to the earth, and heard a voice saying unto him, Saul, Saul, why persecutest thou me ? And he said, Who art thou, Lord ? And the Lord said, I am Jesus whom thou persecutest. It is hard for thee to kick against the pricks. And he, trembling and astonished, said, Lord, what wilt thou have me to do ? And the Lord said unto him, Arise, and go into the city, and it shall be told thee what thou must do. And the men which journeyed with him stood speechless, hearing a voice, but seeing no man. And Saul arose from the earth ; and when his eyes were opened, he saw no man : but they led him by the hand, and brought him into Damascus. And he was three days without sight, and neither did eat nor drink. And there was a certain disciple at Damascus, named Ananias ; and to him said the Lord in a vision, Ananias. And he said, Behold, I am here, Lord. And the Lord said unto him, Arise, and go into the street which is called Straight, and inquire in the house of Judas for one called Saul of Tarsus : for behold, he prayeth, and hath seen in a vision a man named Ananias, coming in and putting his hand on him, that he might receive his sight. . . . And Ananias went his way, and entered into the house : and putting his hands on him, said, Brother Saul, the Lord (even Jesus that appeared unto thee in the way as thou camest) hath sent me, that thou mightest receive thy sight, and be filled with the Holy Ghost. And immediately there fell from his eyes as it had been scales : and he received sight forthwith, and arose, and was baptized. And when he had received meat, he was strengthened. Then was Saul certain days with the disciples which were at Damascus. And straightway he preached Christ in the synagogues, that he is the Son of God. *Acts* 9, 1–12 and 17–20.

Him that is weak in the faith receive ye, but not to doubtful disputations. For one believeth that he may eat all things :

another, who is weak, eateth herbs. Let not him that eateth despise him that eateth not; and let not him which eateth not judge him that eateth : for God hath received him. Who art thou that judgest another man's servant? to his own master he standeth or falleth. Yea, he shall be holden up : for God is able to make him stand. One man esteemeth one day above another : another esteemeth every day alike. Let every man be fully persuaded in his own mind. . . . For none of us liveth to himself, and no man dieth to himself. For whether we live, we live unto the Lord; and whether we die, we die unto the Lord; whether we live therefore, or die, we are the Lord's. For to this end Christ both died and rose, and revived that he might be Lord both of the dead and living. But why dost thou judge thy brother? or why dost thou set at nought thy brother? for we shall all stand before the judgement seat of Christ. For it is written, As I live, saith the Lord, every knee shall bow to me, and every tongue shall confess to God. So then every one of us shall give account of himself to God. Let us not therefore judge one another any more : but judge this rather, that no man put a stumbling block . . . in his brother's way. . . . Let us therefore follow after the things which make for peace, and things where-with one may edify another. For meat destroy not the work of God. All things indeed are pure; but it is evil for that man who eateth with offence. It is good neither to eat flesh, nor to drink wine, nor any thing whereby thy brother stumbleth, or is offended, or is made weak. *Rom.* 14, 1–5, 7–13, 19–21.

Ye are not in the flesh, but in the Spirit, if so be that the Spirit of God dwell in you. Now, if any man have not the Spirit of Christ, he is none of his. And if Christ be in you, the body is dead because of sin; but the Spirit is life because of righteousness. But if the Spirit of him that raised up Jesus from the dead dwell in you, he that raised up Christ from the dead shall also quicken your mortal bodies by his Spirit that dwelleth in you. Therefore, brethren, we are debtors not to the flesh, to live after the flesh. For if ye live after the flesh, ye shall die : but if ye through the Spirit do mortify the deeds of the body, ye shall live. For as many as are led by the Spirit of God, they are the sons of God. . . . What shall we then say to these things? If God be for us, who can be against us? He that spared not his own Son, but delivered him up for us all, how shall he not with him also freely give us all things ? Who shall lay anything to the charge of God's elect ? It is God that justifieth : who is he that condemneth ? It is Christ that died, yea rather, that is risen again, who is even at the right hand of God, who also maketh intercession for us. Who shall separate us from the love of Christ ? shall tribulation, or distress, or persecution, or famine, or nakedness, or peril, or sword ? As it is written, For thy sake we are killed all the day long; we are accounted as sheep for the slaughter. Nay, in all these things we are more than conquerors, through him that loved us. For I am persuaded, that neither death, nor life, nor angels, nor principalities, nor powers, nor things present, nor things to come, nor height, nor depth, nor any other creature, shall be able to separate us from the love of God which is in Christ Jesus our Lord. *Rom.* 8, 9-14, 31-9.

Let love be without dissimulation. Abhor that which is evil; cleave to that which is good. Be kindly affectioned one to another with brotherly love; in honour preferring one another; not slothful in business; fervent in spirit; serving the Lord; rejoicing in hope; patient in tribulation; continuing instant in prayer; distributing to the necessity of saints; given to hospitality. Bless them which persecute you; bless, and curse not. Rejoice with them that do rejoice, and weep with them that weep. Be of the same mind one toward another. Mind not high things, but condescend to men of low estate. Be not wise in your own conceits. Recompense to no man evil for evil. Provide things honest in the sight of all men. If it be possible, as much as lieth in you, live peaceably with all men. Dearly beloved, avenge not yourselves, but rather give place unto wrath: for it is written, Vengeance is mine; I will repay, saith the Lord. Therefore if thine enemy hunger, feed him; if he thirst, give him drink; for in so doing thou shalt heap coals of fire on his head. Be not overcome of evil, but overcome evil with good. *Rom.* 12, 9-21.

Though I speak with the tongues of men and of angels, and have not charity, I am become as sounding brass, or a tinkling cymbal. And though I have the gift of prophecy, and understand all mysteries, and all knowledge; and though I have all faith, so that I could remove mountains, and have not charity, I am nothing. And though I bestow all my goods to feed the poor, and though I give my body to be burned, and have not charity, it profiteth me nothing. Charity suffereth long, and is kind; charity envieth not; charity vaunteth not itself, is not puffed up, doth not behave itself unseemly, seeketh not her own, is not easily provoked, thinketh no evil; rejoiceth not in iniquity, but rejoiceth in the truth; beareth all things, believeth all things, hopeth all things, endureth all things. Charity never faileth : but whether there be prophecies they shall fail; whether there be tongues, they shall cease; whether there be knowledge, it shall vanish away. For we know in part, and we prophesy in part. But when that which is perfect is come, then that which is in part shall be done away. When I was a child, I spake as a child, I understood as a child, I thought as a child; but when I became a man I put away childish things. For now we see through a glass darkly; but then face to face; now I know in part; but then shall I know even as also I am known. And now abideth faith, hope, charity, these three; but the greatest of these is charity. *I Cor.* 13.

Brethren, if a man be overtaken in a fault, ye which are spiritual, restore such an one in the spirit of meekness; considering thyself, lest thou also be tempted. Bear ye one another's burdens, and so fulfil the law of Christ. For if a man think himself to be something, when he is nothing, he deceiveth himself. But let every man prove his own work, and then shall he have rejoicing in himself alone, and not in another. For every man shall bear his own burden. Let him that is taught in the word communicate unto him that teacheth in all good things. Be not deceived; God is not mocked : for whatsoever a man soweth, that shall he also reap. For he that soweth to his flesh shall of the flesh reap corruption; but he that soweth to the Spirit shall of the Spirit reap life everlasting. And let us not be weary in well doing : for in due season we shall reap, if we faint not. *Gal.* 6, 1–9.

Finally, my brethren, be strong in the Lord, and in the power of his might. Put on the whole armour of God, that ye may be able to stand against the wiles of the devil. For we wrestle not against flesh and blood, but against principalities, against powers, against the rulers of the darkness of this world, against spiritual wickedness in high places. Wherefore take unto you the whole armour of God, that ye may be able to withstand in the evil day, and having done all, to stand. Stand therefore, having your loins girt about with truth, and having on the breastplate of righteousness; and your feet shod with the preparation of the gospel of peace; above all taking the shield of faith, wherewith ye shall be able to quench all the fiery darts of the wicked. And take the helmet of salvation, and the sword of the Spirit, which is the word of God : praying always with all power and supplication in the Spirit, and watching thereunto with all perseverance and supplication for all saints; And for me, that utterance may be given unto me, that I may open my mouth boldly, to make known the mystery of the gospel, for which I am an ambassador in bonds : that therein I may speak boldly, as I ought to speak. *Eph.* 6, 10–20.

Love not the world, neither the things that are in the world. If any man love the world, the love of the Father is not in him. For all that is in the world, the lust of the flesh, and the lust of the eyes, and the pride of life, is not of the Father, but is of the world. And the world passeth away, and the lust thereof : but he that doeth the will of God abideth for ever. . . Behold what manner of love the Father hath bestowed upon us, that we should be called the sons of God! therefore the world knoweth us not, because it knew him not. Beloved, now are we the sons of God, and it doth not yet appear what we shall be : but we know that, when he shall appear, we shall be like him; for we shall see him as he is. And every man that hath this hope in him purifieth himself, even as he is pure. . . . But whoso hath this world's good, and seeth his brother have need, and shutteth up his bowels of compassion from him, how dwelleth the love of God in him ? My little children, let us not love in word neither in tongue, but in deed and in truth. . . . Beloved, let us love one another : for love is of God; and every one that loveth is born of God, and knoweth God. He that loveth not, knoweth not God; for God is love. In this was manifested the love of God towards us, because that God sent his only begotten Son into the world, that we might live through him. Herein is love, not that we loved God, but that he loved us, and sent his Son to be the propitiation for our sins. Beloved, if God so loved us, we ought also to love one another. No man hath seen God at any time. If we love one another, God dwelleth in us, and his love is perfected in us. *I John* 2, 15–17; 3, 1–3, 17–18; 4, 7–12.

And I saw a new heaven and a new earth : for the first heaven and the first earth were passed away; and there was no more sea. And I John saw the holy city, new Jerusalem, coming down from God out of heaven, prepared as a bride adorned for her husband. And I heard a great voice out of heaven saying, Behold, the tabernacle of God is with men, and he will dwell with them, and they shall be his people, and God himself shall be with them, and be their God. And God shall wipe away all tears from their eyes; and there shall be no more death, neither shall there be any more pain : for the former things are passed away. And he that sat upon the throne said, Behold, I make all things new. And he said unto me, Write : for these words are true and faithful. And he said unto me, It is done. I am Alpha and Omega, the beginning and the end. I will give unto him that is athirst of the fountain of the water of life freely. He that over-cometh shall inherit all things; and I will be his God, and he shall be my son. But the fearful, and unbelieving, and the abominable, and murderers, and whoremongers, and sorcerers, and idolaters, and all liars, shall have their part in the lake which burneth with fire and brimstone : which is the second death. And there came unto me one of the seven angels which had the seven vials full of the seven last plagues, and talked with me, saying, Come hither, I will shew thee the bride, the Lamb's wife. And he carried me away in the spirit to a great and high mountain, and shewed me that great city, the holy Jerusalem, descending out of heaven from God, having the glory of God : and her light was like unto a stone most precious, even like a jasper stone, clear as crystal; And had a wall great and high, and had twelve gates, and at the gates twelve angels, and names written thereon, which are the names of the twelve tribes of Israel : on the east three gates; on the north three gates; on the south three gates : and on the west three gates. And the wall of the city had twelve foundations, and in them the names of the twelve apostles of the Lamb. And he that talked with me had a golden reed to measure the city, and the gates thereof, and the wall thereof. And the city lieth foursquare, and the length is as large as the breadth : and he measured the city with the reed, twelve thousand furlongs. The length and the breadth and the height of it are equal. And he measured the wall thereof, an hundred and forty and four cubits, according to the measure of a man, that is, of the angel.

And the building of the wall of it was of jasper : and the city was pure gold, like unto clear glass. And the foundations of the wall of the city were garnished with all manner of precious stones. The first foundation was jasper; the second, sapphire; the third, a chalcedony; the fourth, an emerald; the fifth, sardonyx; the sixth, sardius; the seventh, chrysolyte; the eighth, beryl; the ninth, a topaz; the tenth, a chrysoprasus; the eleventh, a jacinth; the twelfth, an amethyst. And the twelve gates were twelve pearls; every gate was of one pearl : and the street of the city was pure gold, as it were transparent glass. And I saw no temple therein : for the Lord God Almighty and the Lamb are the temple of it. And the city had no need of the sun, neither of the moon, to shine in it : for the glory of God did lighten it, and the Lamb is the light thereof. And the nations of them which are saved shall walk in the light of it : and the kings of the earth do bring their glory and honour into it. And the gates of it shall not be shut at all by day : for there shall be no night there. And they shall bring the glory and honour of the nations into it. And there shall in no wise enter into it any thing that defileth, neither whatsoever worketh abomination, or maketh a lie : but they which are written in the Lamb's book of life. *Rev.* 21.

Prayer of St. Francis of Assisi.

Lord, make me an instrument of Thy Peace. Where there is hatred, let me sow love. Where there is injury, pardon. Where there is doubt, faith. Where there is despair, hope. Where there is darkness, light. Where there is sadness, joy.

O Divine Master, grant that I may not so much seek to be consoled as to console; to be understood, as to understand; to be loved, as to love; for it is in giving that we receive, it is in pardoning that we are pardoned, and it is in dying that we are born to Eternal Life. *Written 700 years ago.*

11

ISLAM
(Muhammadanism)

WE come now to the third major religion of the world, a religion which began about six hundred years after the inception of Christianity and which was its last serious rival, Muhammadanism or Islam. As the various names used here are somewhat puzzling, it may be well to run through them.

Islam is the name that the Founder himself gave to his faith : it means complete surrender to the revelation and to the will of God. Muhammadanism is the term more generally used in the West; this incorporates the name of the founder, Muhammad. Islam is the infinitive form of an Arabic verb meaning " To submit," and followers of Muhammad therefore called themselves Muslims or Moslems, which is the past participle of the same verb and signifies " those who have so submitted themselves." It is more usual in the West to speak of Muhammadans, but it should be noticed that they themselves never employ this term. The religion is for them *Islam*, and the adherents *Muslims* or *Moslems*. Mussulman is another word sometimes used by Westerns : this is actually a corruption of the word Muslimin, the plural of Muslim, and is therefore incorrect.

Not only are the various terms rather puzzling, but there is even greater confusion in the matter of spelling. The founder of Islam, who is often referred to simply as The Prophet, may be Mohammad or Mohammed, Muhammad or Mohomet, and adherents, Mohammedans, Mahometans, Muhammadans or Muhammedans; the sacred city Mecca, Mekkah or Makkah, the shrine it contains, the Cabaa, Kaabah, or Ka'ba; the sacred book, the Qur'an, Qoran, or Koran, the religious head the Caliph, Khalif, or Khalifa(h). These divergences are due to variations of pronunciation and dialect and also to the difficulty of rendering certain Arabic letters into English equivalents. Some scholars employ various apostrophes and dots as qualifications, but even these are not consistent. The spelling " Muhammad " and

" Muhammadan " will be used here, and words long naturalized into English will retain their traditional form, i.e., Koran and Caliph, rather than Qur'an and Khalifa(h).

The number of Muhammadans has been reckoned as about 300,000,000, which would be approximately the same as that of the Hindus. But Hinduism is the faith of one people, and is confined to a particular country, just as Confucianism, with 400,000,000, is the culture of the Chinese. Muhammadanism, like Christianity and Buddhism, is in a different category : it is a major religion which has spread over many countries and absorbed many peoples, and it purports to offer a universal truth which may be accepted by all men. It therefore ranks next to Christianity and Buddhism as a world religious power : it is the third and latest major living religion.

In a very general sense, Muhammadanism belongs to the Near and Middle East, just as Christianity belongs to Europe and Buddhism to Asia. Its culture south of Russia divides that of Europe from the farther parts of Asia and also from the southerly parts of Africa. Once, indeed, it had a great Empire extending all along the Mediterranean and from India in the east to Spain and Morocco in the west. Though its frontiers have receded from Europe it has never lost its original stronghold, as both Christianity and Buddhism did theirs, and it is still on the increase today, especially in Africa, where it continues to absorb backward peoples. To give some details : more than half the Moslems in the world are Asiatics (in Arabia, Turkey, Persia (Iran), Iraq, Syria, Afghanistan, Soviet Asia, the Malay States, the East Indies and China), and more than a quarter are Africans (including the whole of North Africa from Morocco to Egypt and southward to the Equator). The remainder are to be found in Europe, chiefly in Bosnia and about Istanbul (Constantinople), and in various parts of America, Australia, and Oceania.

Muhammad was born in Mecca in Arabia, the date usually given for his birth being A.D. 570. His name was rare, though not unknown; it means The Praised One. His father was a member of a tribe called the Koreish, who were not, as is sometimes imagined, pastoral wanderers, but engaged in commerce and handicrafts. The Arabs themselves are a Semitic people who became isolated in the Arabian Peninsula and who there preserved notable purity of breed. When Muhammad was born, Mecca was already a sacred city, for it contained the Black Stone (probably a volcanic or meteorite stone), which was revered by the Arabs and associated with their principal god, named Allah (Al-Ilah), which means the Strong One. The shrine was a cube-shaped house, and was therefore called the Kaaba, from the word " cube." There were other objects of worship in Mecca, which had become an important and wealthy centre owing to the number of pilgrims who paid temple taxes and otherwise enriched the city. The Koreish tribe was in charge of the temple, so that the young Muhammad would have been in touch with the religious centre of his country from his earliest years. His father, whose name was Abdullah, died before his birth, and his mother, Aminah, is said to have died when he was six years old. For a time he was cared for by his influential grandfather, Abdal-Mottalib, but when he also died, a paternal uncle, Abu Talib, became the new guardian. Abu Talib was less wealthy, and the family fortunes seem to have waned. It is doubtful whether Muhammad ever learned to read or write : in any case, his education was slight. When he was twelve years old he accompanied his uncle on a business journey by caravan to Syria, and there came into contact with Christianity, for Syria was nominally a Christian country. A story tells how he listened to the disputes between various sects as to the nature of the Trinity : whether, indeed, the Three Persons were Father, Son, and Holy Ghost, or Father, Son, and Virgin Mary. We can imagine that he was affected by this experience, coming, as he did, from a family essentially interested in religious questions— questions which, as we shall see, were becoming increasingly important in his own city. During the later phases of his youth he followed various callings—among others those of a shepherd and a camel-driver—and at various times he came into contact with the Jews, who were scattered about the country, and learnt from them something of another form of Monotheism. He was instructed in business and trade by his uncle, and at the age of twenty-five offered to lead a caravan to Syria on behalf of a wealthy widow named Khadijah. This was a very successful trip, for on his return, the lady, who was then forty and had been married twice before, offered him her hand in marriage. Although she was fifteen years his senior, the union proved a very happy one, and several children were born, some accounts giving six, two sons and four daughters; some giving only three. In any case, it appears that the boys died early. With this wealthy marriage the fortunes of Muhammad greatly improved, but he continued to work at trade and business till he was nearly forty. He began, however, to show an increasing interest in religion, and spent long hours in solitary meditation in the cave of Hira, about three miles north of Mecca. We may obtain some idea of the state of his religious consciousness at that time by recalling his background. The Arabs had been, like all other people in the early stages, animistic—that is, worshippers of spirits located in trees, stones, rivers, sun, moon, stars and so on—but by the seventh century they had evolved a clear idea of a supreme Deity, whom they called Allah and who was the guardian of moral order. The spirits still existed, but were subservient to him. Three daughters of Allah were also revered as goddesses, and, of these, the most important was a kind of female Allah, Alilat. But Allah himself was Lord, and the Meccans were thus moving from Polytheism into the Monotheistic stage. Muhammad was familiar with these latest developments, besides having had considerable contact with both Jews and Christians. It is probable that he felt acutely the need of his own country for a great prophet of Monotheism, who would correspond to the Jewish Moses and to the Jesus of the Christians.

The practice of solitary meditation was well known. There were, indeed, a large number of ascetics in Arabia, who were given to forms of religious ecstasy. These wanderers were called " hanifs." At a certain stage, however, Muhammad underwent a great spiritual experience, an experience which led to a change in the history of the world. The story tells that, after hearing voices, which declared " You are the chosen one, proclaim the Name of the Lord," a climax came one night (later called the night Al Qadr) when a voice called to him " Iqra " [1]—" recite." Then came a vision of the opening passage of the Koran written in letters of fire upon a cloth. Muhammad stepped out of the cave and then saw the two great eyes of the Angel Gabriel. Fearing that he might have become possessed of an evil spirit, he fled in terror to his home, where he was comforted and reassured by his wife. Shortly afterwards a second section of the Koran was revealed to him, and the revelations continued. He resumed

[1] The word also means read, preach, or proclaim.

his life as a merchant, however, and only talked to his wife and his intimate friends about his experiences. Whatever was the origin of these visions, there is no doubt that Muhammad underwent at that time great spiritual experiences, from which he derived strong and lasting convictions. The principal of these was the Unity, Power, and absolute Sovereignty of a Single God, combined with a passionate hatred of idolatry : then followed the certainty of the Life to Come, Resurrection, Hell, and the reward of the Faithful in Paradise, and of his own mission as the Prophet of God. After a while he began to preach, but only to a few relatives and friends, who for three or four years formed a kind of secret society in Mecca. Khadijah was the first convert : a very important early one was Abu Bekr, a wealthy merchant, who afterwards became Muhammad's successor, the first Caliph (i.e., successor). But gradually the little sect became known, and at last one day Muhammad is said to have marched into the Kaaba and uttered his famous phrase : " There is but one God." He immediately incurred the hostility of the Meccans, who feared for the prestige of the goddesses and also for the sanctuary with its various objects of veneration. The Prophet would have been persecuted, perhaps even killed, but for the protection afforded him by his uncle, who nevertheless besought him to abandon this form of teaching. His followers were severely handled, and some of them fled to Abyssinia, where they were well treated by the Abyssinian King, possibly under the impression that they were persecuted Christians. Muhammad, with some of his followers who remained, was besieged in the " House of Arcam " near the Kaaba, and would have starved to death (no bloodshed was allowed in the sacred city), but that he appeared and made a partial recantation, acknowledging the claims of the Meccan goddesses. Shortly afterwards, however, he withdrew this declaration, and the exiles to Abyssinia, who had returned believing that a compromise had been reached, again fled, and Muhammad himself sought refuge in the outlying country. Though a truce was made later and he returned to Mecca, hostility arose when he began to preach once more. He was now a man of fifty, and misfortunes crowded in upon him. The devoted wife who had done so much to help him died; later his faithful guardian also. Moreover, he found himself once more in straitened circumstances. When he fled to a neighbouring town, he was stoned and driven back again. Yet he persisted in protesting against idolatry, and in A.D. 622 his chance came. Pilgrims had visited him the previous year from a city named Yathrib, which was in an oasis north of Mecca, and had taken an oath to be faithful to his doctrines. They returned and invited him to go to Yathrib as their leader and teacher. This he gladly did, fleeing in secret, and Yathrib, a town which had been founded by the Jews, thenceforth became known as al-Medinah (the city). An attempt to follow and murder him was frustrated, and thereafter his successes were almost unbroken. This flight to Medina is known as the Hijra (flight), incorrectly spelt in English as the Hejira or Hegira, and the Muhammadan chronology dates from this time. Thus our A.D. 622 is A.H.1 (Anno Hegirae 1.) according to the reckoning of Islam. The Jews of Yathrib, on whom he had pinned his hopes, had refused to co-operate with him, and he therefore substituted Mecca for Jerusalem as the city towards which the faithful should now prostrate themselves. The Christians (for there were some Christians also in the town) were hostile too, so, abandoning these two groups of monotheists with whom he had hoped to join, he developed his doctrine of the One True God independently. In this he met with remarkable success, and was soon accepted as despot in Medina (Yathrib). Nevertheless, he and his followers, having abandoned their native industries, did not find it easy to maintain themselves, and a series of raids on travelling caravans began. The Meccans turned out in force to try to prevent this; but on one occasion about a thousand of them were defeated by three hundred of Muhammad's fighting men, and this event was afterwards named the Day of Deliverance. The surrounding tribes, fired by this success, flocked to Muhammad's banner and, when strong enough, he marched on Mecca and entered the city in triumph in A.D. 629 (A.H. 7). By the treaty which followed, Mecca was to adopt the worship of Allah only and to accept Muhammad as his Prophet, but adherents of the new faith were still to make the pilgrimage to Mecca, thus ensuring the continuance of the vital pilgrim traffic. The idols were destroyed, the goddesses lost their power, but the Black Stone, which Muhammad now declared that God had given to Abraham, was preserved, and is honoured to this day. A strange story, by the way, tells that it was originally white, but that it had become black from the tears of penitents. This compromise shows Muhammad's power of diplomacy, and his successes continued amongst the settlements of Jews in various parts of Arabia; those who had previously mocked and scorned him now had to make terms with him as best they could. On the eve of his entry into Mecca he sent letters to all the known rulers in the world, promising them safety if they would accept his doctrines. Three years later, when making preparation for a raid on Syria, which had rejected his advances, Muhammad was seized with a fever from which he died in Medina. His last act had been to make a ceremonial pilgrimage to Mecca. This was in A.D. 632 (A.H. 10), and at that time he was master of nearly all Arabia.

The character of Muhammad is a remarkable one. He was a man of amazing force of personality. Tradition asserts that he had a striking appearance with a fine, intelligent face, dark, piercing eyes with a red tint in them, and a flowing beard. The impression he made, nevertheless, was that of being a kindly man devoted to children. His methods have been much criticized, and also his character in its later phases. It certainly seems as if after the deaths of his wife and guardian, when he was left friendless and alone, his outlook changed. It was then that, having previously been the leader of a peaceful theocratic community, he evolved the idea of the "Holy War" (Jihad) and of using force to promulgate his doctrines. Not only so, but he is said to have taken unfair advantages, such as attacking in the Holy Month, when his enemies were unprepared and resorting to other kinds of trickery. Again, having been devotedly faithful to Khadijah while she lived, he took to himself a large number of wives in his declining years, at least nine of these—some say as many as fifteen. As he had decreed that a Moslem might marry four but no more, he justified this by announcing that he had permission from God in a special revelation. Actually these wives were, in many cases, elderly widows of his followers who had died fighting, and he thus gave them protection and security sorely needed in so turbulent a time. With regard to pillage, we have to remember that the Arab raid was a generally accepted feature of the time; and concerning his other methods, he probably sincerely felt that the end—the destruction of idolatry and the enthronement of the religion of the One True God—justified the means. Personal ambition does not appear to have been a leading motive. Muhammad disdained grandeur, disclaimed all power to work miracles, and took great pains to ensure that he should not be worshipped after his death. He lived simply, performing menial tasks with his own hands, wearing neither gold nor silver, and living, we are told, on a diet of barley, bread, dates, and water, with the occasional addition of milk and honey. He believed intensely in his own mission and in the mercy, majesty, and omnipotence of the One True God. For this cause he risked assassination many times and suffered great privation when he might have enjoyed power and influence in Mecca. His belief in force has encouraged comparison with some of the dictators of later times, who have also been single-hearted and personally abstemious. But the answer to this is that such men tend to fall, whereas Muhammad founded a religion which has guided millions of men of many nationalities for thirteen hundred years and which is still on the increase. Mere power-seeking fanatics are unable to influence later generations no longer subject to their personal magnetism. After the death of Muhammad there was one of the most remarkable outbursts of conquest the world has ever seen. Abu Bekr, his successor, the first Caliph, set as his goal nothing less than the subjugation of the whole world to Allah. Starting with little armies of three thousand to four thousand men, he first gave unity to Arabia, which had hitherto been a land of small, bickering, nomadic tribes, and then proceeded to conquer Syria. So rapidly did Muhammadanism spread that within a hundred years it had swept along the whole of the Mediterranean to Spain and Morocco in the west and to India in the east. With the religion went the rule, culture, and language of the Arabs. The methods of conquest varied. Sometimes the conquerors were content with political submission and the payment of tribute, but more often conversion to Islam was a condition. The march of the Caliph's power was so swift that the religious doctrines suffered little in the process of adaptation to new conditions.

The amazing success of Muhammadanism can be explained principally by two things : (1) its simplicity, (2) its fanaticism. By fanaticism is meant such devotion to a single idea that almost any means, certainly that of force, seems justified in promoting it. Fighting was a natural activity of the Arabs, but hitherto their fearlessness and physical energy had been dissipated in constant bickering among themselves. Now they were united and, moreover, provided with a good reason for the exercise of their warlike qualities. The idea that they were called upon to promote was simple enough for anyone to understand. It had no profound philosophy, nor complicated doctrines : it needed no sacraments nor rituals; it allowed of no images. All energy was centred on the assertion that there was but One God, and that Muhammad was his Prophet. Beyond this there were only certain rules, and a Sacred Book said to have been revealed to Muhammad himself, which contained promises of rewards or punishments after death, according to whether the Creed was accepted and followed or not.

It is interesting to speculate as to what would have happened if Muhammad had come to an understanding with the Jews when he first went to Yathrib, for this is what he seems to have ardently desired. It is possible that Arabia might then have embraced some form of Judaism, for the two religions share the same passionate hatred of idolatry, the same intense devotion to a single Deity " without a partner," and the same belief in Abraham and the prophets of the Old Testament. But Muhammad also took over much from current Christianity, especially that part of it which shows most clearly the influence of the old faith of Persia, such as the final opposition of Good and Evil, the Judgment at the last Day, with the everlasting separation between the righteous and sinners, Heaven and Hell, Satan with his devils, and guardian angels. A single earth-life was predicted for every individual soul, and an absolute certainty of physical resurrection, which extended even to the animal kingdom. Muhammad also retained something of the religion of his own country, the name of Allah, the pilgrimage to Mecca, and the veneration of the Black Stone as the gift of God to Abraham. To this blend of the three religions with which he had come into contact, he added but two elements which were new : the belief in himself as the last of the prophets and the doctrine of the Holy War (Jihad). A process of rejection also helped in building up a new standpoint. Muhammad sternly condemned the Christian doctrine of the Trinity, because it suggested that God had " partners," and taught that Jesus Christ, though virgin-born and sinless, and the greatest of the prophets before himself, was not a Saviour or a partaker of the Divine Nature. Yet, owing to the honour paid to him, Muhammadanism has sometimes been described as a Christian heresy.

The Sacred Book that expounds the teaching of Muhammad
is called the Koran (or Qu'ran), which means " that which is to
be read." This is held to have been revealed to Muhammad in
sections at different times, either by the angel Gabriel or by Allah
Himself. Every word of it is believed, not only to be divinely
inspired (in the traditional manner of the Christian Bible), but
actually to have existed in the mind of God from all eternity. All
sects of Moslems are prepared to defend its complete infallibility.
It consists of 114 *suras* or chapters of very varying lengths, which
were taken down at dictation, as they fell from the lips of the
Prophet, on any material that happened to be handy—flat stone,
pieces of leather, bones or palm leaves. Abu Bekr, the first
Caliph, had a collection made of these, which he compiled into
one volume, and within twenty years of the Prophet's death this
had received its final form. The *suras* were not uttered in the
order in which we now have them : probably the shortest were
the earliest. The Koran cannot be said to be easy reading for
Westerners. The original Arabic is said to be very beautiful,
the form being a kind of rhyming prose which cannot be con-
veyed in another language. As translated, it seems discursive
and repetitive, dealing without much sequence with all kinds of
subjects : doctrine, morals, civil law, manners, and also matters
concerning Muhammad himself. Some of it resembles in style
the writings of the Old Testament, but it differs from any other
Scripture in the world in that it is the work of one man. It
contains many fine passages, and throughout runs the passionate
monotheism of Muhammad like a bright thread, every *sura*
beginning : " In the Name of the most merciful God." Muhammad himself regarded the Koran as a miracle greater even than
that of his divine mission. The materialistic and sensuous
descriptions of Heaven and Hell in the Koran have been read
with such astonishment and even dismay by adherents of other
religions that it is necessary to comment specially on these. Thus
in Paradise, we are told, there will be exquisite jewels, magnificent
fruits, and flowing streams of water, milk, wine, and honey, women
created of pure musk, splendidly apparelled, and eternally young,
while ravishing songs will be sung by the archangel, Israfil.
These, and many other delights, though they will pass human
imagination, will, it is only fair to add, be eclipsed by the joy of
beholding the face of the Almighty, morning and evening. The

pains of Hell are equally vividly described : most terrible in the inventiveness of detailed frightfulness. There is, however, a point almost always forgotten when criticizing these anthropomorphic and highly coloured passages. The Arabs were essentially poets : they esteemed their language highly, and vied with one another in the resourcefulness with which they used highly decorative and elaborate expressions. Frequent contests were held for skilled poets, and these florid chapters of the Koran were considered so beautiful that none dared compete with them. Muhammad, if neither a deep thinker nor what we should call a " saintly " man, had a poetic sense, and when he arrived at appropriate parts of his book he gave his oriental imagination full play, employing all the linguistic devices at his command. The stern reality of Heaven and Hell existed for him without doubt, but the detailed descriptions, which appear to us distressing and even at times ridiculous, should be read as paraphrased poetry, of which the beauty is lost in translation. As regards life in this world, the directions in the Koran are austere enough. Prohibitions, still observed by strict Moslems, include all games of chance, betting, usury, wine, and fermented drinks, the eating of pork, or meats killed in a certain way, and the making of images. When the use of tobacco became general, this, too, was rejected by the most pious as being a form of drug, and coffee has sometimes been excluded on the same grounds. These rules have been relaxed somewhat in the course of time, especially those concerning the drinking of wine. It is interesting to note, in passing, that the game of chess, so beloved by the Arabs, survived with difficulty, many Moslems using blocks of wood to avoid the making of images. The injunction against images led Moslem artists to concentrate their skill on decoration and architectural features. Many of their mosques—buildings which correspond to our churches—are among the most beautiful in the world. In addition to these special prohibitions, there are those of the great Commandments, common to all religions : injunctions against murder, theft, sexual irregularities and excesses, and slander. Three of the most important reforms which the Prophet tried to bring about in his own day were the attempt to break down the blood-feud between tribes, whereby one death led to a series of wars; infanticide, which meant the destruction of girl babies by burying them alive, and, if tradition be correct, the granting to women of the right to inherit property.

The duties of a Muhammadan are very simple. He must recite the profession of belief, " There is no God but Allah, and Muhammad is the Prophet of Allah." This need only be done once in a life-time, and is sufficient, if uttered with full conviction and understanding. In the Kalimah (profession of creed), however, certain verses from the Koran usually follow, and an early theologian has thus summed up the dogmas involved : " I believe in God (Allah), His Angels, His Books and His Messengers, the Last Day, the Resurrection from the Dead, Predestination by God, Good and Evil, the Judgment, the Balance, Paradise, and Hell-fire." The messengers here include the six super-prophets : Adam, Noah, Abraham, Moses, Jesus, and lastly Muhammad himself. The other four duties are Prayer, Almsgiving, Fasting, and Pilgrimage. These, with the Kalimah, are the five pillars of Islam. Prayer must be made five times a day—morning, noon, afternoon, evening, and night—and must be preceded by ablutions, which, if water cannot be obtained, may be made with sand. They include a series of postures and repeated phrases and recitations. There is a public Call at the special hours from the minarets of all mosques, and this Moslems must obey immediately, wherever they are. The noon prayer on Friday takes the form of a public service in the mosque, usually including an address, Friday being the sacred day of the Moslems. Almsgiving involves giving up a portion, not less than a fortieth part— that is, in our familiar phraseology, $2\frac{1}{2}$ per cent.—of the adherent's goods to the poor. Money thus raised has been largely applied to the redemption of slaves. Additional alms are meritorious, and Muhammad himself is said to have been exceedingly generous, an example which has been well followed. The great Moslem fast is that of Ramadan, a whole month, during which eating and drinking are forbidden in the daytime, though nourishment may be taken at night. Ramadan may fall at any season, since the Muhammadan year follows the changes of the moon, and in the long days of the summer it is very exacting. The pilgrimage to Mecca should be performed by every Moslem, man or woman, at least once in a life-time, but the proviso, which absolves the infirm or very poor, is added, " provided able to do so." The phrase " man or woman " should be noticed. It is a common, though mistaken, belief that Muhammadan women "have no souls" and are ignored by their religion. This is probably because in most parts they do not attend mosques, but it must be remembered that *public* worship is not an essential duty. There are no sacraments nor corporate rituals. The Koran abounds in phrases such as : "Whoso doeth good works, *whether he be male or female*, and is a true believer, shall be admitted into Paradise," and it is also taught that women will regain their youth there. Muhammad himself greatly venerated his first wife, who helped him so much and who was his first convert, and, as we have seen, he promoted benefits to wives in the case of inheritance. The belief that women are excluded from the religion is a misinterpretation.

Soon after the death of Muhammad the world of Islam split up into two sects—the Sunnite and the Shi'ite. The dispute originally concerned the succession to the Caliphate, but certain differences gradually arose in matters of doctrine. The Sunnites, who are by far the larger division, accepted the Sunna, a body of tradition which, for them, supplemented the Koran. The Shi'ites (who derive their name from the Caliph whom they supported) reject this : they are less strict regarding the Pilgrimage, the use of wine, and the making of images. Theirs is the official religion of Persia, and they tend to allegorize the Koran and to show the influence of Eastern religions. There are subdivisions of these sects and also other movements within Islam notably that of the Sufis (probably derived from Suf-wool, owing to the coarse garments they wore), a highly mystical sect.

A few words may be said in conclusion about the attributes of Allah himself. In the confession of faith quoted above, the phrase "predestination by God" occurs, and of predestination no mention has yet been made. The Oriental is naturally more fatalistic than the Occidental; we have become familiar with the tendency through the Arabic word *Kismet* or Fate. The Muhammadan form of fatalism is the belief that all happenings—bad, good, or indifferent—are the will of Allah. Everything is preordained, predestined. Yet consistency is lacking, for the Koran often speaks as though men were free to choose their own salvation or damnation, nor, indeed, are the two main sects agreed as to how much free will, if any, man has, or how such would operate. All religions which predicate a righteous and all-powerful Deity become involved, at this difficult stage, in contradictions. Suffice it to say here that complete submission is the central feature of Islam, and that the Muhammadan is content to explain all events, whether happy or disastrous, as the will of Allah. The outstanding attribute of the Muhammadan Divinity may thus be said to be Will, unconditioned, incomprehensible. Moslems have always been reluctant to discuss the Nature of God, but it is agreed that, besides Will, He has Power, Knowledge, and Life. He is Single and Alone, and can never become incarnate or express Himself in any secondary manifestation. Nevertheless, He is merciful, beloved of His worshippers, and whole-heartedly adored by the entire Moslem world.

Verses from the Scriptures

ABBREVIATIONS TO REFERENCES [1]

B.	= Bahai	*Mis.*	= Mishkat-el-Masabih
B.S.	= Bahai Saying	*Qur.*	= Qur'an
Gul.	= Gulshan-i-Raz	*S.*	= Sufism
Mas.	= Masnavi	*T.*	= Traditions

Your exhorting mankind to virtuous deeds is **alms**; and your prohibiting the forbidden is alms; and your showing men the road when they lose it is alms; and your assisting the blind is alms; and your removing stones, thorns, and bones, which are harmful to man is alms; and pouring water from your bucket into that of your brother is alms for you. *Mis.*

The best of **alms** are those given by a man of small means who gives of that which he has earned by labour, and gives as much as he is able. *Mis.*

Verily, whether it be of those who **believe,** or those who are Jews or Christians or Sabaeons, whosoever believe in God, and the last day and act aright, they have their reward at their Lord's hand, and there is no fear for them nor shall they grieve. *Qur.* 2, 59 and 5, 73.

Let go the things in which you are in doubt for the things in which there is doubt. Leaving alone things which do not concern him is one of the good things in a man's Islam. No one of you

---

[1] Dr. Champion has retained the forms Qur'an and Mohammed in the following quotations.

is a **believer** until he loves for his brother what he loves for himself. *An-Nawawi.*

All **believers** are brothers. *Qur.* 249, 10.

No **burden-bearing soul** has borne the burden of another; no person has reaped until he has sown something. . . . How does earning a livelihood preclude the acquisition of treasure? Do not desist from work; that treasure indeed will follow upon it. Beware lest you become a slave to " If ", saying to yourself, " If I had only done this or the other." *Mas.*

He is the first and the last; the seen and the hidden; and he knoweth all things! it is he who in six days **created the heavens** and the earth, then ascended his throne. He knoweth that which entereth the earth, and that which goeth forth from it, and what cometh down from heaven, and what mounteth up to it: and wherever ye are, he is with you; and God beholdeth all your actions. *Qur.* 57, 3–4.

The six articles of **faith** :

1. God.
2. The angels of God.
3. The books of God.
4. The prophets of God.
5. The day of judgment.
6. Predestination.

A man asked the Prophet what was the mark whereby a man might know the reality of his **faith**. He said, " If thou derive pleasure from the good which thou hast done, and be grieved for the evil which thou hast committed, thou art a true believer." The man said, " What doth a fault really consist in ? " He said, " When anything pricketh thy conscience forsake it." *Table-Talk of Mohammed.*

And every man's **fate** have we (God) fastened about his neck; and on the day of resurrection will we bring forth to him a book, which shall be proffered to him wide open: " Read thy book: there needeth none but thyself to make out an account against thee this day." *Qur.* 17, 14–15.

If every one saw his own **faults** first, how should he be neglectful of correcting himself. These people are thoughtless as to, and unacquainted with themselves; and consequently they speak of the faults of one another. *Mas.*

Forgive thy servant seventy times a day. *Mis.*

There is no deity but **God** : and Mohammed is the apostle of God. *Kalimah or Creed.*

God it is who has made for you the night to repose therein, and the day to see by; verily, God is Lord of grace to men, but most men give no thanks. *Qur. 40, 63.*

Dost thou not see that **God** knoweth all that is in the heavens and all that is in the earth ? Three persons speak not privately together, but he is their fourth; nor five, but he is their sixth nor fewer nor more, but wherever they be he is with them. Then on the day of resurrection he will tell them of their deeds : for God knoweth all things. *Qur. 58, 8.*

God, most high, says : he who approaches near to me one span, I will approach near to him one cubit; and he who approaches near to me one cubit, I will approach near to him one fathom; and whoever approaches me walking, I will come to him running; and he who meets me with sins equivalent to the whole world, I will greet him with forgiveness equal to it. *Mis.*

Hast thou not seen how all in the Heavens and in the Earth uttereth the praise of **God** ?—the very birds as they spread their wings ? Every creature knoweth its prayer and its praise! and God knoweth what they do. *Qur. 24, 41.*

Verily, **God** will say in the day of resurrection, O ye sons of men! I was sick and ye did not visit me. And the sons of men will say, O thou defender, how could we visit thee, for thou art the Lord of the universe, and art free from sickness ? and God will say, O ye sons of men, did you not know that such a one of my servants was sick and ye did not visit him ? *Mis.*

Islam is built on five points :—the witness of there being no deity except Allah, and of Mohammed being the apostle of Allah; the performing of prayer; the giving of alms; the pilgrimage to the house (Mecca) and the fast of Ramadan. *T.*

Be **just** : the unjust never prosper. Be valiant : die rather than yield. Be merciful : slay neither old men, children, nor women. Destroy neither fruit trees, grain, nor cattle. Keep your word even to your enemies. *Abu Bekr.*

The **law of life** requires : sincerity to God, severity to self, justice to all people, service to elders. Kindness to the young, generosity to the poor. Good counsel to friends. Forbearance with enemies. Indifference to fools. Respect to the learned. *S. Abdullah Ansari.*

We have prescribed for thee therein " a **life** for a life, and an eye for an eye, and a nose for a nose, and an ear for an ear, and a tooth for a tooth, and for wounds retaliation. *Qur. 5, 49.*

Those who are patient, craving their **Lord's face** and are steadfast in prayer, and expend in alms of what we have bestowed upon them, secretly and openly, and ward off evil with good— these shall have the recompense of the abode, gardens of Eden, into which they shall enter with the righteous amongst their fathers and their wives and their seed; and the angels shall enter in unto them from every gate. *Qur. 13, 20.*

Bitter things become sweet through **love,** copper things become golden through love. Dregs become clear and bright through love; pains become salutary through love. Through love a dead person is made living; through love a king is made a slave. This love too is the result of knowledge; when has foolishness ever sat upon such a throne ? *Mas.*

All beside **love** is but words. *B. Abbas Effendi.*

Love is this—that thou should'st account thyself very little and God very great. *S. Abu Yazid Bistami.*

Do unto all men as you would they should do unto you, and reject for **others** what you would reject for yourself. *Mis.*

God is great! I bear witness that there is no god but God! I bear witness that Mohammed is the Apostle of God! Come to **prayers**! Come to salvation! There is no other god but God. (The Azan, or " call to prayer " by the mu-azzin or crier from the minaret of the mosque at the time of public prayer.)

Let there be no compulsion in **religion.** *Qur. 2, 257.*

Any object of adoration is better than **self-worship**. *S. Hafiz.*

To be a cause of healing for every **sick one**; a comforter for every sorrowful one; a pleasant water for every thirsty one; a heavenly table for every hungry one; a guide for every seeker;

rain for cultivation; a star to every horizon; a light for every
lamp; a herald to every yearning one for the kingdom of God.
B.S.

He who **slayeth** anyone . . . shall be as though he had slain
all mankind; but he who saveth a life shall be as though he had
saved all mankind alive. *Qur.* 5, 35.

A certain person, in your eyes, is like a **snake**; the same
person, in the eyes of some other, is a picture of beauty; because
in your mind there is the thought of his infidelity; and in the
mind of his friend there is the thought of his belief. *Mas.*

That **spring** is involved in autumn; that autumn is an introduction to the spring; flee not from it. Be the companion of
grief, and put up with discomfort; seek in death eternal life.
Mas.

Thou thinkest thou art but a small thing whereas in thee is
involved the whole **universe**. *S. Gul.*

Know that everything is **vanity** but God. *Mis.*

Readings from the Scriptures

Verily, they who believe (Muslims), and they who follow the
Jewish religion, and the Christians, and the Sabeites—whoever
believeth in God and the Last Day, and doeth that which is right,
shall have their reward with their Lord : and fear shall not come
upon them, neither shall they be grieved. . . . And observe
prayer and pay the legal impost : and whatever good thing ye
have sent on before for your soul's sake, ye shall find it with God.
Verily God seeth what ye do. . . . But, they who set their face
with resignation Godward, and do what is right,—their reward
is therefore with their Lord, and no fear shall come on them,
neither shall they be grieved. . . . We believe in God, and that
which hath been sent down to us, and that which hath been sent
down to Abraham and Ismael and Isaac and Jacob and the tribes;
and that which hath been given to Moses and to Jesus, and that
which was given to the prophets from their Lord. No difference
do we make between any of them : and to God are we resigned
(Muslims). It is prescribed to you when any one of you is at the
point of death, that if he leave goods, he bequeatheth equitably

to his parents and kindred; this is binding on those who fear God. O believers! a Fast is prescribed to you, as it was prescribed to those before you, that ye may fear God, for certain days. But he among you who shall be sick, or on a journey, shall fast that same number of other days : and for those who are able to keep it and yet break it, there shall be as an expiation the maintenance of a poor man. And he who of his own accord performeth a good work, shall derive good from it : and that ye fast is good for you—if ye but knew it. As to the month Ramadan in which the Qur'an was sent down to be man's guidance, and an explanation of that guidance, and an illumination, as soon as any one of you observeth the moon, let him set about the fast; but he who is sick, or upon a journey, shall fast a like number of other days. God wisheth you ease and wisheth not your discomfort, and that you fulfil the number of days, and that you glorify God for his guidance : and haply you will be thankful. And when my servants ask thee concerning Me, then verily will I be nigh unto them—will answer the cry of him that crieth, when he crieth unto Me : but let them hearken unto Me, and believe in Me, haply they will proceed aright. . . . God! There is no god but He; the Living, the Self-subsisting; neither slumber seizeth Him, nor sleep; his, whatsoever is in the Heavens and whatsoever is in the Earth! Who is he that can intercede with Him but by his own permission? He knoweth what is present with his creatures, and what is yet to befall them; yet nought of his knowledge do they comprehend, save what He willeth. His throne reacheth over the Heavens and the Earth, and the upholding of both burdeneth Him not; and He is the High, the Great! Let there be no compulsion in Religion. . . . O ye who believe! make not your alms void by reproaches and injury, like him who spendeth his substance to be seen of men, and believeth not in God and in the latter day. The likeness of such an one is that of a rock with a thin soil upon it, on which a heavy rain falleth, but leaveth it hard : no profit from their works shall they be able to gain; for God guideth not the unbelieving people. And the likeness of those who expend their substance from a desire to please God, and through their own steadfastness, is as a garden on a hill, on which the heavy rain falleth, and it yieldeth its fruits twofold; and even if a heavy rain fall not on it, yet is there a dew : and God beholdeth your actions. . . . God will not burden any soul beyond its power. It shall enjoy the good which it hath acquired, and shall bear the evil for the acquirement of which it laboured. O our Lord! punish us not if we forget, or fall into sin; O our Lord! and lay not on us a load like that which Thou hast laid on those who have been before us; O our Lord! and lay not on us that for which we have not strength : but blot out our sins and forgive us, and have pity on us. Thou art our protector : help us then against the unbelievers. *Qur.* 2, 59, 104, 106, 130, 176, 179–82, 256–7, 266–7, 286.

And the good that ye shall give in alms shall redound unto yourselves; and ye shall not give but as seeking the face of God; and whatever good thing ye shall have given in alms, shall be repaid you, and ye shall not be wronged. There are among you the poor, who being shut up for fighting for the cause of God, have not in their power to strike out into the earth for riches. Those who know them not, think them rich because of their modesty. By this their token thou shalt know them—they ask not of men with importunity; and of whatever good thing ye shall give them in alms, of a truth God will take knowledge. *Qur.* 2, 273–4.

Seemly unto men is a life of lusts, of women, and children, and hoarded talents of gold and silver, and of horses well bred, and cattle, and tilth :—that is the provision for the life of this world; but God, with him is the best resort. Say, but shall we tell you of a better thing than this ? For those who fear are gardens with their Lord, beneath which rivers flow; they shall dwell therein for aye, and pure wives and grace from God; the Lord looks on his servants, who say, " Lord, we believe; pardon thou our sins and keep us from the torment of the fire "—upon the patient, the truthful, the devout, and those who ask for pardon at the dawn. *Qur.* 3, 12–15.

And worship God, and join not aught with Him in worship. Be good to parents, and to kindred, and to orphans, and to the poor, and to a neighbour, a kinsman or near neighbour, and to a familiar friend and to the wayfarer, and to the slaves whom your right hands hold : verily, God loveth not the proud, the vain boaster. . . . and those who bestow their substance in alms to be seen of men, and believe not in God and in the Last Day.

Whoever hath Satan for his companion, an evil companion hath
he! . . . God truly will not wrong any one of the weight of a
mote; and if there be any good deed, He will repay it doubly.
. . . Let those then fight in the cause of God who barter this
present life for that which is to come; for whoever fighteth on
God's path, whether he be slain or conquer, we will in the end
give him great reward. . . . Whatever good betideth thee is
from God, and whatever betideth thee of evil is from thyself;
and we have sent thee to mankind as an apostle : and God is thy
sufficing witness. . . . If ye are greeted with a greeting, then
greet ye with a better greeting, or at least return it; verily God
taketh count of all things. . . . And who hath a better religion
than he who resigneth himself (his face) to God, who doth what
is good, and followeth the faith of Abraham, the sound in faith—
and God took Abraham for his friend. *Qur.* 4, 40, 42, 44, 76, 81,
88, 124.

No kind of beast is there on earth nor fowl that flieth with its
wings, but is a folk like you : nothing have we passed over in
the Book : then unto their Lord shall they be gathered. They
who gainsay our signs are deaf, and dumb, in darkness : God
misleadeth whom He will, and whom He pleaseth doth He place
upon the right path. . . . And with Him are the keys of the secret
things; none knoweth them but He : and He knoweth whatever
is on the land and in the sea; and no leaf falleth but He knoweth
it; neither is there a grain in the darknesses of the earth, nor a
thing green or sere, but it is noted in the perspicuous Book.
And it is He who taketh you to Himself at night, and knoweth
what ye have merited in the day : then He awaketh you therein,
that the set life-term may be fulfilled : then unto Him is your
return; and then shall He declare to you that which ye have
wrought. . . . Verily God causeth the grain and the date-stone
to break forth : He bringeth forth the living from the dead, and
the dead from the living! This is God! Why, then, are ye
turned aside from Him ? He causeth the dawn to break, and
hath ordained the night for rest, and the sun and the moon for
computing time! This is the ordinance of the Mighty, the
Wise! And it is He who hath ordained the stars for you, that
ye may be guided thereby in the darkness of the land and of the
sea! clear now have we made our signs for men of knowledge.

And it is He who hath produced you from one man, and hath
provided for you an abode and resting-place! Clear now have
we made our signs for men of insight. And it is He who sendeth
down rain from Heaven: and we bring forth by it the germs of
all the plants, and from them bring we forth the green foliage,
and the close-growing grain; and from the palm-trees the low-
hanging date-clusters out of their sheaths: and gardens of grapes,
and the olive and the pomegranate, like and unlike. Look ye on
their fruits when they fruit and ripen. Truly herein are signs
unto people who believe. . . . As for me, my Lord hath guided
me into a straight path; a true religion, the creed of Abraham,
the sound in faith; for he was not one of those who join gods
with God. Verily my prayers and my worship and my life and
my death are unto God, Lord of the Worlds. He hath no
associate, and this am I commanded, and I am the first of the
Muslims. Shall I seek any other Lord than God, when He is
Lord of all things? No soul shall labour but for itself; and no
burdened one shall bear another's burden. At last ye shall
return to your Lord, and He will declare that to you about which
you differ. *Qur.* 6, 38–9, 59–60, 95–9, 162–4.

O men! if ye are in doubt as to my religion, then I worship
not whom ye worship beside God; but I worship God, who will
cause you to die: and I am commanded to be a believer. And
set thy face toward the true religion, sound in faith (Hanyf), and
be not of those who join other gods with God: neither invoke
beside God that which can neither help nor hurt thee: for if
thou do, thou wilt certainly then be one of the unjust. And if
God lay the touch of trouble on thee, there is none to remove it
but He: and if He would confer good upon thee, there is none
to keep back his bounty: He will confer it on such of his servants
as He chooseth: and He is the Gracious, the Merciful! O mankind! how hath the truth come unto you from your Lord. He
therefore who is guided aright, is guided only for his own behoof:
but he who is in error erreth only against the same; and I am not
guardian over you! And follow what is revealed to thee: and
persevere steadfastly till God shall judge, for He is the best of
Judges. *Qur.* 10, 104–9.

And who, from desire to behold the face of their Lord, are
constant amid trials, and observe prayer and give alms in secret

and openly out of what we have bestowed upon them, and turn aside evil by good : for these is the recompense of the Abode, Gardens of Eden—into which they shall enter together with the just of their fathers, and their wives, and their descendants : and the angels shall go in unto them at every portal. *Qur.* 13, 22–3.

And let not thy hand be tied up to thy neck; nor yet open it with all openness, lest thou sit thee down in rebuke, in beggary. Verily, thy Lord will provide with open hand for whom He pleaseth, and will be sparing. His servants doth He scan, in- spect. Moreover, kill not your children for fear of want : for them and for you will we provide. Verily, the killing them is a great wickedness. Have nought to do with adultery; verily it is a foul thing and an evil way : neither slay any one whom God hath forbidden you to slay, unless for a just cause : and whoso- ever shall be slain wrongfully, to his heir have we given powers; but let him not outstep bounds in putting the manslayer to death; he verily will be assisted and avenged. And touch not the sub- stance of the orphan, unless in an upright way, till he attain his age of strength : and perform your covenant; verily the covenant shall be inquired of : and give full measure when you measure, and weigh with just balance; this will be better, and fairest for settlement. And follow not that of which thou hast no know- ledge; verily the hearing and the sight and the heart,—each for this shall be inquired of : and walk not proudly on the earth : truly thou canst by no means cleave the earth, neither canst thou reach to the mountains in height. *Qur.* 17, 31–9.

The knowledge thereof is with my Lord in the Book of his decrees. My Lord erreth not, and doth not forget, who hath spread the earth for you as a bed, and hath made you to walk therein by paths, and hath sent down rain from the heaven, and by it we bring forth the kinds of various herbs, saying, " Eat ye, and feed your cattle "—Of a truth in this are signs unto men endued with understanding—From it have we created you, and into it will we return you, and out of it we bring you forth a second time. *Qur.* 20, 54–7.

O men! if ye are in doubt about the Resurrection, yet, of a truth, have we created you of dust, then of the moist germs of life, then of clots of blood, then of pieces of flesh shapen and unshapen, that we might give you proofs of our power! And we cause one sex or the other, at our pleasure to abide in the womb until the appointed time; then we bring you forth infants; then permit you to reach your age of strength; and one of you dieth, and another of you liveth on to an age so abject that all his former knowledge is clean forgotten! And thou hast seen the earth barren : but when we send down the rain upon it, it stirreth and swelleth, and groweth every kind of beauteous herb. This, for that God is the Truth, and that it is He who quickeneth the dead, and that He hath power over everything. *Qur.* 22, 5–6.

Happy now the believers, who humble them in their prayer, and who keep aloof from vain words, and who are doers of alms-deeds, and who restrain their appetites, (save with their wives, or the slaves whom their right hand possess; for in that case they shall be free from blame but thou whose desires reach further than this are transgressors :) and who tend well their trusts and their covenants, and who keep them strictly to their prayers : these shall be the heritors, who shall inherit the paradise, to abide therein for ever. *Qur.* 23, 1–11.

God is the light of the heavens and the earth; his light is as a niche in which is a lamp, and the lamp is in a glass, the glass is as though it were a glittering star; it is lit from a blessed tree, an olive neither of the east nor of the west, the oil of which would well nigh give light though no fire touched it,—light upon light. God guides to his light whom he pleases; and God strikes out parables for men, and God all things doth know. *Qur.* 24, 35.

They whom ye worship, ye and your fathers of old, are my foes; but not so the Lord of the Worlds, who hath created me, and guideth me, who giveth me food and drink; and when I am sick, then He healeth me, and who will cause me to die and again quicken me, and who, I hope, will forgive me my sins in the day of reckoning. My Lord! bestow on me wisdom and unite me to the just, and give me a good name among posterity, and make me one of the heirs of the garden of delight, and forgive my father, for he was one of the erring, and put me not to shame on the day when mankind shall be raised up, the day when neither wealth nor children shall avail, save to him who shall come to God with a sound heart, and Paradise shall be brought near the pious, and Hell shall be laid open to those who have gone astray. *Qur.* 26, 75–91.

Yes, and God is well acquainted with those who have believed, and He is well acquainted with the hypocrites. . . . The likeness for those who take to themselves guardians besides God is the likeness of the spider who buildeth her a house : but verily, frailest of all houses surely is the house of the spider. Did they but know this! . . . Dispute ye not, unless in kindliest sort, with the people of the Book; save with such of them as have dealt wrongfully with you : and say ye, "We believe in what hath been sent down to us and hath been sent down to you. Our God and your God is one, and to Him are we self-surrendered" (Muslims). And thus have we sent down the Book of the Qur'an to thee : and they to whom we have given the Book of the law believe in it : and of these Arabians there are those who believe in it : and none, save the Infidels, reject our signs. . . . God is a sufficient witness between me and you : He knoweth all that is in the Heavens and the Earth, and they who believe in vain things and disbelieve in God—these shall suffer loss. . . . Every soul shall taste of death : afterwards to us shall ye return. But those who have believed and wrought righteousness will we assuredly lodge in gardens with lofty apartments, beneath which the rivers flow, to abide therein for ever. Goodly the reward of those who labour, who patiently endure, and put their trust in their Lord! . . . And this present life is no other than a pastime and a disport : but truly the future mansion is life indeed! Would that they knew this! Then when they embark on shipboard, they call upon God, professing to Him the purity of their faith; but when He bringeth them safe to land, behold they join partners with Him, believing not in our revelation and yet take their fill of good things : but in the end they shall know their folly. Do they not see that we have established a safe precinct while all around them men despoil? Will they then believe in vain idols, and not own the goodness of God? *Qur.* 29, 10, 40, 45–6, 51–2, 57–9, 64–7.

O my son! join not other gods with God, verily, the joining gods with God is a great impiety. . . . O my son! verily God will bring everything to light, though it were but the weight of a grain of mustard-seed, and hidden in a rock or in the heavens or

in the earth; verily God is sharp-sighted, informed of all. O my
son! observe prayer, and enjoin the right and forbid the wrong,
and be patient under whatever shall betide thee : verily this is a
bounden duty. And distort not thy face at men; nor walk thou
loftily on the earth; verily God loveth no arrogant vain-glorious
person; but let thy pace be middling; and lower thy voice :
verily the least pleasing of voices is surely the voice of asses. . . .
And if all the trees that are upon the earth were to become pens,
and if God should after that swell the sea into seven seas of ink,
his words would not be exhausted : of a truth God is Mighty,
Wise. *Qur.* 31, 12, 15–18, 24–6.

If any one desireth greatness, greatness is wholly with God.
The good word riseth up to Him, and the righteous deed doth
He exalt. But a severe punishment awaiteth the plotters of evil
things; and the plots of such will be in vain. Moreover God
created you of dust—then of the germs of life—then made you
two sexes : and no female conceiveth or bringeth forth without
his knowledge; and the aged ageth not, nor is aught minished
from man's age, but in accordance with the Book. An easy thing
truly is this to God. Nor are the two seas alike : the one is fresh,
sweet, pleasant for drink, and the other salt, bitter; yet from
both ye eat fresh fish, and take forth for yourselves ornaments
to wear; and thou seest the ships cleaving the waters that ye
may go in quest of his bounties; and haply ye will be thankful.
He causeth the night to enter in upon the day, and the day to enter
in upon the night; and He hath given laws to the sun and to the
moon, so that each journeyeth to its appointed goal : this is God
your Lord : all power is his : but the gods whom ye call on beside
Him have no power over the husk of a date-stone! If ye cry to
them they hear not your cry, and if they heard they would not
answer you ; and in the day of Resurrection they will disown
your joining them with God. And none can instruct thee like
Him who is informed of all. O men! ye are but paupers in need
of God; but God is the Rich, the Praiseworthy! . . . And the
burdened soul shall not bear the burden of another : and if the
heavy-laden soul cry out for its burden to be carried, yet shall
not aught of it be carried, even by the near of kin! Thou shalt
only warn those who fear their Lord in secret, and observe prayer.
And whoever shall keep himself pure, he purifieth himself only

to his own behoof : for unto God shall be the journey back. . . .
Who of his bounty hath placed us in a mansion that shall abide
for ever : therein no toil shall reach us, and therein no weariness
shall touch us. But for unbelievers is the fire of Hell; to die
shall never be decreed them, nor shall aught of its torment be
made light to them. Thus reward we every infidel. . . . If
moreover, God should chastise men according to their deserts,
He would not leave even a reptile on the back of the earth ! *Qur.*
35, 11-16, 19, 32-3, 44.

O my people! this present life is only a passing joy, but verily
the life to come, that is the mansion that abideth. Whoso hath
wrought evil shall not be recompensed but with its like; but
whoso hath done the things that are right, whether male or female,
and is a believer—these shall enter paradise : without reckoning
shall they be supplied therein. And, O my people! how is it
that I bid you to salvation, but that ye bid me to the fire ? Ye
invite me to deny God, and to join with Him that of which I know
nothing; but I invite you to the Mighty, the Forgiving. *Qur.*
40, 42-5.

All that you receive is but for enjoyment in this life present :
but better and more enduring is a portion with God for those who
believe and put their trust in their Lord; and who avoid the
heinous things of crime, and filthinesses, and when they are
angered, forgive; and who hearken to their Lord, and observe
prayer, and whose affairs are guided by mutual counsel, and who
give alms of that with which we have enriched them; and who,
when a wrong is done them, redress themselves; yet let the
recompense of evil be only a like evil—but he who forgiveth and
maketh peace, shall find his reward for it from God; verily He
loveth not those who act unjustly. *Qur.* 42, 34-8.

Mohammed is the Apostle of God; and his comrades are most
vehement against unbelievers, but full of tenderness among
themselves. Thou mayest see them bowing down, prostrating
themselves, imploring favours from God and his good pleasure in
them. Their tokens are on their faces, the traces of their prostra-
tions. This is their picture in the Law, and their picture in the
Evangel—they are as the seed which putteth forth its stalk; and
strengtheneth it, and it groweth stout, and riseth upon its stem,

rejoicing the sowers—to incense unbelievers by their means. To such of them as believe and do good works, hath God promised forgiveness and a noble recompense. *Qur.* 48, 29.

Shall man have whatever he wisheth? The future and the present are in the hand of God: and many as are the Angels in the Heavens, their intercession shall be of no avail save after God hath permitted it to whom He shall please, and whom He will accept. Verily, it is they who believe not in the life to come, who name the angels with names of females: but herein they have no knowledge: verily they follow a mere conceit; and truly mere conceit can profit nothing against the truth. Withdraw then from him who turneth his back on our warning and desireth only this present life. This is the sum of their knowledge. Truly thy Lord best knoweth him who erreth from his way, and He best knoweth him who hath received guidance. And whatever is in the Heavens and in the Earth is God's, that He may recompense those who do evil according to their deeds, and recompense those who do good with good things. . . . That no burdened soul shall bear the burdens of another, and that nothing shall be reckoned to a man but that for which he hath striven, and that his efforts shall at last be seen in their true light: then he shall be recompensed with the most exact recompense. *Qur.* 53, 24–33, 39–42.

But God measureth the night and the day:—He knoweth that ye cannot count its hours aright, and therefore turneth to you mercifully. Recite then so much of the Qur'an as may be easy to you. He knoweth that there will be some among you sick, while others travel through the earth in quest of the bounties of God; and others do battle in his cause. Recite therefore so much of it as may be easy. And observe the Prayers and pay the legal Alms, and lend God a liberal loan: for whatever good works ye send on before for your own behoof, ye shall find with God. This will be best and richest in the recompense. And seek the forgiveness of God: verily, God is forgiving, Merciful. *Qur.* 73, 20.

O thou enwrapped in thy mantle! Arise and warn! And thy Lord—magnify Him! And thy raiment—purify it! And the abomination—flee it! And bestow not favours that thou mayest receive again with increase; and for thy Lord wait thou patiently. For when there shall be a trump on the trumpet, that then shall

be a distressful day, a day, to the unbelievers, devoid of ease. . . .
Thus God misleadeth whom He will, and whom He will doth
He guide aright; and none knoweth the armies of thy Lord but
He; and this is no other than a warning to mankind. Nay, by
the Moon! And by the Night when it retreateth! And by the
Morn when it brighteneth! Verily, Hell is one of the most
grievous woes, fraught with warning to man, to him among you
who desireth to press forward, or to remain behind. *Qur.* 74,
1–10, 34–40.

But man chooseth to go astray as to his future. He asketh,
" When this day of Resurrection ? " When then the eyesight
shall be dazzled, and the moon shall be darkened, and the sun and
the moon shall be together, on that day man shall cry, " Where
is there a place to flee to ? " But in vain—there is no place of
refuge—with thy Lord on that day shall be the sole asylum. On
that day shall man be told of all that he hath done first and last;
yea, a man shall be the evidence against himself : and even if he
put forth his pleas. *Qur.* 75, 5–15.

Have we not made the Earth a couch ? and the mountains its
tent-stakes ? and we have created you of two sexes, and ordained
your sleep for rest, and ordained the night as a mantle, and
ordained the day for gaining livelihood, and built above you
seven solid heavens, and placed therein a brightly-burning lamp;
and we send down water in abundance from the rain-clouds, that
we may bring forth by it corn and herbs, and gardens thick with
trees. Lo! the day of Severance is fixed; the day when there
shall be a blast on the trumpet, and ye shall come in crowds, and
the heavens shall be opened and be full of portals, and the mountains shall be set in motion, and become thin vapour. Hell truly
shall be a place of snares, the home of transgressors, to abide therein
ages; no coolness shall they taste therein nor any drink, save
boiling water and running sores; meet recompense! Verily they
looked not forward to their account; and they gave the lie to our
signs, charging them with falsehood; but we noted and wrote
down all; " Taste this then : and we will not give you increase
but of torment." . . . Verily, we warn you of a chastisement close
at hand; the day on which a man shall see the deeds which his
hands have sent before him; and when the unbeliever shall say,
" Oh! would I were dust! " *Qur.* 78, 6–30, 40–1.

When the sun shall be folded up, and when the stars shall fall, and when the mountains shall be set in motion, and when the she-camels shall be abandoned, and when the wild beasts shall be gathered together, and when the seas shall boil, and when souls shall be paired with their bodies, and when the female child that had been buried alive shall be asked for what crime she was put to death, and when the leaves of the book shall be unrolled, and when the heaven shall be stripped away, and when hell shall be made to blaze, and when paradise shall be brought near, every soul shall know what it hath produced. *Qur.* 18, 1–14.

Verily thy Lord is upon a watch-tower; but as to man, when his Lord trieth him, and honoureth him, and is bounteous to him, then saith he, "My Lord honoureth me:" but when He proveth him and limiteth his gifts to him, he saith, "My Lord despiseth me." Nay, but ye honour not the orphan, nor urge ye one another to feed the poor, and ye devour heritages, devouring greedily, and ye love riches with exceeding love. *Qur.* 89, 13–21.

By the night when she spreadeth her veil; by the Day when it appeareth in glory; by Him who made male and female; verily your aims are indeed different! As then for him who giveth alms and feareth God, and yieldeth assent to the Good; to him will we therefore make easy the path to happiness. But as to him who is covetous and bent on riches, and calleth the Good a lie, to him will we make easy the path to distress; and what shall his wealth avail him when he goeth down headlong? Truly man's guidance is with us, and ours, the next life and this life Present. I warn you therefore of the flaming fire, none shall be burned at it but the most wretched,—who hath called the truth a lie and turned his back. But the greatly God-fearing shall escape it,— who giveth away his substance that he may become pure; and who offereth not favours to any one for the sake of recompense, but only as seeking the face of his Lord the Most High. And assuredly in the end he shall be well content. *Qur.* 92, 1–21.

By the noonday brightness, and by the night when it darkeneth! Thy Lord hath not forsaken thee, neither hath he been displeased. And surely the future shall be better for thee than the past, and in the end shall thy Lord be bounteous to thee and thou be satisfied. Did he not find thee an orphan and gave thee a home? And found thee erring and guided thee, and found

thee needy and enriched thee. As to the orphan therefore wrong
him not; and as to him that asketh of thee chide him not away;
and as for the favours of thy Lord tell them abroad. *Qur.* 93,
1–11.

> READ! in the name of thy Lord who created;—
> Created man from Clots of Blood :—
> Read! For thy Lord is the most beneficent,
> Who hath taught the use of the pen :—
> Hath taught man that which he knew not.
>
> Nay, verily, man is most extravagant in wickedness
> Because he seeth himself possessed of wealth.
> Verily unto the Lord is the return of all.
> What thinkest thou of him who forbiddeth
> A servant of God when he prayeth ?
> What thinkest thou ? that he hath followed the true guidance
> of enjoined piety ?
> What thinkest thou, if he hath treated the truth as a lie and
> turned his back ?
> Doth he not know that God seeth ?
>
> Nay, verily, if he desist not, we will assuredly seize him by the
> forelock!
> The lying sinful forelock!
> Then let him summon his associates;
> We too will summon the guards of hell :
> Nay! obey him not; but adore, and draw nigh to God.
>
> *Qur.* 96, 1–19.

When the earth is shaken with its shaking, and when the Earth
hath cast forth her burdens, and man shall say, What aileth her ?
On that day shall she tell out her tidings, because thy Lord hath
inspired her. On that day shall men come forward in bands to
behold their works, and whosoever shall have wrought an atom's
weight of good shall behold it, and whosoever shall have wrought
an atom's weight of evil shall behold it. *Qur.* 99, 1–8.

Are you less than a piece of earth ? When a piece of earth
finds a friend, that is, the spring, it gains a hundred thousand
flowers. The tree if it be associated with a friend, the pleasant
breezes, will be covered and adorned with blossoms. When it

sees a false friend in the autumn, it draws its head and face under cover. A bad friend is an exciter of calamity; when such comes, my course is to sleep. . . . When the crows pitch their tents upon the winter, the nightingales conceal themselves and are silent. For without the rose-garden the nightingale is silent: the absence of the sun dispels wakefulness. O sun, you abandon this rose-garden in order to illumine the parts beneath the earth. But the Sun of spiritual knowledge suffers no change of place: its point of rising is only the soul and intellect. Especially that perfect Sun which is the best, whose action day and night is the giving of light. *Mas.*

Do not cherish malice, for those whom malice leads astray— their graves are placed by the side of the malicious. The origin of malice is hell, and your malice is a part of that whole, and an enemy to your religion. If you are a part of hell, then bear in mind that the part settles towards its whole. And if, O you of good fame, you are a part of paradise, you will have permanent pleasure through paradise. The bitter is assuredly joined to those who are bitter; how can false words be associated with the true? You, O brother, are only thought; as regards the rest of you, you are merely bone and fibre. If your thought is a rose, you are a rose-garden; and if it is a thorn, you are fuel for the furnace. If you are rose-water, they put you on their head and bosom; and if you are as urine they throw you out. See the trays in front of perfumer-grocers,—how the latter put kind and kind together : mingling together articles of one kind with those of the same, and bringing out a charm through this homogeneity. If lentils should get mixed with their pieces of sugar, they separate them from each other one by one. The trays broke, and the souls were scattered : good and bad were mingled with one another. God sent prophets with inspired leaves, that He might separate these different grains from one another on the tray. Before this, we were one great community; no one knew whether we were good or bad. False coin and true were equally current in the world, since it was all night, and we were as travellers in the night. Until the Sun of the prophets arose, and said, Begone you who are alloyed; you who are true come forth! The eye knows how to distinguish between colours; the eye knows rubies and common stones. The eye knows the gem, and it knows bits of straw and dust; for that reason bits of straw and dust prick the eye. These persistent forgers of coin are enemies of the day; but those pieces of gold fresh from the mine are lovers of the day. *Mas.*

The unbeliever and the believer utter the name of God; but between the two there is a good difference. That beggar uses the name of God for the sake of bread; the pious man utters it from his very soul. If the beggar knew anything of the word he utters, neither less would remain before his eyes nor more. For years that beggar of bread utters God's name : like an ass he bears the Qur'an for the sake of chopped straw. If the words on his lips had shone in his heart, his body would have become as motes. *Mas.*

If you flee in the hope of some relief, a calamity meets you on that side also. No corner is without wild beasts; except in the house of communion with God there is no rest. No corner of that inevitable prison, the world, is exempt from guerdon to those who come to you, and from mat-treading. By Allah! if you go even into a mouse-hole, you will be troubled by one who has claws like a cat. A man has fatness and health from his thoughts if his thoughts are beautiful; but if his thoughts exhibit anything unpleasant, he melts away as wax from a fire. *Mas.*

How happy is he who takes advantage of early days, and pays his debt :—Those days when he has power, health, energy of heart, and strength; that state of youth, like a verdant and fresh garden, yielding produce and fruit unstintingly; the springs of strength and eager desire flowing, and the soil of the body verdant through them; a house well-built, with lofty roof, its walls in just proportion, and without addition or stay;—before the days of old-age come on, and bind the neck with " a cord of woody fibre "; before the soil becomes barren, dry, and poor :—never do fine plants grow from barren soil; when the water of energy, and the water of eager desire cut off, he derives no benefit from himself or from others. *Mas.*

A certain unfeeling person of pleasant speech planted a bramble-bush in the middle of the road. The passers by reproached him, and repeatedly told him to dig it up; but he did not do so. And every moment that bramble-bush was getting larger, and the feet of the people were covered with blood from the wounds it inflicted. The clothes of the people were torn by its thorns; and the feet of the poor were miserably wounded. When the Governor enjoined him seriously to dig it up, he answered, "Yes, I will dig it up some day." For a good time he promised to do it to-morrow and to-morrow; and in the mean time his bramble-bush grew firm and robust. The Governor said to him one day, "O promise-breaker, come forward in my business; do not creep back." He rejoined, "O uncle, the days are between us." The Governor said, "Hasten; defer not the payment of my debt. You who say 'To-morrow,' learn you this, that in every day which time brings, that evil tree grows younger, and this digger of it up gets more old and helpless. The bramble-bush is gaining strength and on the rise; whilst the proposed digger of it up is getting old and on the decline. The bramble-bush every day and every moment more green and fresh; the digger of it up every day more emaciated and withered. It is becoming younger, and you are becoming older; be quick therefore, and do not waste your time. Consider the bramble-bush as any bad habit of yours; its thorns at last will often wound your feet." *Mas.*

The being of man is like a forest;—be full of caution of this being if you are of that Breath. In our being there are thousands of wolves and hogs. In our being there is the righteous, the unrighteous; the fair and the foul. That trait which is predominant decides the temperament; when gold exceeds copper in quantity, the substance is gold. The quality which is predominant in your being,—you will have to rise in the very form of that same quality. At one moment wolfishness comes into man; at another moment, the moon-like beauty of the face of Joseph. Feelings of peace and of enmity go by a hidden road from bosom to bosom. Nay, indeed, wisdom, knowledge, and skill pass from man even into the ox and the ass. The untrained horse, rough and unformed, becomes of good easy paces and docile; the bear dances, and the goat also salutes. From men the desire of doing something enters into the dog: he becomes a shepherd, or a hunter, or a guard. From those Sleepers a moral nature passed to the dog of the Companions of the Cave, so that he became a seeker of God. Every moment a new species appears in the bosom; sometimes a demon, sometimes an angel, and sometimes wild beasts. From that wonderful Forest with which every Lion is acquainted there is a hidden road to that snare, the bosoms of men. *Mas.*

I am independent of the acknowledgment of the world: what care has he in whose favour God is a witness? If a bat finds anything agreeable and consonant in a sun, it is a proof that that supposed sun is not a sun. The aversion of the little bats is a proof that I am a resplendent, glorious sun. If the beetle is eager for some supposed rose-water, that is a proof of its not being rose-water. If a counterfeit coin seeks a supposed touch-stone, there is imperfection in the latter as a touchstone, and doubt as to its being one. The thief wishes for night, not day :— know this therefore that I am not night; I am day, which shines in the world. I am a discerner, a great discriminator, and like a sieve; so that straw does not pass through me. I distinguish the flour from the bran, to show clearly that the latter is only the external form, the former the soul. I am like God's balance in the world: I distinguish every light thing from that which is heavy. The calf considers the cow as its God: the ass is a seeker, and an unripe melon as its fitting aim and object. I am not a cow that the calf should seek me: I am not a thorny bramble that a camel should browse upon me. He thinks that he has inflicted injury upon me; but indeed he has brushed away the dust from my mirror. *Mas.*

Then consider that visiting friends is a necessary custom, whatever they be, on foot, or mounted. And if it be an enemy, this act of kindness is still good, for many an enemy by kindness becomes a friend. And even if he do not become a friend, his enmity is lessened, since kindness is a salve to enmity. Besides these, there are many advantages in visiting, but I am fearful of prolixity, good friend. The sum and substance is this: be the friend of all: like an idol-maker carve out a friend from stone; because the multitude and concourse of a caravan will break the backs and the spears of highway-robbers. *Mas.*

If there were not blemished goods in the world, all merchants would be fools. Then the appreciation of goods would be excessively easy. When there is nothing faulty what is the difference between the unworthy and the worthy? And if there

is nothing but fault, there is no advantage in intelligence : when
there is nothing but common wood here, there is no aloes-wood.
He who says that all are right and true,—it is in folly; and he
who says all are wrong and false,—he is accursed. The merchants
of the prophets have gained profit; the merchants of the world
are unfortunate and wretched. That which is really a snake
appears wealth in your eyes : rub both your eyes well, and see
it as it is. *Mas.*

Your sincere feeling led you to seek; my seeking led me to
sincere feeling. I was really sowing the seed of good fortune in
the ground, but I thought at first my work was nothing but
labour without pay. It was not labour without pay; it was a
fine gain : for every single grain I sowed a hundred grew. A
thief, for instance, goes secretly toward a house; when he enters
it he sees it is his own house. Be ardent, cold man, that ardour
may come to you. Put up with hardship, that ease may come to
you. *Mas.*

When you are not a perfect master do not take a shop by
yourself alone. Submit to be kneaded, in order that you may become paste. . . . The beginning of pride and hatred is from worldly
desire; the stability of your worldly desire comes from habit
and custom. When your evil quality has become strengthened
by habit, you get angry with the person who restrains you. When
you have become a clay-eater, every one who restrains you from
the clay is in your opinion an enemy to you. Since idolaters are
devoted to their idols, they are inimical to those who impede the
way to them. . . . Since you are always thinking of leadership
and superiority, whoever mortifies and checks you is an in-
veterate enemy. When a person says anything opposed to your
habitual feeling, great hatred arises in your heart against him. . . .
Until copper becomes gold it does not know that it was copper :
until the heart becomes king it does not know that it was a bank-
rupt. *Mas.*

A man gave a diram to four persons; one of them a Persian
said, " I will spend this on ' angur '." Another of them was an
Arab; he said, " No, you rogue; I want ' inab ', not ' angur '."
A third was a Turk; he said, " I do not want ' inab ', dear friend,
I want ' uzum '." The fourth was a Greek; he said, " Stop

this altercation; I wish for 'istafil'." Those persons began to fight against one another, because they were ignorant of the secret of the names. Through sheer ignorance they struck one another with their fists; they were full of ignorance and devoid of knowledge. If one who knew the inner truth, an estimable man versed in many tongues, had been there, he would have reconciled them. He would have said, "With this one diram I will gratify the desire of all of you. If in all sincerity you entrust your hearts to me, this diram of yours will do so much for you. Your one diram will become as four, which is what is wanted; four enemies will become as one by concord. The words of each of you lead you to contention and disagreement; my words bring your agreement. Therefore be you silent, keep silence, in order that I may be your tongue in speech. Although your words appear uniform and in harmony, they are the source in their effect of contention and anger. (The contention as to grapes of four persons, each of whom knows grapes by a different name.) *Mas.*

Do not be envious of each other; and do not outbid each other; and do not hate each other; do not oppose each other; and do not undersell each other; and be, O slaves of Allah, as brothers. A Muslim is a brother to a Muslim, not oppressing him and not forsaking him; not lying to him and not despising him. Here is true piety (and he, Mohammed, would point to his breast three times)—it is quite bad enough for a man to despise his brother Muslim. A Muslim's life, property and honour are inviolate to a Muslim. He who dispels from a believer one of the griefs of the world, Allah will dispel for him a grief on the Day of Resurrection; he who cheers up a person in difficulties, Allah will cheer him in this world and the next; he who shields a Muslim, Allah will shield him in this world and the next. Allah is there to help his slave, so long as he is out to help his brother, and he who walks a path seeking therein knowledge, Allah will make easy for him a path to paradise through it. And when a company meets together in one of the houses of Allah to pore over the book of Allah and to study it together amongst themselves, the Shechinah comes down to them and mercy overshadows them; and the angels surround them; and Allah remembers them among them that are his; and the one whose work makes him procrastinate will not be hastened along by the nobility of his ancestry. Be in the world as if you were a stranger or a traveller; when evening time comes, expect not the morning; and when morning time comes expect not the evening; and prepare as long as you are in good health for sickness, and so long as you are alive for death. So long as you call upon me and hope in me, I forgive you all that originates from you; and I will not heed, O son of man, should your sins reach the horizon of the heavens, and then you asked my pardon and I would pardon you. O son of man, were you to come to me with almost an earthful of sins, and then you met me without joining anything with me in the godhead, then would I come to you with an earthful of forgiveness. *An-Nawawi.*

There are seven people whom God will draw under his own shadow, on that day when there will be no other shadow, on a just king; another, who hath employed himself in devotion from his youth; the third, who fixeth his heart on the Mosque till he return to it; the fourth, two men whose friendship is to please God, whether together or separate; the fifth, a man who remembereth God when he is alone, and weepeth; the sixth, a man who is tempted by a rich and beautiful woman, and saith, Verily, I fear God! the seventh, a man who hath given alms and concealed it, so that his left hand knoweth not what his right hand doeth. *Mis.*

Ye must not say your prayers at the rising or the setting of the sun : so when a limb of the sun appeareth, leave your prayers until her whole orb is up : and when the sun beginneth to set, quit your prayers until the whole orb hath disappeared; for, verily she riseth between the two horns of the Devil. . . . When a Muslim performeth the ablution, it washeth from his face those faults which he may have cast his eyes upon; and when he washeth his hands, it removeth the faults they may have committed, and when he washeth his feet, it dispelleth the faults towards which they may have carried him : so that he will rise up in purity from the place of ablution. *Table-Talk of Mohammed.*

Keep fast and eat also, stay awake at night and sleep also, because verily there is a duty on you to your body, not to labour overmuch, so that ye may not get ill and destroy yourselves; and verily there is a duty on you to your eyes, ye must sometimes sleep and give them rest; and verily there is a duty on you to your wife, and to your visitors and guests that come to see you; ye must talk to them; and nobody hath kept fast who fasted always; the fast of three days in every month is equal to constant fasting : then keep three days fast in every month. *Table-Talk of Mohammed.*

Verily the best things which ye eat are those which ye earn yourselves or which your children earn. Verily it is better for one of you to take a rope and bring a bundle of wood upon his back and sell it, in which case God guardeth his honour, than to beg of people, whether they give him or not; if they do not give him, his reputation suffereth and he returneth disappointed; and if they give him, it is worse than that, for it layeth him under obligations. *Table-Talk of Mohammed.*

My son, fear God both secretly and openly; speak the truth, whether you be calm or angry; be economical, whether you be poor or rich; be just to friend and foe; be resigned alike in times of adversity and prosperity. My son, he who sees his own faults has no time to see the faults of others; he who is satisfied with the allotments of Providence does not regret the past; he who unsheaths the sword of aggression will be killed by it; he who digs a pit for his brother will fall into it; he who forgets his own sin makes much of the sin of another; he who takes to evil ways will be despised; he who commits excesses will be known to do them; he who associates with the base will be subject to constant suspicion; he who remembers death will be content with little in this world; he who boasts of his sins before men, God will bring him to shame. *Instructions of Ali Ibn-abi Talib, the first Khalif, to his son. Wortabet's Arabian Wisdom.*

I have heard many sermons and had many counsels, but I have heard no preacher so effective as my grey hairs, and no counsellor so effectual as the voice of my own conscience. I have eaten the most choice food, and drunk the best kinds of wine, and enjoyed the love of the most beautiful women; but I found no pleasure so great as that of sound health. I have swallowed the bitterest food and drink, but I found nothing so bitter as poverty. I have worked at iron, and carried heavy weights, but I found no burden so heavy as that of debt. I have sought wealth in all its form, but found no riches so great as those of contentment. (*The experiences of an old man.*) *Wortabet's Arabian Wisdom.*

12

SIKHISM

WITH the rise of Islam, an account of which was given in the previous chapter, it may well seem that the last word in monotheism had now been uttered. Reacting against Christianity, with its doctrine of the threefold manifestation in the Trinity and the necessity for divine Incarnation, Islam had reasserted the Singleness, Aloneness, and Unity of God with all the fervour and passion of the Jews of old. It may seem strange, therefore, that, in the fourteenth century, yet another religion arose in which the Oneness of God was the leading doctrine. This was the religion of the Sikhs, and it is the last which will be considered in this book.

Sikhism does not compete, however, with Muhammadanism for world domination. Its numbers are few, and it is confined entirely to India : it has never made converts outside that country. Indeed, the view is sometimes taken that it is simply one of the many sects of the Hindus, and it will be useful here to recall what was said in Chapter 8 about the nature of a sect. A sect is a subdivision of some larger religion, and it accepts the same scriptures, the same prophets, and the same general doctrine as the parent body. The Quakers and Congregationalists are sects of the Christians : because they all rely on the authority of the Bible and the teaching of Christ : only in matters of *interpretation* do they break away from the larger body. In the same way Sunnites and Shi-ites are sects of the Muhammadans, and both refer to the authority of the Koran and of the prophet Muhammad. The Sikh claim to independence is that they have their own Scriptures, observances, and special way of life, their own sacred city, and, above all, their own founder and line of prophets. It is true that much of the background of Hinduism is assumed in Sikhism, and it is this which distinguishes it from the monotheism of Muhammad, which was explained in the last chapter. This will become clearer as the religion is examined.

Sikhism arose in North-West India, where Islam contacted the older religion of the Brahmans. It may be said to owe much to this impact, for the exponents of both religions were disputing with one another, and it seemed to some of the religious searchers of the time that neither was giving the right solution. There had already been monotheistic movements within Hinduism itself. These were gaining strength as protests against the polytheism of the masses on the one hand, and the mystical and impersonal monism of the Brahmans on the other. Notably there was the teaching of Kabir, a weaver, who was born in North-West India and who was brought up by Muhammadans. Kabir was a fine poet, and he uttered many hymns in praise of the One True God : yet, though influenced no doubt by Islam, he lived and died within the pale of Hinduism. The Sikhs owe much to Kabir, and some of his hymns are included in their Scriptures. The true founder of Sikhism, however, the man who really broke away from the authority of Brahmanism and evolved a new monotheistic creed, was Nanak, called by the faithful, Baba, or Father, Nanak. The word " Sikh " simply means disciple.

Nanak was born in the year 1496, at a little town called Talwandi, about thirty miles south-west of Lahore in the Punjab. The village still stands, but it has been renamed Nanaka, in honour of the founder of the Sikh religion. Nanak's father, Kalu, and mother, Tripta, were strict Hindus of the Khatri caste, but the Governor of the district, Rai Bular, who lived on a hill above. was an enlightened Muhammadan. Very early, Nanak showed an interest in religion, and he probably acquired a favourable view of Islam. When, at nine years old, the Brahman priest came to invest him with the Sacred Thread, which was to initiate him into his caste, he protested, uttering a hymn which is preserved in the Scriptures. Nanak went to the village school, but he spent much time disputing in the surrounding forests with holy men whom he found there. When he refused to take up regular work his parents doubted his sanity, but he eventually took service with Rai Bular, and it is possible that he even became a Moslem for a time. At the age of fourteen he married Sulakhami, and later had two sons by her, but little beyond this is known of his married life. Contact with Islam did not satisfy the young Nanak for long. He left the Governor's service and went out into the forest to adopt the life of a wandering preacher.

In order perhaps to show that he desired to blend the two religions, he wore a remarkable mixture of Muhammadan and Hindu dress, and he took with him his minstrel, Mardana. It is said that at first he was severely tempted by the Devil, who tried to persuade him to return to his home. He triumphed, however, and then received a vision of God, Who gave him instructions for his mission. Thereafter he proclaimed his teaching by means of improvising and chanting hymns, which were accompanied on the rebeck by the minstrel. These hymns are preserved in the Sikh writings, and from them we can get the main ideas of the new doctrines, which are as follows:

There is but one God—infinitely holy, wise, and lovable, who can be approached by prayer and praise and devotion of the whole heart. He needs no ascetic practices, but neither can He be found by the worldly and self-indulgent. The caste system has no importance in his eyes, and all persons, including women and even outcasts, are equal. Hindus and Muhammadans, too, are all alike. The one thing needful is to worship with absolute simplicity and sincerity. The gods of the Hindus may exist as vassal spirits, creations of the Supreme Deity, but they have no importance as compared with Him. Pilgrimages and the honouring of idols are of no avail. Men should marry and live the ordinary life of the world, but remember God all the time. If they do this, God can save them from having to be born again and again, and they will find rest and deliverance from suffering in Him. Wine and drugs should be avoided, but meat should be eaten, and there was no merit in having food cooked in a particular way or by a particular person, as the Brahmans taught.

Nanak thus rejected the entire Hindu social system, but he accepted much of the cosmology of the Hindus, that part of the religion which explains how the world came into being and the nature of the human soul. The Hindus believed, as we saw in Chapter 2, that God created Maya, Illusion, and that Illusion resulted in the false appearance of material things and the separateness of individual souls. The fate of these human souls is governed by Karma (lit., Works), that law of cause and effect which compels a man to be born over and over again, according to the deeds which he has committed, until at last be becomes purified from all worldly association, *bad or good*, and reabsorbed into the divine life. Nanak accepted the doctrine of Maya and

the working of the Law of Karma, but held that by trust in the
One God, and by worshipping Him with absolute sincerity and
simplicity, this circle, this " wheel of transmigration," could be
broken and the soul, however before imperfect, could return to
God without having to be reincarnated in the world. Nirvana,
the Hindu Heaven, reabsorbtion into the divine life, was the
goal, though the later Sikh Scriptures also make mention of Sach
Khand, a kind of Paradise. Thus the background of Nanak's
teaching had more in common with Hinduism than Muhammadanism, but, on the other hand, his rejection of the caste
system and his fervour of devotion to the One True God showed
the influence of Islam. His doctrine was, however, much
simpler than either Hinduism or Muhammadanism, as he found
them in his time. He advocated the middle way, in which the
extremes both of asceticism and self-indulgence were to be avoided.
He promised no luxurious Paradise, such as that described in the
Koran : the love of God was all-sufficient, both here and hereafter. There was one Hindu ritual, however, which was retained
by Nanak, and that was the repetition of God's Name. This was a
general Hindu practice, many people repeating the name of their
particular deity many thousands of times daily. Nanak believed
that if this were done with sincerity and simplicity it would help
to keep the mind of the worshipper fixed on God. The new name
was Wah-Guru, which means Great Teacher.

Having formulated his creed, Nanak went on through the
forest teaching and preaching. He met holy men who were
engaged in life-long meditation and in ascetic practices, and many
of these inquired whether he were a Muhammadan or a Hindu.
To this he always replied that he worshipped the One God, Who
took no account of either religion. All his life was spent in this
way. Sometimes he went home and saw his family, who became
his disciples. It is said that he travelled as far south as Ceylon
and as far west as Mecca. He met with little opposition, at least
not of a violent kind, and seems to have been generally beloved.
When he died, it is said that Hindus and Muhammadans quarrelled
as to which should have the honour of disposing of his body.
His death occurred in 1538, and he appointed his servant and
disciple Angad to be his successor.

Angad lived much as Guru Nanak had done. He, too, was
married, but much of his time was spent wandering and preach-

ing. A special work of his was the creation of Gurumukhi, literally the Guru's tongue, which was a modification of the Punjabi alphabet. This he used for the transcription of Guru Nanak's hymns, and it has been employed for Sikh sacred literature ever since. This first collection of hymns, to which Angad added some of his own, was the beginning of the Scriptures, which finally became the Granth Sahib, or Noble Book, of the Sikhs. Angad died in 1552, and appointed his servant, Amar Das, as his successor.

Amar Das lived a more settled life than the first two Gurus, and established headquarters at Goindwal. There he stressed Nanak's attitude to caste by refusing to see anyone who had not first eaten from his kitchen. He also began the foundation of a great lake, called Amritsar (lit., the Lake of Nectar). He died in 1574, bestowing the Guruship on his servant and son-in-law, Jetha, who took the name of Ram Das.

Ram Das continued the excavation of the lake and laid the foundation of the Golden Temple, which was to stand in the middle of it. The site had been granted by the Moghul Emperor Akbar, who, unlike most of his dynasty, was tolerant towards all religions. For this work money was needed, and Ram Das began to collect regular offerings from his followers. He appointed officials, who were called Masands and who played a prominent part in the organization of the Sikh religion. Later on these men became dishonest and were abolished by the tenth Guru. When Ram Das died in 1581, he chose one of his sons as his successor, and thereafter the office of Guru became hereditary. On this occasion, however, the eldest son, Pirthi Chand, was passed over, though he made some effort to assert his claim and founded an order of his own.

Arjun, the fifth Guru, was, with the exceptions of Nanak, the first, and Gobind-Singh the tenth, the greatest of all the Gurus. Having completed the tank of Amritsar, he began to build the Mandar, or Golden Temple, the foundations of which had been laid by Ram Das. He also edited and enlarged the collection of Sikh religious poems, adding a number of his own. He was a fine poet, and actually half the completed work was written by him. Hymns by earlier reformers, both Hindus and Muhammadans, were admitted, notably those by Kabir, the monotheistic Hindu who had been brought up by Muhammadans. The volume was now considered complete; it received the title of Granth Sahib and became the Bible of the Sikh religion. Later it was called the *Adi*, or first, Granth, to distinguish it from a volume that was compiled in the name of the tenth Guru.

The Sikhs now possessed a sacred volume written in their special script, they had a large number of adherents, some wealth, a holy lake, and the beginnings, at least, of a temple with a city around it. The attention of both Hindus and Muhammadans was directed to their organization, and complaints of impiety were made to the Emperor Akbar. This tolerant monarch examined the Scriptures, dismissed the complaints, and paid the Guru a reverent visit. His fanatical son, Jehangir, was, however, much more bigoted, and excessively cruel. His own son Khusru rebelled against him, and Guru Arjan unfortunately received this prince with hospitality and lent him money. This gave Jehangir an excuse to summon the Guru to Delhi. When there he was ordered to erase certain passages from the Granth Sahib. This he refused to do, and was subjected to terrible tortures, from which he died in 1606. The Sikhs now claimed their first martyr, and the sixth Guru, Har Gobind, surrounded himself with a bodyguard and ordered his followers to take up arms. This they were well qualified to do, for their rule of life had made them stronger than the peoples round them. They rose early, bathed in cold water, ate meat, and abstained from wine, drugs, and tobacco. They took no part in pilgrimages (so prolific a cause of disease in India) or in any extremes of self-indulgence or asceticism. Thus they had the makings of good warriors, and Sikhism now passed from a quietistic body to a militant theocracy. Har Gobind was imprisoned in the fortress of Gwaldor for twelve years, but he afterwards resisted the new Emperor, Shah Jehan, and claimed various victories over the Imperial troops. He was Guru for thirty-nine years and died in 1645; neither he nor his grandson, Har Rai, who succeeded him, left any hymns.

Har Rai upheld the cause of the Sikhs against oppression for sixteen years, and when he died in 1661, his eldest son was a hostage at the Court of the Emperor. For this reason Har Krishan, a boy only five years old, became Guru. When this child died of small-pox less than three years later, the question of a successor presented a difficulty, but at last a great-uncle of Har Krishan's was found in a remote village and persuaded to take office. This man, named Teg Bahadur, though old, was exceedingly courageous, and he protested to the fanatical Emperor Aurangzeb against his persecution of the Hindus. Aurangzeb, who was cruel and violent, was burning down Hindu temples and destroying sacred places greatly beloved by the people. This protest caused the Guru to be summoned to Delhi, and when imprisoned there he uttered a prophecy about the coming of the Europeans. He was accused of looking in the direction of the Zenana where the Queens lived, and he then replied, addressing the Emperor, " I was not looking at the Imperial Zenana; I was looking in the direction of the Europeans, who are coming from beyond the seas to tear down thy pardas and destroy thy Empire."

Some of these words were used in the battle-cry of the Sikhs in the siege of Delhi in 1857. Teg Bahadur was offered honour and freedom if he would become a Muhammadan, but, refusing to do this, he was beheaded in 1675. The fifth and ninth Gurus had now been martyred by Moghul Emperors, and Sikh military zeal became greater than ever.

The tenth and last Guru, Gobind Rai, son of Teg Bahadur, surrounded himself with a large army, and every new disciple was enrolled as a soldier and received what was known as the Khanda-di-Pahul, the Baptism of the Sword. The title Singh (lion) was then added to their names. Some Sikhs refused the Baptism, and were known as Sadhijdharis, or livers-at-ease. These were not warriors, but traders or agriculturists, and this was the first split in the organization. The followers of Gobind Singh received the name of *Khalsa*, which comes from the Arabic word meaning " pure," and they were distinguished by the wearing of five articles, the names of which all began with a K. These were *Kes*, long hair; *Kangha*, a comb; *Kripan*, a sword; *Kachh*, knee-breeches; and *Kara*, a steel bracelet. Each had a symbolical significance, and the strict Sikh can still be recognized by these five things. When Aurangzeb died, Guru Gobind Singh made friends with the new Emperor, Bahadur Shah, and the two went hunting together. But there was still fighting among their followers, and it is said that the Guru himself was stabbed by a Muhammadan, a wound from which he eventually died in 1708. Both Gobind Singh's sons having been killed, he announced that he would appoint no successor, but that the Khalsa and the Granth Sahib between them would carry on the work. The

Noble Book, which was placed in the centre of the Golden Temple at Amritsar, was thenceforth honoured as Guru. Thus the line of the ten Gurus came to an end. Gobind Singh wrote many hymns, in praise of the Sword and other weapons, but he also wrote poems of a highly mystical religious character. He made greater personal claims than his predecessors, for he says: " I am the Son of the Immortal God, Who has sent me into the world to restore religion. . . . I did not desire to come, for my attention was fixed on God's feet. . . . God remonstrated earnestly with me."

The foregoing account of the Sikh Gurus will have given some idea of the development of the religion, and shows how it passed from a peaceful quietistic creed to a militant force. This was largely due to the opposition of the Moghul Emperors. At first very friendly to Muhammadanism, Sikhism became an enemy through persecution. There was inevitably something of a re-action towards Hinduism, to which it was in so many ways at first opposed. This reaction has gone on ever since, and Sikhism has tended more and more to become part of the general Hindu system. Sikhs have called in Brahman priests to officiate at marriages and funerals, ignoring their own special offices for these occasions. But they still have their sacred city, their sacred book, their temple and college at Amritsar, and their own rules. The distinct part they have played in history is well known, for they became magnificent warriors and their devotion and bravery in warfare have never been surpassed. They have a fine ethical code, which embodies all the great virtues, and in their early opposition to such things as the burning of widows, the veiling of women, infanticide, and so on, they put forward a social system which was in advance of their time. The key-note has always been the middle way. Whereas the Hindu Reformer, Kabir, would not permit the picking of a flower, in order to preserve life, the Sikhs encouraged the eating of meat, though, on the other hand, they severely condemned the use of drugs, wine, and tobacco. In a land given to extremes of all kinds, this moderation led to greatly increased health and strength; but, above all, and giving sanction to everything, was the passionate and selfless devotion to the One True God. Sikhism is the last fine example of Monotheism.

Verses from the Scriptures

ABBREVIATIONS TO REFERENCES

J. = Samuel Johnson, *Oriental Religions and their Relation to Universal Religion*, 2 vols.

M. = M. A. Macauliffe, *The Sikh Religion*. 6 vols.

P.S. = Puran Singh, *The Book of the Ten Masters*

T. = Trumpp's translation, *The Adi Granth or The Holy Scriptures of the Sikhs*

What thou considerest thine **advantage** shall not go with thee an inch. Naked didst thou come, naked shalt thou go; thou shalt become a morsel for death, and return to a body again and again. *Arjan M.* 3, 152.

Being **beautiful** one should not be charmed by it: it is the light of the Lord, that shines in all bodies. Being rich why should one be proud, as all wealth is the gift of him. *Arjan T.* 405.

Live in harmony, utter the **Creator's name**, and if any one salute you therewith, return his salute with the addition true, and say " Sat Kartar ", the True Creator, in reply. There are four ways by which, with the repetition of God's name, men may reach Him. The first is holy companionship, the second truth, the third contentment, and the fourth restraint of the senses. By whichsoever of these doors a man entereth, whether he be a hermit or a householder, he shall find God. *Nanak M.* 1, 49.

Of all **devotions** the best devotion is to utter the name of God. *Arjan M.* 3, 307.

Burn worldly love, grind its ashes and make it into ink; turn superior intellect into paper.

Make **divine love** thy pen, and thy heart the writer; ask thy guru and write his instruction.

Write God's name, write His praises, write that He hath neither end nor limit. . . .

One man cometh, another goeth; we give them great names.

Some men God created to beg, and some to preside over great courts.

When they have departed, they shall know that without the Name they are of no account. *Nanak M.* 1, 8–9.

Eat little, sleep little, love mercy and forbearance. *Gobind Singh M.* 5, 324.

Were the earth to become paper, the forests pens, and the wind a writer, the end of the **endless one** could not be described. *Arjan M.* 3, 323.

Nay, O Lalu, listen to the following qualities :—
Forgiveness is my mother, contentment my father,
Truth by which I have subdued my heart my uncle,
Love of God my brother, affection mine own begotten son,
Patience my daughter—I am pleased with such relations—
Peace my companion, wisdom my disciple—
This is my **family** in whom I ever rejoice. *Nanak M.* 26.

Even if I have gone astray, I am thy child, O God; thou art my **father and mother.** *Arjan M.* 3, 107.

None can erase what was written on the **forehead** in the beginning :
What was written happeneth; he who hath spiritual insight understandeth this. *Amar Das M.* 2, 79.

Thank him by whose **gifts** thou liveth. *Asa ki War* 22; *M.* 1, 247.

Know that all reliance on man is vain;
It is **God** alone who bestoweth,
By whose gifts we remain satisfied,
And not again feel thirst.
The one God alone destroyeth and protecteth;
There is nothing in man's power.
Happiness cometh from understanding the will of God.
                    Arjan's Sukhmani, Ashtapadi 14; *M.* 3, 239.

Many millions search for **God** and find him in their hearts. *Arjan M.* 3, 229.

Nobody hath found **God** by walking his own way. *Ram Das M.* 2, 346.

We see, and hear, and know that **God** cannot be found in worldly pleasures;
How can man without feet, arms, and eyes run to embrace Him ?
Make feet out of fear, hands out of love, and eyes out of understanding. *Angad M.* 1, 46.

Where there is divine knowledge there is virtue; and where there is falsehood there is sin; where there is covetousness there is death; where there is forgiveness there is **God** himself. *Kabir M.* 6, 302.

God is concealed in every heart, his light is in every heart. *Nanak M.* 1, 330.

It is not by the practice of perpetual silence, nor by the ostensible relinquishment of pride, nor by the adoption of a religious dress, nor by shaving the head,

Nor by wearing a wooden necklace, nor by twisting matted hair round the head that **God** is found. *Gobind Singh M.* 5, 289.

God is in the water, God is in the dry land, God is in the heart, God is in the forest, God is in the mountain, God is in the cave. God is in the earth, God is in heaven. . . . Thou art in the tree, thou art in its leaves, thou art in the earth, thou art in the firmament. *Gobind Singh M.* 5, 269.

God is in thy heart, yet thou searchest for Him in the wilderness. *Arjan M.* 3, 39.

God though ever apart dwelleth everywhere, and is contained even in thee.

As in flowers there is odour and in a mirror reflection.

So God dwelleth continually in thy heart; search for Him there, O brother. *Teg Bahadur M.* 4, 402.

Fight with no weapon but the word of **God**; use no means but a pure faith. *Nanak J.* 2, 313.

It is **God** who arrangeth marriages . . . Those whom he hath once joined he joineth for ever. *Nanak M.* 1, 100.

It is the one **God** who created Brahma;

It is the one God who created our understanding;

It is from the one God the mountains and the ages of the world emanated;

It is the one God who bestoweth knowledge.

It is by the word of God man is saved.

It is by the name of the one **God** the pious are saved.

Nanak M. 1, 63.

O father, dispel such doubts. It is **God** who doeth whatever is done; all who exist shall be absorbed in Him. The different forms, O God, which appear are ever Thine, and at the last they shall all be resolved in Thee. He who is absorbed in the Guru's word, shall thoroughly know Him who made this world, Thine, O Lord, is the word; there is none but Thee; where is there room for doubt? *Amar Das M.* 1, p. 1.

There is but one **God** whose name is true, the creator, immortal, unborn, self-existent. *Japji M.* 1, 195.

God will not ask man of what race he is. He will ask what he has done. *Adi Granth J.* 2, 162.

They who make truth their fasting, contentment their place of pilgrimage, divine knowledge and meditation their ablutions, mercy their idol, and forgiveness their rosary, are foremost in **God's favour.** *Nanak M.* 1, 374.

Behold Him without thee as He is within thee; there is none other.

Under the Guru's instruction regard all men as equal, since **God's light** is contained in the heart of each. *Arjan M.* 4. 237.

Without the **Guru** man is ruined by wandering. *Nanak M.* 1, 335.

I wandered through the whole world calling out for my beloved, yet my thirst departed not: but on meeting the true **Guru**, O Nanak, my thirst departed and I found my beloved in my own home on my return. *Amar Das M.* 2, 214.

They who worship not the true **Guru** or ponder on his words, never obtain divine knowledge in their hearts, and are as dead in the world. They wander in the eighty-four lakhs of existence, and are ruined by transmigration. *Amar Das M.* 2, 168.

Everybody asketh for **happiness**; nobody asketh for misery.

Great misery attendeth on happiness, but the perverse understand it not.

They who consider happiness and misery the same, and know the secret of the Word shall be happy. *Nanak M.* 1, 270.

Everything is found at **home**, nothing abroad:

He who searcheth abroad is lost in doubt. *Arjan M.* 3, 116.

Consider thy **house** altogether as the forest, and remain an anchoret at heart. *Gobind Singh M.* 5, 324.

Become a **husbandman**, make good works thy soil, and the word of God thy seed; ever irrigate with the water of truth.

Faith shall germinate, and thus even a fool shall know the distinction between heaven and hell.

Think not that thou shalt find the Lord by mere words.

In the pride of wealth and the splendour of beauty life hath been wasted. *Nanak M.* 1, 21.

He who deemeth himself **lowly**,
Shall be deemed the most exalted of all. *Arjan M.* 3, 206.

Mammon is a serpent which twineth herself round the world;
She devoureth him at last who waiteth upon her.

A few holy men are snake-charmers who trample on her with their feet.

Nanak, they are saved who continue to fix their attention on the True One. *Amar Das M.* 2, 202.

Make **mercy** thy cotton, contentment thy thread, continence its knot, truth its twist. *Nanak M.* 1, 16.

Mercy to human beings is more acceptable than bathing at the sixty-eight places of pilgrimage, and than all alms offered there. (Sixty-eight is the number of sacred places of pilgrimage in the estimation of the Hindus.) *Arjan M.* 3, 129.

The whole world is dead repeating " **mine, mine**," yet worldly wealth departeth with no one.

Man suffereth for worldly love; Death is on the watch for every one. *Amar Das M.* 2, 163.

Make kindness thy **mosque**, sincerity thy prayer-carpet, what is just and lawful thy Qur'an,

Modesty thy circumcision, civility thy fasting, so shalt thou be a Musalman;

Make right conduct thy Kaaba, truth thy spiritual guide, good works thy creed and thy prayer,

The will of God thy rosary, and God will preserve thine honour, O Nanak. *Nanak M.* 1, 38.

Treat **others** as thou wouldst be treated thyself. *Angad M.* 2, 29.

Make thy mind the **ploughman**, good acts the cultivation, modesty thy irrigating water, and thy body the field to till,

The Name the seed, contentment thy harrow, and the garb of humility thy fence;

By the work of love the seed will germinate; thou mayest behold happy the homes of persons who thus act.

O father, mammon accompanieth not man when he departeth. *Nanak M.* 1, 22.

When the world is in distress, it heartily **prayeth**. The True One attentively listeneth and with His kind disposition granteth consolation. He giveth orders to the Cloud and the rain falleth in torrents. *Amar Das M.* 1, xli.

Man **preacheth** and dictateth to others, but practiseth not what he preacheth;

But, on meeting the company of the saints, obtaineth staunchness of faith, and God's name saveth him. *Ram Das M.* 2, 339.

To the **pure** all things are pure, nothing can defile them. *Farid M.* 6, 380.

They who **quarrel** with others, instead of quarelling with their own hearts, waste their lives. *Amar Das M.* 2, 167.

Some in their hearts accept incarnations of God, but I have renounced all vain **religion**. *Gobind Singh M.* 5, 318.

Hopes and desires are entanglements, my brother; **thy religious ceremonies** are also entanglements. Man, my brother, is born in the world as the result of bad and good acts, he perisheth when he forgetteth the name. Maya bewitched the world, my brother; all thy religious ceremonies are worthless.

(Man is destined to rebirth through good deeds as well as bad ones. If he would escape transmigration he must learn nonattachment through the Name and the teaching of the Guru.) *Nanak M.* 1, 334.

There is no greater penance than patience, no greater happiness than contentment, no greater evil than greed, no greater virtue than mercy, and no more potent weapon than forgiveness. Whatever man **soweth** that shall he reap. If he sow trouble, trouble shall be his harvest. If a man sow poison, he cannot expect ambrosia. *Amar Das M. (Lectures on the Sikh Religion)*, p. 18.

Make honesty thy **steed**, truth thy saddle, continence thine equestrian armour;

The five virtues thine arrows, and truth thy sword and shield. *Nanak M.* 1, 127.

Three things—**truth, patience, and reflection** are put into a dish; and when kneaded with the water of God's name, become perfect ambrosial food.

By partaking of them man is satisfied, and attaineth the gate of salvation.

This food is rare, O saints, but it can be obtained by the Guru's instruction. *Amar Das M.* 2, 221.

Utter not one disagreeable **word**, since the true Lord is in all men.

Distress no one's heart; every heart is a priceless jewel. *Farid M.* 6, 414.

Readings from the Scriptures

[The *Japji* is considered by the Sikhs a key to their sacred volume and an epitome of its doctrines. It is silently repeated by the Sikhs early in the morning. Every Sikh must have it by heart otherwise he is not deemed orthodox. It is the duty of all Sikhs, even if they cannot read, to have themselves taught this great morning divine service. The composition appears to have been the work of Guru Nanak in advanced age.]

There is but one God whose name is true, the Creator, devoid of fear and enmity, immortal, unborn, self-existent; by the favour of the Guru.

The True One was in the beginning; the True One was in the primal age. The True One is now also, O Nanak; the True One also shall be.

By thinking I cannot obtain a conception of Him, even though I think hundreds of thousands of times.

Even though I be silent and keep my attention firmly fixed on Him, I cannot preserve silence.

The hunger of the hungry for God subsideth not though they obtain the load of the worlds.

If man should have thousands and hundreds of thousands of devices, even one would not assist him in obtaining God.

How shall man become true before God? How shall the veil of falsehood be rent?

By walking, O Nanak, according to the will of the Commander as preordained.

By His order bodies are produced; His order cannot be described.

By His order souls are infused into them; greatness is obtained.

Men are high or low; they obtain preordained pain or pleasure.

Some obtain their reward; others must ever wander in transmigration.

All are subject to His order; none is exempt from it.

He who understandeth God's order, O Nanak, is never guilty of egoism.

Who can sing His power? Who hath power to sing it?

Who can sing His gifts or know His signs?

Who can sing His attributes, His greatness, and His deeds?

His knowledge whose study is arduous?

Who fashioneth the body and again destroyeth it?

Who taketh away life and again restoreth it?

Who appeareth to be far, but is known to be near?

Who is all-seeing and omnipresent?

In describing Him there would never be an end.

Millions of men give millions upon millions of descriptions of Him, but they fail to describe Him.

The Giver giveth; the receiver groweth weary of receiving.

In every age man subsisteth by His bounty. *Japji* 1–3; *M.* 1, 195–7.

If I please Him that is my place of pilgrimage to bathe in; if I please Him not, what ablutions shall I make?

What can all the created beings I behold obtain without previous good acts?

Precious stones, jewels, and gems shall be treasured up in thy heart if thou hearken to even one word of the Guru. . . .

Were man to live through the four ages, yea ten times longer;

Were he to be known on the nine continents, and were everybody to follow in his train;

Were he to obtain a great name and praise and renown in the world;

If God's look of favour fell not on him, no one would notice him.

He would be accounted a worm among worms, and even sinners would impute sin to him. *Japji* 6, 7; *M.* 1, 199.

By hearing the Name, truth, contentment, and divine knowledge
are obtained.

Hearing the Name is equal to bathing at the sixty-eight places
of pilgrimage. . . .

By hearing the Name a blind man findeth his way.

The unfathomable becometh fathomable. . . .

Sorrow and sin are no more. *Japji* 10–11; *M.* 1, 200.

When the hands, feet, and other members of the body are
covered with filth,

It is removed by washing with water.

When thy clothes are polluted,

Apply soap, and the impurity shall be washed away.

So when the mind is defiled by sin,

It is cleansed by the love of the Name.

Men do not become saints or sinners by merely calling themselves so.

The recording angels take with them a record of man's acts.

It is he himself soweth, and he himself eateth. . . .

But he who heareth and obeyeth and loveth God in his heart,

Shall wash off his impurity in the place of pilgrimage within him.

All virtues are Thine, O Lord; none are mine.

There is no devotion without virtue. *Japji* 20–1; *M.* 1, 205–6.

What is that gate, what is that mansion where Thou, O God,
sittest and watchest over all things?

How many various and countless instruments are played! How
many musicians,

How many musical measures with their consorts,[1] and how
many singers sing Thee!

Wind, water, and fire sing Thee; Dharmrāj[2] sings at Thy
gate.

The recording angels, who know how to write, and on whose
record Dharmrāj judgeth, sing Thee.

Ishar,[3] Brahma, and Devi,[4] ever beautiful and adored by Thee,
sing Thee.

Indar, seated on his throne with the gods at Thy gate, sing
Thee.

---

[1] Indian musical measures were allotted wives and daughters, i.e.,
variations of these tunes.

[2] God of death.   [3] A name of Shiv.   [4] A Hindu goddess.

Sidhs [1] in meditation sing Thee; holy men in contemplation sing Thee.

The continent, the true, and the patient sing Thee; unyielding heroes sing Thee.

The Pandits and the supreme Rikhis,[2] reading their Veds, sing Thee in every age.

The lovely celestial maids who beguile the heart in the upper, middle and nether regions sing Thee.

The jewels created by Thee with the sixty-eight places of Hindu pilgrimage sing Thee.

Mighty warriors and divine heroes sing Thee; the four sources of life sing Thee.

The continents, the worlds, and the universe made and supported by Thy hands sing Thee.

The saints who please Thee, and who are imbued with Thy love sing Thee.

The many others who sing Thee I cannot remember; how could Nanak recount them?

That God is ever true, He is the true Lord, and the true Name.

He who made this world is and shall be; He shall neither depart nor be made to depart.

He who created things of different colours, descriptions, and species,

Beholdeth His handiwork which attesteth His greatness.

He will do what pleaseth Himself; no order may be issued to Him.

He is King, the King of kings, O Nanak; all remain subject to his will. *Japji* 27; *M.* 1, 210–12.

Make contentment and modesty thine earrings, self-respect thy wallet, meditation the ashes to smear on thy body;

Make thy body, which is only a morsel for death, thy beggar's coat, and faith thy rule of life and thy staff.

And the conquest of thy heart the conquest of the world. . . .

Make divine knowledge thy food, compassion thy storekeeper, and the voice which is in every heart the pipe to call to repast. . . . Union and separation is the law which regulateth the world. By destiny we receive our portion. *Japji* 28–9; *M.* 1, 212–13.

---

[1] An ancient order of Jogis.   [2] Ancient sages.

God created nights, seasons, lunar days, and week days,
Wind, water, fire and the nether regions.
In the midst of these He established the earth as a temple.
In it He placed living beings of different habits and kinds.
Their names are various and endless.
And they are judged according to their acts. *Japji* 34; *M.* 1,
215.

Make continence thy furnace, resignation thy goldsmith,
Understanding thine anvil, divine knowledge thy tools,
The fear of God thy bellows, austerities thy fire,
Divine love thy crucible, and melt God's name therein.
In such a true mint the Word shall be coined. *Japji* 38; *M.* 1,
217.

The sun and moon, O Lord, are Thy lamps; the firmament
Thy salver; the orbs of the stars the pearls enchased in it.

The perfume of the sandal is Thine incense, the wind is Thy
fan, all the forests are Thy flowers, O Lord of light.

What worship is this, O Thou Destroyer of birth? Unbeaten
strains of esctasy are the trumpets of Thy worship.

Thou hast a thousand eyes and yet not one eye; Thou hast a
thousand forms and yet not one form;

Thou hast a thousand stainless feet and yet not one foot; Thou
hast a thousand organs of smell and yet not one organ. I am
fascinated by this play of Thine.

The light which is in everything is Thine, O Lord of light.

From its brilliancy everything is brilliant;

By the Guru's teaching the light becometh manifest.

What pleaseth Thee is the real worship.

O God, my mind is fascinated with thy lotus feet as the bumble-
bee with the flower; night and day I thirst for them.

Give the water of Thy favour to the sarang [1] Nanak, so that he
may dwell in Thy name.

From the *Sohila* (repeated at bed-time), *Nanak M.* 1, 259.

Religion consisteth not in a patched coat, or a Jogi's staff, or
in ashes smeared over the body; religion consisteth not in earrings worn or a shaven head, or in the blowing of horns. Abide
pure amid the impurities of the world; thus shalt thou find the

---

[1] The pied Indian Cuckoo, a bird famous in Indian literature.

way of religion. Religion consisteth not in mere words; he who
looketh on all men as equal is religious. Religion consisteth not
in wandering to tombs or places of cremation, or sitting in attitudes
of contemplation; religion consisteth not in wandering in foreign
countries, or in bathing at places of pilgrimage. Abide pure
amid the impurities of the world; thus shalt thou find the way
of religion. *Nanak M.* 1, 60.

In the beginning there was indescribable darkness;
Then was not earth or heaven, naught but God's unequalled
Order.
Then was not day, or night, or moon, or sun; God was medita-
ting on the void.
Then were not continents, or hells, or seven seas, or rivers, or
flowing streams.
Nor was there paradise, or a tortoise, or nether regions; or the
hell or heaven of the Muhammadans, or the Destroyer Death;
Or the hell or heaven of the Hindus, or birth or death; nor did
any one come or go.
Then was not Brahma, Vishnu, or Shiv;
No one existed but the One God.
Then was not female, or male, or caste, or birth; nor did any
one feel pain or pleasure.
There was no caste or religious garb, no Brahman or Khatri.
No hom,[1] no sacred feasts, no places of pilgrimage to bathe in,
nor did any one perform worship.
There was no love, no service, no Shiv, or Energy of his;
Then were not Veda or Muhammadan books, no Simitris, no
Shastars;
The Imperceptible God was Himself the speaker and preacher;
Himself unseen He was everything.
When He pleased He created the world;
Without supports He sustained the sky.
He created Brahma, Vishnu, and Shiv, and extended the love
of Mammon.
He issued His order and watched over all. *Nanak M.* 1, 165–7.
Remember God and banish neglect of Him from thy heart.
Accursed the life of him in this world who breatheth without
uttering the Name. . . .

[1] Burnt sacrifice.

Be humble before every one, and call no one bad.

Repent with sincerity of heart lest thou afterwards grieve.

Thy body shall perish; thy mouth shall be buried with it; what canst thou do then?

Praise God very much; draw not thy breath without doing so. . . .

Put together travelling expenses, and pack up wherewithal to go with thee:

Without the Lord thou shalt trudge about wearily.

Embrace humility, renounce the pride of thy heart;

Restrain thy wandering mind, and every moment remember thy Creator.

They were traitors who forgot their Creator;

Their minds were bent on the hoarding of wealth, and they bore loads of sin upon their heads.

Be honest, O man, and sleep not during the eight watches of day and night.

Awake for one watch and hold converse with God. . . .

Search thy heart; the Lord is in thee.

The body is a vessel which He wrought, and into which He infused His workmanship and skill.

Thou shalt obtain martyrdom if thou die for the love of the dear One. . . .

God's splendour is lost for those who associate themselves with worldly affairs.

Arise, look before thee, and regard not the play of the world. . . .

The wealth of those, saith Nanak, who have not given alms shall slip away.

Look to truth alone, and know that the world is false.

They who think the world is true shall die confounded.

They become saints who associate with the true.

The more they remember God, the more they love Him.

Nanak M. 1, 12–14.

Were I to live for millions of years and drink the air for my nourishment;

Were I to dwell in a cave where I beheld not sun or moon, and could not even dream of sleeping,

I should still not be able to express Thy worth; how great shall I call Thy Name?

O true Formless One, Thou art in Thine Own Place—

As I have often heard I tell my tale—if it please Thee, show Thy favour unto me.

Were I to be felled and cut in pieces, were I to be ground in a mill;

Were I to be burned in a fire, and blended with its ashes,

I should still not be able to express Thy worth; how great shall I call Thy name?

Were I to become a bird and fly to a hundred heavens;

Were I to vanish from human gaze and neither eat nor drink,

I should still not be able to express Thy worth; how great shall I call Thy Name?

Nanak, had I hundreds of thousands of tons of paper and a desire to write on it all after the deepest research;

Were ink never to fail me, and could I move my pen like the wind,

I should still not be able to express Thy worth; how great shall I call Thy Name? *Nanak M.* 1, 34-5.

Man is first conceived in flesh, he dwelleth in flesh.

When he quickeneth, he obtaineth a mouth of flesh; his bone, skin, and body are made of flesh.

When he is taken out of the womb, he seizeth teats of flesh.

His mouth is of flesh, his tongue is of flesh, his breath is in flesh.

When he groweth up he marrieth, and bringeth flesh home with him.

Flesh is produced from flesh; all man's relations are made from flesh. . . .

Fools wrangle about flesh, but know not divine knowledge or meditation on God.

They know not what is flesh, or what is vegetable, or in what sin consisteth. . . .

Ye were produced from the blood of your parents, yet ye eat not fish or flesh. . . .

A fœtus is conceived from flesh; we are vessels of flesh. . . .

All animals have sprung from flesh, and the soul taketh its abode in flesh. . . .

In flesh we are conceived, from flesh we are born; we are vessels of flesh. *Nanak M.* 1, 47-9.

Covetousness is a dog, falsehood a sweeper, food obtained by deceit carrion;

Slander of others is merely others' filth in our mouths; the fire of anger is a sweeper.

Pleasures and self-praise—these are mine acts, O Creator.

My friends, doth any one obtain honour by mere words ?

Call them the best, who are the best at the gate of the Lord; they who do base acts sit and weep.

There is pleasure in gold, pleasure in silver and in women, pleasure in the perfume of sandal;

There is pleasure in horses, pleasure in couches and in palaces, pleasure in sweets, and pleasure in meats.

When such are the pleasures of the body, how shall God's name obtain a dwelling therein ? . . .

They who please God are good; what more can be said ?

They in whose heart God is contained possess wisdom, honour, and wealth.

What need is there of praising them ?   What further decoration can they obtain ?

Nanak, they who are beyond God's favouring glance love not charity or His Name. *Nanak M.* 1, 71-2.

Were a mansion of pearls erected and inlaid with gems for me;

Perfumed with musk, saffron, fragrant aloes and sandal to confer delight;

May it not be that on beholding these things I may forget Thee, O God, and not remember Thy name!

My soul burneth without Thee.

I have ascertained from my Guru that there is no other shelter than in God.

Were the earth to be studied with diamonds and rubies, and my couch to be similarly adorned;

Were fascinating damsels whose faces were decked with jewels to shed lustre and enhance the pleasure of the scene;

May it not be that on beholding them I may forget Thee and not remember Thy Name!

Were I to become a Sidh and work miracles; could I command the wealth of the universe to come to me ;

Could I disappear and appear at pleasure, and were the world to honour me;

May it not be that on beholding these things I may forget Thee and not remember Thy Name!

Were I to become a monarch on my throne and raise an army; Were dominion and regal revenue mine—O Nanak, they would be all worthless—

May it not be that on beholding these things I may forget Thee and not remember Thy Name! *Nanak M.* 1, 79–80.

God hath given fixed time for all events, and fully established the nine regions, the seven seas, the fourteen worlds, the three qualities, and the four ages.

He put four lamps one by one into the hands of the four ages. O kind God, such is Thy power.

The dwellers at every hearth are Thy slaves, and religion is their ruler.

The earth is Thy cooking-pot, Thou gavest once for all; destiny is Thy storekeeper.

Instigated by their hearts men lose patience and beg again and again to their ruin.

Covetousness is a black dungeon, demerits the fetters on the feet.

Wealth ever beateth the soul with its mallet, while sin sitteth as judge.

Man shall be either good or bad, O Lord, as Thou lookest on him. *Nanak M.* 1, 116.

It is the one God Who hath commissioned me.
Every one partaketh of His Gifts.
He who looketh for human support
Loseth both this world and the next.
There is but one Giver, the whole world are beggars.
They who forsake Him and attach themselves to others lose all their honour.
Kings and Emperors are all made by Him.
There is none equal to Him. *Nanak M.* 1, 122.

What manner of resting-place is the world?
Tie up the practice of sincerity as thy travelling expenses, and remain attached to the Name.
Jogis sit in devotional postures, mullas dwell at places of rest;
Pandits read books; sidhs sit in the palaces of the gods;

Demigods, sidhs, heavenly musicians, munis, saints, shaikhs, pirs, and commanders

Have gone stage by stage, and others too are departing.

Emperors, kings, princes, nobles have marched away.

Man must depart in a ghari or two; O my heart, understand that thou too must go.

This is told in hymns, yet few are they who understand it.

Nanak humbly asserteth, God is contained in sea and land, in the upper and lower regions;

He is unseen, inscrutable, omnipotent, the kind Creator.

The Merciful alone is permanent; the whole world beside is transitory.

Call Him permanent on whose head no destiny is recorded.

The heavens and the earth shall pass away; He the one God alone is permanent.

By day the sun travelleth, by night the moon; hundreds of thousands of stars pass away.

The one God alone is our resting-place, Nanak saith verily. *Nanak M.* 1, 154.

Wealth, youth, and flowers are guests only for four days; They wither and fade like the leaves of the water lily.

Enjoy God's love, O dear one, in the freshness of youth.

Few are thy days; thou art wearied and the vesture of thy body hath grown old.

My merry friends have gone to sleep in the grave.

I too shall depart in sorrow, and weep with a feeble voice.

O fair one, why not attentively listen to this message?

Thou must go to thy father-in-law's; thou mayest not dwell for ever in thy father's house.

Nanak, know that she who sleepeth in her father's house, is robbed at an untimely season.

She hath lost her bundle of merits and departed with a load of demerits. *Nanak M.* 1, 187.

Men act as they see others act: the perverse acquire not understanding.

The service of the pious whose hearts are pure is acceptable to God.

They sing God's praises, ever read them, and by singing them become absorbed in Him. . . .

To serve God is to love Him, if pious men reflect on it.

God is not served by hypocrisy : the words of the double-dealer are despised.

He in whose heart are discrimination and reflection uniteth not with him.

He is called the servant of God who claspeth Him to his heart.

The holy man who placeth before Him and entrusteth to Him his soul and body, and rooteth out pride from within him,

Is blest and acceptable, and shall never suffer defeat.

God is obtained by his own favour; without it He is not obtained.

Eighty-four lakhs of species thirst for God, but only he whom He blendeth with Himself shall meet Him.

Nanak, the pious man who is ever absorbed in God's Name shall find him. *Nanak M.* 2, 154–5.

Beautiful is the bird on the tree, which pecketh at truth by the Guru's favour.

It drinketh the essence of God's Name, abideth in happiness, and flieth not hither and thither.

It obtaineth a dwelling in its own nest, and is absorbed in God's name.

O man, do the Guru's service.

If thou walk in the way of the Guru, thou shalt be day and night absorbed in God's Name.

Can the birds on the tree be prized which fly in every direction ?

The more they fly, the worse they suffer; they ever burn and scream.

Without the Guru they cannot behold God's court or obtain the ambrosial fruit.

For the pious who are naturally true, God is an evergreen tree.

They reject the three branches and attach themselves to the Word which is the trunk.

The Name of God alone is ambrosial fruit; He Himself giveth it to be eaten.

The perverse even while erect are withered; they have no fruit or shadow.

Sit not near them; they have neither house nor village.

They are ever cut down and burnt as dry wood; they have neither the Word nor God's Name.

Men act according to God's order and wander according to their previous acts.

By His order they obtain a sight of Him, and whither He sendeth them thither they go. *Amar Das M.* 2, 158–9.

When very great troubles befall, and nobody receiveth one;
When enemies pursue, and relations flee away;
When all from whom man looked for assistance have fled, and all succour is at an end,
If he then remember God, no hot wind shall strike him.
God is the strength of the strengthless.
He neither cometh nor goeth; He is permanent ever; by the Guru's instruction know Him as the True One.
If man be weak from the pangs of nakedness and hunger,
If he have not a paisa in his purse, and there be none to console him,
If no one gratify his aims and desires, and he be never successful,
Yet, if he remember God, he shall obtain a permanent kingdom.
If any one have excessive anxiety, and bodily suffering,
If bound up in household and family, he feel alternate joy and sorrow,
If he wander in every direction, and cannot rest even for a moment,
Yet if he think upon God, his body and soul shall be happy.
Man may be in the power of lust, wrath, and covetousness; he may become a miser through love of greed;
He may have committed the four great sins and all venial sins; he may be a demon to destroy;
He may never have listened to sacred books, hymns, and poetry;
Yet shall he be saved if he think upon God and repeat His Name even for a moment. . . .
Yet if he think not of the supreme God, he shall be taken and consigned to the abode below. . . .
He to whom the supreme God is merciful obtaineth the society of the saints.
The more that association increaseth, the greater his love for God. *Arjan M.* 3, 95–7.

The love of mammon is mental impurity,
By which men are led astray in doubt and suffer transmigration.

The impurity of the perverse never departeth
Until they become saturated with the Word and with God's
name.
Whatever taketh the form of worldly love is all impurity:
On this account man dieth and is born again and again.
There is impurity in fire, in wind, and in water;
There is impurity in whatever is eaten;
There is impurity in religious ceremonies and in worship.
Only the heart which is dyed with the Name is pure.
By serving the True Guru impurity departeth. *Amar Das M.
2, 76.*

Abandon obstinacy and pride, serve the saints, prepare sacred
food according to the rules of our religion, feed the hungry,
clothe the naked, rise before day, repeat the *Japji*, bestow a little
of your time and wealth on God's service, associate with the
saints, meditate on the Word, perform the duties of your religion,
hurt no one's feelings, sing the Guru's hymns, be lowly and
abandon pride, recognize only the Creator as the one God, and
all your desires shall be fulfilled. If a man be weighed down
with worldliness, he shall sink like an overladen boat in the
world's ocean; but, if worldliness lie not heavily on him, his bark
shall float, and he shall obtain deliverance. *Amar Das. M. 2, 85.*

He is called a holy man and perfect saint who is filled with the
following six pairs of qualities—
Who possesseth the spell of God's Name, and meditateth on
Him who filleth every place;
Who deemeth woe and weal as the same, and whose life is pure
and without enmity;
Who is compassionate to all creatures, and who hath expelled
the five deadly sins;
Who subsisteth on God's praises, and who abideth in the world
untouched by it as the lotus in the water; who instructeth friend
and enemy alike, who loveth God's service;
Who heareth not slander of others, and abandoning pride
becometh the dust of all men's feet. *Arjan M. 3, 431–2.*

Know that according to the Musalmans everything is produced
from air, fire, water, and earth;
But the pure God created the world out of five elements.

However high man may leap, he shall fall on the earth again.

Even though a bird fly, it cannot compete in endurance with the torrent and the wind which move by God's will.

How great shall I call God? to whom shall I go to inquire regarding Him?

He is the greatest of the great, and great is His word; men depart in their pride.

I have consulted the four Veds, but these writings find not God's limits.

I have consulted the four books of the Muhammadans, but God's worth is not described in them.

I have consulted the nine regions of the earth; one improveth upon what the other saith.

Having turned my heart into a boat, I have searched in every sea;

I have dwelt by rivers and streams and bathed at the sixty-eight places of pilgrimage;

I have lived among the forests and glades of the three worlds and eaten bitter and sweet;

I have seen the seven nether regions and heavens upon heavens.

And I, Nanak, say man shall be true to his faith if he fear God and do good works. *Nanak M.* 1, 178–9.

O man, in God's image is he

Who is unaffected by weal or woe, by covetousness, worldly love, or pride. . . .

Who uttereth neither praise nor blame, and to whom gold and iron are the same. . . .

Who feeleth neither joy nor sorrow, and who treateth an enemy and a friend as the same. . . . .

Who inspireth no fear, and who hath no fear of others. . . .

Who hath abandoned mammon and selfishness, and renounced everything. . . .

Man shall find many companions in weal, but none in woe. . . .

Man maketh many efforts to obtain happiness, but none to obtain misery. . . .

I have particularly observed that in this world no one is another's friend;

Nanak, only devotion to God is permanent; preserve that in thy heart. *Teg Bahadur* 13, 14, 15, 16, 18, 22, 39, 48; *M.* 4, 415–20.

Lord! thou art the Hindu, the Moslem, the Turk and the Feringhi; thou art the Persian, the Sanskritian, the Arabian; thou art the poet, the skilled dancer, the songster supreme. Thou art the speech; and thou art the avdhuta. The adept. Thou art the warrior clad in shining armour, and thou art the peace supreme! Thou art man, woman, child and God! Thou art the flute-player, the herdsman that goes grazing his dumb cows! Thou bestoweth love, and thou givest thyself to all! Thou art the protector of life and the giver of all prosperity! Thou art the cure of all sorrow and suffering; thou art the net of the charms of youth, and high summit of all fulfilment: Thou art the form of a beautiful princess and thou art the emaciated form of the Brahmachari with the wooden beads hanging from his neck! Thou art the Muezzin that cries from the roof of the Mosque, the Yogi that lies wrapt in silence of deep thought, unthinking in the soul-lit cave. The Vedas art thou, and the Qur'an! In all shapes and everywhere, thou art dear to me; in every form thou art thyself! Thou art my vow, my Dharma! my beginning, and my end. *Gobind Singh P.S.* 148.

Fall at the feet of the great God; He is not a stone. He liveth in water, in the dry land, in all things, and in all monarchs. He is in the sun, in the moon, in the sky. Wherever thou lookest, thou mayest fix thy gaze on Him. He is in fire, in wind, and beneath the earth. In what place is He not? He is contained in everything. Were all the continents to become paper and the seven seas ink; were all the vegetables to be cut down and employed as pens; were Saraswati the goddess of eloquence, to dictate and all beings to write for sixty ages, they could not in any way describe God. Yet, O fool, thou supposest Him to be a stone. *Gobind Singh M.* 5, 69.

I shall now tell my own history.
How God brought me into the world as I was performing penance
On the mountain of Hem Kunt,
There I performed very great austerities
And worshipped Great-death.
I performed such penance
That I became blended with God.
When God gave me the order,
I assumed birth in this Kal age.

I did not desire to come,
As my attention was fixed on God's feet.
God remonstrated earnestly with me,
And sent me into this world with the following orders. . . .
(God then tells the Guru how He had created the demi-gods
and the various prophets, but how they had all been false to their
religion, and had attracted glory to themselves.)

" None of them recognized Me, the Supreme Being.
I have cherished thee as My son,
And created thee to extend My religion.
Go and spread My religion there,
And restrain the world from senseless acts."
I stood up, clasped my hands, bowed my head, and replied :
" Thy religion shall prevail in the world when Thou vouch-
safest assistance."

On this account God sent me.
Then I took birth and came into the world.
As He spoke to me so I speak unto men :
I bear no enmity to any one.
All who call me the Supreme Being
Shall fall into the pit of hell.
Recognize me as God's servant only :
Have no doubt whatever of this.
I am the slave of the Supreme Being,
And have come to behold the wonders of the world.
I tell the world what God told me,
And will not remain silent through fear of mortals. *Gobind
Singh M.* 5, 296–300.

Every one talketh of happiness, but true happiness can only be
known from the Guru ;
If the beloved Guru be merciful, happiness shall ever be known
from him.
The Guru being merciful cut away my sins, and put into mine
eyes the salve of divine knowledge ;
The True One hath adorned with the Word those whose hearts
have parted with worldly love.
Saith Nanak, that is the real happiness which is known from the
Guru.

O Father, he to whom Thou givest happiness obtaineth it;

He obtaineth it to whom Thou givest it; what else can poor mortal do?

Some led astray by error wander in every direction, others are adorned by attachment to Thy name;

Through the Guru's favour pure are the hearts of those to whom the will of God is agreeable.

Saith Nanak, the man on whom Thou, O Beloved, conferreth happiness obtaineth it. *Nanak, The Anand*, 7, 8; *M.* 2, 119–20.

Foul within and fair without;

They who are fair without and foul within, have lost their human lives at play.

They have contracted the great disease of avarice and forgotten death.

The Name, which is the best thing in the Veda, they hear not; they wander like demons.

Saith Nanak, they who have renounced truth, and attached themselves to falsehood, have lost their human lives at play.

Fair within and fair without;

They who are fair without and fair within, do good acts through the true Guru.

Even the very name of falsehood reacheth them not, and truth is the object of their desires.

The merchants who have earned the jewel of human birth are prosperous.

Saith Nanak, the hearts of those who abide with the Guru are ever pure. *Nanak, The Anand*, 19, 20; *M.* 2, 123.

The perverse are spiritually blind, foolish and proud.

In their hearts is wrath; they lose their senses in play.

They commit the sins of falsehood and unrighteousness.

What can they hear and what can they tell others?

They are blind and deaf; they lose their way and stray into the desert.

The blind unbeliever suffereth transmigration.

He obtaineth no place without meeting the true Guru.

Nanak, man obtaineth what is written for him from the beginning.

He who through the Guru's instruction obtaineth divine knowledge, discrimination, and intelligence,

Shall sing God's praises and string a garland in his heart.

He shall be the purest of the pure and possess the highest intelligence.

He who meeteth such a person shall be saved by him.

He whose heart containeth the perfume of God's Name,

Shall utter great and exalted words to make happy those who hear them;

And he himself shall obtain honour at God's court.

Nanak, on meeting the true Guru, the Name is obtained as wealth and property. *Amar Das I* ; *M.* 2, 189–90.

Let him who calleth himself a Sikh of the true Guru, rise early and meditate on God;

Let him exert himself in the early morning, bathe in the tank of nectar,

Repeat God's name under the Guru's instruction, and all his sins and transgressions shall be erased.

Let him at sunrise sing the Guru's hymns, and whether sitting or standing meditate on God's name.

The disciple who at every breath meditateth on God, will please the Guru's heart.

The Guru communicateth instruction to that disciple of his to whom my Lord is merciful.

The slave Nanak prayeth for the dust of the feet of that Guru's disciple who himself repeateth God's name and causeth others to do so. *Nanak M.* 2, 264.

The whole world is God's field; God Himself causeth tillage to be performed.

The holy man hath made God's grace germinate; the perverse have lost their capital.

Every one cultivateth for his own advantage; if it please God, He causeth the field to germinate.

The Guru's disciples sow ambrosia, and obtain God's Name as the ambrosial fruit.

Death the mouse ever gnaweth the produce; but God the Creator killeth and expelleth it.

With God's love the tillage succeedeth, and the harvest-heap is produced by His favour,

God hath removed all the trouble and anxiety of those who have meditated on Him.

The slave Nanak hath worshipped the Name; he is saved himself, and saveth the whole world. *Nanak M.* 2, 302–3.

In God's asylum there is rest. . . .
The man who is untouched by covetousness, worldly love, selfishness, joy, and sorrow,
And who is not a slave to his passion, is the image of God;
So is he who deemeth heaven and hell, ambrosia and poison, gold and copper, as the same;
And so also is he who deemeth praise and blame as the same, and who is not enslaved by avarice and worldly love :
Recognize him as possessed of divine knowledge who hath not the entanglements of pain and pleasure. *Teg Bahadur M.* 4, 395.

Were man to move the earth, that would not induce God to grant him undeserved favours. . . .
Were I to put on a dress of fire, construct a house of snow and eat iron;
Were I to turn all my troubles into water, drink it, and drive the earth as a steed;
Were I able to put the firmament into one scale and weigh it with a tank;
Were I to become so large that I could be nowhere contained; and were I to lead every one by the nose;
Had I such power in myself that I could perform such things or cause others to perform them, it would be all in vain.
As great as the Lord is, so great are His gifts; He bestoweth according to His pleasure.
Nanak, he on whom God looketh with favour obtaineth the glory of the True Name. *Nanak M.* 1, 157–8.

Man washeth his clothes and his body, and mortifieth himself.
Knowing not of the filth attaching to his heart, he rubbeth and cleanseth himself externally.
Being blind he is led astray, and falleth into Death's noose.
He deemeth the property of others as his own, and suffereth for his pride.
Nanak, when pride is dispelled under the Guru's instructions, man meditateth on God's name.
Repeateth the Name, adoreth the Name, and through the Name is absorbed in happiness. *Nanak M.* 1, 280.

The one Lord who created the world is the Lord of all.

Fortunate is their advent into the world, whose hearts remain attached to God's service.

O foolish man, why hast thou forgotten Him?

When thou adjustest thine account, my friend, thou shalt be deemed educated.

The primal Being is the Giver; He alone is true.

No account shall be due by the pious man who understandeth by means of these letters.

Praise Him whose limit cannot be found.

They who practise truth and perform service shall obtain their reward.

He who knoweth divine knowledge is the learned pandit.

He who knoweth the one God in all creatures would never say " I exist by myself."

When the hair groweth white, it shineth without soap. . . .

The servant who performeth the Guru's work, who remaineth obedient to His commands,

Who deemeth bad and good as the same, shall in this way be absorbed in Him. . . .

Why die of grief, O mortal? What God hath to give He continueth to give.

He giveth, beholdeth and issueth His orders how living things are to obtain sustenance.

When I look carefully I see no other than God.

The one God pervadeth all places; the one God dwelleth in the heart.

O mortals, why practise deceit? Ye shall have to depart in a ghari [1] or two.

Lose not the play of your lives, run and fall under God's protection. . . .

He himself destroyeth and buildeth; He acteth as He pleaseth.

He beholdeth the work of His hands, issueth His orders, and saveth those on whom He looketh with favour.

He in whose heart God dwelleth singeth His praises.

The Creator blendeth men with Himself, and they are not born again. . . .

The whole world is entangled with a noose and bound by Death's chain.

[1] Period of 24 minutes.

They who by the Guru's favour have run to God for protection, are saved. *Nanak M. 1, 3–6.*

Man may perform all devotion, all penance, and resort to every expedient;

Yet he is as if he wandered in a wilderness, and could not find the way.

Without knowing God, no one is acceptable.

Without the Name man is despised.

The Lord is permanent; the world cometh and goeth.

Mortals shall be emancipated by being the holy man's slaves.

The world is bound by worldly love and many desires. . . .

Without a guru man forgetteth God and suffereth transmigration.

Him whom God regardeth favourably He blendeth with Himself. *Nanak M. 1, 312–13.*

By meeting the true Guru worldly hunger departeth; but it departeth not by merely putting on a sectarial garb.

Through the pain of hunger the Tapa wandereth from house to house; in the next world he shall obtain twofold punishment.

His appetite is not satisfied, and he never eateth in comfort what he obtaineth.

He ever beggeth with persistency and annoyeth the giver.

Leading the life of a householder, by which somebody may gain, is better than putting on such a sectarial dress.

They who are imbued with the Word acquire understanding; others are led astray by doubt.

They act as they were destined; it is of no use to address them.

Nanak, they who please God are fortunate; they are honoured and acceptable. *Amar Das M. 2, 37.*

Reading and study are worldly acts if the sin of avarice be in the heart.

All who read through pride grow weary, and are ruined by worldly love.

He is learned, he is a wise pandit who pondereth on the Guru's word:

He searcheth in his heart, findeth the Real Thing there, and reacheth the gate of deliverance:

He tranquilly meditateth on God, and findeth Him who is the treasury of excellences.

Nanak, blessed is that trader who by the Guru's instruction obtaineth the Name as his support. *Amar Das M. 2, 223.*

He who in adversity heedeth it not,
Who in prosperity feeleth neither affection nor fear, and who deemeth gold as dross;
Who uttereth neither praise nor blame, and who suffereth not from avarice, worldly love, or pride;
Who is unaffected by joy or sorrow, by honour or dishonour;
Who hath renounced all hopes and desires, and expecteth nothing from the world;
Whom lust and wrath touch not—in such a person's heart God dwelleth. . . .
And shall be blended with God, O Nanak, as water with water. . . .
The whole world is entangled in its own pleasures; nobody is any one else's friend.
In prosperity many persons come and sit together by one, encircling him on all sides;
When adversity befalleth him, all abandon him and nobody cometh near him. *Teg Bahadur M. 4, 402.*

The Unseen, Infinite, Inaccessible, Inapprehensible God is not subject to death or destiny.
He is of no caste, unborn, self-existent, without fear or doubt. . . .
He hath no form, or colour, or outline; He becometh manifest by the true Word.
He hath no mother, father, son, or kinsman; He feeleth not lust, and hath no wife
Or family; He is pure, endless, and infinite; all light is Thine, O Lord.
God is concealed in every heart; His light is in every heart. *Nanak M. 1, 330.*

What religious acts can he perform who hath greed in his heart?
He uttereth falsehood and eateth poison.
O Pandit, if thou churn coagulated milk, butter shall be produced;
If thou churn water, thou shalt obtain but water; this is the way of the world.

The unseen God dwelleth in every heart, yet without the Guru man is ruined by wandering.

Maya hath bound this world on all sides with her cable:

Without a guru its knot cannot be untied; man groweth weary in striving.

This world is led astray by superstition; words are of no avail.

By meeting the Guru, my brother, the fear of God entereth the heart. To die in the fear of God is man's true destiny.

In God's court the Name is superior to ablutions, alms, and similar religious acts. *Nanak M.* 1, 335.

The Guru hath the key of the lock, the heart is the storeroom, the body is its roof;

Nanak, without the Guru the doors of the heart cannot be opened, since nobody else hath the key. . . .

Thou Thyself, O God, didst create, saith Nanak, Thou Thyself didst put creatures in their different places;

Whom shall I call inferior since all have the same Master?

There is one Master of all; He appointeth men to their various duties and watcheth over them—

Some to small, some to great duties; none departeth empty.

Men come naked, they depart naked, yet during their lives they make a display;

Nanak, it is not known what duty God will order for them in the next world. *Angad M.* 2, 53.

Tell me where there is any one in whom God is not.

The Creator who is full of mercy conferreth all happiness: ever meditate on that God.

Sing the praises of that God on whose thread creatures are strung.

Remember that God who gave thee everything; to whom else shouldst thou go?

Profitable is the service of my God; from it thou shalt obtain the fruit thy heart desireth.

Saith Nanak, take the gain and profit of service, and thou shalt go home happy. *Arjan M.* 4, 99.

Trees which grow near sandal are perfumed like sandal. If any of the eight metals be touched by the philosopher's stone, it becometh gold. As rivers, streams, and water-courses which fall into the Ganges become the Ganges, so doth the society of holy men save sinners and wash away the filth of sin. It saveth countless souls from hell, and associateth with itself hundreds of thousands of the lost. . . . The sandal-tree perfumeth other trees whether they bear fruit or not. Rain falleth everywhere whether the ground be good or bad. When the sun riseth, it diffuseth its beams through the warp and woof of the world. The earth hath the capacity of endurance. Though the ruby, jewels, gems, gold, iron, the philosopher's stone are all produced from it, it regardeth not outrages. In the same way the company of the saints conferreth on men indiscriminately benefits which cannot be estimated. *Bhai Gur Das M.* 4, 241.

Devotion, penance, hom, feasts, fasting, austerities, pilgrimages, alms-gifts, the service of gods and goddesses, ceremonies, are all inferior to truth, and so are hundreds of thousands of devices. . . . Deal in truth and thou shalt gain. Why deal in falsehood which causeth loss ? Truth is a current coin, falsehood is counterfeit copper. Hundreds of thousands of stars in a dark night afford light, but when one sun riseth they all disappear. In the same way falsehood disappeareth before truth. Truth and falsehood stand to one another in the relation of a stone to an earthen vessel. If a stone be thrown at an earthen vessel it is the earthen vessel which will break. If the earthen vessel be thrown at a stone it is again the earthen vessel which will break. In either case it is the earthen vessel that suffereth. *Bhai Gur Das M.* 4, 259.

It is the speciality of a tree that it returneth good for evil. He who loppeth its branches sitteth in its shade, and it returneth him good for evil. It giveth fruit when clods are thrown at it. When carved into a boat, it saveth him who carved it. The perverse who have not the endurance and generosity of trees, obtain not fruit, while for the worshipper countless fruit is produced. . . . The custom of the world is to return good for good, but the custom of the Guru is to return good for evil. *Bhai Gur Das M.* 4, 260.

God will regenerate those in whose hearts there is love;
He will make them happy with gifts, and cause them to forget their sorrows.
There is no doubt that He will assuredly save them.

The Guru cometh to meet those for whom such destiny hath been recorded.

And will give them for their instruction God's ambrosial Name.

They will walk as it pleaseth the true Guru, and never wander a-begging.

Why should he, for whom God's court is at hand, bow to any one else?

The porter at God's gate will ask him no questions whatever.

Man shall be saved by the words of those on whom God looketh with favour.

There is no one to advise Him who sendeth and recalleth man.

God knoweth how to do all things; He destroyeth, constructeth, and createth.

Nanak, the Name is the reward of him to whom the Gracious One showeth favour. *Nanak M. 2, 7.*

Where God is remembered, there He becometh a friend and helper.

God dwelleth in the heart by the favour of the Guru; He is not otherwise obtained.

Amass God's wealth, my brethren,

So that God may assist you in this world and the next.

God's wealth is earned in the company of the holy; God's wealth is not obtained elsewhere or by other effort.

The holy who deal in God's jewels purchase the jewel of God's wealth : dealers in glass acquire not God's wealth by idle words.

God's wealth is as jewels, ornaments, and gems :

God's saints fix their attention on it at the suitable ambrosial hour.

When God's wealth is sown at the ambrosial hour, God's saints eat it, spend it, and it never faileth.

Both in this world and the next the saints who deal in God's wealth are congratulated.

There is no fear for God's wealth; it ever remaineth immovable and permanent; it cannot be destroyed by fire, or by water; it is not the prey of thieves or of Death's myrmidons.

Pickpockets cannot approach God's wealth, nor can the tax-gatherer Death impose a tax on it.

The apostates through sin have amassed sinful wealth, but not a particle of it shall go with them.

In this world the apostate is miserable when wealth slippeth from his hands : the apostate shall not find entrance into God's court hereafter.

The dealer in this wealth of God, O saints, is God Himself; he to whom He giveth it, loadeth it and taketh it away.

This wealth of God shall never suffer deficiency; the Guru hath given this knowledge to the slave Nanak. *Ram Das M.* 2, 332–3.

My mind is ever and ever troubled.

In many troubles my body pineth away and ever groweth worse.

The body which forgetteth God's word,
Screameth like a real leper.
To make many complaints is to talk folly,
Without our complaining everything is known to God,
Who made our ears, our eyes, and our noses;
Who gave us tongues wherewith to speak;
Who preserved us in the fire of the womb;
And through whom the breath moveth and speaketh everywhere.
Worldly love, affection, and dainties
Are all blackness and stains.
If man depart with the brand of sin on his face,
He will not be allowed to sit in God's court.
If he meet Thy favour, O God, he repeateth Thy Name.
By attaching himself to it he is saved; he hath no other resource.
Even if he be drowning in sin, God will still take care of him.
Nanak, the True One is beneficent to all. *Nanak M.* 1, 107.

O silly man, as thou camest so shalt thou depart; as thou wert born so shalt thou die;
As thy enjoyment so shall be thy suffering; through forgetfulness of the Name thou shalt fall into the terrible ocean.
Thou art proud on beholding thy beauty and wealth.
Thou hast extended thy love to gold and woman; why hast thou forgotten the Name and gone astray ? . . .
Alms-gifts, ablution, and austerities are of no avail; without association with the saints, thou hast been born in vain. . . .
Man cometh when God sendeth him, and he goeth away when God calleth him. . . .

The pious consider woe and weal as the same, and are free from joy or sorrow. *Nanak M.* 1, 353-5.

O servant of God the Inscrutable,
Cease to think of worldly occupations.
Become the dust of the feet of poor travellers; thus shall the darwesh be accepted at God's door.
Make truth thy prayer, faith thy prayer-carpet; chasten desires, and subdue thy feelings.
Make thy body the mosque, thy conscience the Mulla, and the very pure God thy creed. . . .
Make the subjection of thy ten organs the rosary by which God is remembered in thy heart;
Good conduct and great restraint over thyself, thy circumcision.
Know thy heart that everything is for the moment.
Sports, banquets, and sodalities are all entanglements.
Kings, rulers, and nobles are perishable; God's gate alone is the stable place.
Let first God's praises, second patience,
Third mildness, fourth almsgiving,
Fifth the five evil passions restrained in one place be thy five most precious times of prayer.
Make the knowledge that God is everywhere thy daily worship;
The abandonment of evil deeds the water-pot in thy hand;
The knowledge that there is but one God thy call to prayer; such a Muezzin shall have an excellent reward.
What is honestly obtained eat thou as thy food;
Wash away thy filth in the river of thy heart. . . .
Make good works thy body, faith thy spouse.
And obedience to God thy pleasures and spectacles.
Purify what is impure, make God's presence thy Hadis;[1] let a complete body be the turban on thy head. *Arjan M.* 3, 18-19.

Let none be proud of his caste.
He who knoweth God is a Brahman.
O stupid fool, be not proud of thy caste;
From such pride many sins result.
Everybody saith there are four castes,

---

[1] Hadis—traditional sayings of the Prophet, which have the force of law among Moslems.

But they all proceeded from God's seed.
The world is all made out of one clay,
But the potter fashioned it into vessels of many sorts.
The body is formed from the union of five elements;
Let any one consider if he hath less or more in his composition.
Saith Nanak, the soul is fettered by its acts.
Without meeting the true Guru salvation is not obtained.
Arjan M. 2, 238.

O Thou perfect in miracles, eternal, beneficent, Bestower of grace, maintenance, salvation, and mercy; Dispenser of bliss, Pardoner, Saviour, Remitter of sins, dear to the heart, King of kings, Bestower of excellence, Indicator of the way, without colour and without equal, Lord, who giveth heavenly bliss to him who hath no property, no retinue, no army, and no comforts. Distinct from the world, powerful, whose light is everywhere diffused, Thou bestowest gifts as if Thou wert present in person. Pure Cherisher, Bestower of favours, Thou art merciful, and Provider of sustenance in every land. Thou art Lord of every clime, the greatest of the great. Perfect in beauty, merciful, Master of knowledge, Support of the unhappy, Protector of the Faith, Fountain of eloquence, Searcher of hearts. Author of revelation, Appreciator of wisdom, Lord of intelligence, Diviner of secrets. Omnipresent God, Thou knowest the affairs of the world. Thou resolvest its difficulties, Thou art its great Organizer. *Gobind Singh M.* 5, 201.

O man with the garb, religion consisteth not in wearing a garb.
It consisteth not in wearing matted hair and long nails, or in smearing ashes on the body, or dyeing thy raiment.
If man obtain Jog by dwelling in the forest, the bird ever dwelleth there.
The elephant ever throweth dust on his head; consider this in thy heart.
Frogs and fishes ever bathe at places of pilgrimage.
The cat, the wolf, and the crane meditate; what know they of religion?
As thou endurest pain to deceive men, do so also for God's sake. *Gobind Singh M.* 5, 314.

Practise asceticism in this way :—

Consider thy house altogether as the forest, and remain an anchoret at heart.

Make continence thy matted hair, union with God thine ablutions, thy daily religious duties the growth of thy nails.

Divine knowledge thy spiritual guide; admonish thy heart and apply God's name as ashes to thy body.

Eat little, sleep little, love mercy and forbearance.

Ever practise mildness and patience, and thou shalt be freed from the three qualities.

Attach not to thy heart lust, wrath, covetousness, obstinacy, and worldly love. . . .

Make truth thy horn, sincerity thy necklace, and apply meditation as ashes to thy body;

Make restraint of thy heart thy lyre, and the support of the Name thine alms;

Play the primal essence as thy strings, and thou shalt hear God's sweet song. *Gobind Singh M.* 5, 324.

DISTRIBUTION OF THE WORLD'S RELIGIONS

This table has been reprinted, with some alterations in the Distribution column, from *The Eleven Religions and their Proverbial Lore*, by kind permission of Messrs. Routledge.

Religion	No. of Adherents	Distribution
Hinduism	300,000,000	India, Pakistan, Ceylon, Bali, Siam (or Thailand), South Africa.
Shinto	About 17,000,000 (1936 census)	Japan.
Judaism	16,000,000 at the outbreak of war 1939	Europe, U.S.A., Palestine (or Israel), and the other countries of the world.
Zoroastrianism (Parseeism)	125,000	India (chiefly Bombay), Pakistan (chiefly Sind). There are still adherents in Persia (or Iran), chiefly in Kerman and Yazd.
Taoism	Impossible to estimate	China, Korea and Manchuria.
Confucianism	400,000,000	China, Korea and Manchuria.
Jainism	1,500,000	India (chiefly Bombay, Central Provinces and Berar and Orissa), Pakistan (chiefly Sind).
Buddhism	520,000,000	Ceylon, Burma, Siam (or Thailand), Indo-China (or Viet Nam), China, Tibet, Korea, Japan, Mongolia, Kalmucks of Russia.
Christianity	500,000,000	Europe, North and South America; the British Commonwealth Countries, British, French, Italian, and Portuguese Africa, Abyssinia, Syria and Lebanon, Madagascar, Netherlands East Indies, with wide permeations elsewhere.
Islam	300,000,000	Arabia, North Africa (from Morocco to Egypt and southwards almost to the Equator, where it is still spreading), Somaliland and the East Coast of Africa, Syria, Turkey, Iraq, Persia (or Iran), Afghanistan, Pakistan, India, Malay States, East India Islands, parts of China, Asiatic Russia, and the Balkans.
Sikhism	5,700,000	India (chiefly East Punjab, a few in Central Provinces and Berar, and Orissa), Pakistan (chiefly Baluchistan and Sind).

COMPARATIVE CHART

Name of Religion	Country of Origin	Date of Origin	Name of Founder	Title of Founder	Social Position and/or Avocation	Origin of Name of Religion	Type of Religion
1. Hinduism	India	Prehistoric	—	—	—	After a race	Monistic. Pantheistic; also Monotheistic and Polytheistic
2. Shintoism	Japan	Prehistoric	—	—	—	After the leading aspect of doctrine	Polytheistic
3. Judaism	Palestine	Giving of the law at Sinai. 13th Century B.C.	—	—	—	After a race	Monotheistic
4. Zoroastrianism (Parseeism)	Persia	7th Century, B.C.	Zarathustra (Zaratust Zoroaster)	—	Spitama Clan (Pastoral Tribe)	After the Founder	Dualistic
5. Taoism	China	6th Century, B.C.	Li-poh-Yang	*Lao-Tse* (Old Master)	Court-Librarian and Recorder Historiographer?	After the leading aspect of doctrine	Monistic
6. Confucianism	China	6th Century, B.C.	K'ung-Fu-Tzu (Latin form) *Confucius*	The Perfect Sage; the First Holy One	Teacher, Holder of minor official posts. Father a Soldier	After the Founder	Ethical System founded on Ancient Monotheism.
7. Jainism	India	Prehistoric. Final form. 6th Century, B.C.	Vardhamana	*Mahavira* (Great Hero)	Kshatriya Caste (Jnata Clan)	After an aspect of doctrine	No Theology. Following the Tirthankaras will reveal the Truth
8. Buddhism	India	6th Century, B.C.	Siddartha; Family name *Gautama*	*Buddha* (the Enlightened One)	Kshatriya Caste (Sayka Clan.) Landowners. Father a Chieftain	After the Founder's title	No Theology. Truth will be found in spiritual experience
9. Christianity	Palestine	B.C. 4	*Jesus*	*Christ* (Anointed One)	Carpenter's family	After the Founder's title	Monotheistic. Trinitarian
10. Islam (Muhammadanism)	Arabia	7th Century, A.D.	*Muhammad*	*The Prophet*	Koreish Tribe (influential merchants and in charge of temple at Mecca)	After the leading aspect of doctrine (after the name of Founder)	Monotheistic
11. Sikhism	India	15th Century, A.D.	*Nanak*	Baba (Father) *Guru*	Kshatriya Caste Father a village Accountant and Steward	After those who practised it (Sikh = disciple)	Monotheistic
(a)	(b)	(c)	(d)	(e)	(f)	(g)	(h)

Name of Religion	Special Way	Name of Deity	The Future Life	Lives on Earth	Leading Scriptures	Main Divisions	Whether Proselytizing
1. Hinduism	Knowledge of Brahma (also devotion to Vishnu and Siva)	Brahma; also Vishnu and Siva	Absorption in Brahma (Nirvana)	Many	Vedas Vedanta	Vaishnavism Saivism	No
2. Shintoism	Devotion to the Kami	The Kami	Survival as spirits	One	Kojiki Nihongi	State Shinto Sectarian Shino	No
3. Judaism	Worship of Jahweh. Obedience to the Law of Moses	Jahweh (Jehovah)	Individual survival (resurrection of the body). Paradise	One	The Bible (Old Testament), The Torah, Talmud	—	Not now
4. Zoroastrianism (Parseeism)	Assistance to the Good God	Ahura-Mazda (Ormuzd)	Individual survival. Resurrection of the body. Heaven or Hell. Paradise	One	Avesta	[Parsees] Shahanshahis Kadmis	Not now
5. Taoism	Quietism and close contact with Nature	The Tao	The Tao	One	Tao Te Ching	—	No
6. Confucianism	Return to virtue of the Ancients. Evolution of the Superior Man	Shang-Ti T'sien	T'sien. Individual survival as spirits	One	The five King The four Shu	—	No
7. Jainism	Asceticism, Ahinsa. (Non-injury to living beings)	None. The Tirthankaras are honoured in temples	Individual survival in Nirvana	Many	Agamas Kalpa Sutra	Digambaras Svetambaras	Not now
8. Buddhism	The Noble Eightfold Path	None. The Buddha is honoured in temples	Release from bonds of self. Nirvana may be attained in this life	Many	Tripitakas (the Three Baskets)	Himayana Mahayana	Yes. By permeation
9. Christianity	Redemption through life and death of Christ	God (Father, Son, and Holy Spirit)	Individual survival. Heaven, Hell, or Purgatory. Resurrection of the body	One	The Bible, especially New Testament	Catholic Protestant Eastern	Yes
10. Islam (Muhammadanism)	Acceptance of One God and Muhammad as His Prophet	Allah	Individual survival. Heaven or Hell. Resurrection of the body	One	The Koran	Shiahs Sunnis	Yes
11. Sikhism	Following the Guru and the repetition of God's Name	Wah-Guru	Absorption into the Divine Life. (Nirvana.) Temporary Paradise—Sachs Khand	Many	The Granth Sahib	Singhs Sahijdharis	Not now
	(i)	(j)	(k)	(l)	(m)	(n)	(o)

333

GLOSSARY

A short glossary of words of doctrinal significance as used in the text.

Agnosticism : The belief that nothing is known or likely to be known about the existence of God or of anything beyond material phenomena.

Animatism : The belief that a soul or spirit has a special power over certain natural objects or happenings and may dwell within these as well as beyond them.

Animism : The belief that there is a soul or spirit in natural objects.

Atheism : The belief that there is no God.

Anthropomorphism : The belief that God has human attributes, personality, or form.

Asceticism : The practice of severe self-discipline and austerity, in the belief that this will assist spiritual progress.

Deism : The belief that God exists, independently of any special revelation (cf. Theism).

Dualism : The belief that there are two independent principles in the universe, as, for instance, good and evil.

Materialism : The belief that nothing exists but matter and its movements and modifications.

Monarchism : Attachment to principle of monarchy. In religion the belief in a king-god who rules over other gods.

Monism : The belief that there is but one Being in the universe.

Monotheism : The belief that there is only one God.

Mysticism : Spiritual apprehension of truth by means beyond the reason and understanding.

Pantheism : The belief that God is everything and everything is God.

Polytheism : The belief that there are many gods.

Quietism : Practice of a passive attitude with devotional contemplation.

Theism : Belief in a God Who has been revealed to man (cf. Deism).

Trinitarianism : Belief that there is a union of three Persons in one God.

BIBLIOGRAPHY

The late Dr. Champion wished to express appreciation to the authors, compilers, and publishers (and in some cases executors), who kindly granted him permission to use material from the works preceded by an asterisk below.

HINDUISM

HALE-WORTHAM (B.). *Hitopadesa or The Book of Good Counsel.* (Routledge) London. N.D.
HOPKINS (E. W.). * *Ordinances of Manu.* (Routledge) London, 1884.
MONIER-WILLIAMS (M.). *Hinduism.* (S.P.C.K.) London, 1885.
MONIER-WILLIAMS (M.). *Brahmanism and Hinduism.* (John Murray) London, 1891.
* *Sacred Books of the East.* Laws of Manu by Buhler. (Clarendon Press) Oxford, 1886.
* *Sacred Books of the East.* Bhagavadgita, Sanatsugatiya, Anugita. (Clarendon Press). Trans. by Kashinath Trimbak Telang. Oxford, 1882.

SHINTOISM

ASTON (W. G.). * *Shinto, the Ancient Religion of Japan.* (Constable) London, 1907. * *Shinto (The Way of the Gods).* (Longmans, Green.)
HARADA (TASUKU). *The Faith of Japan.* (Macmillan Co.) N.Y., 1914.
GENCHI KATO. *A Study of Shinto, The Religion of the Japanese Nation* (Meiji Japan Society) Tokyo, 1937.

JUDAISM

The Holy Bible. (Authorised version.)
The Apocrypha.

ZOROASTRIANISM

MOULTON (J. H.). * *Early Zoroastrianism.* Hibbert Lectures. (Williams & Norgate) London, 1913.
* *Sacred Books of the East.* Ed. by Max Muller. (Clarendon Press) Oxford, 1880, 1883, 1887. *The Zend-Avesta*, Parts 1, 2, and 3.

TAOISM AND CONFUCIANISM

DOUGLAS (R. K.). *Confucianism and Taoism.* (S.P.C.K.) London, 1879.
GILES (H. A.). * *Chuang Tzu. Mystic Moralist and Social Reformer.* 2nd Edition. (B. Quaritch) London, 1926. (Kelly & Walsh) Shanghai.
GILES (L.). *The Sayings of Confucius.* (John Murray) London, 1907.
LEGGE (J.). *The Chinese Classics* (including Tao Te King and The Great Learning). Vols. 1–7. (Routledge) London, 1861.

LYALL (L. A.). *Mencius.* (Longmans, Green) London, 1932.
* *Sayings of Confucius and Mencius.* (Longmans, Green). By kind permission of the Executors of the late L. A. Lyall.
OLD (W. G.). *Shu King.* The Theosophical Publishing Society, London & Benares. (John Lane) New York, 1904.
WALEY (A.). * *The Way and its Power.* (Allen & Unwin) London, 1934.
YUTANG (LIN). *The Wisdom of China.* (Michael Joseph) London, 1944.

JAINISM

SHRI GUNA-BHADRA ACHARYA. *The Sacred Books of the Jainas,* Vol. 7. *Atmanushasana,* 1928. (Pandit Ajit Prasad) The Central Publishing House, Lucknow, India.
SHRIMAT AMRITA CHANDRA SURI. *The Sacred Books of the Jainas,* Vol. 4. *Purushartha-Siddhyupaya,* 1933. (Abhinandan Prasada Jindal) The Central Jaina Publishing House, Lucknow, India.

BUDDHISM

BEAL (S.) *Texts from the Buddhist Canon (Dhammapada).* (Routledge) London, 1878.
RHYS-DAVIDS (T. W.). * *Buddhism.* (S.P.C.K.) London, 1925.
THOMAS (E. J.). *Early Buddhist Scriptures.* (Routledge) London, 1935.
* *Sacred Books of the East* (including Dhammapada). Ed. by Max Muller. (Clarendon Press) Oxford, 1879–1910.

CHRISTIANITY

The Holy Bible. (Authorised version.)

ISLAM

LANE-POOLE (S.). * *The Speeches and Table-Talk of the Prophet Mohammad.* (Macmillan) London, 1882.
RODWELL (J. M.). * *The Koran.* (Dent) London, 1909.
PALMER (E. H.). * *The Koran.* (World's Classics). Oxford Univ. Press.
WILSON (C. E.). * *The Masnavi.* Book 2. (Arthur Probsthain) London, 1910.
WORTABET (J.). *Arabian Wisdom.* (John Murray) London, 1910.

SIKHISM

FIELD (D.) [Dorothy Dudley Short]. *The Religion of the Sikhs.* Wisdom of the East Series (John Murray) London, 1914.
MACAULIFFE (M. A.). * *The Sikh Religion,* 6 Vols. (Clarendon Press) Oxford, 1909.

GENERAL

BALLOU (R. O.). * *The Pocket World Bible.* (Routledge) London, 1948.
CHAMPION (S. G.). * *The Eleven Religions and their Proverbial Lore.* (Routledge) London, 1944.
* *Wisdom of the East* (7 vols.). (John Murray).

A CATALOG OF SELECTED
DOVER BOOKS
IN ALL FIELDS OF INTEREST

A CATALOG OF SELECTED DOVER
BOOKS IN ALL FIELDS OF INTEREST

CONCERNING THE SPIRITUAL IN ART, Wassily Kandinsky. Pioneering work by father of abstract art. Thoughts on color theory, nature of art. Analysis of earlier masters. 12 illustrations. 80pp. of text. 5⅜ x 8½. 23411-8

ANIMALS: 1,419 Copyright-Free Illustrations of Mammals, Birds, Fish, Insects, etc., Jim Harter (ed.). Clear wood engravings present, in extremely lifelike poses, over 1,000 species of animals. One of the most extensive pictorial sourcebooks of its kind. Captions. Index. 284pp. 9 x 12. 23766-4

CELTIC ART: The Methods of Construction, George Bain. Simple geometric techniques for making Celtic interlacements, spirals, Kells-type initials, animals, humans, etc. Over 500 illustrations. 160pp. 9 x 12. (Available in U.S. only.) 22923-8

AN ATLAS OF ANATOMY FOR ARTISTS, Fritz Schider. Most thorough reference work on art anatomy in the world. Hundreds of illustrations, including selections from works by Vesalius, Leonardo, Goya, Ingres, Michelangelo, others. 593 illustrations. 192pp. 7⅛ x 10¼. 20241-0

CELTIC HAND STROKE-BY-STROKE (Irish Half-Uncial from "The Book of Kells"): An Arthur Baker Calligraphy Manual, Arthur Baker. Complete guide to creating each letter of the alphabet in distinctive Celtic manner. Covers hand position, strokes, pens, inks, paper, more. Illustrated. 48pp. 8¼ x 11. 24336-2

EASY ORIGAMI, John Montroll. Charming collection of 32 projects (hat, cup, pelican, piano, swan, many more) specially designed for the novice origami hobbyist. Clearly illustrated easy-to-follow instructions insure that even beginning papercrafters will achieve successful results. 48pp. 8¼ x 11. 27298-2

THE COMPLETE BOOK OF BIRDHOUSE CONSTRUCTION FOR WOOD-WORKERS, Scott D. Campbell. Detailed instructions, illustrations, tables. Also data on bird habitat and instinct patterns. Bibliography. 3 tables. 63 illustrations in 15 figures. 48pp. 5¼ x 8½. 24407-5

BLOOMINGDALE'S ILLUSTRATED 1886 CATALOG: Fashions, Dry Goods and Housewares, Bloomingdale Brothers. Famed merchants' extremely rare catalog depicting about 1,700 products: clothing, housewares, firearms, dry goods, jewelry, more. Invaluable for dating, identifying vintage items. Also, copyright-free graphics for artists, designers. Co-published with Henry Ford Museum & Greenfield Village. 160pp. 8¼ x 11. 25780-0

HISTORIC COSTUME IN PICTURES, Braun & Schneider. Over 1,450 costumed figures in clearly detailed engravings–from dawn of civilization to end of 19th century. Captions. Many folk costumes. 256pp. 8⅜ x 11¾. 23150-X

THE CLARINET AND CLARINET PLAYING, David Pino. Lively, comprehensive work features suggestions about technique, musicianship, and musical interpretation, as well as guidelines for teaching, making your own reeds, and preparing for public performance. Includes an intriguing look at clarinet history. "A godsend," *The Clarinet,* Journal of the International Clarinet Society. Appendixes. 7 illus. 320pp. 5⅜ x 8½. 40270-3

HOLLYWOOD GLAMOR PORTRAITS, John Kobal (ed.). 145 photos from 1926-49. Harlow, Gable, Bogart, Bacall; 94 stars in all. Full background on photographers, technical aspects. 160pp. 8⅜ x 11¼. 23352-9

THE ANNOTATED CASEY AT THE BAT: A Collection of Ballads about the Mighty Casey/Third, Revised Edition, Martin Gardner (ed.). Amusing sequels and parodies of one of America's best-loved poems: Casey's Revenge, Why Casey Whiffed, Casey's Sister at the Bat, others. 256pp. 5⅜ x 8½. 28598-7

THE RAVEN AND OTHER FAVORITE POEMS, Edgar Allan Poe. Over 40 of the author's most memorable poems: "The Bells," "Ulalume," "Israfel," "To Helen," "The Conqueror Worm," "Eldorado," "Annabel Lee," many more. Alphabetic lists of titles and first lines. 64pp. 5³⁄₁₆ x 8¼. 26685-0

PERSONAL MEMOIRS OF U. S. GRANT, Ulysses Simpson Grant. Intelligent, deeply moving firsthand account of Civil War campaigns, considered by many the finest military memoirs ever written. Includes letters, historic photographs, maps and more. 528pp. 6⅛ x 9¼. 28587-1

ANCIENT EGYPTIAN MATERIALS AND INDUSTRIES, A. Lucas and J. Harris. Fascinating, comprehensive, thoroughly documented text describes this ancient civilization's vast resources and the processes that incorporated them in daily life, including the use of animal products, building materials, cosmetics, perfumes and incense, fibers, glazed ware, glass and its manufacture, materials used in the mummification process, and much more. 544pp. 6¹⁄₈ x 9¹⁄₄. (Available in U.S. only.) 40446-3

RUSSIAN STORIES/RUSSKIE RASSKAZY: A Dual-Language Book, edited by Gleb Struve. Twelve tales by such masters as Chekhov, Tolstoy, Dostoevsky, Pushkin, others. Excellent word-for-word English translations on facing pages, plus teaching and study aids, Russian/English vocabulary, biographical/critical introductions, more. 416pp. 5⅜ x 8½. 26244-8

PHILADELPHIA THEN AND NOW: 60 Sites Photographed in the Past and Present, Kenneth Finkel and Susan Oyama. Rare photographs of City Hall, Logan Square, Independence Hall, Betsy Ross House, other landmarks juxtaposed with contemporary views. Captures changing face of historic city. Introduction. Captions. 128pp. 8¼ x 11. 25790-8

AIA ARCHITECTURAL GUIDE TO NASSAU AND SUFFOLK COUNTIES, LONG ISLAND, The American Institute of Architects, Long Island Chapter, and the Society for the Preservation of Long Island Antiquities. Comprehensive, well-researched and generously illustrated volume brings to life over three centuries of Long Island's great architectural heritage. More than 240 photographs with authoritative, extensively detailed captions. 176pp. 8¼ x 11. 26946-9

NORTH AMERICAN INDIAN LIFE: Customs and Traditions of 23 Tribes, Elsie Clews Parsons (ed.). 27 fictionalized essays by noted anthropologists examine religion, customs, government, additional facets of life among the Winnebago, Crow, Zuni, Eskimo, other tribes. 480pp. 6⅛ x 9¼. 27377-6

CATALOG OF DOVER BOOKS

ANATOMY: A Complete Guide for Artists, Joseph Sheppard. A master of figure drawing shows artists how to render human anatomy convincingly. Over 460 illustrations. 224pp. 8⅜ x 11¼. 27279-6

MEDIEVAL CALLIGRAPHY: Its History and Technique, Marc Drogin. Spirited history, comprehensive instruction manual covers 13 styles (ca. 4th century through 15th). Excellent photographs; directions for duplicating medieval techniques with modern tools. 224pp. 8⅜ x 11¼. 26142-5

DRIED FLOWERS: How to Prepare Them, Sarah Whitlock and Martha Rankin. Complete instructions on how to use silica gel, meal and borax, perlite aggregate, sand and borax, glycerine and water to create attractive permanent flower arrangements. 12 illustrations. 32pp. 5⅜ x 8½. 21802-3

EASY-TO-MAKE BIRD FEEDERS FOR WOODWORKERS, Scott D. Campbell. Detailed, simple-to-use guide for designing, constructing, caring for and using feeders. Text, illustrations for 12 classic and contemporary designs. 96pp. 5⅜ x 8½. 25847-5

SCOTTISH WONDER TALES FROM MYTH AND LEGEND, Donald A. Mackenzie. 16 lively tales tell of giants rumbling down mountainsides, of a magic wand that turns stone pillars into warriors, of gods and goddesses, evil hags, powerful forces and more. 240pp. 5⅜ x 8½. 29677-6

THE HISTORY OF UNDERCLOTHES, C. Willett Cunnington and Phyllis Cunnington. Fascinating, well-documented survey covering six centuries of English undergarments, enhanced with over 100 illustrations: 12th-century laced-up bodice, footed long drawers (1795), 19th-century bustles, 19th-century corsets for men, Victorian "bust improvers," much more. 272pp. 5⅜ x 8¼. 27124-2

ARTS AND CRAFTS FURNITURE: The Complete Brooks Catalog of 1912, Brooks Manufacturing Co. Photos and detailed descriptions of more than 150 now very collectible furniture designs from the Arts and Crafts movement depict davenports, settees, buffets, desks, tables, chairs, bedsteads, dressers and more, all built of solid, quarter-sawed oak. Invaluable for students and enthusiasts of antiques, Americana and the decorative arts. 80pp. 6½ x 9¼. 27471-3

WILBUR AND ORVILLE: A Biography of the Wright Brothers, Fred Howard. Definitive, crisply written study tells the full story of the brothers' lives and work. A vividly written biography, unparalleled in scope and color, that also captures the spirit of an extraordinary era. 560pp. 6⅛ x 9¼. 40297-5

THE ARTS OF THE SAILOR: Knotting, Splicing and Ropework, Hervey Garrett Smith. Indispensable shipboard reference covers tools, basic knots and useful hitches; handsewing and canvas work, more. Over 100 illustrations. Delightful reading for sea lovers. 256pp. 5⅜ x 8½. 26440-8

FRANK LLOYD WRIGHT'S FALLINGWATER: The House and Its History, Second, Revised Edition, Donald Hoffmann. A total revision–both in text and illustrations–of the standard document on Fallingwater, the boldest, most personal architectural statement of Wright's mature years, updated with valuable new material from the recently opened Frank Lloyd Wright Archives. "Fascinating"–*The New York Times*. 116 illustrations. 128pp. 9¼ x 10¾. 27430-6

THE STORY OF THE TITANIC AS TOLD BY ITS SURVIVORS, Jack Winocour (ed.). What it was really like. Panic, despair, shocking inefficiency, and a little heroism. More thrilling than any fictional account. 26 illustrations. 320pp. 5⅜ x 8½.
20610-6

FAIRY AND FOLK TALES OF THE IRISH PEASANTRY, William Butler Yeats (ed.). Treasury of 64 tales from the twilight world of Celtic myth and legend: "The Soul Cages," "The Kildare Pooka," "King O'Toole and his Goose," many more. Introduction and Notes by W. B. Yeats. 352pp. 5⅜ x 8½.
26941-8

BUDDHIST MAHAYANA TEXTS, E. B. Cowell and others (eds.). Superb, accurate translations of basic documents in Mahayana Buddhism, highly important in history of religions. The Buddha-karita of Asvaghosha, Larger Sukhavativyuha, more. 448pp. 5⅜ x 8½.
25552-2

ONE TWO THREE . . . INFINITY: Facts and Speculations of Science, George Gamow. Great physicist's fascinating, readable overview of contemporary science: number theory, relativity, fourth dimension, entropy, genes, atomic structure, much more. 128 illustrations. Index. 352pp. 5⅜ x 8½.
25664-2

EXPERIMENTATION AND MEASUREMENT, W. J. Youden. Introductory manual explains laws of measurement in simple terms and offers tips for achieving accuracy and minimizing errors. Mathematics of measurement, use of instruments, experimenting with machines. 1994 edition. Foreword. Preface. Introduction. Epilogue. Selected Readings. Glossary. Index. Tables and figures. 128pp. 5⅜ x 8½.
40451-X

DALÍ ON MODERN ART: The Cuckolds of Antiquated Modern Art, Salvador Dalí. Influential painter skewers modern art and its practitioners. Outrageous evaluations of Picasso, Cézanne, Turner, more. 15 renderings of paintings discussed. 44 calligraphic decorations by Dalí. 96pp. 5⅜ x 8½. (Available in U.S. only.)
29220-7

ANTIQUE PLAYING CARDS: A Pictorial History, Henry René D'Allemagne. Over 900 elaborate, decorative images from rare playing cards (14th–20th centuries): Bacchus, death, dancing dogs, hunting scenes, royal coats of arms, players cheating, much more. 96pp. 9¼ x 12¼.
29265-7

MAKING FURNITURE MASTERPIECES: 30 Projects with Measured Drawings, Franklin H. Gottshall. Step-by-step instructions, illustrations for constructing handsome, useful pieces, among them a Sheraton desk, Chippendale chair, Spanish desk, Queen Anne table and a William and Mary dressing mirror. 224pp. 8⅛ x 11¼.
29338-6

THE FOSSIL BOOK: A Record of Prehistoric Life, Patricia V. Rich et al. Profusely illustrated definitive guide covers everything from single-celled organisms and dinosaurs to birds and mammals and the interplay between climate and man. Over 1,500 illustrations. 760pp. 7½ x 10⅛.
29371-8

Paperbound unless otherwise indicated. Available at your book dealer, online at **www.doverpublications.com**, or by writing to Dept. GI, Dover Publications, Inc., 31 East 2nd Street, Mineola, NY 11501. For current price information or for free catalogues (please indicate field of interest), write to Dover Publications or log on to **www.doverpublications.com** and see every Dover book in print. Dover publishes more than 500 books each year on science, elementary and advanced mathematics, biology, music, art, literary history, social sciences, and other areas.